DATE OF RETUR
UNLESS RECALLED BY  KU-288-941

1 8 MAR 2011

THE POLITICS OF EUROPEANIZATION

The Politics of Europeanization

edited by

KEVIN FEATHERSTONE

and

CLAUDIO M. RADAELLI

OXFORD

UNIVERSITY PRESS

OXFORD
UNIVERSITY PRESS

Great Clarendon Street, Oxford OX2 6DP

Oxford University Press is a department of the University of Oxford.
It furthers the University's objective of excellence in research, scholarship,
and education by publishing worldwide in

Oxford New York

Auckland Cape Town Dar es Salaam Hong Kong Karachi Kuala Lumpur
Madrid Melbourne Mexico City Nairobi New Delhi Shanghai Taipei Toronto

With offices in

Argentina Austria Brazil Chile Czech Republic France Greece
Guatemala Hungary Italy Japan South Korea Poland Portugal
Singapore Switzerland Thailand Turkey Ukraine Vietnam

Oxford is a registered trade mark of Oxford University Press
in the UK and in certain other countries

Published in the United States
by Oxford University Press Inc., New York

© The several contributors, 2003

The moral rights of the authors have been asserted

Database right Oxford University Press (maker)

First published 2003

All rights reserved. No part of this publication may be reproduced,
stored in a retrieval system, or transmitted, in any form or by any means,
without the prior permission in writing of Oxford University Press,
or as expressly permitted by law, or under terms agreed with the appropriate
reprographics rights organization. Enquiries concerning reproduction
outside the scope of the above should be sent to the Rights Department,
Oxford University Press, at the address above

You must not circulate this book in any other binding or cover
and you must impose this same condition on any acquirer

British Library Cataloguing in Publication Data

Data available

Library of Congress Cataloging in Publication Data

Data available

ISBN 978-0-19-925208-4 (hbk.)
ISBN 978-0-19-925209-1 (pbk.)

Typeset by Newgen Imaging Systems (P) Ltd., Chennai, India
Printed in Great Britain
on acid-free paper by
the MPG Books Group

UNIVERSITY
OF SHEFFIELD
LIBRARY D

CONTENTS

Preface   vii
List of Figures   viii
List of Tables   ix
List of Contributors   x
List of Abbreviations   xi

I. Theorizing Europeanization

1. Introduction: In the Name of 'Europe'   3
   KEVIN FEATHERSTONE
2. The Europeanization of Public Policy   27
   CLAUDIO M. RADAELLI
3. Conceptualizing the Domestic Impact of Europe   57
   TANJA A. BÖRZEL AND THOMAS RISSE

II. Comparing Institutional Contexts

4. Meeting the Demands of EU Membership: The
   Europeanization of National Administrative Systems   83
   HUSSEIN KASSIM
5. Variable Geometry, Multilevel Governance: European
   Integration and Subnational Government in the New Millennium   112
   MIKE GOLDSMITH
6. Europeanization in Comparative Perspective: Institutional
   Fit and National Adaptation   134
   MARCO GIULIANI

III. Europeanization and Policy Analysis

7. Europeanization as Interpretation, Translation, and
   Editing of Public Policies   159
   ULRIKA MÖRTH

8. Europeanization as Convergence: The Regulation of
   Media Markets in the European Union   179
   ALISON J. HARCOURT

9. The Impact of the European Union on Environmental Policies   203
   MARKUS HAVERLAND

IV. Interest Groups and Europeanization

10. Europeanization and Organizational Change in National Trade
    Associations: An Organizational Ecology Perspective   225
    JÜRGEN R. GROTE AND ACHIM LANG

11. Differentiated Europeanization: Large and Small Firms
    in the EU Policy Process   255
    DAVID COEN AND CHARLES DANNREUTHER

V. Understanding 'Europe' as a Policy Model

12. The Idea of the European Social Model: Limits and
    Paradoxes of Europeanization   279
    DANIEL WINCOTT

13. Europeanization Goes East: Power and Uncertainty in the
    EU Accession Process   303
    HEATHER GRABBE

VI. Conclusions

14. A Conversant Research Agenda   331
    KEVIN FEATHERSTONE AND CLAUDIO M. RADAELLI

Index   342

PREFACE

The present volume has its origins in an international workshop on Europeanization we organized whilst at the University of Bradford in May 2000 and a panel at the Political Studies Association Annual Conference the previous month. These initiatives were taken in the context of us establishing the 'Research Unit on Europeanization' at the University of Bradford as a forum for activity in this area.

Our interest in 'Europeanization' covers both its conceptualization and its empirical application. We could not fail to recognize the fashionable nature of the term, but we were intent on establishing how far the term has a distinctive meaning and useful application. The present volume reflects these interests, in that substantial space is devoted to the definition of 'Europeanization' and then to its empirical utility in different contexts. The intention is to provide the reader with a comprehensive account of what is meant by 'Europeanization' and the extent to which it clarifies important processes of change in contemporary Europe.

We would like to record our gratitude to the participants in the earlier workshop and panel, to the contributors to the volume, and to Dominic Byatt and his colleagues at OUP. The efficiency and support of the latter has made this project less arduous than would otherwise have been the case. We would also like to thank the University of Bradford for supporting the May 2000 workshop.

Finally, the volume is dedicated to our families, for their tolerance, support, and affection.

Kevin Featherstone
Claudio M. Radaelli

LIST OF FIGURES

2.1. (a) Domains of Europeanization and change
  (b) Europeanization and the institutional analysis of policy change 35
2.2. Mechanisms of Europeanization 41
2.3. Key intervening variables explaining the likelihood and
  direction of Europeanization 47
3.1. The domestic effect of Europeanization 60
3.2. Two logics of domestic change 69
3.3. The different degrees of domestic change 71
4.1. Systems for the coordination of EU policy by degree
  of centralization and coordinating ambition 93
6.1. National adaptation to the EU (1986–2000) 138
6.2. Veto players and EU adaptation 144
8.1. Number of ECJ media decisions 1974–2001 184
8.2. Number of MTF media decisions 1989–2001 189

LIST OF TABLES

1.1. Number of academic articles referring to 'Europeanization'   5
1.2. Focus of articles on 'Europeanization', 1981–2000   6
4.1. Functions of the permanent representations   99
4.2. Type of EU coordination system, European policy, and structure of domestic polity   106
6.1. Mean and range values of main independent and dependent variables   141
6.2. Institutional variables and national adaptation (correlation coefficients)   143
6.3. Partial correlations: national adaptation and institutional variables   148
6.4. Partial correlations: veto players or majoritarian democracy?   149
6.5. An institutional model (stepwise regression)   150
10.1. Different types of challenges (general and from within different levels)   246
10.2. Allocation of resources to different organizational tasks   248

LIST OF CONTRIBUTORS

Tanja A. Börzel, Humboldt University of Berlin
David Coen, University College London
Charles Dannreuther, University of Leeds
Kevin Featherstone, London School of Economics
Marco Giuliani, Università degli Studi di Milano
Mike Goldsmith, University of Salford
Heather Grabbe, Centre for European Reform and Wolfson College, Oxford
Jürgen R. Grote, Konstanz University
Alison J. Harcourt, University of Bradford
Markus Haverland, University of Nijmegen
Hussein Kassim, Birkbeck College
Achim Lang, Konstanz University
Ulrika Mörth, SCORE, University of Stockholm
Claudio M. Radaelli, University of Bradford (on leave at the European University Institute)
Thomas Risse, Free University of Berlin
Daniel Wincott, University of Birmingham

LIST OF ABBREVIATIONS

AI	Access to Information
BDB	British Digital Broadcasting
CEE	Central and Eastern Europe
CFSP	Common Foreign and Security Policy
DEI	Domestic Encompassing Interest
EBC	European Builders Confederation
EBU	European Broadcasting Union
ECJ	European Court of Justice
EFTC	European Federation of Timber Construction
EIA	Environmental Impact Assessment
EIoP	European Integration online Papers
EMAS	Environmental Management and Audit system
EMU	European Monetary Union
EPC	European Political Cooperation
EPG	European Policy Group
EPRA	European Platform of Regulatory Authorities
ERT	European Round Table
ESM	European Social Model
ESPN	European Sports Network
EU	European Union
FCO	Foreign and Commonwealth Office
FEDLO	Federation of European Dental Laboratory Owners
FRANREP	French Permanent Representation
HMG	Holland Media Group
IR	International Relations
ISPO	International Society Project
ITV	Independent Television Publications
LCP	Large Combustion Plant
MTF	Merger Task Force
NAFTA	North Atlantic Free Trade Area
NSD	Nordic Satellite Distributor
OMC	Open Method of Coordination
PMI	Pari Mutuel International
TABD	Transatlantic Business Dialogue

TDC	Transnational Defence Company
TWF	Television Without Frontiers
UK	United Kingdom
UKREP	UK Permanent Representation
UNICE	Union of Industrial and Employees Conference of Europe
US	United States

I

Theorizing Europeanization

1

Introduction: In the Name of 'Europe'

KEVIN FEATHERSTONE

What does 'Europeanization' mean? How does it affect domestic politics and policies? More particularly, how is it evident in the ideas, interests, behaviour, and settings of domestic politics? Is 'Europeanization' an irreversible process? Does it mean convergence across Europe? How and why do differences remain? These questions are at the heart of this volume.

'Europeanization' has gained widespread currency amongst scholars as a newly fashionable term to denote a variety of changes within European politics and international relations. Interestingly, other branches of the social sciences use the term much less often. Yet, the faddish use of 'Europeanization' in different contexts can easily obscure its substantive meaning. The purpose of this volume is to bring recognized experts in the field together to distinguish the conceptual meaning of 'Europeanization' and to analyse its empirical implications.

In order to set the context, this chapter seeks to chart the uses of the term 'Europeanization' and to clarify how it will be used in the rest of the volume. The aim is to provide some structure to the potential confusion of the uninitiated reader, whilst also mapping out key research areas.

'Europeanization'—like 'globalization'—can be a useful entry-point for greater understanding of important changes occurring in our politics and society. The obligation of the researcher is to give it a precise meaning. 'Europeanization' has little value if it merely repeats an existing notion. It is not a simple synonym for European regional integration or even convergence, though it does overlap with aspects of both. As a term for the social sciences, it can range over history, culture, politics, society, and economics. It is a process of structural change, variously affecting actors and institutions, ideas and interests. In a maximalist sense, the structural change that it entails must fundamentally be of a phenomenon exhibiting similar attributes to those that predominate in, or are closely identified with, 'Europe'. Minimally, 'Europeanization' involves a response to the policies of the European Union (EU).[1] Significantly, even in the latter context, the

---

[1] The impact of these policies may not necessarily be one of convergence, however (Héritier and Knill 2000).

scope of 'Europeanization' is broad, stretching across existing member states and applicant states, as the EU's weight across the continent grows.

Empirical analysis can gauge the scope and significance of the adjustments involved: 'Europeanization' is, to put it somewhat crudely, a matter of degree. It also has a dynamic quality: its structural effects are not necessarily permanent or irreversible. With respect to regional integration, this is one major reason why 'Europeanization' is not a new label for 'neofunctionalism' (Haas 1958). The impact of Europeanization is typically incremental, irregular, and uneven over time and between locations, national and subnational. Profound disparities of impact remain—it is inherently an asymmetric process—and the attraction for researchers is to account for them. The ontology of 'Europeanization' is also complex. Within the international system, the relationship between 'Europeanization' and 'globalization' is often difficult to distinguish in case studies of domestic adaptation, obscuring the key independent variable (for a preliminary discussion, see Hennis 2001). In addition, Caporaso (1996) has argued that 'the study of European integration is moving into a post-ontological stage', meaning that 'scholars are less concerned with how to categorize [the EU] than how to explain process and outcome' (1996: 30). Within this frame, analytical difficulties remain. Cause and effect in the 'Europeanization' process can be deceptive: for example, relatively 'small' and technical EU obligations may have widespread domestic ramifications in certain settings and be a subterfuge for further changes.[2] Further, the relationship between structure and agency is by no means simple. Actors can be of different types: individual, collective, or corporate. Within the process of 'Europeanization', structure and agency are best understood as being inherently relational concepts (Bhaskar 1979; Giddens 1984; Checkel 1998). Agency within the 'Europeanization' process is not only structured, but may also be structuring, as actors 'lead' (Dyson and Featherstone 1999: 776–82). Dauntingly, the study of 'Europeanization' does not fit easily 'the language of dependent and independent variables and the logic of regression analysis' (Olsen 1996: 271). Transformation may occur on the basis of 'a multitude of coevolving, parallel and not necessarily tightly coupled processes' (Olsen 1996: 271).[3]

Given these general characteristics, how might 'Europeanization' be applied in the social sciences? A survey of the literature over the last two

---

[2] For example, EU transparency rules for the financial accounts of institutions have had major implications for pension fund bodies in Greece (Featherstone *et al.* 2001).

[3] In a more recent study, Olsen has further refined the research agenda (2002). Included in his agenda is a focus on 'how institutional transformation may be understood as an ecology of mutual adaptation and coevolving institutions, including a (varying) number of interacting processes of change' (2002: 23).

decades that has referred to 'Europeanization' reveals the diversity of applications attached to the term.

A Typology of 'Europeanization'

The usage of the term 'Europeanization' in the social science literature has increased rapidly in recent years. Table 1.1 is based on a survey of some 116 academic journal articles as listed in the 'Social Sciences Citation Index'. It indicates that only five articles (4 per cent) referring to 'Europeanization' were published in the 1980s. Four of these were concerned with foreign policy. By contrast, twenty-seven articles (23 per cent) were published between 1990–5 and 1984 (73 per cent) since. The breadth of application has been wide-ranging. Table 1.2 categorizes the main focus of the articles published between 1981 and 2000. Combining the individual entries, the table indicates that 'Europeanization' is applied within four broad categories: as an historical process; as a matter of cultural diffusion; as a process of institutional adaptation; and as the adaptation of policy and policy processes. The first two are maximalist interpretations and have little direct connection to the impact of the European Union. The other two categories are minimalist and are more

TABLE 1.1 *Number of academic articles referring to 'Europeanization'*[a]

1981–8	3
1989	2
1990	1
1991	4
1992	2
1993	9
1994	8
1995	3
1996	5
1997	6
1998	7
1999	20
2000	24
2001	22

[a] The table shows the total number of articles with 'Europeanization' or 'Europeanization' as a subject term, in all languages, listed for each year in the Social Sciences Citation Index, as reported via the 'ISI Web of Science' database.

TABLE 1.2 *Focus of articles on 'Europeanization',*
1981–2000[a]

Focus category	% of total
Historical process	5.6
Cultural diffusion	12.5
Central government	8.3
NGOs	8.3
Subnational authorities	11.1
Political parties	4.2
Policy and policy process	33.3
Foreign relations	16.7

[a] Articles categorized by author according to journal abstract,
$N = 70$.

closely linked to the operation of the European Union. The conclusions from both tables are that the increasing usage of 'Europeanization' appears to reflect a shift of research agenda, as well as of fashion. The general trends in the literature can be considered within this fourfold typology.

'Europeanization' as a Historic Phenomenon

'Europeanization' has taken on different meanings throughout modern history (Mjoset 1997). It has referred to the 'export' of European authority and social norms: imperial control, institutional organization and practices, social and cultural beliefs, values, and behaviour. 'Europeanization' is used in this way by historians to describe the export of cultural norms and patterns (e.g. Kohout 1999). Imperial endeavours by Britain, France, Spain, and Portugal linked civilization with the spread of European norms and habits.

But what constitutes 'Europe' and who are 'Europeans' has also been the basis, historically, of the separation of social identities and interests within the broad geographical area understood today as 'Europe'. Anthropologists, for example, use 'Europeanization' to characterize changes in early human society and the shift of ethnic groups (e.g. Cesnys 1991; Poruciuc 1993). In later history, religious cleavages reinforced such points of distinction. The religious affiliations of southern Europe, for example, would in the past have been both mutually exclusive and the basis of a clear divide with the present 'core' EU states, questioning the meaning of 'Europe' and 'Europeans'. Orthodox Greece, Muslim Turkey, Catholic Italy, Spain, and Portugal stand in contradistinction to the mix of Catholicism and Protestantism in the north. In the modern period, 'Europeanization' has often meant adaptation to west

European norms and practices, acknowledging the 'pull' to convergence of the major powers of the region (Diamandouros 1994).

Transnational Cultural Diffusion

A second category of application sees 'Europeanization' as increasing transnationalism: that is, the diffusion of cultural norms, ideas, identities, and patterns of behaviour on a cross-national basis within Europe. The usage of 'Europeanization' in this category tends to be very broad. At a cultural level, 'Europeanization' has been applied to a shift in drinking habits in Iceland (Olafsdottir *et al.* 1997) and identities in relation to engagement with football (Maguire *et al.* 1999). 'Europeanization' affects wider social activities such as education (Seitter 1993). It has been used to describe changes in political culture (Pamir 1994; Borneman and Fowler 1997); and, more specifically, a redefinition of citizenship (Joppke 1995) and a shift in ideology (Gransow 1982). An interesting case of 'Europeanization' is that involving the cultural assimilation of European-based notions of human rights and citizenship by Turkish immigrants in Germany (Soysal 1994). In each of these examples, the factors prompting 'Europeanization' appear to have at best an indirect linkage to the activities of the European Union.

Institutional Adaptation

The above examples notwithstanding, 'Europeanization' today is most often associated with domestic adaptation to the pressures emanating directly or indirectly from EU membership. This perspective can be seen as refracting the integration-building processes underway at the EU level or as part of a 'second-image reversed' process (Gourevitch 1986). The first category of applications here refers to how actors and institutions have been affected.

With respect to the latter, 'Europeanization' is used to denote how public administrative institutions at the centre have adapted to the obligations of EU membership (Benoit 1997; Wessels 1998; Agh 1999; Harmsen 1999; Bulmer and Burch 2001). 'Historical institutionalism' lends itself to studies in which domestic (and/or EU) institutions have an intervening effect on actor preferences and interests in the short term, and a sufficiently stronger impact over the longer term, to establish distinct paths of development in policies and institutions (Bulmer and Burch 1998). In a more distinctive approach, Rometsch and Wessels (1996) went further and argued that there has been a 'fusion' of national and European institutions in the policy cycle, though only a partial convergence of political systems.

'Europeanization' is also identified with the adaptation of other institutional actors in the domestic political process. Significantly, a change at the level of parliamentary politics (Agh 1999*a*,*b*) and in the behaviour of organised interests in central Europe (Finkhafner 1998) connects 'Europeanization' with the transition to democracy in the region. Some authors have detected a shift towards 'Europeanization' on the part of political parties (Ladrech 1994; Daniels 1998; Holden 1999; cf. Mair 2000; Cole 2001). In a similar vein, 'Europeanization' has been applied to a transformation in the roles of non-governmental actors: such as trade unions (Turner 1996); universities (Dineen 1992); the legal system (Levitsky 1994); and the wider public sector (Jorgensen 1999). This is an area in which it is especially important to differentiate the processes of 'Europeanization' with respect to a change in elite behaviour from the assumptions of neofunctionalism, which posited a shift by elites in favour of integration. Some years ago, Kerr (1973) referred to the cognitive and affective response of actors participating within European institutions. If written now, no doubt their response would be seen as being one of 'Europeanization'.

A large number of studies relate 'Europeanization' to the strengthening of subnational governance (Goldsmith 1993; Martin 1993; Goetz 1995; John and LeGalès 1997; John and Whitehead 1997). This interpretation is consistent with the notion that the European Union is encouraging 'the emergence of "multilevel governance"... [drawing] some previously centralized functions of the state up to the supranational level and some down to the local/regional level' (Marks 1993: 392). Case studies have given further empirical support to this thesis: for example, in otherwise centralizing states in southern Europe (Kazamias and Featherstone 2000) and the United Kingdom (John 1996; see also Goldsmith and Sperling 1997; for a comparison, see Goldsmith and Klausen 1997). Goetz (1995) found that Europeanization had affirmed, if not reinforced, key structural principles of German federalism. Goldsmith (this volume) surveys the state of the current literature on this aspect.

The notion of power and participation being dispersed is also found in studies of EU policy making which identify actors engaged in policy networks of a horizontal and vertical nature (Rhodes *et al.* 1996). In one of the most comprehensive accounts of this approach, Kohler-Koch and Eising (1999: 268) have argued that 'we are currently witnessing a transformation towards a network mode of governance at the level of the European Community'. Given the peculiar characteristics of the EU polity (its multilevel structure; the combination of supranational and inter-governmental elements; the strength of the judiciary; the functional and technocratic style; the heterogeneity and fluidity of the actors involved over the different policy phases), the emergence of a predominantly network mode of governance—as opposed to pluralism, statism, and corporatism—is seen as inevitable. The focus here is on how EU policies develop and the role of EU actors in the process, rather than domestic impacts and response. The precise impact of the new mode of governance on the distribution of power is not always closely defined, however, nor the appropriate 'test' for the falsification of the argument.

The restructuring of power within bargaining relations is most readily accounted for within the framework of 'rational choice institutionalism' (e.g. Scharpf 1988, 1997; Tsebelis 1994, 1995; Garrett and Tsebelis 1996). 'Europeanization' emphasizes how interests and capabilities might be redefined across a 'two-level' bargaining structure (Putnam 1988) or as involving 'nested games' (Tsebelis 1990). This complex interpenetration between the 'domestic' and the 'European' level creates a variety of opportunities for actors to exploit. First, governments can identify strategic advantages in being bound by EU commitments (Grande 1994, 1995; Moravcsik 1994). Second, differentiation may be made between 'core' and 'peripheral' states according to their relative impact on bargaining and policy outcomes. For example, individually, and even collectively, the southern states managed to have little distinctive impact on the elaboration of the EMU agreement of 1991 (Dyson and Featherstone 1999; Featherstone *et al.* 2000). Third, domestic actors may seek to be bound by EU constraints in order to obtain otherwise elusive reform at home and strategic advantage over their rivals, within or beyond government institutions. Dyson and Featherstone (1996, 1999) termed this strategy one of seeking to exploit a 'vincolo esterno' (external tie). They noted how technocrats in Italy viewed membership of EMU as an external constraint by which to impose fiscal and monetary discipline on the often-errant instincts of politicians in the old 'partitocrazia'. Giuliani (2000) found domestic empowerment in Italy from the European Union across a broader range of actors and policy spheres. Case studies in Ross and Martin (forthcoming) gave further evidence of a vincolo esterno strategy. By contrast, Featherstone *et al.* (2001), in their study of attempted pension reform in Greece, reported the weakness of technocratic empowerment resulting from the EMU commitment in the face of wider social and political obstacles ('veto-points'). The restructuring of bargaining relations is explicitly incorporated into several conceptual frameworks of 'Europeanization', as will be seen later.

'Europeanization' can also be seen as a defensive strategy with respect to the onset of 'globalization', and the neoliberalism associated with it. EMU offers currency stability within Europe and a defence against the US dollar. More generally, globalization is seen as a threat to the 'European social model' and joint action within the European Union might enable the latter to be sustained. Wincott's contribution to this volume discusses the clash of paradigms involved in this social policy debate and the ability of European states to exert regulatory authority. Such a focus illustrates the overlap between discussions of institutional settings and of policy adaptation.

Adaptation of Policies and Policy Processes

It is clear from Table 1.1 that the largest single category of contemporary applications relates to the public policy impacts of EU membership, though this grouping includes a variety of perspectives. Some emphasize the constraints on domestic policy posed by EU regulation. Examples here are Rothstein *et al.* (1999), Lecher and Rub (1999), Jordan (1998), Radaelli (1997), Eberlein (1997), Featherstone (1998), and Mangen (1996). A variant of this perspective is to note the juxtaposition of European Union and national regulatory systems, with the former in a process of replacing the latter (Abraham and Lewis 1999) or even potentially vice versa (Mazey 1998). Others note the indirect effects of the EU's role on national policy: e.g. Radaelli (1997) again, Chapman and Murie (1996), Benington and Taylor (1993), Nilson (1993), and Doogan (1992).

The recognition of domestic inputs into EU policy making as 'Europeanization' properly equates with more traditional notions of integration. Andersen (1995) examined the conditions under which the European Union could establish common policies. Venturelli (1993) analysed the scope for EU policy specifically in broadcasting, Mazey (1998) the difficulties of an EU regime for women's rights, and Lawton (1999) the development of a European airline policy. Groux *et al.* (1993) focused on the role of the ETUC as an EU-level actor. The common thread here is of building something new at the EU level, possibly involving a transfer of sovereignty.

Amongst scholars of international relations, the use of 'Europeanization' as a term has reflected the evolution of EU foreign policy coordination itself. Keatinge (1983: 138) was one of the first authors to refer to the 'Europeanization of foreign policy', in his study of how Irish policy had been reoriented as a consequence of EC entry. Shortly afterwards, Saeter (1984) applied a similar perspective to West Germany. Such usage was rare, however, as a result of the late, modest, and faltering development of EC competencies in this area. In the different context of NATO, a shift in its mode of operation, towards strengthening the European 'pillar', has been regarded as a process of 'Europeanization' (Charles and Albright 1984; Wallace 1994; Knutsen 1996). Such usage is unusual in suggesting 'Europeanization' as a synonym for regional cooperation, though it has a particular relevance juxtaposed to 'Atlanticism'. Allen (1998: 56–7) prefers the term 'Brusselization' to denote the emergence of the EU as a foreign policy actor. 'Europeanization' has also been linked to the involvement of European states in conflicts taking place elsewhere in the world. Gurbey (1999) referred to the 'Europeanization' of the Kurdish conflict; Salih (1989) the war in Africa. Here, the meaning relates to both cooperation and external intervention.

'Europeanization' as a process of domestic adaptation in the area of foreign policy became a more frequently used term with the growing importance of the 'European Political Cooperation' (EPC) process in the late 1980s, the development of the Common Foreign and Security Policy (CFSP) after Maastricht in 1991, and shifts consequent on the collapse of Communism. Heimann (1990) and Langewiesche (1999) identify such a shift on the part of

Germany, whilst Yost (1996) does so for France, and Torreblanca (2001) for Spain. Many of the case studies of national foreign policies in the European Union, contained in the volume edited by Manners and Whitman (2000), use 'Europeanization' to denote domestic adaptation as a result of EU membership. Yet a contrast probably still exists between the significance of EU pressures in this sphere and those in many areas of economic and social policy, as a result of foreign policy cooperation remaining the preserve of national sovereignty. Whilst 'the delegation of policy competences (in foreign affairs)... has had a limited impact on domestic policy choices' (Hix and Goetz 2000: 6), the more general impact of EU membership, or even the prospect of it, has in some cases led to a profound national reorientation. These more general effects are most glaring in states aspiring to join the club. Agh (1999*b*) detects such a change in 'East Central Europe', Kazan and Waever (1994) on the part of Turkey, Featherstone (2000) for Cyprus. Each of these cases refers to the strengthening of European institutions and/or the convergence of national policies to what are perceived to be the needs of 'Europe'. The relationship between these two dimensions is a matter that will be pursued further below.

Participation in EU institutions and processes is often linked to a domestic policy convergence or mimicry between member states. There are several aspects here that would need to be 'unpacked' for careful analysis (Bennett 1991; Radaelli this volume). Andersen and Eliassen identify the European Union 'as a system of transnational authority and policy-making', and they describe the effect, rather awkwardly, as 'Europeification' (1993: 255–6). In another comparative volume, Hanf and Soetendorp apply 'Europeanization' to 'a process in which Europe, and especially the European Union, become an increasingly more relevant and important point of political reference for the actors at the level of the member states', and the latter engage in intergovernmental and transnational policy networks that reach from Brussels into the domestic sphere (1998: 1). Mény *et al.* (1996) take a wider perspective. They posit a convergence process in which there is a 'progressive emergence of a bundle of common norms of action, the evolution of which escapes the control of any particular member state and yet decisively influences the behaviour of public policy actors' (1996: 8–9). Evidence for convergence can be found at three levels: the emergence of a European political agenda (the process of problem definition shifts to the European level); the forms of interest representation (for example, corporatism threatened by more open and competitive modes of representation); and the modes of operation of various actors. They do indeed find a convergence of public policies in Europe, but argue that in the absence of an arbitrating agency at the top, this constitutes a 'kind of cooperative federalism without a state' (1996: 17).

The key point here is that of causality, between structure and agency: convergence may occur as a loose transnational phenomenon and may be described as 'Europeanization'; but for the European Union to be identified as a prime agent, or facilitating structure, in this process requires evidence of direct causal effect. Convergence as a result of EU participation is far from being inevitable. Integration has significant asymmetrical effects (Héritier and Knill 2000) and has been incremental, irregular, and uneven. It is these qualities of differentiation that serve to restructure the interests and ideas of actors at the domestic level, providing the scope for advocacy coalitions on particular policies (Sabatier 1998).

'Europeanization' as a Conceptual Framework

This bibliographical survey has explored the range of different dimensions along which 'Europeanization' has been applied. It would be misleading, however, to suggest that 'Europeanization' has been widely used as a stand-alone conceptual framework. Instead, relevant studies—as already indicated above— are often couched within longer-established meta-theoretical frames—'new institutionalism'; liberal intergovernmentalism; multilevel governance; and policy networks (Marks 1996: 39–63; cf. Peterson and Bomberg 1999)—with 'Europeanization' as a loose epithet.

Whilst many use the term 'Europeanization', few writers have sought to define its precise meaning. Ladrech (1994) provided one of the first definitions and this has been widely cited. He saw 'Europeanization' as 'a process reorienting the direction and shape of politics to the degree that EC political and economic dynamics become part of the organizational logic of national politics and policy-making' (1994: 69). Inherent in this conception is the notion that actors redefine their interests and behaviour to meet the imperatives, norms, and logic of EU membership. Whilst it has the strength of incorporating both 'politics' and 'policy-making', it remains a somewhat loose definition. It is generally compatible with the domestic dimension of earlier neofunctionalist theory. It is unclear how this helps the analyst to gauge the extent of 'Europeanization'.

The analysis of 'Europeanization' in relation to foreign policy cooperation and adaptation has been obliged to take into account the relative weakness of EU competencies in this area, as compared to many aspects of market regulation. Perhaps as a result, the perspective developed by authors in this area has been wide, sometimes cutting across different strands of 'new institutionalism'. Tonra (Manners and Whitman 2000: 245) identified 'Europeanization' of foreign policy as: 'a transformation in the way in which national foreign policies are constructed, in the ways in which professional roles are defined and pursued and in the consequent internalization of norms and expectations arising from a complex system of collective European policy making'.

Smith (2000: 617–28) elaborated four major indicators of domestic adaptation to EU foreign policy cooperation: elite socialization; bureaucratic reorganization; constitutional change; and the increase in public support for EPC/CFSP. Participation in EU processes has impacts on national foreign policy cultures, because of their inherent features: they involve regular communication and consultation between states; the latter remain confidential and develop trust; decisions are made by consensus; and issues that are highly sensitive to one or more states are considered 'off-limits' (2000: 616). These features promote a focus on 'problem solving' that is conducive to the forging of common positions. He argues that procedure and culture are important—EU norms reorient those found at the domestic level—but there remains some ambiguity over whether he is also claiming an impact on national policy preferences.

It is what Goetz (2000: 222) terms the 'missing link' between (EU-level) pressures for change and the perceived (domestic) substantive adaptations that connects studies of Europeanization in different fields. The ontological challenge is to clarify the role of structure and agency within the Europeanization process, whilst identifying the mechanisms that are the interactive link between the 'domestic' and the 'EU' spheres of activity.

Olsen (1996) sought to capture 'Europeanization' for comparative politics, relating it to earlier perspectives on national integration and differentiation. In this perspective, European nation-states 'are integrating and disintegrating in non-synchronized ways', and Europeanization highlights an important dimension to the changes underway in domestic systems (March and Olsen 1995). Olsen saw the process in a largely EU-centric and top-down fashion, arguing that the future impact of the EU is still to be determined according to its own evolving policy balance.[4] In a more recent paper, Olsen (2002) distinguishes five possible uses of the term 'Europeanization' that parallel the typology developed here in the previous section. This new schema is broader than the European Union and is not exclusively 'top-down', in that it incorporates institution building at the European level.

'Europeanization' is most often placed within some type of institutional perspective. In a large comparative study, Caporaso *et al.* (2001) see 'Europeanization' as political institutionalization. This 'involves the development of formal and informal rules, procedures, norms, and practises governing politics at the European, national, and subnational levels'. Their focus is on cross-level political interactions, interpreted within the framework of historical institutionalism.

---

[4] The impact of Europeanization on the nation-state, he argued, 'will depend on the future emphasis of political, economic, cultural, and social integration; that is, the relative priority given to building a European polity, a market, a welfare society, or a culture' (1996: 264). With this in mind, he differentiates between a political agenda of developing institutions for market regulation; reallocation of resources; reinterpretation and reeducation of citizens and culture; and reorganization of the democratic polity.

They recognize different levels on which Europeanization may take place: institution-building at the European level; the impact of EU membership at the national level; and as a response to globalization. This is a useful and broad perspective, though some will not like the focus extending beyond domestic impacts. In any event, its specific empirical application again depends on further interpretation.

In one of the most explicit frameworks developed to date, Knill and Lehmkuhl (1999) outline three mechanisms of 'Europeanization'. By contrast to Caporaso *et al.*, their focus is exclusively 'top-down'. Each mechanism involves (policy) constraints from the European level that may yield domestic institutional change. Other forms of 'Europeanization'—as institutionalization at the EU level, as transnationalism between states—are not accounted for. The first mechanism they identify takes the form of 'positive integration' and is found when EU obligations prescribe an institutional model to which domestic arrangements have to be adjusted, with limited national discretion. They cite EU policy on environmental protection; health and safety at work; consumer protection; and some aspects of social policy. Europeanization here rests on the institutional 'goodness of fit' of domestic and European arrangements. The second mechanism is labelled 'negative integration' and occurs where EU legislation alters the domestic rules of the game. They cite the single market as an example. The impact is to alter the 'domestic opportunity structures' entailed in the distribution of power and resources between actors. Here, it is not a question of institutional fit or misfit, but rather 'the extent to which European policies have altered the strategic position of domestic actors' (1999: 3). The third, and weakest, mechanism is where European policy alters the beliefs and expectations of domestic actors, which may in turn involve a change of preferences and strategies, as well as institutional adaptation. They see this mechanism as one of 'framing integration', affecting perceptions.

The typology builds on much of the existing literature. The first mechanism reflects a new institutionalist (especially historical institutionalist) perspective on adaptation. The second can be related to multilevel bargaining games and rational choice. Sidney Tarrow (1994) applied the notion of 'political opportunity structures' to the analysis of social movements. The explanation of outcomes on the basis of actors seizing 'opportunities' may run a teleological risk: can opportunities be identified independently of the outcome? It can serve, though, a heuristic purpose. The third mechanism can be linked to sociological institutionalism (Checkel 1997, 1999) and to the work of Schoen and Rein (1994) on frame reflection. Although the typology does not cover all aspects of what might be reasonably termed 'Europeanization', as a schema of domestic structural transformation it represents significant conceptual refinement and it offers a set of empirical questions to the researcher. Not least, it stresses the potential significance of divergences between different national settings, accommodating the asymmetries of the process.

This aspect is taken further in the recent work of Schmidt. In an early article, she identified three key dimensions of adjustment: the economic, the institutional, and the ideational (1997). More recently, she has explored further the 'mechanics' of economic policy adjustment, thereby addressing the concerns raised by Goetz that were noted above. The impact of EU policies, Schmidt argues, has had different domestic effects in member states, depending on a number of intervening variables (2002). The primary attribute of EU policies, in this regard, is how narrowly they specify rules of implementation. The mirror-image is set by the mediating factors found within each domestic setting:

- (i) the economic vulnerability to global and European pressures;
- (ii) the political institutional capacity to respond as necessary;
- (iii) the 'fit' of EU policies with national policy legacies and preferences; and,
- (iv) the discourses that influence policy preferences and thus affect the sense of vulnerability and capacity.

The combination of these factors explains the outcomes of inertia, absorption, or transformation across states. Again, the approach builds on the works of several authors and it presents a clearly articulated (new institutionalist) framework, incorporating a range of independent variables, to explain differential outcomes.

Like Schmidt, the Caporaso *et al.* and the Knill and Lehmkuhl studies each draw heavily on 'new institutionalist' arguments. These need to be distinguished in order to clarify the framework of analysis (Hall and Taylor 1996). The first aspect is that each study examines '*the goodness of fit*', between EU-level processes, policies, and institutions and those found at the domestic level. The second aspect of new institutionalism that is relevant here is the notion of there being two 'logics' in the operation of institutions. This notion is based on the now classic study of March and Olsen (1984,1989). They posited a '*logic of appropriateness*', in which institutions affect actor behaviour by the latter internalizing the norms of the institution and developing identities that are compatible with it. In other words, actors develop a commitment to the institution or are persuaded of the legitimacy of its claims. A second logic—of '*consequentialism*'—affects the opportunities and constraints of actors within institutions; in other words, the distribution of power. Each of these aspects has been very influential in the elaboration of 'Europeanization' processes.

In this volume, Börzel and Risse begin with the 'goodness of fit' notion and seek to combine the two logics of March and Olsen. The logic of appropriateness, and the processes of persuasion, is placed within the sociological institutionalist approach. The logic of consequentialism, dealing with differential empowerment, is placed within 'rationalist institutionalism', drawing on rational choice precepts. The core of their argument is that the two logics of March and Olsen are not incompatible. This is a distinctive position to adopt: ideas and interests normally give rise to separate frameworks. They argue—rather persuasively—that both logics often occur simultaneously or they characterize different phases of the Europeanization process. Moreover, the impact of Europeanization is differential across policies, polities, and politics. The determining factors of the two logics differ, however: the logic of appropriateness depends on the activities of norm entrepreneurs and the nature of political culture; the logic of consequentialism rests on the existence of multiple veto points and the distribution of institutional resources between actors.

Other contributions in this volume question the interpretation of 'goodness of fit' in relation to adaptational pressure. Haverland argues that even with a misfit at the domestic level, other conditions must exist before shifts occur. Government reluctance to implement the appropriate policy changes may not be due to lack of will, but rather the result of being held back by domestic veto points. The argument refines the understanding of the strategic dilemmas faced by governments. Indeed, it would be fruitful to enrich the analytical framework further, by disaggregating 'government' into distinct actors. Börzel and Risse in this volume acknowledge that 'misfit' is a necessary, but not a sufficient, condition of domestic change. Moreover, in a crucial qualification to their framework they note that 'goodness of fit' is not a static phenomenon. This is important in that both the institutional settings of the European Union and of the member states are evolving, not fixed, and the task is to show the reciprocal effects on each.

Radaelli offers a more fulsome critique, noting the limits to the application of the 'goodness of fit' perspective, developing a similar point made by Knill and Lehmkuhl. 'Goodness of fit' is relevant when an EU model exists to be implemented. However, the impact of the EU can be felt via softer mechanisms and others, such as regulatory competition. Radaelli highlights several types of cases. First, with respect to 'negative integration' (the removal of internal market barriers), the stimulus to change is not the 'goodness of fit' between domestic and the EU commitments, but rather regulatory competition, for example, as a result of mutual recognition. Second, in policy areas like that of railways, the European Union has developed minimalist directives or non-compulsory regulations, which do not themselves create adaptational pressure, but may prepare the ground for major cognitive shifts in the domestic policy debate. Innovations in regulatory policy affected national debates on media ownership policy. Third, the European Union can affect national policy by creating policy forums and socialization processes that lead to cognitive convergence. Radaelli develops his argument further: the 'goodness of fit' notion must be qualified according to the type of domestic institutional setting that exists, taking account of strong/weak institutional differences, the institutional conditions that can resist or be thwarted by EU impacts.

It is tempting to see Radaelli's contribution as a refinement of the 'goodness of fit' perspective, rather than a refutation. It extends the understanding of how EU developments can be transmitted into domestic politics and it focuses attention on the need to differentiate institutional settings. It is a much subtler elaboration of the mechanisms of Europeanization operating in public policy processes. The two logics of appropriateness and of consequentialism remain valid: they should not be seen in a narrow, mechanistic sense. Moreover, as noted earlier, the role of structure and agency in the Europeanization process is mutually constitutive.

'Europeanization' as a research agenda

The chapter by Börzel and Risse in this volume ably outlines a general analytical framework for investigating the ramifications of Europeanization in terms of the domestic institutional setting. By extension, 'Europeanization' entails absorption, accommodation, and transformation of this setting in response to the demands of EU membership. Their incorporation of rationalist and sociological institutionalism leads them to combine a stress on actor interests and ideas, following the two logics of consequentialism and appropriateness. It is important, though, not to neglect the norms, rules, and procedures highlighted by the historical institutionalist perspective (Pierson 1996). Moreover, the Börzel and Risse formulation essentially provides an outline of potential mechanisms: the research task is to evaluate the significance of the different components of their framework in particular cases.

The design of the present volume reflects a sense that this perspective, broad as it already is, does not capture all the major features of how the EU affects member states. In particular, it may not be the best starting point for the study of how the EU impacts upon policies and policy processes. Here, Radaelli offers an alternative and insightful definition. 'Europeanization', he writes, consists of

processes of (a) construction (b) diffusion and (c) institutionalization of formal and informal rules, procedures, policy paradigms, styles, 'ways of doing things', and shared beliefs and norms which are first defined and consolidated in the EU policy process and then incorporated in the logic of domestic (national and subnational) discourse, political structures, and public policies.

The stress here on construction, diffusion, and institutionalization is itself wide-ranging. Some operational issues arise here. The emphasis on phenomena that are first set at the EU level and then impact domestically begs a 'chicken and egg' question: which comes first? Or, who is affecting whom? It may also not adequately reflect the emergence of cross-national policy networks that are not directly 'defined and consolidated in the EU policy process'. Finally, the 'logic of...discourse, structures and policies' remains somewhat ambiguous—'logic' here needs careful definition—and gives less emphasis to actors themselves. Yet, the prime advantage of Radaelli's conceptualization is that it fills some of the gaps left in the Börzel and Risse formulation—notably, in the treatment of the policy process—whilst it overlaps in other areas. Mörth in her contribution to this volume extends the coverage of Europeanization of public policy, by delineating processes of 'interpretation, translation, and editing' at the domestic level.

The two formulations—of, crudely, institutional settings and policy processes—are well grounded in the wider political science literature. Nevertheless, breadth and specificity are difficult bedfellows in this context. Authors working with other meta-theoretical frames would give more emphasis than either provides explicitly to the impact of the EU on the processes of central government administration, on subnational authorities (multilevel governance), and on policy networks. Later chapters in this volume do precisely that. Kassim investigates how national governments have sought to coordinate their EU policy at home, to be more effective at the EU level. Goldsmith's chapter addresses the impact of EU membership on regional and local governments.

More generally, the chapter by Grabbe makes the point that Europeanization effects are felt beyond the current member states. The so-called 'preaccession states' of central Europe have already experienced the impact of EU regulation, financial incentive, monitoring, political participation, and the like. Often the relationship between the EU and the applicant states can appear akin to that of David and Goliath, albeit with the former having no effective sling in this case. The contrast can be most stark for the microstates seeking EU entry (Cyprus, Malta). Featherstone (2000) examined the onset of 'Europeanization' for Cyprus, noting the extent of domestic structural transformation and government adaptation. A distinctive feature in this case is the strategic usage of the planned accession by the Cyprus Government to gain advantage over Turkey and its pariah 'statelet', the Turkish Republic of Northern Cyprus. The external dimension of 'Europeanization' is of major and continuing significance, but to encapsulate both this and the internal dimension in a single formulation is problematic.

Fundamentally, contrasts of this type affirm the relevance of examining the asymmetries of 'Europeanization' across settings, be it national or policy sector. Patterns may exist in national responses to 'Europeanisation', according to shared state characteristics. The studies contained in the volume by

Featherstone and Kazamias (2000) analyse the patterns of 'Europeanization' in southern Europe, noting likely core–periphery differences. Later contributions in the present volume investigate the nature of 'Europeanization' in specific and varied policy sectors. Haverland reflects on the state of current knowledge of the impact of the EU on environmental policies; Harcourt discusses the processes through which the EU has become a major actor in shaping national media regulation; and Wincott considers the role of the EU in shaping domestic social policies, in a context of competing international pressures on the state's regulatory capacity. An alternative lens by which to view sector impacts is that of gauging the response of interest groups to 'Europeanization'. The two chapters by Grote and Schneider and by Coen and Danreuther examine how the European Union has affected business groups in EU processes. Together, these chapters provide a rich empirical base on which to draw out key features of the 'Europeanization' process. This is a task taken up by Featherstone and Radaelli in the conclusion to this volume.

Conclusion: The Utility of 'Europeanization

Why use the term 'Europeanization'? The foregoing survey has highlighted the range of usage, the complex ontology, and the problems of research design inherent in the study of 'Europeanization'. Against this background, the utility of 'Europeanization' as a term in political science may be questioned. Yet, by using 'Europeanization', the researcher can provide a gateway to developments across the continent that are both current and complex. It is precisely the breadth of application and the demanding explanatory framework needed that attests to the value and importance of the term. The contemporary reality of asymmetrical patterns of absorption, accommodation, and transformation— to use the Börzel and Risse outline of institutional impacts in response to pressures emanating within the dynamics of EU integration—requires careful investigation. Crucially, as is evident from the works discussed above, such developments necessitate two prime types of innovation: first, the revision and/or synthesis of existing conceptual frameworks in political science and international relations; and, second, an empirical focus that cuts across traditional analytical dimensions (European, national, subnational, etc.). As a term for such innovation, 'Europeanization' acknowledges the dynamism, imbroglio, and limits to determinism in present-day Europe.

In this context, 'Europeanization' as an analytical focus stresses key changes in contemporary politics. Most notably, it highlights the:

- adaptation of institutional settings in the broadest sense (of rules, procedures, norms, practices) at different political levels in response to the dynamics of integration;

- role of the preaccession process in the continued democratization and 'marketization' of central Europe;
- emergence of new, cross-national policy networks and communities;
- nature of policy mimicry and transfer between states and subnational authorities;
- shifts in cognition, discourse, and identity affecting policy in response to European developments;
- restructuring of the strategic opportunities available to domestic actors, as EU commitments, having a differential impact on such actors, may serve as a source of leverage.

Such foci create a challenging research agenda and the chapters in this volume address many of the key questions that arise:

- How does Europeanization affect the interests and ideas, actors and institutions within the European Union? As noted here, the chapter by Börzel and Risse and that by Radaelli develop competing arguments on these questions.
- What is the impact of the European Union on policy processes?
- How significant is transnational learning in policy processes?
- Can we delineate how actors in different national settings 'translate' and 'edit' EU policy obligations?
- Why does adaptational pressure lead to policy convergence between states in some sectors, but not in others?

Radaelli provides a general analytical framework for this discussion, and more specific issues are examined in the empirical case studies provided in the chapters by Harcourt, Haverland, Mörth, and Wincott.

- What is the impact of the European Union on institutions and modes of governance?
- Are EU pressures prompting states to manage and coordinate their EU policies in a similar fashion?
- What is the impact of Europeanization on subnational authorities?
- How have interest groups responded to the new forms of EU politics?
- Are the impacts of the European Union in Central Europe comparable to those in existing member states?

These issues are taken up in the chapters by Kassim; Goldsmith; Grote and Schneider; Coen and Danreuther; and Grabbe.

The discussions that follow provide a convincing argument that the study of 'Europeanization' is central to an understanding of the contemporary politics of the continent, as Europe faces the new challenges of the twenty-first century.

REFERENCES

Abraham, J. and Lewis, G. (1999). 'Harmonizing and Competing for Medicines Regulation: How Healthy are the European Union's Systems of Drug Approval?' *Social Science and Medicine* 48(11): 1655–67.

Agh, A. (1999*a*). 'Europeanization of Policy-Making in East Central Europe: The Hungarian Approach to EU Accession', *Journal of European Public Policy* 6(5): 839–54.

——(1999*b*). 'Processes of Democratization in the East Central European and Balkan States: Sovereignty Related Conflicts in the Context of Europeanization', *Government and Post-Communist Studies* 32(3): 263–79.

Allen, D. (1998). 'Who Speaks for Europe? The Search for an Effective and Coherent External Policy', in J. Peterson and M. Sjursen (eds), *A Common Foreign Policy for Europe? Competing Visions of CFSP* (London: Routledge), 44–58.

Andersen, S. S. (1995). 'Europeanization of Policy Making' *Tidsskrift for Samfunnsforskning* 36(4): 495–518.

—— and Eliassen, K. A. (1993) (eds). *Making Policy in Europe: The Europeification of National Policy-Making* (London: Sage).

Benington, J. and Taylor M. (1993). 'Changes and Challenges Facing the UK Welfare State in the Europe of the 1990s', *Policy and Politics* 21(2): 121–34.

Bennett, C. (1991). 'Review Article: What Is Policy Convergence and What Causes It?' *British Journal of Political Science* 21: 215–33.

Benoit, B., Keeler, J. T. S., and Schain, M. A. (1997). 'Chirac's Challenge: Liberalization, Europeanization and Malaise in France', *Millenium Journal of International Studies* 26(2): 555–7.

Bhaskar, R. (1979). *The Possibility of Naturalism* (Brighton: Harvester).

Borneman, J. and Fowler, N. (1997). 'Europeanization' *Annual Review of Anthropology* 26: 487–514.

Bulmer, S. and Burch, M. (1998). 'Organizing for Europe: Whitehall, the British State and European Union', *Public Administration* 76, Winter, 601–28.

——(2001). 'The "Europeanisation" of Central Government: The UK and Germany in Historical Institutionalist Perspective', in G. Schneider and M. Aspinwall (eds), *The Rules of Integration: Institutionalist Approaches to the Study of Europe* (Manchester: Manchester University Press).

Caporaso (1996). 'The European Union and Forms of State: Westphalian, Regulatory or Post-Modern?' *Journal of Common Market Studies* 34(1): 29–52.

Checkel, J. (1997). 'International Norms and Domestic Politics: Bridging the Rationalist-constructivist Divide', *European Journal of International Relations* 3: 473–95.

——(1998). 'The Constructivist Turn in International Relations Theory', *World Politics* 50(2): 324–48.

——(1999). 'Social Construction and Integration', *Journal of European Public Policy* 6(4): 545–60.

Cesnys, G. (1991). 'The Neolithic and Bronze-Age Man in South-East Baltic Area', *Homo* 42(3): 232–43.

Chapman, M. and Murie, A. (1996). 'Housing and the European Union', *Housing Studies* 11(2): 307–18.

Charles, D. and Albright, D. (1984). 'Europeanization of NATO', *Bulletin of the Atomic Scientists* 40(9): 45–6.

Cole, A. (2001). 'National and Partisan Contexts of Europeanisation', *Journal of Common Market Studies* 39(1): 15–36.

Daniels, P. (1998). 'From Hostility to "Constructive Engagement": The Europeanisation of the Labour Party', *West European Politics* 21(1): 72–96.

Diamandouros, N. (1994). 'Cultural Dualism and Political Change in Post-Authoritarian Greece', *Estudios-Working Papers* 50, Madrid: Centro de Estudios Avanzados en Ciencias Sociales.

Dineen, D. A. (1992). 'Europeanization of Irish Universities', *Higher Education* 24(3): 391–411.

Doogan, K. (1992). 'The Social Charter and the Europeanization of Employment and Social Policy', *Policy and Politics* 20(3): 167–76.

Dyson, K. and Featherstone, K. (1996). 'Italy and EMU as a "*Vincolo Esterno*": Empowering the Technocrats, Transforming the State', *South European Society and Politics* 1(2): 272–99.

——(1999). *The Road to Maastricht: Negotiating Economic and Monetary Union* (Oxford: Oxford University Press).

Eberlein, B. (1997). 'The Decline of French Statism: The Case of Research and Technology Policy', *Politische Vierteljahresschrift* 38(3): 441–86.

Featherstone, K. (1998). ' "Europeanization" and the Centre Periphery: The Case of Greece in the 1990s', *South European Society and Politics* 3(1): 23–39.

——(2000). 'Cyprus and the Onset of Europeanization: Strategic Usage, Structural Transformation and Institutional Adaptation', *South European Society and Politics* 5(2): 141–65.

——and Kazamias, G. (2000). *Europeanization and the Southern Periphery* (London: Frank Cass). Also published as special issue of *South European Society and Politics*.

——and Papadimitriou, D. (2000). 'Greece and the Negotiation of Economic and Monetary Union: Preferences, Strategies, and Institutions', *Journal of Modern Greek Studies* 18: 393–414.

Featherstone, K. Kazamias, G. and Papadimitriou, D. (2001). 'The Limits of External Empowerment: Greece, EMU and Pension Reform', *Political Studies* 49: 462–80.

Finkhafner, D. (1998). 'Organized Interests in the Policy-making Process in Slovenia', *Journal of European Public Policy* 5(2): 285–302.

Garrett, G. and Tsebelis, G. (1996): 'An Institutional Critique of Intergovernmentalism', *International Organization* 50: 269–300.

Giddens, A. (1984). *The Constitution of Society* (Cambridge: Polity Press).

Giuliani, M. (2000). 'Europeanization and Italy: A Bottom-Up Process?' *South European Society and Politics* 5(2): 47–72.

Goetz, K. (1995). 'National Governance and European Integration: Inter-Governmental Relations in Germany', *Journal of Common Market Studies* 33(1): 91–116.

——(2000). 'European Integration and National Executives: A Cause in Search of an Effect?' *West European Politics* 23(4): 211–40.

——and Hix, S. (2000). 'Introduction: European Integration and National Political Systems', *West European Politics*, special issue 'Europeanised Politics? European Integration and National Political Systems', 23(4) (Oct.).

Goldsmith, M. (1993). 'The Europeanisation of Local Government', *Urban Studies* 30(4/5): 683–99.

——and Klausen, K. (1997) (eds). *European Integration and Local Government* (Cheltenham: Edward Elgar).

——and Sperling, E. (1997). 'Local Governments and the EU: The British Experience', in Goldsmith and Klausen (eds).

Gourevitch, P. (1986). *Politics in Hard Times: Comparative Responses to International Economic Crises* (Ithaca, NY: Cornell University Press).

Grande, E. (1995). 'Das Paradox der Schwaeche, Forschungspolitik und die Einflusslogik europaischer Politikverflechtung' [The Paradox of Weakness: Research Policy and the Logic of Influence of Interlinked European Politics], in M. Jachtenfuchs and B. Kohler-Koch (eds), *Europaische Integration* [*European Integration*] (Opladen: Leske and Budrich).

Gransow, V. (1982). 'The End of the Ideological Age: The Europeanization of Europe', *Argument* 24(Mar.); 299–300.

Groux, G., Mouriaux, R. and Pernot, J. M. (1993). 'L'européanisation du mouvement syndical: la confédération, européene des syndicats': *Mouvement Social*, 162, 41–67.

Haas, E. B. (1958). *The Uniting of Europe: Political, Social and Economic Forces 1950–57* (Stanford, CA: Stanford University Press).

Hall, P. and Taylor, R. (1996). 'Political Science and the Three New Institutionalisms', *Political Studies* 44: 936–57.

Hanf, K. and Soetendorp, B. (1998). *Adapting to European Integration: Small States and the European Union* (London: Longman).

Harmsen, R. (1999). 'The Europeanization of National Administrations: A Comparative Study of France and the Netherlands'. *Governance* 12(1): 81–113.

Heimann, G. (1990). 'The Weakening of Blocks and the Europeanization of Germany', *Europa Archiv* 45(5): 167–72.

Hennis, M. (2001). 'Europeanization and Globalization', *Journal of Common Market Studies* 39(5): 829–50.

Héritier, A. and Knill, C. (2000). 'Differential Responses to European Policies: a Comparison', *Max Planck Projektgruppe Recht der Gemeinschaftsgüter Preprint 2000–3*, Bonn.

Holden, R. (1999). 'Labour's Transformation: Searching for the Point of Origin–the European dynamic', *Politics* 19(2): 103–8.

John, P. (1996). 'Europeanisation in a Centralising State: Multi-Level Governance in the U.K.', *Regional and Federal Studies* 6(2).

——and LeGalès, P. (1997). 'Is the Grass Greener on the Other Side? What Went Wrong with French Regions, and the Implications for England', *Policy and Politics* 25(1): 51–60.

——and Whitehead, A. (1997). 'The Renaissance of English Regionalism in the 1990s', *Policy and Politics* 25(1): 7–17.

Joppke, C. (1995). 'Toward a New Sociology of the State: On Brubaker, Roger', *Archives Europeennes de Sociologie* 36(1): 168–78.

Jordan, A. (1998). 'Private Affluence and Public Squalor? The Europeanization of British Coastal Bathing Water Policy', *Policy and Politics* 26(1): 33–54.

Jorgensen, T. B. (1999). 'The Public Sector in an In-Between Time: Searching for New Public Values', *Public Administration* 77(3): 565–84.

Kazan, I. and Waever, O. (1994). 'Turkey between Europe and Europeanization', *Internasjonal Politikk* 52(2): 139–75.

Keatinge, P. (1983). 'European Political Cooperation: Towards a Foreign Policy for Europe', *Journal of Common Market Studies* 21(3).

Kerr, H. (1973). 'Changing Attitudes Through International Participation: European Parliamentarians and Integration', *International Organization* 27: 45–83.

Knill, C. and Lehmkuhl, D. (1999). 'How Europe Matters: Different Mechanisms of Europeanization', *European Integration Online Papers* 3(7).

Knutsen, B. O. (1996). 'The Europeanization of NATO and a Common European Defence Policy', *Internasjonal Politikk* 54(4): 501–26.

Kohler-Koch, B. and Eising, R. (eds) (1999). *The Transformation of Governance in the European Union* (London: Routledge).

Kohout, J. (1999). 'On Patocka's Philosophy on History', *Filosoficky Casopis* 47(1): 97–103.

Ladrech, R. (1994). 'The Europeanization of Domestic Politics and Institutions: The Case of France', *Journal of Common Market Studies* 32(1): 69–88.

Lawton, T. (1999). 'Governing the Skies: Conditions for the Europeanisation of Airline Policy', *Journal of Public Policy* 19(1): 91–112.

Lecher, W. and Rub, S. (1999). 'The Constitution of European Works Councils: From Information Forum to Social Actor?' *European Journal of Industrial Relations* 5(1): 7–25.

Levitsky, J. E. (1994). 'The Europeanization of the British Legal Style', *American Journal of Comparative Law* 42(2): 347–80.

Maguire, J., Poulton, E., and Possamai, C. (1999). 'The War of the Words? Identity Politics in Anglo-German Press Coverage of EURO '96', *European Journal of Communication* 14(1): 61–89.

Mair, P. (2000). 'The Limited Impact of Europe on National Party Systems', *West European Politics* 23(4): 27–51.

Mangen, S. (1996). 'The Europeanization of Spanish Social Policy', *Social Policy and Administration* 30(4): 305–23.

Manners, I. and Whitman, R. G. (2000). (eds), *The Foreign Policies of the European Union Member States* (Manchester: Manchester University Press).

March, J. and Olsen, J. P. (1984). 'The New Institutionalism: Organizational Factors in Political Life', *American Political Science Review* 78(3): 734–49.

——(1989). *Rediscovering Institutions: The Organizational Basis of Politics* (New York: The Free Press).

——(1995): *Democratic Governance* (New York: Free Press).

Marks, G. (1993). 'Structural Policy and Multilevel Governance in the EC', in A. Cafruny and G. Rosenthal (eds) *The State of the European Community II: The Maastricht Debates and Beyond* (Boulder: Lynne Rienner).

——(1996). 'An Actor-Centred Approach to Multi-Level Governance', *Regional and Federal Studies* 6(2): Summer, 20–38.

Martin, S. (1993). 'The Europeanization of Local Authorities: Challenges for Rural Areas', *Journal for Rural Studies* 9(2): 153–61.

Mazey, S. (1998). 'The European Union and Women's Rights: From the Europeanization of National Agendas to the Nationalization of a European Agenda?' *Journal of European Public Policy* 5(1): 131–52.

Mény, Y. (1996). 'Introduction', in Y. Mény, P. Muller, and J-L. Quermonne (eds), *Adjusting to Europe: The Impact of the European Union on National Institutions and Policies* (London: Routledge).

—— Muller, P., and Quermonne, J. L. (1996). *Adjusting to Europe: The Impact of the European Union on National Institutions and Policies* (London: Routledge).

Mjoset, L. (1997). 'The Historical Meanings of Europeanization', *Arena Working Paper* 24 (Oslo: University of Oslo).

Moravcsik, A. (1994). 'Why the European Community Strengthens the State: Domestic Politics and International Cooperation', *Center for European Studies Working Paper* 52 (Cambridge, Mass: Harvard University).

Nilson, H. R. (1993). 'European Integration and Environmental Cooperation in the Barents Region: The Baltic Sea Cooperation—A Model for Europeanization', *Internasjonal Politikk* 51(2): 185–98.

Olafsdottir, H., Gudmundsdottir, A., and Asmundsson, G. (1997). 'The Europeanization of Drinking Habits in Iceland after the Legalization of Beer', *European Addiction Research* 3(2): 59–66.

Olsen, J. P. (1996). 'Europeanization and Nation-state Dynamics', in S. Gustavsson and L. Lewin (eds), *The Future of the Nation-State* (Stockholm: Nerenius and Santérus Publishers).

—— (2002). 'The Many Faces of Europeanization', *Arena Working Papers*, 01/2, Oslo.

Pamir, M. (1994). 'Turkey between Europe and Europeanization', *Internasjonal Politikk* 52(2): 177–9.

Peterson, J. and Bomberg, E. (2000). *Decision-Making in the European Union* (London: Macmillan).

Pierson, P. (1996). 'The Path to European Integration: A Historical Institutionalist Analysis', *Comparative Political Studies* 29: 123–63.

Poruciuc, A. (1992). 'Problems and Patterns of the Southeast European Ethnogenesis and Glottgenesis (*c.*6500BC–AD1500)', *Mankind Quarterly* 33(1): 3–41.

Putnam, R. (1988). 'Diplomacy and Domestic Politics: The Logic of Two-Level Games', *International Organization* 42: 427–60.

Radaelli, C. (1997). 'How Does Europeanization Produce Domestic Policy Change? Corporate Tax Policy in Italy and the United Kingdom', *Comparative Political Studies* 30(5): 553–75.

Rhodes, R. A. W., Bache, I., and George, S. (1996). 'Policy Networks and Policy Making in the European Union: A Critical Appraisal', in L. Hooghe (ed.), *Cohesion Policy and European Integration* (Oxford: Clarendon Press), 367–87.

Risse, T., Caporaso, J., and Green Cowles, M. (2001). 'Introduction', in M. Green Cowles, J. Caporaso and T. Risse (eds), *Transforming Europe: Europeanization and Domestic Change* (Ithaca, NY: Cornell U.P.).

Rometsch, R. and Wessels, W. (eds) (1996). *The European Union and Member States: Towards Institutional Fusion?* (Manchester: Manchester University Press).

Rothstein, H., Irwin, A., Yearley, S., and McCarthy, E. (1999). 'Regulatory Science, Europeanization and the Control of Agrochemichals', *Science Technology and Human Values* 24(2): 241–64.

Sabatier, P. (1998). 'The Advocacy Coalition Framework: Revisions and Relevance for Europe', *Journal of European Public Policy* 5(1): 98–130.

Saeter, M. (1984). 'Germany in European Politics: East–West Confrontation or Europeanization?', *Internasjonal Politikk* SIS2: 63–91.

Salih, MAM (1989). 'The Europeanization of War in Africa: From Traditional to Modern Warfare', *Current Research on Peace and Violence* 12(1): 27–37.

Scharpf, F. (1988). 'The Joint-Decision Trap: Lessons from German Federalism and European Integration', *Public Administration* 66(3): 239–78.

——(1997). *Games Real Actors Play* (Boulder, Col.: Westview Press).

Schmidt, V. A. (1997). 'Discourse and (Dis)integration in Europe: The Cases of France, Germany and Great Britain', *Daedalus* 126(3): 167–99.

——(2001). 'The Politics of Economic Adjustment in France and Britain: When does Discourse Matter'? *Journal of European Public Policy* 8(2): 247–64.

——(2002). 'Europeanization and the Mechanics of Economic Policy Adjustment', *Journal of European Public Policy*, forthcoming.

Schoen, D. and Rein, M. (1994). *Frame Reflection* (New York: Basic Books).

Seitter, W. (1993). 'Adult Education between Europeanization and National Traditions', *Zeitschrift fur Padagogik* 39(3): 427–42.

Smith, M. E. (2000). 'Conforming to Europe: The Domestic Impact of EU Foreign Policy Co-operation', *Journal of European Public Policy* 7(4).

Soysal, Y. (1994). *Limits of Citizenship: Migrants and Postnational Membership in Europe* (Chicago: University of Chicago Press).

Tarrow, S. (1994). *Power in Movement: Social Movements, Collective Action and Politics* (Cambridge: Cambridge University Press).

Torreblanca, J. I. (2001). 'Ideas, Preferences and Institutions: Explaining the Europeanization of Spanish Foreign Policy', *Arena Working Papers*, Oslo, 01/26.

Tsebelis, G. (1990). *Nested Games: Rational Choice in Comparative Politics* (Berkeley: University of California Press).

——(1994). 'The Power of the European Parliament as a Conditional Agenda-setter', *American Political Science Review* 88: 128–42.

——(1995). 'Conditional Agenda Setting and Decision Making Inside the European Parliament', *Journal of Legislative Studies* 1: 65–93.

Turner, L. (1996). 'The Europeanization of Labour: Structure before Action', *European Journal of Industrial Relations* 2(3): 325–44.

Venturelli, S. S. (1993). 'The Imagined Transnational Public Sphere in the European Community Broadcast Philosophy: Implications for Democracy', *European Journal of Communication* 8(4): 491–518.

Yost, D. S. (1996). 'France's Nuclear Dilemmas', *Foreign Affairs* 75(1): 108–20.

Wallace, W. (1994). 'Rescue or Retreat: The Nation State in Western Europe, 1945–1993', *Political Studies* 42: 52–76.

Wessels, W. (1998). 'Comitology: Fusion in Action—Politico-Administrative Trends in the EU System', *Journal of European Public Policy* 5(2): 209–34.

2

The Europeanization of Public Policy

CLAUDIO M. RADAELLI

Introduction

This chapter deals with the Europeanization of public policy, with emphasis on the problems that researchers encounter when they try to get to grips with the concept of Europeanization, the issue of explanation, the measurement of effects, and the control of alternative rival hypotheses. The chapter covers the domestic impact of the public policy of the European Union (EU), hence one could use the term 'EU-ization' in this context. As shown by Featherstone, in his introduction, the scope of Europeanization can go beyond EU-isation— for example, it can include the transfer of policy from one European country to several other countries. But here I am primarily concerned with how the EU impacts on the domestic policy systems of member states. The reference to member states is indicative of another limitation of this chapter. Indeed, the analysis presented here is based on evidence coming from the EU member states. The reader interested in Europeanization in the context of enlargement should refer to Grabbe's chapter in this volume.

Before we start our discussion of the Europeanization of *public policy*, it is useful to look at the status of the concept of Europeanization and the place of public policy therein. Empirical analysis is essential. However, it has to be accompanied by a delimitation of the concept. Research on Europeanization runs the risk of conceptual stretching. As shown by the introduction to this volume, the scope of Europeanization as a research agenda is broad. The question arises whether this scope is so broad as to stretch the concept of Europeanization beyond the limit of what is acceptable in the social sciences. Indeed, the implications of sloppy conceptual frameworks should not be overlooked.

The section 'The Concept', therefore, exposes these implications and suggests ideas in the direction of conceptual precision. Concepts are relevant in the

I am grateful to European Integration online papers (EIoP) and *Politique Européenne* for the opportunity to present a draft of this chapter to their readership.

context of analytical frameworks, mechanisms of explanation, and theories. Thus, the next step is to make the concept of Europeanization amenable to empirical analysis and to connect it to explanation, although theoretical work on Europeanization is still in its early days. Accordingly, the section 'What is Europeanized and to What Extent?' 'unpacks' the concept of Europeanization by using a simple taxonomy. The section 'Vertical and Horizontal Mechanisms' illustrates the main mechanisms involved in Europeanization of public policy, before the key explanatory variables are discussed in section 'Towards Explanation?' The section 'Conclusions' presents suggestions for future research. The key argument throughout this chapter is that research on Europeanization presents an opportunity to bring EU scholars closer to 'normal' political science. As shown by Hassenteufel and Surel (2000), this is an important item in the agenda of EU studies, in order to avoid intellectual segregation and contribute to cumulative knowledge in the social sciences. By focusing on the Europeanization of public policy, I will discuss some prerequisites for 'normal' analysis, that is, the definition of concepts, the methodology, the identification of research designs, and questions and puzzles amenable to theoretical public policy analysis. There is no need to invent ad hoc theories and models that do not travel beyond Europeanization. Quite the opposite indeed, the goal in this chapter is to show how several important aspects of Europeanization can be handled by using standard analysis of concepts and the methodology of comparative policy analysis. As such, Europeanization has potential for conversation with (as opposed to segregation from) the main research agendas in contemporary political science—a point that will be developed in the conclusions of this volume.

The Concept

Conceptual analysis is a fundamental step in comparative political science, as shown by the recommendations formulated by Sartori in several essays (Sartori 1970, 1984, 1991). Concepts that are not well-defined lead to confusion and elusive language. Concepts that do not specify the level of analysis generate mistakes in terms of the 'ladder of abstraction', that is, they obfuscate the relations between *genus* and *species*. Concepts without negation are universals: they point to everything, 'conceptions without specified termination or boundaries' (Sartori 1970: 1042).

What is the state of the current research on Europeanization in the light of conceptual analysis? The problem is not that different authors assign different meanings to Europeanization—this is an indicator of a vibrant debate. Instead, the potential risks refer to (a) concept misformation, (b) conceptual stretching, and (c) 'degreeism'.

Definitions and their Problems

Lawton (1999), for example, suggests that Europeanization is the *de jure* transfer of sovereignty to the EU level, and distinguishes this concept from 'Europeification', that is, the de facto sharing of power between national governments and the European Union. Thus, Europeanization and 'Euro-peification' are identified with the emergence of EU competencies and the pooling of power. Börzel (1999: 574) instead draws attention to what happens once power has been transferred to Brussels. She defines Europeanization as a 'process by which domestic policy areas become increasingly subject to European policy-making'. This notion goes in the right direction. However, it requires further specification, if one wants to distinguish between the simple fact that there is more 'Europe' in domestic policies and the more profound impact of the European Union in policy areas which have now become dominated by a European logic of behaviour. Additionally, the reference to an 'increasing' role of European policy making may complicate things in terms of degreeism (see below): at the level of member states, most political phenomena seem to show at least a minimum degree of Europeanization. How does one distinguish between Europeanized policies and the ones which are still eminently domestic?

Risse, Cowles, and Caporaso, in their introduction to Cowles *et al.* (2001: 3), have provided yet another option with the following definition:

We define Europeanization as the emergence and development at the European level of distinct structures of governance, that is, of political, legal, and social institutions associated with political problem-solving that formalize interactions among the actors, and of policy networks specializing in the creation of authoritative European rules.

To begin with, the reader is struck by the emphasis on policy networks. Arguably, the authors use the notion of networks with wide latitude, that is, networks as patterns of social interaction present everywhere except under conditions of extremely autocratic rule. Yet the EU debate displays different positions on the usefulness of the network approach (see Kassim 1994 for a critical position). Additionally, networks are one possible 'mode' of governance (as opposed to corporatism, pluralism, and statism; see Kohler-Koch 1999), not an ever-present phenomenon. Thus, one would think that the relevance of policy networks is a matter of empirical (rather than definitional) analysis. More importantly still, the emphasis on the 'creation of rules' and 'the European level' suggests an extremely broad notion of Europeanization, inclusive of both EU policy and politics and their repercussions on national systems. But if Europeanization has to have a precise meaning, it has to be different and more selective than the notions of EU policy formation and European integration. Common sense indicates that Europeanization has something to do with the penetration of the European dimension in national arenas of politics and policy, a point raised by Börzel (1999).

Ladrech heads towards a promising direction when he puts emphasis on Europeanization as process. He argues that Europeanization is an:

Incremental process re-orienting the direction and shape of politics to the degree that EC political and economic dynamics become part of the organizational logic of national politics and policy-making. (Ladrech 1994: 69)

By 'organizational logic' he means the 'adaptive processes of organizations to a changed or changing environment' (Ladrech 1994: 71). In doing so, he underlines the role of adaptation, learning, and policy change. The emphasis on organizations is broad enough as to accommodate both processes wherein networks play a role and instances of Europeanization in which there are no networks at work. The drawback is that too much emphasis on organizations may obfuscate the role of individuals and policy entrepreneurs. Further, the object of Europeanization is limited to 'national politics and policy making'. One could add identities and the cognitive component of politics. Drawing upon Ladrech's definition, I would argue that the concept of Europeanization refers to:

Processes of (a) construction, (b) diffusion, and (c) institutionalization of formal and informal rules, procedures, policy paradigms, styles, 'ways of doing things', and shared beliefs and norms which are first defined and consolidated in the making of EU public policy and politics and then incorporated in the logic of domestic discourse, identities, political structures, and public policies.

This definition stresses the importance of change[1] in the logic of political behaviour. Europeanization involves the domestic assimilation of EU policy and politics, hence the definition refers to processes of institutionalization (Stone Sweet *et al.* 2001). Another point: the definition does not mention organizations. By contrast, it accommodates both organizations and individuals. It is sufficiently broad to cover the major interests of political scientists, such as political structure, public policy, identities, and the cognitive dimension of politics. It can be applied both to EU member states and to other countries (see Grabbe, this volume). The definition does not mention EU laws or decisions of a similar level, but 'EU public policy' because it includes modes of governance which are not targeted towards law making, such as the open method of coordination. As Wincott argues in his contribution to this volume, it would be a mistake to assume that the EU level has a high level of coherence from which Europeanization proceeds. Rather, 'the European Union is always still in formation, built through political contests and struggles' (Wincott, this volume). Therefore, the definition stresses the *making* of policy, without

---

[1] The process can be more or less incremental. Indeed, one the most interesting areas of research on Europeanization concerns the time, timing, and tempo of the process. See below, Towards Explanation?

assuming that there is a coherent, rational layer of 'EU decisions' from which Europeanization descends.

The sceptical reader may observe that this definition of Europeanization is too restrictive as it ignores processes that go beyond the EU dimension. Research themes such as the development of the European identity and culture, and the imitation and transfer of policy between one European country and another (without the involvement of the European Union) are not covered by my definition. Europe is an area of regional integration where processes of identity formation, public policy diffusion, and institutional change can take place independently of the European Union. This is certainly true, but I would still defend this definition by introducing the difference between a preanalytic focus on the broad notion of 'what is Europe' and an analytic focus leading to definition, operationalization, and explanation.

More precisely, I would point out to the reader the difference between *background concepts* and *systematized concepts* (Adcock and Collier 2001). A background concept represents 'the constellation of potentially diverse meanings associated with a given concept' (Adcock and Collier 2001: 530). Background concepts do not typically refer to explicit definitions. At this level, Europeanization covers a collection of diverse research themes and understandings relevant to a wide community of scholars (political scientists, sociologists, and historians). By contrast, the systematized concept is a specific formulation adopted by a particular group of researchers *and* is 'commonly formulated in terms of an explicit definition' (Adcock and Collier 2001: 530). Think of the difference between a 'dictionary definition' of a concept and the broader encyclopedic knowledge within which the meaning of the concept is embedded. An encyclopedic (or preanalytic) focus is fully legitimate but it does not help scholars to understand and explain complex phenomena. We need to be explicit about what we want to investigate. Systematized concepts can do a better job, although 'dictionary definitions' can vary according to the specific community of scholars involved. This chapter addresses one community of scholars (namely, political scientists interested in the European Union); hence, I opt for a systematized concept centered on the European Union. As mentioned above, I acknowledge that Europeanization can take on broader meanings within other communities of scholars, as shown by Featherstone in this volume. This is not a problem, provided that the conceptual elements of empirical analysis are clarified upfront.

Concept Stretching

Turning to conceptual stretching, according to elementary logic a concept can be described by two fundamental properties, that is, extension and intension

(Sartori 1970). Intension refers to the collection of properties covered by a concept. Extension represents the class of entities to which the concept applies. There is a trade-off between intension and extension. The more properties are included in the concept of Europeanization, the smaller will be the class of empirical instances. Although there are no priorities in the choice between intension and extension, a concept with high intension has high discriminatory power. Most studies of Europeanization, however, seem to privilege extension. This is probably the result of an early stage of research, when the analytic grid has to be broad enough as to accommodate a wide range of empirical observations that may have something to do with Europeanization. Thus, we have read that Europeanization is supposed to explain processes of cultural change, new identity formation, policy change, administrative innovation, and even modernization. It covers the formation of European public policy and the effects of EU decisions on national systems. It affects member states but also the wider world.

However, the more we know about Europeanization, the more exigent we should be in terms of intension, that is, the properties of the concept. Otherwise the risk of degreeism may loom large. Degreeism, as defined by Sartori (1970, 1991), occurs when differences in kind are replaced by differences of degrees. As we are not able to see the difference between a cat and a dog, we speak of different degrees of cat-dogs (Sartori 1991). The metaphor of Europeanization as a continuum and the notion of domestic political systems being 'increasingly' penetrated by EU policy make the distinction between the cat and the dog difficult. Without boundaries, it is impossible to define Europeanization. But the literature is somewhat reluctant to tell us what falls outside Europeanization. If everything is Europeanized to a certain degree, what is *not* Europeanized? In this case again, political scientists in the early days of research on a new topic have been hesitant to exclude possible indirect, unforeseen, and simply odd instances of Europeanization. They tend to argue that 'a certain degree of Europeanization' may be found almost everywhere. In terms of sociology of knowledge, one can understand this cautious approach. Political scientists do not want to preclude innovation by posing a rigid fence around a developing area of research. But this strategy has the cost of conceptual sloppiness and degreeism.

Shall one then stick to a very narrow definition of Europeanization, thus limiting the scope of analysis? Connotative precision (i.e. high intension) is vital in this stage of research, but one does not need to narrow the analysis to a few selective aspects of Europeanization. The best strategy—I argue—is to unpack the concept and to distinguish between Europeanization and other terms (thus, showing what Europeanization is not). To unpack a concept—Sartori explained—is to decompose 'mental compounds into orderly and manageable sets of component units' (Sartori 1970: 1083).

Europeanization and Contiguous (but Different) Terms

In the next section, I will present my own 'unpacking' proposals. At the onset, however, it is indispensable to draw the line between Europeanization and other concepts, namely convergence, harmonization, integration, and policy formation.

To begin with, Europeanization is not convergence. The latter can be a consequence of Europeanization. Convergence is not Europeanization because there is a difference between a process and its consequences. However, Europeanization can also produce divergence or convergence limited to a family of countries. Policy studies have detected considerable variability. Some authors have found consistent convergence of media markets regulation induced by Europeanization (Harcourt, this volume), but the Europeanization of transport policy has resulted in striking domestic differences (Héritier and Knill 2001).

Europeanization should not be confused with harmonization. In a study of French environmental policy for the agricultural sector, Montpetit concludes that 'Europeanization encourages domestic policy change, but not all member states will opt for the same types of change. Europeanization does not necessarily accord with harmonization. (Montpetit 2000: 590). Harmonization reduces regulatory diversity, typically by providing a level playing field (see Leebron 1996 on types, claims, and goals of harmonization). Europeanization leaves the issue of diversity open. The outcome of Europeanization can be regulatory diversity, intense competition, even distortions of competition.

Finally, Europeanization is not political integration. Typically, theories of integration address the question: 'why do different countries join forces and build up supranational institutions?' Europeanization would not exist without European integration. But the latter concept belongs to the ontological stage of research, that is, the understanding of a process in which countries pool sovereignty, whereas the former is post-ontological, being concerned with what happens once EU institutions are in place and produce their effects (on EU 'ontology' and post-ontological perspectives see Caporaso 1996). This begs the question of the relationship between Europeanization and general theories of integration. As shown by Börzel (1999: 576–7), theories of integration focus on the issue whether European integration strengthens the state (intergovernmentalism), weakens it, or triggers 'multilevel governance' dynamics. The post-ontological focus of Europeanization brings us to other, more specific, questions, such as the role of domestic institutions in the process of adaptation to Europe. In the literature on Europeanization, the final results in terms of 'strengthening' or 'hollowing out' of the state are always conditional—for example, it depends on the configuration and response of domestic institutions.

Europeanization and EU policy formation should be kept distinct at the conceptual level. But in the real world they are interconnected. European policy is not a mysterious deus ex machina situated 'up there'. Instead, it originates from processes of conflict, bargaining, imitation, diffusion, and interaction between national (and often subnational) and EU level actors. 'The European Union'—Goetz argues—'is best understood as an arena rather than an actor' (Goetz 2002: 4).

Further, the outcomes of Europeanization can feed back into the process of EU policy reformulation. National actors can draw lessons from Europeanization and seek to change or adapt EU policy. Thus, Börzel (2001) and Bulmer and Burch (2001) argue that Europeanization is a two-way process. Member states upload their preferences to Brussels via complex negotiations and download them from various EU policy menus. Goetz (2002: 4) concludes that 'Europeanization is circular rather than unidirectional, and cyclical rather than one-off'.

However, *analytically* one should distinguish between the process leading to the formation of a certain policy, and the reverberation of that policy in national arenas. Otherwise, the concept of Europeanization—in the sense of Börzel and Bulmer and Burch—would be exactly the same as the concept of 'EU policy process', which includes both uploading and downloading. Parsimony and elementary logic would suggest that we do not use two concepts—that is, Europeanization and policy process—for the same thing. In empirical research, one can go beyond Europeanization and show how EU policy was first formulated: but this is a matter concerning the scope of one's empirical research, not a matter of definition. More generally, I do not see why one cannot treat Europeanization as an example of 'second-image reversed' process (Gourevitch 1978). If 'second-image reversed' research designs are legitimate tools of scientific inquiry, then Europeanization is nothing but an instance of these designs.

What is Europeanized and to What Extent?

As mentioned above, concepts are just a component of a wider explanatory toolbox. In order to proceed towards explanation, one has to make concepts useful in terms of empirical analysis. This is the role performed by taxonomies. A taxonomy is a simple device that organizes research and makes complex concepts amenable to empirical analysis. Therefore, the ideas presented in this section serve the purpose of assisting research design. To repeat: the emphasis at this stage is on the organization of research, not on explanation.

Bearing in mind the definition of Europeanization adopted in the previous section, one can approach the study of this phenomenon by raising the questions '*what is Europeanized?*' (i.e. the domains where the effects of Europeanization are supposed to materialize) and '*to what extent*'? (i.e. extension and direction of Europeanization). Figure 2.1a—inspired by but different from Morlino's proposal (Morlino 1999)—provides a suggested taxonomy for the empirical investigation of these two dimensions.

Let us begin with the domains of Europeanization (Figure 2.1a). The first important distinction is between macrodomestic structures, public policy, and

(a)

Domains of Europeanization	Extent and direction of Europeanization
Domestic structures 1. Political structures 　　a) Institutions (e.g. cabinet-assembly relations) 　　b) Public administration 　　c) Intergovernmental relations 　　d) Legal structure 2. Structures of representation and cleavages 　　a) Political parties 　　b) Pressure groups 　　c) Societal-cleavage structures	
Public policy 　　a) Actors 　　b) Policy problems 　　c) Style 　　d) Instruments 　　e) Resources	
Cognitive and normative structures 　　a) Discourse 　　b) Norms and values 　　c) Political legitimacy 　　d) Identities 　　e) State traditions—understanding of governance 　　f) Policy paradigms, frames, and narratives	

(b)

	Direction of policy change Retrenchment　inertia　absorption　transformation <-------------------------------------> －　　　0　　　+　　　++ **Empirical analysis of four processes:** Interaction　robustness　equilibration　discourse
Policy a (e.g.: EMU) Policy b Policy c ...	

FIGURE 2.1. (a) Domains of Europeanization and change. (b) Europeanization and the institutional analysis of policy change

cognitive–normative structures. Domestic structures include the political and legal structures of a country, namely institutions (e.g. the relations between cabinet and assembly), inter-governmental relations, and the legal structure. In terms of representation and cleavages, one can distinguish between political parties, pressure groups, and the social dimension of political cleavages (Figure 2.1a). Let us turn to public policy now. Public policy is not the mere output of the political system and it may have dynamic effects on political structures. But analytically, and specifically in a static exercise on taxonomies, one is allowed to differentiate between policy and domestic structures.

Public Policy

The Europeanization of public policy can take different forms. In principle, it can affect all the elements of public policy, such as actors, resources, and policy instruments (see Figure 2.1). Additionally, Europeanization can affect the policy style, for example, by making it more or less conflictual, corporatist, or pluralist, or more or less regulative.

It is impossible to review the considerable amount of research on the Europeanization of public policy. The essential point, however, is simple. When contrasted with the literature on domestic structures, studies at the policy level reveal a greater impact of Europe. This impact takes different forms, such as convergence (Harcourt, this volume, on media markets regulation; Schneider 2000 on telecommunications), direct and indirect transfer of models from Brussels (Radaelli 2000*b* on monetary policy, tax policy, and regulatory policy), and a profound impact of EU regulation on national competition policy and regulatory approaches (Majone 1996).

Cognitive and Normative Dimensions

The cognitive and normative dimensions of Europeanization should be kept distinct from the others. The main reason for that is twofold. On the one hand, there is the simple observation that not only can Europe affect formal political structures, it can also influence the values, norms, and discourses prevalent in member states. On the other, and most importantly, the 'cognitive and normative frames' (Surel 2000) may trigger transformative effects on all the elements of politics and policy. For example, discourse may change the interpretation of a political dilemma facing a political party. It may alter the perception of what is at stake in a policy controversy. It may transform the interests and preferences upon which negotiations are structured. Further, policy discourses can be decisive in terms of securing legitimacy for choices in line with EU policy (Schmidt 2001; Schmidt and Radaelli 2002).

The Institutional Analysis of Policy Change

Ideally, research on Europeanization should be organized in a matrix similar to the one portrayed in Figure 2.1a. On the one hand, one has to specify 'what' is Europeanized; on the other, there is the question of 'how much change' has been brought about by Europeanization. Frankly, I do not know how the analysis of change should be tackled in general terms, that is, with reference to the whole set of elements portrayed in Figure 2.1a, from political parties to norms. However, theoretical policy analysis has produced a number of propositions and hypotheses on the more specific question of *policy* change. Given that this chapter is eminently concerned with the Europeanization of public policy, we will now turn to the issue of measuring policy change.

(a) Four Possible Outcomes: Retrenchment, Inertia, Absorption, and Transformation

Drawing upon Börzel (1999), Cowles *et al.* (2001), Héritier (2001), and Héritier and Knill (2001), four possible outcomes of Europeanization can be discerned (see Figure 2.1b): inertia, absorption, transformation, and retrenchment. Taken together, they cover both *the magnitude of change and its direction* (retrenchment being an example of 'negative' Europeanization, hence the sign minus in Figure 2.1b).

Inertia is a situation of lack of change. This may simply happen when a country finds that EU political architectures, choices, models, or policy are too dissimilar to domestic practice. Inertia may take the forms of lags, delays in the transposition of directives, implementation as transformation, and sheer resistance to EU-induced change. In the long term, however, inertia can become impossible to sustain (economically and politically). Therefore, one can submit that long periods of inertia should produce crisis and abrupt change (Olsen 1996).

Absorption indicates change as adaptation. Domestic structures and policy legacy provide a mixture of resiliency and flexibility. They can absorb certain non-fundamental changes, but maintain their 'core'. Absorption—as specified by Héritier (2001)—is accommodation of policy requirements[3] without real modification of the essential structures and changes in the 'logic' of political behaviour.

The 'accommodation' of Europe should not be confused with transformation. This is similar to what Hall labels 'third order' change, that is, paradigmatic

---

[2] Hall (1993) provides a different typology, suitable for the analysis of policy change, based on paradigmatic change, change of instruments, and change in the levels of instruments.

[3] For example, economic incentives instead of command and control regulation, the introduction of a new policy instrument, the formal separation between infrastructures and provision of service in railways, or the modification of the legal status of public employees' contracts.

change (Hall 1993). Paradigmatic change occurs when the fundamental logic of political behaviour changes—for example, a change in the format and mechanics of party systems or the adoption of a new orthodoxy in monetary policy.

However, Europeanization can also induce retrenchment. This is a very paradoxical effect, as it implies that national policy becomes less 'European' than it was. Kerwer (2001) shows that—in the Italian case at least—EU pressure to liberalize road haulage has objectively strengthened coalitions of domestic actors opposing reform. Therefore, the direction of change has been one of increased intervention, rather than liberalization. How this may happen depends on the mechanisms and the factors explaining Europeanization, two issues examined below in sections 'Vertical and Horizontal Mechanisms' and 'Towards explanation?'

(b) The Problem of Measuring the Four Outcomes . . . and
a Tentative Solution

The four outcomes outlined so far cover the whole spectrum of possibilities. So far, so good. The problem is: how does one go about the empirical measurement of these four outcomes? The vocabulary of adaptation, transformation, and inertia is becoming very popular, but how does one know that there is mere adaptation but not transformation? For example, where is the 'fence', the *empirical indicators* that tell us whether Greece and Italy have been transformed by Economic and Monetary Union (EMU), instead of simple adaptation? Is transformation in the eye of the beholder, a matter of very qualitative assessment, or can political scientists be more precise? When does marginal change falls under the rubric of inertia rather than absorption?

I would suggest a tentative answer to this problem. The idea is to supplement what has been already said with insights from the literature on learning and cognitive psychology (Bateson 1973) applied to policy analysis (Laird 1999). This literature makes a useful distinction between simple coping strategies (i.e. how to get around an obstacle by using a menu of well-known responses in various ingenious ways) and deutero learning or learning to learn. This can be used to determine—to continue with my example of EMU—whether there have been simple coping strategies or deutero learning. Absorption implies learning some clever strategies as a response to stimulation (typical of behavioural psychology). In a sense, this is a 'thin' form of learning. To 'think' differently, by contrast, postulates a 'thick' effect of Europeanization on learning dynamics in that it implies a modification of belief systems, preferences, and values.

Drawing upon cognitive psychology, Laird (1999) differentiates between learning and cognitive development. The former indicates a gradual, incremental process, whereas the latter designates a discontinuous jump towards new ways of organizing knowledge. Laird explains that:

Development [as opposed to learning] denotes qualitatively different stages of cognition. When children go from one stage of development to another, they reorganize their knowledge and the way they think about the world in a drastic way. (Laird 1999: 4)

The distinction between simple learning and cognitive development is useful. First, it chimes with the distinction between adaptation and transformation. Second, Laird provides a clear focus on institutions, which provides more precision than terms such as transformation. 'Transformation of what?'— a sceptical reader may indeed ask! The focus on transformation as institutional development brings institutions (in the sense of March and Olsen 1989) back into the analysis. As such, it leads to the empirical analysis of policy change in its institutional context. Indeed, when political scientists say that 'EU environmental policy has transformed environmental policy in country A' they mean that the *institutions* of environmental policy 'think' and perform along European tracks. Third, and perhaps more importantly still, it provides clues in terms of empirical research. In fact, there are four processes of transformation that can be traced out empirically. They are political experience, robustness, equilibration, and discourse.

1. *Interaction*. This is the dimension of political experience (Laird 1999) or, simply, interaction. In terms of empirical analysis of EMU as Europeanization (to continue with the same example), one could think of the interactions between core executive and other actors. One way of detecting transformation is to look at how institutions become (or do not become) stronger in relation to other institutions in the context of their interactions. To illustrate: the interaction between the core executive and Parliament, organized interests, and the electorate can be studied empirically by looking at EMU-induced reforms of the finance bill, pension reforms, the reregulation of the labour market, and so on.

2. *Robustness*. The second process revolves around the question to what extent has Europeanization brought about 'institutional robustness' of domestic institutions? Institutions become more robust by dint of advisory structures, improved policy technologies, and stronger bureaucratic structures. In terms of empirical analysis, if the first process concerns the interaction between an institution and its environment, the second process (i.e. robustness) leads to research 'within' the institution itself across time.

3. *Equilibration*. The third process identified by Laird is called equilibration. Institutions develop through equilibration when they face a crisis that does not fit with any of the standard repertoires of action. This is a bit of a limitation, because it casts the theme of development in terms of stimuli (the crisis) and responses. By contrast, the ideas about EMU (sound finance, central bank

independence, low inflation, and policy credibility) have provided a cognitive framework within which institutions can rethink their preferences. This is why I would expand equilibration to capture phenomena such as frame reflection (Schön and Rein 1994). Be that as it may, in terms of empirical analysis the bottom line is that development (as opposed to simple learning) requires a discontinuity with the past. The rules and norms through which institutions learn are transformed and become institutionalized through experience. At this point the link between the previous definition of Europeanization as institutionalization and the analysis of change should be evident.

4. *Discourse*. Discourse is fundamental both in giving shapes to new rules, values, and practices, and in the production of legitimacy. Drawing upon Schmidt (2001), it is useful to distinguish between discourse formation at the level of elites (coordinative discourse) and the forms of political communication directed to the mass public (communicative discourse). Empirically, the analysis of change will detect the presence or absence of transformative discourses as defined by Schmidt (2001).

To sum up the results of this section: research can be organized by using two dimensions, that is, the 'objects' of Europeanization and the dimension (and direction) of change. A typical research design should therefore treat Figure 2.1 as a matrix and fill in the cells with empirical observations. Research conducted so far shows a higher level of Europeanization of policy, whereas structures seem to be less permeable. This brings us to the question of whether policy dynamics feed back into political structures, an issue that can be dealt with by looking at the mechanisms of Europeanization and the explanatory variables. It is to these questions that we now turn.

Vertical and Horizontal Mechanisms

Once the concept of Europeanization and the dimensions of change have been clarified, the next step concerns the possible mechanisms of Europeanization. The literature on the mechanisms is still in its early days. Börzel (1999) and the contributors to Cowles *et al.* (2001) have drawn attention to the so-called 'goodness of fit' (i.e. the degree of institutional compatibility) between domestic institutions and European policy. By focusing on the 'goodness of fit', these authors draw our attention to *explanatory* factors related to *any* mechanism of change. Therefore, their insights on explanation will be dealt with in the next section. Knill and Lehmkuhl (2002) have presented three mechanisms (the first based on the presence of European models, the second on the domestic opportunity structure, and the third on the role of 'minimalist' directives in 'framing' integration). In an article on policy transfer,

Radaelli (2000*b*) draws on institutionalism in organizational analysis and presents the mechanisms of coercion, mimetism, and normative pressures in EU policy diffusion. In another article, he looks at the process of EU-induced cognitive convergence in the absence of direct compulsion from Brussels (Radaelli 1997). Finally, Kohler-Koch (1996) highlights subtle—yet crucial—mechanisms that go beyond the issue of the impact of EU policy on the 'balance of power'. Figure 2.2 combines the insights of the current debate. The purpose is to organize our understanding of Europeanization, bearing in mind that at this stage it is vital to raise the right questions, instead of looking for the ultimate answer.

Basically, there are two types of mechanisms, that is, 'vertical' and 'horizontal' Europeanization. Vertical mechanisms seem to demarcate clearly the EU level (where policy is defined) and the domestic level, where policy has to be metabolized. By contrast, horizontal mechanisms look at Europeanization as a process where there is no pressure to conform to EU policy models. Instead, horizontal mechanisms involve a different form of adjustment to Europe based on the market or on patterns of socialization. In horizontal Europeanization, the process is not one of conforming to EU policy which 'descends' into the domestic policy arena as in a hierarchical chain of command. Horizontal Europeanization is a process of change triggered by the market and the choice of the consumer or by the diffusion of ideas and discourses about the notion of good policy and best practice. More precisely, the vertical mechanisms are based on adaptational pressure; the horizontal mechanisms involve different forms of framing (Figure 2.2). Regulatory competition is a mechanism starting with vertical prerequisites but that has horizontal consequences. In fact, the competition of rules is based on the choices of market players, but it exists only in the context of an institutional choice, 'vertically' enforced by the European Court of Justice, such as mutual recognition.

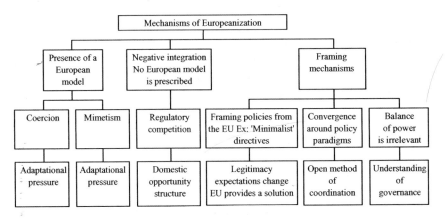

FIGURE 2.2. Mechanisms of Europeanization

UNIVERSITY
OF SHEFFIELD
LIBRARY

Consider first the role of European models and vertical Europeanization (Figure 2.2). In certain policy areas the European Union prescribes the adoption of a specific model. As Knill and Lehmkuhl (2002) argue, member states have to bring domestic arrangements into line with an institutional model designed in Brussels. Examples are provided by new regulatory policies in the areas of consumer protection, environmental policy, and health and safety at work. As the European Union positively prescribes the adoption of a model, one could use the term positive integration to distinguish this mechanism from the cases of negative integration, in which the European Union strikes down national barriers to the emergence of European markets without prescribing models.

When there are EU models, member states are under 'adaptational pressure'. Put differently, they are under pressure to adapt to Europe. Pressure implies coercion—for example, certain directives specify a period of time at the end of which member states are compelled to introduce regulatory arrangements. Adaptational pressure can operate with mechanisms different from coercion. Mimetism illustrates this alternative channel of Europeanization. If the countries adopting EU models provide a critical mass, the remaining countries can feel the force of attraction of the EU 'centre of gravity' and join in. Mimetism and coercion are mechanisms of isomorphism, that is, the tendency to become alike, well known to the new institutionalism in organizational analysis (DiMaggio and Powell 1991).

Let us now turn to other mechanisms of Europeanization. There are cases in which EU policies do not prescribe a model (see Figure 2.2). Policies of 'negative integration' (or 'market-making' policies, as opposed to 'market-shaping') create integrated markets by removing barriers to trade, investment, freedom of establishment, and free circulation of people. They do not say how a market should be governed in terms of institutional models, but typically emphasize the role of mutual recognition once the barriers have been removed. The key mechanism triggered by 'negative integration' is international regulatory competition.

When markets are opened, and certain choices are excluded from the domestic policy menu, existing domestic equilibria are challenged. Negative integration is aimed at achieving results at the national level, of course. However, these objectives are not achieved directly, by prescribing a model, but indirectly, by changing the domestic opportunity structure. The key mechanism is the change in the domestic opportunity structure rather than the compatibility between European Union and domestic and EU policy (Knill and Lehmkuhl 2002: 258). Figure 2.2, accordingly, puts emphasis on this type of change. The overall effect of this indirect mechanism cannot be predicted a priori. It all hinges on who is empowered and disempowered, and how, by 'negative integration' at the national level.

Directly or indirectly, the mechanisms examined so far assume that EU policy has a precise direction and aims to produce specific compliance at the level of the member states. Typically, they are based on the 'hard' instruments of EU public policy, such as directives and decisions of the European Court of Justice. However, there are at least three other soft framing mechanisms of horizontal Europeanization, portrayed on the right-hand side of Figure 2.2. To begin with, in some cases, such as railway policy, the EU proceeds by minimalist directives or non-compulsory regulations. By their nature, these instruments do not create any pressure in terms of adaptation (or 'goodness of fit') or international regulatory competition. Yet they can prepare the ground for major policy change. They do so by providing additional legitimacy to domestic reformers in search of justifications, by 'inseminating' possible solutions in the national debate, and by altering expectations about the future. Additional legitimacy is particularly important when domestic leaders are engaged in radical reforms (Knill and Lehmkuhl 2002). The introduction of new solutions coming from Brussels can alter the perception of problems. New solutions can provide a new dimension to national policy problems and trigger learning dynamics or a different political logic. In the case of media ownership policy, the instrument of audience share was first aired at the EU level and then 'inseminated' in national political systems, with important effects on national legislation in Germany and the United Kingdom (Harcourt 2000). Further, even the vaguest European policy has the potential of altering the expectations of domestic players, for example, by showing that opponents of liberalization are fighting for a 'lost cause' because EU policy is heading in a totally different direction (Knill and Lehmkuhl 2002).

Can the European Union affect national policy even in the absence of EU directives and regulations, albeit minimalist? The answer hinges on the strength of new governance architectures which create the preconditions for the diffusion of shared ideas and policy paradigms. The most important innovation in terms of governance architectures is the open method of coordination (OMC, see de la Porte and Pochet 2002). The OMC is a means of spreading best practice and achieving convergence towards the EU goals. The idea is to use the European Union as a policy transfer platform rather than a law-making system. Thus, the OMC should assist member states in developing their own policies. The 'method' is defined by the following characteristics: the EU guidelines combined with specific timetables and action to be undertaken at the national or regional level; benchmarking and sharing of best practice; qualitative and, when appropriate, quantitative indicators; 'period monitoring, evaluation, and peer review organized as mutual learning processes' (Presidency Conclusions, Lisbon European Council, 23–24 March 2000). As mentioned above, one aim of the OMC is to encourage convergence. Preliminary evidence suggests that the OMC has facilitated convergence on policy paradigms and policy beliefs (Trubek and Mosher 2001; Bertozzi and Bonoli 2002; de la Porte and Pochet 2002; Radaelli 2002). Looking at the future, the key issue is whether it will also produce convergence of national policies and convergence of results.

Finally, Europeanization can produce effects that go beyond the balance of power. Kohler-Koch (1996, 1999) argues that the insistence on the implications of EU policy in terms of the balance of power can be misleading. The crucial effect of Europeanization—she suggests—is on the dissemination of the 'network mode of governance' (as opposed to other modes of governance, such as corporatism, statism, and pluralism) into the member states (Kohler-Koch 1999). EU policy can change the understanding and the practice of what legitimate governance is all about. 'Impact studies', that is, research designs looking at the domestic impact of EU policy, may miss the target because they define the dependent variable in very narrow terms. The 'governance' effect cannot be detected at the level of a single episode; neither can it be investigated in a simple 'balance of power' research design, for example, by looking at the battle between reformers and advocates of the status quo. Yet the long-term implications of new modes of governance can be the most powerful.

Towards Explanation?

Mechanisms shed light on the process of Europeanization. But how does one explain the likelihood and direction of change? Two research projects have recently been concluded (Cowles *et al.* 2001; Héritier and Knill 2001), but more research is needed in this area. At the moment of writing, the best option is, arguably, to examine explanatory variables with the aid of the evidence made available by recent projects, but also with insights and suggestions that, at this stage, are still somewhat speculative. On balance, this section contains more ideas on how to proceed than specific hypotheses corroborated by empirical evidence.

Goodness of Fit: General Explanation or Special Case?

The explanation provided by Börzel (1999) and Cowles *et al.* (2001) is based on the general idea of adaptational pressure. The basic idea is that Europeanization matters only if there is divergence, incompatibility, or 'misfit' between European-level institutional process, politics, and policies, and the domestic level.

The relationship between adaptational pressure and change in domestic structures and policies is curvilinear. When adaptational pressure is low, because the content of EU policy is already present in a member state, there is no need to change domestic institutions. Simply put, there is a good 'fit' between national policy and the European Union. Hence it is easy to absorb 'Europe'. At the other extreme, when the distance between EU policies and national ones is very high, member states will find it very difficult to 'digest' and 'metabolize' European policy. Hence there will be inertia at the domestic level. The degree of change will be high when adaptational pressure falls between the two extremes. An arc on a Cartesian plan, with adaptational pressure on the *x-axis* and domestic change on the *y-axis* can illustrate this relation.

Börzel and Cowles *et al.* explicitly refer to new institutional analysis in their investigation of adaptational pressure. Domestic institutions refract Europeanization by providing dominant strategy in cases of 'misfit' between the European Union and member states. Börzel (1999) shows how Spanish regions reacted with a confrontational strategy to Europeanization, whereas German *Länder* preferred a cooperative strategy. Institutions, in addition, determine the distribution of resources among domestic actors affected by Europeanization. The result is that the impact of Europeanization is contingent on institutional factors. A corollary is that Europeanization will produce diversity rather than convergence, because domestic institutions differ widely.

The 'goodness of fit' argument is not without its problems, however. To begin with, what happens when domestic institutions are fragile (Morlino 1999)? In countries such as Belgium and Italy, domestic institutions have been in crisis or transition in the last decade or so. They have not behaved like rigid posts, capable of fencing or shaping the process of Europeanization. Quite the opposite: in certain episodes Europeanization has been a crucial component of domestic institutional change, as shown by the impact of EMU. The interaction between Europeanization and domestic institutions is therefore dialectic.

Second, the notion of 'goodness of fit' needs further exploration. The metaphor of the 'fit' covers quite a broad range of elements. To illustrate: a country can have a bad or good 'fit' because of the presence–absence of Roman law, strength–weakness of bureaucratic structures, corporatist–pluralist style of decision making, centralization–decentralization of power, and so on. Given this broad range, there is no absolute compatibility or mismatch: it is up to political actors at the European Union and domestic level to define what they are. This definition is part of a process of interpretation and political conflict (Goetz 2002). The notion of mismatch neglects this process.

Third, this explanation seems to work better in the presence of vertical Europeanization. Although the advocates of this explanation claim that they offer a general explanation, it remains to be seen how the 'goodness of fit' approach performs in the various forms of horizontal Europeanization described above. More research is needed before one can answer this question.

To conclude on this third point, the ideas of adaptational pressure and 'goodness of fit' provide a point of departure for general explanations, and future research will hopefully bring more precision to this type of analysis.

Fourth, the 'goodness of fit' does not tell the full story of Europeanization. It is a special case (not a general explanation). As shown by Mark Thatcher (2002) in the case of telecommunications, governments have been under little adaptational pressure from EU regulation. Yet they have used European policy to justify and legitimate change. Governments already seeking reform have been able to use European policy as an opportunity, rather than responding to a 'pressure'. The effects of this type of Europeanization have been large in terms of the clash between the reformers and the advocates of the status quo in telecommunications. But these effects are not captured by the 'goodness of fit' argument. Héritier and Knill (2001) have presented empirical evidence on European policies leading to domestic reforms even in the absence of adaptational pressure. Their argument is that European policies can be exploited by national actors engaged in policy reforms even if European and national arrangements are compatible. The implication is that adaptational pressure is not a necessary condition for Europeanization to cause domestic change.

Fifth, adaptational pressure is not the best predictor of how a country responds to Europeanization. A country can be under strong adaptational pressure, yet it can implement EU policy without too many problems, as shown by the implementation of the packaging waste directive in the United Kingdom (Haverland 2000). The intervening variable in this process is the presence or absence of institutional veto points, as argued by Haverland (2000; see also his contribution to this volume). Institutional veto points available to those opposing EU policy can make Europeanization very problematic even in the presence of low adaptational pressure. It is to the intervening variables that we now turn.

Mapping the Intervening Variables

Héritier and her associates are bringing the debate further in the direction of specific sets of intervening variables. Their first group of variables refers to the institutional capacity to produce change. This is still a very general hypothesis. Accordingly, it is useful to segment it into more specific propositions (see Figure 2.3). To begin with, the presence of veto players constrains the institutional capability to produce change. Conventional analysis of the political systems can be used to show how political processes differ among EU member states. This is a general macrofocus, one centred on the characteristics of the political systems. But Héritier and her associates put emphasis on *informal* veto players as well. For example, in policies of privatization and liberalization of the utilities, pressure groups can represent serious obstacles.

1. Institutional capacity to produce change
- Veto players in the political system
- Scope and type of executive leadership.

2. Timing of European policies

3. Policy structure and advocacy coalitions:
- Technocratic capture potential
- Adoption–implementation balance
- Presence of a legitimating *policy* discourse
- Impact of EU policy on domestic advocacy coalitions.

FIGURE 2.3. Key intervening variables explaining the likelihood and direction of Europeanization

Even small haulage companies can exercise their blackmail potential on certain political systems (Héritier and Knill 2001; Kerwer 2001). By doing so, Héritier and her colleagues switch from the macro-characteristics of the political process to the specific features of public policies.

The interaction between policy dynamics and the macropolitical structure is perhaps one of the most interesting areas of Europeanization. But one cannot see it if the policy level and the macropolitical level are lumped together. Accordingly, one should separate the policy level from the macrocomparative analysis of the political systems and treat the 'informal' veto players within the set of actors operating in policy systems (see below).

After this short digression on policy and politics, let us complete the analysis of macrovariables. The scope and type of executive leadership has to be considered. The leadership—Héritier and Knill (2001) explain—can be integrated or, at the other extreme, fragmented, short-lived, and conflict-ridden. When leadership is integrated and the number of veto players is low, Europeanization hardly makes a difference. Executives willing to promote policy change can do so whether European policy exists or not. At the other extreme, fragmented leadership with strong sectoral veto players makes EU-induced change improbable. Europeanization is instead most likely to have a high impact (in terms of policy change) under conditions of intermediate institutional capacity.

At any rate, the institutional capacity to produce change is a necessary condition, but it is not sufficient. The presence or absence of change—and its direction—depends on more specific variables at the level of the policy structure. Before we examine them, however, it is useful to draw attention to timing (Figure 2.3). The impact of EU public policy is contingent on whether a country is already involved in a process of reform or not. For example, certain policies of liberalization in the European Union have caught some countries unprepared whereas others, most notably the United Kingdom, were already on their way to deregulation and privatization. Put differently, the analysis of the effects of European public policy on national policy systems should be conducted in parallel to the investigation of domestic processes.

At a more general level, the temporal dimension is relevant to the extent that decision-makers can manipulate 'time' by delaying decisions, sequencing the process of adaptation, and controlling the speed of Europeanization (e.g. they can follow a gradualist path or proceed by leaps and bounds). This brings Goetz (2001) to borrow from Schmitter and Santiso (1998) the categories of time, timing, and tempo.[4]

The final set of variables—labelled 'policy structure and advocacy coalitions'—have not received enough attention in projects completed so far. Consequently, the analysis becomes rather speculative from this point onwards. Yet the policy level is crucial because the most surprising effects of Europeanization have taken place via policy change even when formal political structures have remained unchanged (Featherstone 1998; Dyson and Featherstone 1999; Ferrera and Gualmini 2000; Giuliani 2000).

There are four observations on 'policy variables' (see Figure 2.3). The first observation concerns the difference between policies that can be governed by technocratic, elitist circles and policies that by their very nature require a wider constellation of actors. Let us consider the examples of EMU and transport policy. In the case of the single currency, the process of Europeanization has been seized by small technocratic elites. Core executives, central banks, and technocrats with political power have been empowered by Europeanization. They have been able to produce dramatic change in monetary policy, even in countries with low potential for modernization. By contrast, the liberalization of transport policy has become the hostage of small pressure groups with intense preferences, and divisions within the political establishment. One key difference between the two policy areas is—I submit—the diverse degree of the technocratic capture potential. Comparatively, monetary policy can be captured by a small policy elite rather easily. To govern interest rates and the domestic financial markets, one needs clear rules about the competence of the Treasury and the central bank, and the manipulation of very few policy instruments (either a monetary aggregate or the structure of interest rates). Contrast this with road haulage, where different departments (within and outside the core executive), a panoply of policy instruments, and the collaboration of pressure groups with blackmail potential are simultaneously needed. The technocratic capture potential (or insulation from pressure groups and

---

[4] Time refers to when a decision is made, timing to the sequencing of decisions, and tempo to the speed.

societal pressure) of transport policy is inherently low, independently from the macroconstellation of domestic veto players in the political process.

The second observation (not totally independent from the first) concerns the balance between policy formulation–adoption and policy implementation. The management of monetary policy is all about policy formulation. Implementation concerns the reaction of the financial markets, but political and administrative structures are not directly involved. So much so that to announce a monetary policy is often equivalent to produce results via the expectations of market players. Tax policy is completely different. To draft a rule on tax avoidance may require the same length of time required by a decision on interest rates, but to implement anti-tax avoidance schemes is a laborious task involving tax inspectors, banks, and other financial institutions, as well as cooperation with tax administrations abroad. Concluding on this point, my hypothesis is that the more the adoption–implementation balance veers towards implementation, the more problematic the process of Europeanization is.

The third observation is about policy discourse, that is, the discourse that provides a rationale and justifies change at the policy level. Institutional capacity and timing provide the potential for change, but policy change has to be considered legitimate. As the role of discourse has already been discussed in this paper, it is sufficient to remark that the empirical analysis of discourse presents its own problems. One the one hand, there is the risk of reification of discourse. On the other, an empirical determination of discourse based on the press and the official speeches of key politicians remains too superficial and elusive. A possible way out of this dilemma is to draw upon the insights of discourse analysis provided by international relations. Another is to address the specific forms taken by policy discourse, such as policy narratives. Policy narratives are amenable to empirical analysis in a variety of forms (Roe 1994).

The emphasis on legitimacy and discourse brings us to the crucial role played by belief systems. Europeanization processes are filtered and refracted by systems of policy beliefs. As shown by Sabatier and Jenkins-Smith (1993), the belief system can be articulated in three levels, that is, 'deep core' beliefs (normative and axiomatic), 'policy core' beliefs (i.e. empirical and normative beliefs concerning the fundamental policy strategies), and 'secondary' beliefs. An important issue is to what extent and under which conditions Europeanization can change 'policy core' beliefs and facilitate learning and non-incremental change.

Taking these observations together, they put emphasis on the constellation of actors, the characteristics of policy, and the role of belief systems. Turning to the final observation, it is therefore surprising that there has not been systematic analysis of Europeanization in terms of frameworks well grounded in policy theory. To mention only one example, one could think of the advocacy coalition framework.[5] This is not the solution to all the research puzzles raised by Europeanization. But it at least provides a framework for the systematic analysis of policy change over a decade or so. It assigns great importance to belief systems and to the balance between endogenous learning dynamics and exogenous shocks. As such, it is suited to an analysis of the interplay between 'exogenous' EU policy and domestic 'endogenous' factors. Further, it provides an integrated framework for the analysis of constellations of actors, by grouping them into a number of coalitions with different belief systems. In conclusion, the recommendation is to use frameworks which are well grounded in theoretical policy analysis.

Conclusions: Towards Bottom-up Research Designs?

At this preliminary stage of research, it is impossible to draw neat conclusions. However, an important achievement is that fundamental questions on the impact of the European Union on member states have been raised. The risk of conceptual stretching looms large, but improvement is on the way. Taxonomies that 'unpack' concepts and make them amenable to empirical research can reduce the risk of concept misformation. Research can be organized by considering a matrix that includes the political entities affected by Europeanization and the extent (and direction) of change.

Research designs are still too rigid. They are limited to the analysis of 'European effects' in certain areas of change, but they do not control for *rival alternative hypotheses*. As Goetz (2001) observes, future research should focus on the *relative* impact of Europeanization (e.g. in the area of administrative change Europeanization can be an intervening variable in processes of modernization and reform). This requires systematic analysis of alternative or complementary explanations. It may be difficult to undertake multicausal analysis, but this is the best way to be relatively sure that changes observed at the national level are originated by EU dynamics, and not by other forces.

The problem is that to cast the discussion of Europeanization exclusively in terms of its *effects* means to assume that . . . there *are* EU-induced effects! Put differently, there is a serious risk of prejudging the significance of EU variables. The emphasis on effects, indeed, should be accompanied by a *contextualization* of Europeanization and by an explicit treatment of causality. It is difficult to assess the contribution of a single independent EU variable to the process of domestic policy change. Take the case of EMU and Italy. Here the process of macroeconomic convergence with the criteria designed at

---

[5] For recent developments and an illustration of the framework, see Sabatier (1998, 1999).

Maastricht took place in the context of a threefold political crisis (of authority, legitimacy, and distribution between centre and periphery; see Bull and Rhodes 1997). Therefore EMU has to be contextualized in relation to the domestic political transition of the 1990s. At the same time, the process of Europeanization induced by EMU is a major component of this transition. One possible way out of this puzzle is to trace temporal sequences. Historical analysis can show when, why, and how actors responded to EMU and with what effects (see Dyson 2002 for case studies along these lines).

Let me elaborate a little further. The focus on Europeanization can produce serious fallacies when it leads the researcher to adopt a top-down logic in which the only aim is to find out the domestic effects of independent variables defined at the EU level. In this top-down perspective, the problem of domestic policy-makers is all about putting into practice—or 'absorbing'—EU policy. This is a managerial, 'chain-of-command' logic that creates an artificial separation between events such as EMU as 'policy' and domestic absorption as 'implementation'. By contrast, I argue for an 'inside-out' or 'bottom-up' perspective on Europeanization. The implication is that the researcher will trace sequences of events in domestic policy and, drawing upon Elmore's suggestions for bottom-up research, will look at the individual and institutional choices 'that are the hub of the problem to which policy is addressed, to the rules, procedures, and structures that have the closest proximity to those choices, to the policy instruments available to affect those things' (Elmore 1981: 1). It is in the context of domestic choices made 'at the hub of the problem' that one can see if and when processes such as EMU play a role in the logic of economic policy making—or even change this logic. More or less, this corresponds to the so-called bottom-up approach to implementation research. Hence I would use the notion of 'bottom-up perspective' on Europeanization to describe this research strategy.

In terms of substantive change, the jury is still out on critical issues such as whether Europeanization is producing substantive convergence, although current research points to a differential Europe or clustered convergence: some countries exhibit similar outcomes, but others do not—hence the result of different clusters (Börzel and Risse 2000; Börzel 2001). As for the amount of change induced by Europeanization, the answer depends on the level of analysis: macroanalyses at the level of politics and polities detect low levels of Europeanization, whereas studies at the policy level signal a more consistent impact. But future research at the policy level should make a clear distinction between policy outcomes and policy processes (Börzel and Risse 2000). The policy level seems the most exciting. In some countries and some policy areas, the Europeanization of policy has triggered processes of transformation of the state. This dynamic effect of policy upon politics has taken place independently from the macro-characteristics of political systems (be they dirigiste, corporatist, or polarized). In some cases, the Europeanization of public policy has changed the state even in the shadow of institutions that have not changed their formal-constitutional organization, as Giuliani (2000) argues in his analysis of change in the context of stalemate on institutional reforms in Italy. One suggestion is therefore to intensify research at the policy level. Another is to start thinking of Europeanization less in substantive terms (i.e. as an end-state) and more in processual terms. Goetz (2002) and Olsen (2002) argue that political scientists should be less interested in questions of end-state and final outcomes and more in questions of processes and coevolution of domestic and EU structures.

How can policy research be 'intensified' and hopefully improved? Europeanization is a process. It is a process where the cognitive dimension of political life matters. Hence, the current emphasis on mechanisms and variables should not preclude the dimension of evolution, learning, and the social construction of politics. Evolution and learning require frameworks of analysis sensitive to policy change over the medium to long term. One option that researchers may consider is the advocacy coalition framework.[6] This framework is not panacea—as shown by the symposium hosted by the *Journal of European Public Policy* (March 2000) on the theories of the policy process. But it is suitable for studies of policy change centered on belief systems, legitimacy, and the conflict between reformers and advocates of the status quo.

Research on Europeanization could also benefit from the considerable amount of knowledge generated by studies of the international sources of domestic policy change, that is, the so-called second-image reversed perspective on international relations (Gourevitch 1978). The volume edited by Cowles *et al.* (2001) goes in this direction, and in so doing it contributes to cumulative research (as opposed to ad hoc research). Although the European dimension presents significant peculiarities, one does not see the point of starting theoretical research on Europeanization from tabula rasa, and perhaps reinventing propositions already well known on the role of domestic institutions as filters of international forces. Europeanization can therefore contribute to the 'normalization' of research—as advocated by Hassenteufel and Surel (2000). Overall, Europeanization has opened a new avenue for a closer debate between comparative politics, comparative public policy, and more traditional EU studies. If it does not confine itself to ad hoc theorization, research on Europeanization has considerable potential for our understanding of the evolution of governance and public policy.

---

[6] See Dyson and Featherstone (1999) and Radaelli (1998) for applications of this framework to Europeanization.

REFERENCES

Adcock, R. and Collier, D. (2001). 'Connecting Ideas With Facts: The Validity of Measurement', *American Political Science Review* 95(3): 529–46.

Bateson, G. (1973). *Steps to an Ecology of Mind* (Paladin: St Albans).

Bertozzi, F. and Bonoli, G. (2002). 'Europeanisation and the Convergence of National Social and Employment Policies: What can the Open Method of Coordination Achieve'?, *Paper delivered to the ECPR joint sessions of workshops*, Turin, 22–27 March 2002.

Börzel, T. (1999). 'Towards Convergence in Europe? Institutional Adaptation to Europeanisation in Germany and Spain', *Journal of Common Market Studies* 39(4): 573–96.

—— and Risse, T. (2000). 'When Europe Hits Home. Europeanisation and Domestic Change', *Paper presented to the annual meeting of the American Political Science Association, Washington, DC*, 31 August–3 September 2000.

Börzel, T. A. (2001). 'Pace-Setting, Foot-Dragging, and Fence-Sitting: Member State Responses to Europeanisation', *Paper prepared for the ECSA conference*, Madison (USA), May 31–June 2, 2001.

Bull, M. and Rhodes, M. (eds) (1997). *Crisis and Transition in Italian Politics* (London: Frank Cass).

Bulmer, S. and Burch, M. (2001). 'The Europeanisation of Central Government: The UK and Germany in Historical Institutionalist Perspective', in G. Schneider and M. Aspinwall (eds), *The Rules of Integration: Institutionalist Approaches to the Study of Europe* (Manchester: Manchester University Press), 73–96.

Caporaso, J. (1996). 'The European Union and Forms of State: Westphalian, Regulatory or Post-Modern'?, *Journal of Common Market Studies* 34(1): 29–52.

Cowles, M. G., Caporaso, J., and Risse, T. (eds) (2001). *Transforming Europe: Europeanization and Domestic Change* (Ithaca and London: Cornell University Press).

de la Porte, C. and Pochet, P. (eds.) (2002). *Building Social Europe through the Open Method of Coordination* (Brussels: Peter Lang).

DiMaggio, P. J. and Powell, W. W. (1991). 'The Iron Cage Revisited: Institutional Isomorphism and Collective Rationality in Organizational Fields', in W. W. Powell and J. DiMaggio (eds), *The New Institutionalism in Organizational Analysis* (Chicago and London: University of Chicago Press), 63–82.

Dyson, K. (2002) (ed.). European States and the Euro: Europeanization, Variation, and Covergence (Oxford: Oxford University Press).

—— and Featherstone, K. (1999). *The Road to Maastricht. Negotiating Economic and Monetary Union* (Oxford: Oxford University Press).

Elmore, R. (1981). Backward mapping and youth employment, unpublished paper quoted by M. Hill (1997). *The Policy Process in the Modern State* (Hemel Hampstead: Prentice Hall).

Featherstone, K. (1998). 'Europeanisation and the Centre Periphery: The Case of Greece in the 1990s', *South European Society and Politics* 3(1): 23–39.

Ferrera, M. and Gualmini, E. (2000). 'Italy: Rescue from without'?, in F. W. Scharpf and V. Schmidt (eds), *Welfare and Work in the Open Economy. Diverse Responses to Common Challenges* (Oxford: Oxford University Press), 351–98.

Giuliani, M. (2000). 'Europeanisation and Italy: A Bottom-uo Process', *South European Society and Politics* 5(2): 47–72.

Goetz, K. (2001). 'European Integration and National Executives: A Cause in Search of an Effect', in K. Goetz and S. Hix (eds), *Europeanised Politics? European Integration and National Political Systems* (London: Frank Cass), 211–31.

—— (2002). 'Four worlds of Europeanisation', *Paper prepared for the ECPR Joint Sessions of Workshops*. Turin, Italy, 22–7 March 2002.

Gourevitch, P. (1978). 'The Second Image Reversed: The International Sources of Domestic Politics', *International Organization* 32(4): 881–911.

Hall, P. (1993). 'Policy Paradigms, Social Learning and the State. The Case of Economic Policy-Making in Britain', *Comparative Politics* 25(3): 275–96.

Harcourt, A. J. (2000). European institutions and the media industry. European regulatory politics between pressure and pluralism. Ph.D. Dissertation, Department of Government, University of Manchester.

Hassenteufel, P. and Surel, Y. (2000). 'Des politiques publiques comme les autres? Construction de l'objet et outils d'analyse des politiques européennes', *Politique Européenne* 1(1): 8–24.

Haverland, M. (2000). 'National Adaptation to European Integration: The Importance of Institutional Veto Points', *Journal of Public Policy* 20(1): 83–103.

Héritier, A. (2001). 'Differential Europe: Administrative Responses to Community Policy', in Cowles *et al.* (eds), *Transforming Europe: Europeanisation and Domestic Change.*

—— and Knill, C. (2001). 'Differential Responses to European Policies: A Comparison', in A. Héritier, D. Kerwer, C. Knill, D. Lehmkuhl, M. Teutsch, and A. C. Douillet (eds), *Differential Europe: The European Union Impact on National Policymaking* (Lanham, Boulder, New York and Oxford: Rowman and Littlefield), 257–94.

Kassim, H. (1994). 'Policy Networks, Networks and EU Policy Making. A Sceptical View', *West European Politics* 17(4): 17–27.

Kerwer, D. (2001). *Regulatory Reforms in Italy: A Case-Study in Europeanisation* (Aldershot: Ashgate).

Knill, C. and Lehmkuhl, D. (2002). 'The National Impact of European Union Regulatory Policy: Three Europeanization Mechanisms', *European Journal of Political Research* 41(2): 255–80.

Kohler-Koch, B. (1996). 'Catching up with Change. The Transformation of Governance in the European Union', *Journal of European Public Policy* 3(3): 359–80.

—— (1999). 'The Evolution and Transformation of European Governance', in B. Kohler-Koch and R. Eising (eds), *The Transformation of Governance in the European Union* (London: Routledge), 14–35.

Ladrech, R. (1994). 'Europeanisation of Domestic Politics and Institutions: The Case of France', *Journal of Common Market Studies* 32(1): 69–88.

Laird, F. R. (1999). 'Rethinking Learning', *Policy Currents* 9(3,4): 3–7.

Lawton, T. (1999). 'Governing the Skies: Conditions for the Europeanisation of Airline Policy', *Journal of Public Policy* 19(1): 91–112.

Leebron, D. W. (1996). 'Lying Down with Procustes: An Analysis of Harmonization Claims', in J. Bhagwati and R. Hudec (eds), *Fair Trade and Harmonization: Pre-Requisites for Free Trade?* (Cambridge: The MIT Press), 41–117.

Majone, G. D. (1996). *Regulating Europe* (London: Routledge).

March, J. and Olsen, J. P. (1989). *Rediscovering Institutions* (New York: The Free Press).

Montpetit, E. (2000). 'Europeanisation and Domestic Politics: Europe and the Development of a French Environmental Policy for the Agricultural Sector', *Journal of European Public Policy* 7(4): 576–92.

Morlino, L. (1999). Europeanisation and Representation in Two Europes. Local Institutions and National Parties, *Paper given to the conference on Multi-Party Systems: Europeanisation and the Reshaping of National Political Representation*, European University Institute, Florence, 16–18 December 1999.

Olsen, J. P. (1996). 'Europeanisation and Nation-State Dynamics', in S. Gustavsson and L. Lewin (eds), *The Future of the Nation-State* (London: Routledge), 245–85.

——(2002). 'The Many Faces of Europeanisation', ARENA working paper no.2/2002, ARENA: Olso. (http://www.arena.uio.no/).

Radaelli, C. M. (1997). 'How does Europeanisation Produce Policy Change? Corporate Tax Policy in Italy and the UK', *Comparative Political Studies* 30(5): 553–75.

——(1998). 'Networks of Expertise and Policy Change in Italy', *South European Society and Politics* 3(2): 1–22.

——(2000*a*). 'Logiques de pouvoirs et récits dans les politiques de l'Union Européenne', *Revue Française de Science Politique* 50(2): 255–75.

——(2000*b*). 'Policy Transfer in the European Union', *Governance* 13(1): 25–43.

——(2002). 'The Code of Conduct on Business Taxation: Open Method of Coordination in Disguise'? Submitted to *Public Administration*.

Roe, E. (1994). *Narrative Policy Analysis* (Durham: Duke University Press).

Sabatier, P. (ed) (1999). *Theories of the Policy Process* (Boulder: Westview Press).

——and Jenkins-Smith, H. C. (1993). *Policy Change and Learning. An Advocacy Coalition Approach* (Boulder: Westview Press).

Sabatier, P. A. (1998). 'The Advocacy Coalition Framework: Revisions and Relevance for Europe', *Journal of European Public Policy* 5(1): 98–130.

Sartori, G. (1970). 'Concept Misformation in Comparative Politics', *American Political Science Review* 64(4): 1033–53.

——(1984) (ed.). *Social Science Concepts: A Systematic Analysis* (London: Sage).

——(1991). 'Comparing and Miscomparing', *Journal of Theoretical Politics* 3(3): 243–57.

Schmidt, V. A. and Radaelli, C. M. (2002). 'Europeanisation, Discourse, and Policy Change: Mapping the New Research Agenda', *Paper Prepared For the ECPR Joint Sessions of Workshops* Turin, Italy, 22–27 March.

Schmitter, P. and Santiso, J. (1998). 'Three Temporal Dimensions to the Consolidation of Democracy', *International Political Science Review* 19(1): 69–92.

Schneider, V. (2000). 'Institutional Reform in Telecommunications: The European Union in Transnational Policy Diffusion', in Cowles *et al.* (eds), *Transforming Europe: Europeanisation and Domestic Change*.

Schön, D. and Rein, M. (1994). *Frame Reflection. Toward the Resolution of Intractable Policy Controversies* (New York: Basic Books).

Surel, Y. (2000). 'The Role of Cognitive and Normative Frames in Policy-Making', *Journal of European Public Policy* 7(4): 495–512.

Stone Sweet, A., Sandholtz, W., and Fligstein, N. (2001) (eds) *The Institutionalization of Europe* (Oxford: Oxford University Press).

Thatcher, M. (2002). 'Europeanisation and Domestic Institutional Reform: The Regulation of Telecommunications', *Paper delivered to the ECPR joint sessions of workshops*, Turin, Italy, 22–27 March 2002.

Trubek, D. M. and Mosher, J. (2001). New Governance, EU Employment Policy, and the European Social Model, Presented at *Reconfiguring Work and Welfare in the New Economy*. European Union Center, University of Wisconsin-Madison. May 10–12, 2001.

3

Conceptualizing the Domestic Impact of Europe

TANJA A. BÖRZEL AND THOMAS RISSE

Introduction

For decades, European studies have been mostly concerned with explaining European integration and Europeanization processes themselves. Debates between neofunctionalism, (liberal) intergovernmentalism, and the 'multi-level governance' perspective centred around the question of how to account for the emerging European polity. This research, therefore, adopted a 'bottom-up' perspective, in which the dynamics and the outcome of the European institution-building process are the main dependent variable (see e.g. Puchala 1972; Wallace and Wallace 1996; Moravcsik 1998; Héritier 1999). More recently, however, an emerging literature focusses on the impact of European integration and Europeanization on domestic political and social processes of the member states and beyond. This move toward studying 'top-down' processes is desperately needed in order to fully capture how Europe and the European Union (EU) matter. It fits nicely with recent developments in international studies in general, which increasingly study the domestic effects of international institutions and norms. As far as the European Union is concerned, we will get a more comprehensive picture if we study the feedback processes among and between the various levels of European, national, and subnational governance.

While we are aware of these various feedback loops, this paper self-consciously restricts itself to the 'top-down' perspective. How do European integration and Europeanization more generally affect domestic policies, politics, and polities of the member states and beyond? To answer this question,

An earlier version of this paper was presented at the 2000 Annual Convention of the American Political Science Association, Washington DC, and published as a European Integration On-line Paper (http://eiop.or.at/eiop/texte/2000-015a.htm). We thank Klaus Goetz, Christine Ingebritsen, Claudio Radaelli, and two anonymous reviewers for their critical comments and suggestions.

we use the emerging literature on the topic to develop some preliminary hypotheses on the conditions under which we would expect domestic change in response to Europeanization. We seek to simplify various propositions made in the literature and to point out where further research is needed. Our arguments can be summarized as follows.

Whether we study policies, politics, or polities, there are two conditions for expecting domestic changes in response to Europeanization. First, Europeanization must be 'inconvenient', that is, there must be some degree of 'misfit' or incompatibility between European-level processes, policies, and institutions, on the one hand, and domestic-level processes, policies, and institutions, on the other. This degree of fit or misfit leads to adaptational pressures, which constitute a necessary but not sufficient condition for expecting domestic change. The second condition is that various facilitating factors—be it actors, be it institutions—respond to the adaptational pressures, thus inducing the change.

One can conceptualize the adaptational processes in response to Europeanization in two ways, which in turn lead to different emphases concerning these facilitating factors. Here, we refer to two variants of the 'new institutionalism' in political science, rational choice institutionalism, on the one hand, and sociological (or constructivist) institutionalism, on the other (see March and Olsen 1989, 1998; Hall and Taylor 1996; Risse 2002). From a rationalist perspective following the 'logic of consequentialism', the misfit between European and domestic processes, policies, and institutions provides societal and/or political actors with new opportunities and constraints to pursue their interests. Whether such changes in the political opportunity structure lead to a domestic redistribution of power, depends on the capacity of actors to exploit these opportunities and avoid the constraints. Two mediating factors with opposite effects influence these capacities:

1. *Multiple veto points* in a country's institutional structure can effectively empower actors with diverse interests to resist adaptational pressures emanating from Europeanization.
2. *Formal institutions* might exist providing actors with material and ideational resources to exploit new opportunities, leading to an increased likelihood of change.

The logic of rationalist institutionalism suggests that Europeanization leads to domestic change through a differential empowerment of actors resulting from a redistribution of resources at the domestic level.

In contrast, a sociological or constructivist perspective emphasizes a 'logic of appropriateness' (March and Olsen 1998) and processes of persuasion. European policies, norms, and the collective understandings attached to them exert adaptational pressures on domestic-level processes, because they do not resonate well with domestic norms and collective understandings. Two mediating factors influence the degree to which such misfit results in the internalization of new norms and the development of new identities:

1. 'Change agents' or *norm entrepreneurs* mobilize in the domestic context and persuade others to redefine their interests and identities.
2. A *political culture* and other informal institutions exist which are conducive to consensus-building and cost-sharing.

Sociological institutionalism suggests that Europeanization leads to domestic change through a socialization and collective learning process, resulting in norm internalization and the development of new identities.

The two logics of change are not mutually exclusive. They often occur simultaneously or characterize different phases in a process, of adaptational change. Our paper concludes with some suggestions as to how to link the two mechanisms and to specify conditions under which each logic dominates.

The paper proceeds in the following steps. First, we specify what we mean by 'domestic impact' of Europeanization. Second, we develop the concept of 'misfit' and distinguish between differential empowerment and socialization as the two theoretical logics of domestic adaptation to Europe. Third, we discuss the degree and direction of domestic changes to be expected by the two logics and causal mechanisms, focusing on the question of whether we are likely to see convergence or divergence. We conclude with propositions on how differential empowerment and socialization relate to each other.

Europeanization and the 'Goodness of Fit'

Europeanisation and the Dimensions of Domestic Change

Scholars who adopt a 'top-down' perspective have used the concept of Europeanization in different ways, which gave rise to considerable confusion in the literature (for critical discussions see Radaelli 2000; Eising forthcoming). For pragmatic reasons, and since we are interested in understanding both the processes by which European integration affects domestic change and the outcome of this change, we follow the proposal by Risse, Cowles, and Caporaso. They conceptualize Europeanization as the 'emergence and the development at the European level of distinct structures of governance, that is, of political, legal, and social institutions associated with political problem solving that formalizes interactions among the actors, and of policy networks specializing in the creation of authoritative European rules' (Risse *et al.* 2001: 3). Europeanization is understood as a process of institution-building at the European level in order to explore how this Europeanization process impacts upon the member states.

Europeanization
Processes, policies, and institutions

Policies
- Standards
- Instruments
- Problem-solving approaches
- Policy narratives and discourses

Politics
Processes of
- Interest formation
- Interest aggregation
- Interest representation
- Public discourses

Polity
- Political institutions
- Intergovernmental
  relations
- Judicial structures
- Public administration
- State traditions
- Economic institutions
- State–society relation
- Collective identities

FIGURE 3.1. The domestic effect of Europeanization

We use the distinction between policies, politics, and polity to identify three dimensions along which the domestic impact of Europeanization can be analysed and processes of domestic change can be traced (see Figure 3.1).

Whether we focus on policies, politics, or polity, the general proposition that Europeanization affects the member states is no longer controversial. We can also see an emerging consensus that Europeanization has a differential impact on domestic policies, politics, or polities (see Kohler-Koch 1998*a*; Kohler-Koch and Eising 1999; Cowles *et al.* 2001; Héritier *et al.* 2001). Only few authors expect increasing convergence in domestic policies and institutions in response to Europeanization (e.g. Knill and Lehmkuhl 1999; Schneider 2001). The issue is no longer whether Europe matters but how it matters, to what degree, in what direction, at what pace, and at what point of time. In other words, the more recent literature on the domestic impact of Europe has focused on identifying the causal mechanisms through which Europeanization can affect the member states. Most studies draw on several mechanisms to explain the domestic change they observe (see e.g. Héritier *et al.* 1996; Hooghe 1996; Haverland 1999; Knill and Lehmkuhl 1999; Börzel 2002; Héritier *et al.* 2001). We argue below that the different causal mechanisms can be collapsed into two logics of domestic change. In the following, and drawing on Cowles *et al.* (2001) and Börzel (1999), we develop a conceptual framework that allows us to integrate the various mechanisms.

Misfit as a Necessary, but Not Sufficient Condition of Domestic Change

While focusing on different causal mechanisms, most studies share the proposition that Europeanization is only likely to result in domestic change if it is 'inconvenient'. There must be some 'misfit' (Duina 1999) or 'mismatch' (Héritier *et al.* 1996) between European and domestic policies, processes, and institutions. The 'goodness of fit' (Risse *et al.* 2001) between the European and the domestic level determines the degree of pressure for adaptation generated by Europeanization on the member states: *The lower the compatibility between European and domestic processes, policies, and institutions, the higher the adaptational pressure.*

This proposition is rather trivial, since there is no need for domestic changes, if Europeanization fits perfectly well with domestic ways of doing things. If European environmental regulations, for example, match with domestic policies, member states do not need to change their legal provisions. In general, if European norms, rules, and the collective understandings attached to them are largely compatible with those at the domestic level, they do not give rise to problems of compliance or effective implementation more broadly speaking. Nor do they provide new opportunities and constraints to domestic actors that would lead to a redistribution of resources at the domestic level, empowering some actors while weakening others. European policy frames which resonate with domestic policy ideas and discourses are unlikely to trigger collective learning processes which could change actors' interests and identities. The European system of judicial review only empowers national courts and citizens in member states whose legal systems are alien to judicial review (Conant 2001). The Single Market, finally, only provides exit options for firms which used to operate within closed and protected markets. Those firms which already enjoyed open competition across borders had little to gain from the Single Market provisions. In brief, misfit and resulting adaptational pressures constitute the starting point for any causal mechanism discussed in the literature.

Ultimately, adaptational pressures are generated by the fact that the emerging European polity encompasses structures of authoritative decision making which might clash with national structures of policy making, and that the EU member states have no exit option given that EU law constitutes the law of the land. This is a major difference to other international institutions which are simply based on voluntary intergovernmental arrangements. We distinguish two types of misfits by which Europeanization exerts adaptational pressure on the member states.

First, European policies might lead to a *policy misfit* between European rules and regulations, on the one hand, and domestic policies, on the other. Policy misfits essentially equal compliance problems. European policies can challenge national policy goals, regulatory standards, the instruments or techniques used to achieve policy goals, and/or the underlying problem-solving approach (Héritier *et al.* 1996; Börzel 2000). Such policy misfit can also exert adaptational pressure on underlying institutions (Caporaso and Jupille 2001;

Sbragia 2001; Schneider 2001). As policy misfits produce adaptational costs at the domestic level, member states strive to 'upload' their policies to the European level in order to reduce their compliance problems. Regulatory contest results from these efforts, particularly among the powerful member states. Yet, since it is unlikely that the same group of member states succeeds most of the time in uploading its preferences unto the European level, this contest gives rise to a regulatory 'patchwork' of EU rules and regulations following a very diverse pattern of policies, problem-solving approaches, and administrative styles (Héritier 1996). This regulatory patchwork, however, produces significant degrees of misfit for all those member states who did not succeed in uploading their preferences to the European level and, thus, are required to change their policies and even institutional structures in response to Europeanization. As a result, all member states—including the 'big three', Great Britain, France, and Germany—face significant, albeit different degrees of adaptational pressures when they have to download European policies (Börzel 2002; Cowles *et al.* 2001).

This is an important finding which challenges several dominant approaches in the study of European integration. Liberal intergovernmentalism, for example, implies that bargains are struck among the powerful member states at the level of lowest common denominator (Moravcsik 1993, 1998). It follows that Britain, France, and Germany are unlikely to face significant adaptational pressures from Europeanization. This proposition is thoroughly refuted by the available evidence on Europeanization effects (e.g. Duina 1999; Knill and Lenschow 2000; Cowles *et al.* 2001; Héritier *et al.* 2001). From a different theoretical angle, sociological institutionalism would expect that the more institutional structures at the European and domestic levels look alike (structural isomorphism), the less adaptational pressures member states should face (DiMaggio and Powell 1991; Olsen 1995). German domestic structures, for example, show many similarities with the emerging European polity (multilevel system; decentralization; federalism, etc.; see Bulmer 1997; Katzenstein 1997). Yet, Germany has experienced as many misfits with Europeanization processes as other member states (Cowles and Risse 2001).

This latter argument points to a second type of misfit and adaptational pressure which we need to distinguish from policy misfit. Europeanization can cause *institutional misfit*, challenging domestic rules and procedures and the collective understandings attached to them. European rules and procedures, for example, which give national governments privileged decision powers vis-à-vis other domestic actors, challenge the territorial institutions of highly decentralized member states which grant their regions autonomous decision powers (Börzel 2002). The accessibility of the European Commission for societal interests challenges the statist business–government relations in France and the corporatist system of interest mediation in Germany (Conant

2001; Cowles 2001). Europeanization might even threaten deeply collective understandings of national identity as it touches upon constitutive norms such as state sovereignty (Checkel 2001; Risse 2001). Institutional misfit is less direct than policy misfit. Although it can result in substantial adaptational pressure, its effect is more likely to be long term and incremental.

Policy or institutional misfit, however, is only the necessary condition for domestic change. Whether misfits produce a substantial effect at the domestic level depends on the presence of various factors facilitating adaptation and serving as catalysts for domestic change. Only if and when these intervening factors are present can we expect a transformation of policies, politics, or polities in the member states.

Facilitating Factors as Sufficient Conditions for Domestic Change

The domestic effect of Europeanization can be conceptualized as a process of change at the domestic level in which the member states adapt their processes, policies, and institutions to new practices, norms, rules, and procedures that emanate from the emerging European system of governance (Olsen 1996, 1997). Rationalist and sociological institutionalisms identify different mechanisms of institutional change, which can be equally applied to the change of policies and politics.[1] The two logics of change stress different factors facilitating domestic adaptation in response to Europeanization.

Domestic Change as a Process of Redistribution of Resources

Rationalist institutionalism embodies a 'logic of consequentialism' (March and Olsen 1998), which treats actors as rational, goal-oriented, and purposeful. Actors engage in strategic interactions using their resources to maximize their utilities on the basis of given, fixed, and ordered preferences. They follow an instrumental rationality by weighing the costs and benefits of different strategy options taking into account the (anticipated) behaviour of other actors. From this perspective, Europeanization is largely conceived as an emerging political opportunity structure which offers some actors additional resources to exert influence, while severely constraining the ability of others to pursue their goals. Liberal intergovernmentalists have suggested that European opportunities and constraints strengthen the action capacities of national executives enhancing their autonomy vis-à-vis other domestic actors (Moravcsik 1994). Neofunctionalists come to the opposite conclusion that Europeanization provides societal and subnational actors with new resources,

---

[1] The following draws on Olsen (1996), Börzel (2002), and Checkel (1999*b*).

since the European Union enables them to circumvent or bypass the national executives (Marks 1993; Sandholtz 1996). Proponents of multilevel governance approaches in turn argue that Europeanization does not empower one particular group of actors over the others but increases their mutual interdependence, giving rise to more cooperative forms of governance (Grande 1996; Kohler-Koch 1996; Rhodes 1997). The three resource dependency approaches all predict convergence, but around very different outcomes.

Neither can account for the differential impact of Europeanization observed at the domestic level. The evidence suggests that Europeanization does not systematically favour one particular group of domestic actors over others. For instance, while French firms gained more autonomy vis-à-vis their national government by circumventing it (Schmidt 1996), Spanish firms did not (Aguilar Fernandez 1992). The Italian regions have been far less able to ascertain their domestic power than their Austrian or British counterparts (Rhodes 1996; Desideri and Santantonio 1997; Morass 1997). While the Spanish territorial structure is undergoing profound change in response to adaptational pressure, German federalism has been reinforced by Europeanization. While the equal pay and equal treatment directives empowered womens' groups in Great Britain, they had virtually no effect in France (Caporaso and Jupille 2001).

We argue that Europeanization only leads to a redistribution of resources and differential empowerment at the domestic level if (1) there is significant misfit providing domestic actors with additional opportunities and constraints (necessary condition), and (2) domestic actors have the capacities to exploit such new opportunities and avoid constraints, respectively (sufficient condition). Two mediating factors influence these action capacities (cf. Risse *et al.* 2001: 9–10).

1. *Multiple veto points* in a country's institutional structure can empower actors with diverse interests to avoid constraints emanating from Europeanization pressures and, thus, effectively inhibit domestic adaptation (Tsebelis 1995; Haverland 2000; Héritier *et al.* 2001). The more power is dispersed across the political system, and the more actors have a say in political decision making, the more difficult it is to foster the domestic consensus or 'winning coalition' necessary to introduce changes in response to Europeanization pressures. A large number of institutional or factual veto players impinges on the capacity of domestic actors to achieve policy changes and limits their empowerment. The European liberalization of the transport sector, for example, empowered societal and political actors in highly regulated member states, which had been unsuccessfully pushing for privatization and deregulation. But while the German reform coalition was able to exploit European policies to overcome domestic opposition to liberalization, Italian

trade unions and sectoral associations successfully blocked any reform attempt (Héritier *et al.* 2001; Héritier 2001; Kerwer and Teutsch 2001). The variation can be explained if we take into account the large number of veto players in the Italian system.

2. Existing *formal institutions* can provide actors with material and ideational resources necessary to exploit European opportunities and to promote domestic adaptation. The European political opportunity structure may offer domestic actors additional resources. But many are unable to exploit them when they lack the necessary action capacity. Direct relations with European decision-makers provide regions with the opportunity to circumvent their central government in European policy making. But many regions do not have sufficient resources (manpower, money, expertise) to be permanently present at the European level and to exploit the new opportunities. While Bavaria or Catalonia are strong enough to maintain regular relations with EU institutions, Estremadura or Bremen simply lack the action capacity to do this. Many regions then rely on their central governments to channel their interests into the European policy process (Jeffery 2000). In the United Kingdom, public agencies and related complementary institutions, the Equal Opportunities Commission in particular, provided womens' organizations with the means to use EU equal pay and equal treatment directives in furthering gender equality. In the absence of such an institution, French women were not able to overcome domestic resistance to implement the EU equal pay and equal treatment policies (Tesoka 1999; Caporaso and Jupille 2001).

In sum, and following a rationalist institutional logic, we can conceptualize the adaptational pressures or the degrees of misfit emanating from Europeanization as providing new opportunities for some actors and severely constraining other actors' freedom of manoeuvre. Whether actors can exploit these opportunities or circumvent the constraints depends on intervening factors such as the number of veto points in the political system, on the one hand, and the (in-) existence of supporting formal institutions, on the other. These two factors determine whether the new opportunities and constraints resulting from Europeanization in case of misfit translate into an effective redistribution of resources among actors and, thus, whether Europeanization does indeed lead to a differential empowerment of actors.

Domestic Change as a Process of Socialization and Learning

Sociological institutionalism draws on the 'logic of appropriateness' (March and Olsen 1989, 1998) according to which actors are guided by collective understandings of what constitutes proper, that is, socially accepted behaviour in a given rule structure. These collective understandings and intersubjective meanings influence the ways in which actors define their goals and what they perceive as 'rational' action. Rather than maximizing their subjective desires, actors strive to fulfil social expectations. From this perspective, Europeanization is understood as the emergence of new rules, norms, practices, and structures of meaning to which member states are exposed and which they have to incorporate into their domestic practices and structures.

Sociological institutionalism offers two potential explanations for domestic change in response to Europeanization, one more structuralist, the other more agency-centred. The first account focuses on institutional isomorphism, suggesting that institutions which frequently interact, are exposed to each other, or are located in a similar environment develop similarities over time in formal organizational structures, principles of resource allocation, practices, meaning structures, and reform patterns (DiMaggio and Powell 1991; Meyer and Rowen 1991; Scott and Meyer 1994). Institutional isomorphism explains a process of homogenization of organizational structures over time. It ultimately rests on a form of structural determinism assuming that actors strive to match institutions to environmental changes. Rather than adapting to functional imperatives, organizations respond to changes in their normative and cognitive environment giving rise to institutional isomorphism. The conditions for isomorphism can vary. It appears to be most likely in environments with stable, formalized, and clear-cut organizational structures (Scott and Meyer 1994: 118). Provided that institutions are exposed to such an environment, they are expected to respond with similar changes in their institutional structure. This argument is faced with serious problems in explaining variation in institutional adaptation to a similar environment. It cannot account for the differential impact of Europe, since the causal mechanism identified should lead to structural convergence.

There is a second, more agency-centred version of sociological institutionalism which theorizes differences in the degree to which domestic norms and institutions change in response to international institutional arrangements. This version focuses on socialization processes by which actors learn to internalize new norms and rules in order to become members of (international) society 'in good standing' (Finnemore and Sikkink 1998; Checkel 1999*a*). Actors are socialized into new norms and rules of appropriateness through processes of arguing, persuasion, and social learning and to redefine their interests and identities accordingly. This perspective generates expectations about the differential impact of Europeanization, since 'misfit' constitutes the starting condition of a socialization process. While citizenship norms of the Council of Europe resonated well with traditional citizenship practices in France (*ius solis*), they directly contradicted the historical understandings of citizenship in Germany (*ius sanguinis*), thus creating a serious misfit (Checkel 2001). The idea of cooperative governance emulated by the European Commission fitted

German cooperative federalism but challenged statist policy-making practices in Italy and Greece (Kohler-Koch 1998*b*). The more European norms, ideas, structures of meaning, or practices resonate (fit) with those at the domestic level, the more likely it is that they will be incorporated into existing domestic institutions (Olsen 1996: 272), and the less likely it is that the European norms will lead to domestic change. High cognitive or normative misfit as lack of resonance is equally unlikely to cause substantial domestic change since domestic actors and institutions will resist adaptation (see below). We argue in turn that high misfit may lead to processes of socialization and learning resulting in the internalization of new norms and the development of new identities, provided that (one of) two mediating factors are present:

1. 'Change agents' or *norm entrepreneurs* mobilize at the domestic level. Norm entrepreneurs do not only pressure policy-makers to initiate change by increasing the costs of certain strategic options. Rather, they use moral arguments and strategic constructions in order to persuade actors to redefine their interests and identities, engaging them in processes of social learning. Persuasion and arguing are the mechanisms by which these norm entrepreneurs try to induce change (Risse 2000). There are two types of norm- and idea-promoting agents. *Epistemic communities* are networks of actors with an authoritative claim to knowledge and a normative agenda (Haas 1992*b*). They legitimate new norms and ideas by providing scientific knowledge about cause-and-effect relationships. Epistemic communities are more influential in inducing change, the higher the uncertainty about cause-and-effect relationships in the particular issue-area among policy-makers, the higher the consensus among the scientists involved, and the more scientific advice is institutionalized in the policy-making process (Haas 1992*a*; Adler and Haas 1992). In the case of the European single currency, the euro, a coalition of central bankers and national technocrats successfully advocated a monetarist approach which produced dramatic changes in domestic monetary policy, even in countries such as Italy and Greece which had to undergo painful adaptation (Radaelli 1998; Dyson and Featherstone 1999). *Advocacy* or *principled issue networks* are bound together by shared beliefs and values rather than by consensual knowledge (Keck and Sikkink 1998). They appeal to collectively shared norms and identities in order to persuade other actors to reconsider their goals and preferences. Processes of complex or 'double-loop' learning (Agyris and Schön 1980), in which actors change their interests and identities as opposed to merely adjusting their means and strategies, occur rather rarely. They usually take place after critical policy failure or in perceived crises and situations of great uncertainty (Checkel 1999*a*). While persuasion and social learning are mostly identified with processes of policy change, they transform domestic institutions, too. As Checkel argues, Germany underwent

a profound and constitutive change of its citizenship norms resulting from a learning process instigated by an advocacy network (Checkel 2001).

2. A political culture and other *informal institutions* conducive to consensus-building and cost-sharing also facilitate domestic change in response to Europeanization. Informal institutions entail collective understandings of appropriate behaviour that strongly influence the ways in which domestic actors respond to Europeanization pressures. First, a consensus-oriented or cooperative decision-making culture helps to overcome multiple veto points by rendering their use inappropriate for actors. Cooperative federalism prevented the German *Länder* from vetoing the European Treaty revisions which deprived them of core decision powers (Börzel 2002). The German litigational culture encouraged citizens to appeal to national courts for the deficient application of Community Law, while such a culture was absent in France where litigation is much lower (Conant 2001). Second, a consensus-oriented political culture allows for a sharing of adaptational costs which facilitates the accommodation of pressure for adaptation (Katzenstein 1984). Rather than shifting adaptational costs upon a social or political minority, the 'winners' of domestic change compensate the 'losers'. The German government shared its decision powers in European policy making with the *Länder* to make up for their Europe-induced power losses (Börzel 2002). Likewise, the consensual corporatist decision-making culture in the Netherlands and Germany facilitated the liberalization of the transport sector by offering compensation to the employees as the potential losers of the domestic changes (Héritier 2001; Héritier *et al.* 2001). A confrontational and pluralist culture, however, may inhibit domestic change, as the example of the Spanish regions in response to Europeanization pressures documents. The competitive institutional culture initially prevented the regions from cooperating with the Spanish central state in order to reap the benefits of Europeanization and to share its costs, respectively.

Norm entrepreneurs and consensus-oriented cultures affect whether European ideas, norms, and the collective understandings which do not resonate with those at the domestic level, are internalized by domestic actors giving rise to domestic change. This sociological logic of domestic change emphasizes arguing, learning, and socialization as the mechanisms by which new norms and identities emanating from Europeanization processes are internalized by domestic actors and lead to new definitions of interests and of collective identities. The logic also incorporates mimetic processes whereby institutions emulate others to reduce uncertainty and complexity (DiMaggio and Powell 1991; Radaelli 2000). Emulation is a significant mechanism by which member states learn from their neighbours and other Europeans how to respond effectively to adaptational pressures from Europeanization.

The two logics of domestic change as summarized in Figure 3.2 are not mutually exclusive. They often work simultaneously or dominate different

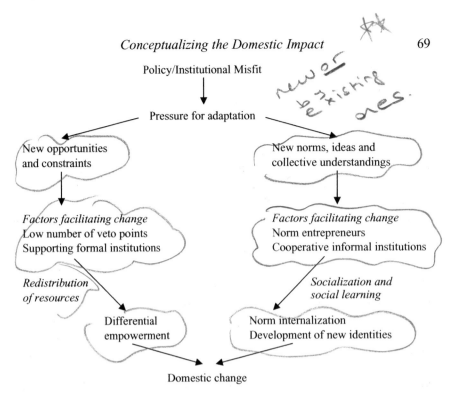

FIGURE 3.2. Two logics of domestic change

phases of the adaptational process. We come back to this point in the concluding part of the paper.

The Outcome of Domestic Change in Response to Europeanization

The two logics generate different propositions about the degree and direction of domestic change. Both take misfit as the necessary condition of domestic change and converge around the expectation that the lower the misfit, the smaller the pressure for adaptation and thus the lower the degree of expected domestic change. But the two logics depart on the effect of high adaptational pressure.

Absorption, Accommodation, or Transformation?

Domestic change in response to Europeanization pressures can be weak or strong. We distinguish here three degrees of domestic change:

1. *Absorption*: Member states incorporate European policies or ideas into their programs and domestic structures, respectively, but without substantially

modifying existing processes, policies, and institutions. The degree of domestic change is low

2. *Accommodation*: Member states accommodate Europeanization pressures by adapting existing processes, policies, and institutions without changing their essential features and the underlying collective understandings attached to them. One way of doing this is by 'patching up' new policies and institutions onto existing ones without changing the latter (Héritier 2001). The degree of domestic change is modest

3. *Transformation*: Member states replace existing policies, processes, and institutions by new, substantially different ones, or alter existing ones to the extent that their essential features and/or the underlying collective understandings are fundamentally changed. The degree of domestic change is high.

The rationalist institutionalist perspective suggests that the more Europeanization provides new opportunities and constraints (high adaptational pressure), the more likely a redistribution of resources is, which may alter the domestic balance of power and which may empower domestic actors to effectively mobilize for policy change by overriding domestic veto points. Medium adaptational pressure is also likely to result in domestic transformation if there are supporting formal institutions. In the presence of multiple veto points, however, medium adaptational pressure will be at best accommodated, if not absorbed, even if this means non-compliance in case of policy misfit. Finally, the mere absorption of low pressure of adaptation may be prevented by formal institutions which support domestic actors in exploiting modest new opportunities.

Sociological institutionalism, by contrast, argues that high adaptational pressure is likely to meet strong institutional inertia preventing any domestic change. New norms, rules, and practices do not simply replace or harmonize existing ones. Profound and abrupt changes should only be expected under conditions of crisis or external coercion (Olsen 1996). Actors are more open to learning and persuasion, if new norms and ideas, albeit 'inconvenient', are compatible with collectively shared understandings and meaning structures. Therefore, medium pressure for adaptation is most likely to result in domestic transformation, at least in the long run. Processes of adaptation evolve along institutional paths.

In sum, the two logics predict opposite outcomes under conditions of high adaptational pressure. Moreover, sociological institutionalism would expect domestic change beyond absorption only as the result of a long-term process of incremental adaptation (cf. Figure 3.3). Unfortunately, the available empirical evidence does not allow us yet to evaluate these propositions. Further systematic research is necessary to link the various causal mechanisms and

	High adaptational pressure	Medium adaptational pressure	Low adaptational pressure
Facilitating factors	RI: Transformation SI: Inertia (unless external shock)	RI: Transformation SI: Gradual transformation	RI: Accommodation SI: Accommodation
No facilitating factors	RI: Accommodation SI: Inertia	RI: Accommodation/ absorption SI: Accommodation/ absorption	RI: Inertia SI: Absorption

FIGURE 3.3. The different degrees of domestic change

intervening factors to the degree of domestic change to be expected in order to evaluate the assumptions.

Convergence or Divergence?

Most of the literature on the domestic impact of Europeanization tends to analyse the outcome of domestic change in terms of the likelihood of convergence of policies and institutions among the member states. But measuring convergence and divergence is extremely tricky. Answers vary according to the level at which one looks for convergence (Knill and Lenschow 2001) and the issue supposedly subject to convergence. What looks like convergence at the marco-level may still show a significant degree of divergence at the micro-level. Economic and Monetary Union gave rise to policy convergence among the twelve members with regard to inflation and budgetary restraints, as well as to institutional convergence concerning the independence of central banks. But it did not lead to similar institutional arrangements in the economic and fiscal policy area. And the means by which the member states reduced their budget deficits varied enormously—from austerity programs to new 'euro' taxes (in the case of Italy, see Sbragia 2001). While all member states responded to the liberalization of telecommunication by creating independent regulatory agencies, they adopted different institutional setups, reflecting variation in administrative structures (Böllhoff 2002; Schneider 2001).

Thus, authors need to specify very clearly at what level of policies and/or institutional arrangements they would expect converging processes or rather continued divergence among the member states. In any case, policy convergence seems to be more likely than institutional convergence as policy changes are more easily achieved (see the chapters in Cowles *et al.* 2001). Moreover, EU rules and regulations require convergence in policy outcomes (such as low inflation or budgetary restraint in the case of EMU), while they leave substantial discretionary power to the member states with regard to the means to ensure compliance. Thus, we need to specify what we mean by 'policy convergence': convergence in outcome (which equals compliance with EU law and, thus, is not particularly interesting to observe) or convergence in policy processes and instruments. This is often confused in the literature, as a result of which we know surprisingly little about the degree of policy convergence not related to policy outcomes.

As to the degree of institutional convergence, resource dependency and sociological institutionalist approaches generally lean towards convergence. Resource dependency predicts a redistribution of resources strengthening one group of actors over the others or reinforcing their mutual dependence. Arguments about institutional isomorphism (see above) suggest that institutions which frequently interact, are exposed to each other, or are located in a similar environment, become more similar over time (DiMaggio and Powell 1991; Meyer and Rowen 1991). However, we have sufficient empirical evidence that the outcome of the domestic effects of Europeanization is much more diverse than either resource dependency or sociological institutionalist approaches would expect.

The most comprehensive empirical studies on the domestic institutional effects of Europeanization so far showed that most empirical instances of domestic institutional change fall in the 'mixed' category whereby some countries converged toward similar policy or system-wide structures, while others retained their specific institutional arrangements, state–society relations, or cultural understandings (Kohler-Koch 1998b; Cowles *et al.* 2001; Héritier *et al.* 2001). There is not a single empirical case in which convergence meant the complete homogenization of domestic structures across member states. There is no evidence that domestic institutional change meant the comprehensive rejection of national administrative styles, legal cultures, societal relationships, and/or collective identities. As to the latter, France did not shed its national identity when adopting a European one. The meanings of 'Europe' differed in the German and French political discourses, even though the elites in both countries have incorporated Europeanness into their collective nation-state identities (Risse 2001). The traditional tensions between the Spanish regions and central government did not disappear as a result of a more cooperative arrangement in territorial matters (Börzel 2002). There is no general convergence toward cooperative federalism in Europe, just a movement toward such structures among federal states such as Germany and Spain.

These findings refute those schools of thought that expect strong structural convergence. According to the economic convergence school (Strange 1996; Woolcock 1996), we would expect increasing similarities in institutional arrangements in areas exposed to global market forces, that is, mostly areas of *negative integration* (Scharpf 1996). While the case of telecommunications confirms the argument, the case of the monetary and economic union does not (except with regard to independent central banks). Once again, one should not confuse convergence in policy outcomes (such as low inflation, budgetary constraints, etc.) with convergence in policy instruments, let alone institutional arrangements. In contrast, others have argued that EU policies of *positive integration* prescribe concrete institutional models for domestic compliance which should then result in institutional convergence (Knill and Lehnkuhl 1999; Radaelli 2000). The studies cited above refute this proposition, too.

Our analytical framework can easily explain why we do not find convergence across the board. First, as argued above, the 'goodness of fit' between Europeanization, on the one hand, and the domestic policies, politics, and institutional arrangements, on the other, varies enormously among the member states. Only those EU countries which exhibit similar domestic arrangements also face similar adaptational pressures as the necessary condition for domestic change. Second, and quite irrespective of the pressures for adaptation, each member state has a different set of institutions and actors facilitating or inhibiting change in response to these pressures. Multiple veto points, supporting formal institutions, norm entrepreneurs, and cooperative formal institutions mediate between the adaptational pressures and the outcome of domestic change. The facilitating factors identified by our two logics of domestic change can explain the absence of full convergence and should lead us to expect only partial, or some 'clustered convergence', where some member states converge toward similar policies or institutions, but others do not. Member states facing similar pressures for adaptation are likely to converge around similar outcomes, because similar actors are empowered and are likely to learn from each other in searching for ways to respond to adaptational pressure. The regions of federal and regionalized member states by now rely on cooperation with their central government to inject their interests into the European policy process, a finding which does not hold for less decentralized member states (Börzel 1999).

Conclusions: Toward Integrating the Two Logics of Domestic Change

We have argued in this chapter in favour of a rather parsimonious approach to the study of the domestic impact of Europeanization. Whether we study policies, politics, or polities, a misfit between European-level and domestic processes, policies, or institutions constitutes the necessary condition for expecting *any* change. But adaptational pressures alone are insufficient. There must be mediating factors enabling or prohibiting domestic change and accounting for the empirically observable differential impact of Europe. We have introduced two pathways leading to domestic changes which are theoretically grounded in rationalist and sociological institutionalisms, respectively. On the one hand, rationalist institutionalism follows a logic of resource redistribution emphasizing the absence of multiple veto points and the presence of supporting institutions as the main factors facilitating change. On the other hand, sociological institutionalism emphasizes a socialization and learning account, focusing on norm entrepreneurs as 'change agents' and the presence of a cooperative political culture as the main mediating factors. We claim that Europeanization might lead to convergence in policy outcomes, but only to partial and 'clustered convergence' with regard to policy processes and instruments, politics, and polities.

We need to be aware, however, that 'goodness of fit', adaptational pressures, and domestic responses to Europeanization are not static phenomena. Europeanization processes are constantly in motion and so are the domestic adaptations to them. There are also continuous feedback processes leading from the domestic levels to the European one. The analytical framework proposed here is not meant to suggest a static picture of Europeanization and domestic change. Rather, it is meant as a tool to enable systematic empirical research on the domestic impact of Europeanization, which would be impossible if we did not keep some variables constant.

Moreover, the two pathways identified in this chapter are by no means mutually exclusive. Of course, we need to distinguish analytically between the two logics of action and interaction emphasized by rationalist institutionalism and sociological institutionalism, respectively. In practice, however, the two logics often occur simultaneously or characterize different phases in processes of adaptational change. Future research has to figure out how the two pathways and causal mechanisms relate to each other. In conclusion, we build upon March and Olsen's (1998: 952–3) interpretations of how the logic of consequentialism and the logic of appropriateness may be linked. First, a clear logic should dominate an unclear one. In the case of Europeanization, this would mean that the 'socialization/learning' pathway is the more likely to be followed, the more the actors are uncertain about their preferences and strategy options. In contrast, the 'resource redistribution' pathway is likely to prevail if actors' preferences are well-defined and the available strategy options known.

Second, the two pathways might relate to each other in a sequential way. For example, norm entrepreneurs might be empowered by supportive institutions, but then start a socialization process of persuasion in order to overcome multiple veto points in the domestic system. In contrast, if domestic change in response to Europeanization involves high redistributional costs, a socialization process might be necessary to overcome stalemate and to develop new rules of fairness on the basis of which actors can then bargain over the distribution of costs.

Finally, the logic of consequentialism exogenizes preferences and identities, while the logic of appropriateness endogenizes them. As a result, the more Europeanization exerts adaptational pressures on constitutive and deeply embedded institutions (such as citizenship rules) and collective identities, the more the socialization/learning pathway is necessary to induce constitutive change. The example of the French elites and their collective identity is instructive in this regard. When the French socialists with President Mitterrand assumed power during the early 1980s, their economic and monetary policies quickly turned out to be incompatible with what was required under the European monetary system (a quite substantial misfit). In response, Mitterrand changed course and adjusted French economic policies accordingly. This change of policies turned out to be incompatible with the Socialist preferences and collective identities of the French left. As a result, the French Socialists adjusted their preferences to Europe and increasingly (re-)defined French state identity as part and parcel of a collective European identity (Risse 2001). In this case, we can explain the original policy change as an instrumental adaptation to reduce economic and political costs. However, it then led to a more profound change of preferences and even collective identities.

It is too early to say which of these propositions hold under which circumstances. Future research needs to specify under which conditions instrumental adaptation to Europeanization pressures suffices for domestic change, and when more profound change of preferences and identities is necessary for member states to adjust to Europe. Yet current empirical work has clearly demonstrated that Europe matters, leading to sometimes quite significant transformations of domestic policies, politics, and polities in the member states.

REFERENCES

Adler, Emanuel and Peter Haas (1992). 'Conclusion: Epistemic Communities, World Order, and the Creation of a Reflective Research Program'. *International Organization* 46(1): 367–90.

Aguilar Fernandez, Susana (1992). 'Environmental Monitoring and Environmental Information in Spain', in Peter Knöpfel, Helmut Weidner, and R. Zieschank (eds), *Environmental Monitoring and Reporting in Selected Countries* (Basel, Frankfurt a/M: Helbing and Lichtenhahn).

Agyris, Chris and Donald A., Schön (1980). *Organizational Learning* (Reading, Mass.: Addison-Wesley).

Böllhoff, Dominik (2002). The New Regulatory Regime—The Institutional Design of Telecommunications Regulation at the National Level', in A. Héritier (eds), *Common Goods: Reinventing European and International Governance* (Lanham: Rowman and Littlefield Publishers), 235–61.

Börzel, Tanja, A. (1999). 'Towards Convergence in Europe? Institutional Adaptation to Europeanization in Germany and Spain', *Journal of Common Market Studies* 37 (4): 573–96.

——(2000). 'Why There Is No Southern Problem. On Environmental Leaders and Laggards in the European Union', *Journal of European Public Policy* 7(1).

——(2002). *States and Regions in the European Union. Institutional Adaptation in Germany and Spain* (Cambridge: Cambridge University Press).

Bulmer, Simon (1997). 'Shaping the Rules? The Constitutive Politics of the European Union and German Power', in Peter J. Katzenstein (ed.), *Tamed Power. Germany in Europe* (Ithaca, NY: Cornell University Press), 49–79.

Caporaso, James, A. and Joseph Jupille (2001). 'The Europeanization of Gender Equality Policy and Domestic Structural Change', in Maria Green Cowles, James A. Caporaso and Thomas Risse (eds), *Transforming Europe. Europeanization and Domestic Change* (Ithaca, NY: Cornell University Press), 21–43.

Checkel, Jeffrey T. (1999*a*). 'International Institutions and Socialization'. Working Paper, 5. Oslo: ARENA, University of Oslo, February.

——(1999*b*). 'Social Construction and Integration'. *Journal of European Public Policy* 6(4).

——(2001). 'The Europeanization of Citizenship'? in Maria Green Cowles, James A. Caporaso, and Thomas Risse (eds), *Transforming Europe. Europeanization and Domestic Change* (Ithaca, NY: Cornell University Press), 180–97.

Conant, Lisa Joy (2001). 'Europeanization and the Courts: Variable Patterns of Adaptation among National Judiciaries', in Maria Green Cowles, James A. Caporaso, and Thomas Risse (eds), *Transforming Europe. Europeanization and Domestic Change* (Ithaca, NY: Cornell University Press), 97–115.

Cowles, Maria Green (2001). 'The Transatlantic Business Dialogue and Domestic Business-Government Relations', in Maria Green Cowles, James A. Caporaso and Thomas Risse (eds), *Transforming Europe. Europeanization and Domestic Change* (Ithaca, NY: Cornell University Press), 159–79.

——James Caporaso, and Thomas Risse eds. (2001). *Transforming Europe: Europeanization and Domestic Change* (Ithaca, NY: Cornell University Press).

——and Thomas Risse (2001). 'Transforming Europe: Conclusions', in Maria Green Cowles, James A. Caporaso and Thomas Risse (eds), *Transforming Europe. Europeanization and Domestic Change* (Ithaca, NY: Cornell University Press), 217–38.

Desideri, Carlo and Vincenzo Santantonio (1997). 'Building a Third Level in Europe: Prospects and Difficulties in Italy', in Charlie Jeffery (ed.), *The Regional Dimension of the European Union. Towards a Third Level in Europe?* (London: Frank Cass), 96–116.

DiMaggio, Paul J. and Walter W. Powell (1991). 'The Iron Cage Revisited: Institutional Isomorphism and Collective Rationality in Organizational Fields', in Walter W. Powell and Paul J. DiMaggio (eds), *The New Institutionalism in Organizational Analysis* (Chicago, London: University of Chicago Press), 63–82.

Duina, Francesco G. (1999). *Harmonizing Europe. Nation-States within the Common Market* (New York: State University of New York Press).

Dyson, Kenneth and Keith Featherstone (1999). *The Road to Maastricht* (Oxford: Oxford University Press).

Eising, Rainer. forthcoming. 'Integration und Europäisierung', in Markus Jachtenfuchs and Beate Kohler-Koch (eds), *Europäische Integration, new edition*.

Finnemore, Martha and Kathryn Sikkink (1998). International Norm Dynamics and Political Change', *International Organization* 52(4): 887–917.

Grande, Edgar (1996). 'The State and Interest Groups in a Framework of Multi-level Decision-making: The Case of the European Union', *Journal of European Public Policy* 3 (3): 318–38.

Haas, Peter M. (1992*a*). Introduction: Epistemic Communities and International Policy Coordination', *International Organization* 46(1): 1–36.

——ed. (1992*b*). *'Knowledge, Power and International Policy Coordination'*, *International Organization, Special Issue*. 1 ed. 46.

Hall, Peter A. and Rosemary C. R. Taylor (1996). 'Political Science and the Three New Institutionalisms', *Political Studies* 44: 952–73.

Haverland, Markus (1999). *National Autonomy, European Integration, and the Politics of Packaging Waste* (Amsterdam: Thela Thesis).

——(2000). 'National Adaptation to European Integration: The Importance of Institutional Veto Points', *Journal of Public Policy* 20(1): 83–103.

Héritier, Adrienne (1996). 'The Accommodation of Diversity in European Policy-Making', *Journal of European Public Policy* 3(2): 149–76.

——(1999). *Policy-Making and Diversity in Europe. Escape from Deadlock* (Cambridge: Cambridge University Press).

——(2001). 'Differential Europe: National Administrative Responses to Community Policy', in Maria Green Cowles, James A. Caporaso and Thomas Risse (eds), *Transforming Europe. Europeanization and Domestic Change* (Ithaca, NY: Cornell University Press), 44–59.

Héritier, Adrienne *et al.* (2001). *Differential Europe—New Opportunities and Restrictions for Policy Making in Member States* (Lanham, MD: Rowman and Littlefield).

Héritier, Adrienne, Christoph Knill, and Susanne Mingers (1996). *Ringing the Changes in Europe. Regulatory Competition and the Transformation of the State. Britain, France, Germany* (Berlin, New York: Walter de Gruyter).

Hooghe, Liesbet (ed.) (1996). *Cohesion Policy and European Integration: Building Multi-Level Governance* (Oxford: Oxford University Press).

Jeffery, Charlie (2000). 'Sub-National Mobilization and European Integration', *Journal of Common Market Studies* 38(1): 1–23.

Katzenstein, Peter J. (1984). *Corporatism and Change. Austria, Switzerland, and the Politics of Industry* (Ithaca and London: Cornell University Press).

Katzenstein, Peter J. (1997). 'United Germany in an Integrating Europe', in Peter J. Katzenstein (ed.), *Tamed Power. Germany in Europe* (Ithaca, NY: Cornell University Press), 1–48.

Keck, Margret and Kathryn Sikkink (1998). *Activists Beyond Borders. Transnational Advocacy Networks in International Politics* (Ithaca, NY: Cornell University Press).

Kerwer, Dieter and Michael Teutsch (2001). 'Elusive Europeanisation. Liberalising Road Haulage in the European Union', *Journal of European Public Policy*.

Knill, Christoph and Dirk Lehnkuhl (1999). How Europe Matters. Different Mechanisms of Europeanization. *European Integration on-line Papers* 3(7): http://eiop.or.at/eiop/texte/1999–007a.htm.

—— and Andrea Lenschow (eds) (2000). *Implementing EU Environmental Policy: New Approaches to an Old Problem* (Manchester: Manchester University Press).

—— (2001). 'Seek and Ye Shall Find'. Linking Different Perspectives on Institutional Change. *Comparative Political Studies* 34: 187–215.

Kohler-Koch, Beate (1996). 'The Strength of Weakness. The Transformation of Governance in the EU', in Sverker Gustavsson and Leif Lewin (eds), *The Future of the Nation State. Essays on Cultural Pluralism and Political Integration* (Stockholm: Nerenius and Santerus), 169–210.

—— (1998a). 'Europäisierung der Regionen: Institutioneller Wandel als sozialer Prozeß', in Beate Kohler-Koch *et al.* (eds), *Interaktive Politik in Europa. Regionen im Netzwerk der Integration* (Opladen: Leske and Budrich), 13–31.

—— (ed.) (1998b). *Interaktive Politik in Europa. Regionen im Netzwerk der Integration.* (Opladen: Leske and Budrich).

—— and Rainer Eising (eds) (1999). *The Transformation of Governance in the European Union* (London: Routledge).

March, James G. and Johan P. Olsen (1989). *Rediscovering Institutions* (New York: The Free Press).

—— (1998). 'The Institutional Dynamics of International Political Orders', *International Organization* 52(4): 943–69.

Marks, Gary (1993). Structural Policy and Multilevel Governance in the European Community. In Alan Cafruny and Glenda Rosenthal (eds), *The State of the European Community II: Maastricht Debates and Beyond* (Boulder: Lynne Riener), 391–410.

Meyer, John W. and Brian Rowen (1991). 'Institutionalized Organizations: Formal Structures as Myth and Ceremony', in Paul J. DiMaggio and Walter W. Powell (eds), *The New Institutionalism in Organizational Analysis* (Chicago: University of Chicago Press), 41–62.

Morass, Michael (1997). 'Austria: The Case of a Federal Newcomer in European Union Politics', in Charlie Jeffery (ed.), *The Regional Dimension of the European Union. Towards a Third Level?* (London: Frank Cass), 76–95.

Moravcsik, Andrew (1993). 'Preferences and Power in the European Community. A Liberal Intergovernmentalist Approach', *Journal of Common Market Studies* 31(4): 473–524.

—— (1994). Why the European Community Strengthens the State: Domestic Politics and International Cooperation. Working Paper, 52 (Cambridge, Mass.: Harvard University).

——(1998). *The Choice for Europe: Social Purpose and State Power from Rome to Maastricht* (Ithaca, NY: Cornell University Press).

Olsen, Johan P. (1995). Europeanization and Nation-State Dynamics. Working Paper, 9. Oslo: ARENA, March 1995.

——(1996). 'Europeanization and Nation-State Dynamics', in Sverker Gustavsson and Leif Lewin (eds), *The Future of the Nation-State* (London: Routledge), 245–85.

——(1997). 'European Challenges to the Nation State', in B. Steunenberg and F. van Vught, *Political Institutions and Public Policy* Hague *et al.* (Dordrecht: Kluwer Academic Publishers), 157–88.

Puchala, Donald J. (1972). 'Of Blind Men, Elephants and International Integration', *Journal of Common Market Studies* 10(3): 267–84.

Radaelli, Claudio (1998). 'Networks of Expertise and Policy Change in Italy', *South European Society and Politics* 3(2): 1–22.

——(2000). Whither Europeanization? Concept Stretching and Substantive Change. *European Integration on-line Papers* 4 (8): http://eiop.or.at/eiop/texte/2000–008 a.htm.

Rhodes, R.A.W. (1996). Governing without Governance: Order and Change in British Politics. Inaugural lecture, Newcastle upon Tyne: University of Newcastle, 18 April 1996.

——(1997). *Understanding Governance. Policy Networks, Governance, Reflexivity and Accountability* (Buckingham and Philadelphia: Open University Press).

Risse, Thomas (2000). ' "Let's Argue!" Communicative Action in International Relations'. *International Organization* 54(1): 1–39.

——(2001). 'A European Identity? Europeanization and the Evolution of Nation-State Identities', in Maria Green Cowles, James A. Caporaso, and Thomas Risse (eds), *Transforming Europe. Europeanization and Domestic Change* (Ithaca, NY: Cornell University Press), 198–216.

——(2002). Constructivism and the Study of International Institutions: Toward Conversations across Paradigms', in Ira Katznelson and Helen V. Milner (eds), *Political Science as Discipline? Reconsidering Power, Choice, and the State at Century's End* (New York: W. W. Norton).

Risse, Thomas, James Caporaso, and Maria Green Cowles (2001). Europeanization and Domestic Change. Introduction, in Maria Green Cowles, James Caporaso and Thomas Risse (eds), *Transforming Europe: Europeanization and Domestic Change* (Ithaca, NY: Cornell University Press), 1–20.

Sandholtz, Wayne (1996). 'Membership Matters: Limits of the Functional Approach to European Institutions', *Journal of Common Market Studies* 34(3): 403–29.

Sbragia, Alberta (2001). 'Italy Pays for Europe: Political Leadership, Political Choice, and Institutional Adaptation', in Maria Green Cowles, James A. Caporaso and Thomas Risse (eds), *Transforming Europe. Europeanization and Domestic Change* (Ithaca, NY: Cornell University Press), 79–98.

Scharpf, Fritz W. (1996). 'Negative and Positive Integration in the Political Economy of European Welfare States', in Gary Marks *et al.* (eds), *Governance in the European Union* (London, Thousand Oaks, New Delhi: Sage), 15–39.

Schmidt, Vivien (1996). *From State to Market? The Transformation of French Business and Government* (Cambridge: Cambridge University Press).

Schneider, Volker (2001). 'Institutional Reform in Telecommunications: The European Union in Transnational Policy Diffusion', in Maria Green Cowles, James A. Caporaso and Thomas Risse (eds), *Transforming Europe. Europeanization and Domestic Change* (Ithaca, NY: Cornell University Press), 60–78.

Scott, W. Richard and John W. Meyer (1994). *Institutional Environments and Organizations—Structural Complexity and Individualism* (London: Sage Publications).

Strange, Susan (1996). *The Retreat of the State. The Diffusion of Power in the World Economy* (Cambridge: Cambridge University Press).

Tesoka, Sabrina (1999). 'Judicial Politics in the European Union: Its Impact on National Opportunity Structures for Gender Equality'. MPIfG Discussion Paper, 99/2, Köln: Max-Planck-Institut für Gesellschaftsforschung.

Tsebelis, George (1995). 'Decision Making in Political Systems. Veto Players in Presidentialism, Parliamentarism, Multicameralism and Multipartism', *British Journal of Political Science* 25(3): 289–325.

Wallace, Helen and William Wallace (eds) (1996). *Policy-Making in the European Union* (Oxford: Oxford University Press).

Woolcock, Stephen (1996). 'Competition among Forms of Corporate Governance in the European Community: the Case of Britain', in Suzanne Berger and Ronald Dore (eds), *National Diversity and Global Capitalism* (Ithaca, NY: Cornell University Press), 179–96.

II

Comparing Institutional Contexts

4

Meeting the Demands of EU Membership: The Europeanization of National Administrative Systems

HUSSEIN KASSIM

This chapter approaches the theme of Europeanization somewhat differently from the other contributions to this volume. Using the term in its broadest sense, it examines the administrative response on the part of member states to the demands of EU membership and considers the institutional arrangements they have put in place to manage their participation in EU decision making. European integration subjects national governments to unique and exacting pressures and imposes strict requirements on their participation in processes of EU decision making. This chapter considers these demands. It examines and compares national responses in terms of the ambitions developed by the member states, their coordination strategies, and the structures they have put in place to manage their involvement in the Union. Finally, it considers the underlying determinants that shape national coordination arrangements.

The Demands of EU Membership

Membership of the European Union confronts governments with a set of particularly testing organizational and managerial challenges. On the one hand,

This chapter draws on the findings of a project jointly convened by the author, Guy Peters, Anand Menon, and the late Vincent Wright. I should like to thank my co-convenors and the participants of the two workshops in Oxford in June 1998 and May 1999 for their contributions to the project, in particular, the detailed case studies. I am grateful to colleagues in the School of Politics and Sociology at Birkbeck College, University of London, for allowing me to take sabbatical leave in 2001–2. This chapter was written while I was a Visiting Scholar at the Center for European Studies, Harvard University. I am grateful to the Director of the Centre and his colleagues for allowing me the pleasure of working in such a congenial and stimulating environment. Thanks are also due to the editors for their helpful comments on an earlier version of this chapter.

the pressure on member states to develop and present a coherent position in Brussels is strong. The Union is an authoritative actor and decision-making arena. The benefit from 'getting things right' can be substantial, while 'getting things wrong' may be costly economically and politically. Participation in EU policy making is extremely demanding. Member states are locked into a 'continuous policy making process of both an active and reactive nature' (Wright 1996: 149) across a broad and expanding terrain where they interact with multiple partners in a complex institutional environment. Action must be coordinated at and between at least two levels, the domestic and the European,[1] so that proposals in Brussels are consistent with national imperatives. Each dimension, moreover, imposes its own requirements and has particular dynamics. As a result, governments find themselves subject to varying, often contradictory, demands.

Why Coordinating National Action in Europe Matters

Across a broad range of activities, the Union has become an important, if not the most important, policy maker or decision-making venue. Decisions taken in Brussels have far-reaching consequences for the member states. EU legislation that is consistent with domestic policy can bring positive benefits (Héritier *et al.* 1996; Kohler-Koch and Eising 1999). For example, the threat of being undercut by its competitors will be reduced if the high-cost national regulations confronted by a firm in a particular member state are extended across the Union. Similarly, companies used to competing in a deregulated environment at home may benefit from Union-wide liberalization that effectively exports the domestic regime. Conversely, the adoption of EU regulations that are out-of-step with long-standing domestic orientations can impose heavy adjustment costs on companies and be politically costly for governments (Héritier *et al.* 1996).

Commission decisions can be similarly consequential. State aid or merger cases often become politicized in the home state of the companies concerned, and governments can be damaged if a ruling goes against one of its 'national champions'. More generally, as 'Europe' has become increasingly salient as a domestic political issue, governments often find themselves under pressure to demonstrate to sceptical publics that they have been suitably vigilant in their defence of the 'national interest'. This applies particularly to key sectors, such as agriculture in France and fisheries in Spain and the United Kingdom. Moreover, the European Union disposes of substantial economic resources, notably in agriculture and regional development. Governments, subnational authorities, businesses, and other domestic actors have an interest in securing

---

[1] See Kassim *et al.* (2000, 2001) for discussion of the demands imposed at domestic and European levels respectively and for detailed discussion of how member states have responded.

a share of the funds available, creating incentives at the national level to establish organizational arrangements that will ensure effective lobbying in these areas. Ireland, for example, gained a reputation for its astute 'grantsmanship'[2] on account of its success in making bids for monies from the cohesion funds.

If the importance of ensuring the effective representation of national interests in Brussels creates a general incentive for member states to make the necessary arrangements, the institutions of the European Union and the obligations that they impose on governments also encourage these efforts. Participation in Union institutions, such as the Council of the Union, calls for coordination on the part of governments. Meetings must be prepared, positions defended, and negotiations undertaken. The European Council's increasingly high profile and the broadening of its agenda, moreover, require that Heads of State and Government have at their disposal the institutional resources necessary for effective participation. Similarly, InterGovernmental Conferences call for careful organization, strategic action, and tactical thinking across a broad front of activities, particularly now that governments have realized that seemingly innocuous institutional changes can have far-reaching consequences on policy outcomes and the balance of power between actors at the European level. Effective coordination on the part of national governments, finally, is necessary to carry out the duties of the Council Presidency (Hayes-Renshaw and Wallace 1997: 134–57).[3]

The Challenge to the Member States

While the benefits and obligations that flow from EU membership create powerful incentives for effective organization on the part of governments, the challenges with which the Union presents national governments are considerable. The European Union is an extremely complex political system that confronts individual governments with a challenging environment in which they lack the resources—authority, agenda control, party discipline, established networks, and administrative traditions—that they can mobilize at home for domestic purposes. Among the features that present particular difficulties are the following:

1. The European Union is 'fluid, ambiguous, and hybrid' (Olsen 1997: 165). It is 'not based on a single treaty, a unitary structure, or a single dominating

---

[2] The term is Brigid Laffan's.

[3] For discussion of the tasks and challenges confronting the Council Presidency, see de Bassompierre (1990), O'Nuallain and Hocheit (1985), Westlake (1995: 37–54), and Hayes-Renshaw and Wallace (1997: 134–57). The official Council guidebook warns that '[m]ajor deployment of the entire national administrative apparatus is required to get the Presidency up and running' (General Secretariat 1997: 6). It adds ominously, 'The size of this extra workload for national administrations ... even for the larger Member States, should not be underestimated' (General Secretariat 1996: 6).

centre of authority and power. Rather, the Union is built on several treaties and a complex three-pillar structure...[where] the pillars are organized on different principles and supranational/intergovernmental mixes' (Olsen, ibid.), their interrelations ill-defined, and their institutions poorly integrated. More broadly, '[t]here is no shared vision or project, or common understanding of the legitimate basis of a future Europe' (Olsen, ibid.). Its membership, its rules, the relationships between, and authority of, its institutions are constantly evolving (Wright 1996; Olsen 1997).

2. The EU policy processes are unusually open (Peters 1994; Wright 1996: 151). Items on its agenda come from a variety of sources, and the policy menu is long, ever changing, and more varied than at the national level. Decision making involves a multiplicity of actors, including, besides the fifteen member governments, the EU institutions and other European bodies and agencies, representatives of regional and local authorities, and a host of lobbyists of varying size and importance (Mazey and Richardson 1993; Greenwood 1997; Greenwood and Aspinwall 1997), each with its own interests and, in the case of EU bodies, an institution with its own rules, code of conduct, and operating style, and an arena in which individuals, groups, and associations compete for influence. Since decisions are not typically the result of action on the part of a single actor or institution, parties must search for allies and create coalitions.

3. The European Union is institutionally and procedurally complex, and lacks a constitutionally defined separation of powers or a tidy division of responsibilities (Lenaerts 1991; Kohler-Koch and Eising 1999). Legislative power is shared by two institutions—the Council and the European Parliament—that form 'a classic two-chamber legislature' (Hix 1999: 56), and executive authority is spread between the member states (individually and collectively) and the Commission.[4] Legislative procedures are long and complex, and combined with the different decision rules that apply to the Council in different policy sectors and subsectors, present a bewildering array of formal processes.[5] Each distributes the power between institutions in different ways,

---

[4] According to Simon Hix, executive power has two elements: '*political*, the leadership of society through the proposal of policy and legislation; and *administrative*, the implementation of law, the distribution of public revenues, and the passing of secondary and tertiary rules and regulations' (1999: 21). The member states' executive responsibilities involve setting the long-term policy goals of the European Union (Council), setting the medium-term policy agenda (European Council), implementing EU legislation through their own bureaucracies, and managing the day-to-day administration of EU policies with the Commission through comitology (Hix 1999: 25); the Commission's responsibilities include developing medium-term strategies for the development of the European Union, drafting legislation and arbitrating in the legislature process, making rules and regulations, managing the EU budget, and scrutinizing the implementation of the Treaty of secondary legislation (Hix 1999: 32).

[5] The Commission in its review of the operation of the Treaty of European Union found twenty-four combinations in operation (CEC 1995).

thereby enshrining variations in the interinstitutional balance between and within sectors according to which procedure is used (Garrett 1995; Scully 1997), encouraging different strategies and imposing different 'bargaining requirements' (Pollack 1994), and privileging certain outcomes over others (Tsebelis 1990). The most intricate of these procedures—codecision—retains its complexity even though simplifications were introduced by the Treaty of Amsterdam and it has been extended to a wider range of policies (Falkner and Nentwich 2000).

4. The European Union is characterized by high degrees of institutional fragmentation—the main institutions are internally differentiated and segmented—and organizational density. Formations of the Council have proliferated, its tripartite structure complicated by the addition of bodies and tiers to handle new competencies; the Commission is segmented into twenty-four directorates general, each with its own operating style (Abélès *et al.* 1993; Cini 1997; Page 1997), while a permanent tension defines relations between the College and the services; and the Parliament is a multiparty chamber, where partisan affiliations cut across the functional allocation of legislative scrutiny between its twenty committees. Intra- and interinstitutional interactions take place in a universe of permanent and ad hoc committees and subcommittees that has only recently begun to be charted (Buitendijk and Van Schendelen 1995; Dogan 1997; Van Schendelen 1999). As Wright (1996: 151–2) has noted, '[t]hese committees are largely responsible for the mass of microlevel sectoral decisions... and... are interwoven with a set of overlapping bargaining networks'. Systematic control over these committees and subcommittees has yet to be exercised, and their relative functions and status have fluctuated considerably over time.

5. Sectoralization is strongly pronounced (Mazey and Richardson 1993; Menon and Hayward 1996). Although a feature of domestic policy making, 'the extent and nature of these problems in Brussels is of a different order' (Wright 1996: 130). The main distinction is between polity issues, such as treaty reform, the power of institutions, external relations, and enlargement, and more technical areas (Derlien 2000; Maurer and Wessels 2001), which can be separated into regulatory, redistributive, and distributive (Lowi 1964), each with its own logic and conflict potential and its own demands in terms of technical expertise. The EU competence varies from sector to sector, different legislative procedures and decision rules apply, and distinct constellations of actors are engaged. The scope and pace of policy development varies accordingly (Wright 1996; Menon and Hayward 1996).

If the general characteristics of the European Union make it difficult for national coordinators to negotiate, a further difficulty for governments is the need simultaneously to ensure that action taken in Brussels is acceptable at home. What may be desirable for domestic policy purposes may be not be feasible at the European level. One prominent view is that the constraints at one level may be transformed into opportunities at the other: 'National bargaining positions in Brussels may be reinforced by invoking "problems back home" whilst essential but unpalatable politics...are imposed on domestic constituencies which readily finger Brussels as the real culprit' (Wright 1996: 149).[6] In practice, however, governments no longer enjoy, if in fact they ever did, the far-reaching autonomy in European policy with respect to domestic constituencies that is implied by earlier versions of intergovernmentalism. Europe's salience as a domestic political issue ensures that government are kept under the glare of the national press. Moreover, governments are no longer the gatekeepers of the 'national interest' (Marks *et al.* 1996). Domestic interests—private actors, such as businesses and pressure groups, but also public sector bodies, such as bankers, regions, and local authorities—are active in Brussels, making direct contact with EU institutions and counterparts from other member states (Mazey and Richardson 1993; Pedlar and Van Schendelen 1993; Greenwood 1997; Greenwood and Aspinwall 1997). Although they continue to lobby their national governments, they are also ready to exploit the possibilities that Brussels presents, to challenge domestic policies to which they are opposed and to take advantage of the new political opportunity structure that European integration has brought about (Marks *et al.* 1996; Favell 1998).

Comparing National Responses

The comparison of national arrangements inevitably raises the question of the extent to which member states pursue similar ambitions, follow similar strategies, and have put in place similar structures. Existing theoretical perspectives conflict on this issue. One set of approaches suggests that there is good reason to expect a convergence of institutions, structures and procedures. Another contends that there are strong grounds to anticipate divergence between national systems.

Convergence or Divergence?

The expectation of convergence arises from two different perspectives: from rational choice institutionalism (Hall and Taylor 1998) and from the new institutionalism in organizational analysis (DiMaggio and Powell 1991).

---

[6] See Hoffmann (1982), Putnam (1992), Moravcsik (1993, 1994), and Smith (1997).

According to the former, institutions in a shared institutional environment are likely to grow increasingly similar, as they converge around the most efficient organizational form. 'Optimization' (Harmsen 1999: 84) takes place as member states copy from their counterparts the structures or procedures that have proved to be the most successful. The result is 'a gradual convergence of national practices around the most effective solutions to . . . common problems' (Harmsen 1999: 84). According to the latter, organizations in a common institutional environment are likely to become increasingly similar as a result of two additional factors: coercion—in an EU context, the obligations and pressures that flow from hard and 'soft' rules (DiMaggio and Powell 1991); and mimicry—the copying by some organizations of the mechanisms or features of other organizations. Socialization is a third mechanism (Haas 1958; Kerremans 1996; Wessels 1997; Lewis 1998). Frequent contact and interaction between national officials can, moreover, be expected to lead to the development of common norms, as officials are 'gradually socialized into the shared values and practices of the EU system' (Harmsen 1999: 84),[7] resulting in a 'gradual diffusion of those shared values within national administrative systems' and a common culture that leads eventually to the 'emergence of increasingly similar national structures and processes' (ibid.). In short, 'institutions that frequently interact or are exposed to each other over time develop similarities in organizational structures, processes, recruitment patterns, structures of meaning, principles of resource allocation, and reform patterns' (Olsen 1997: 161).[8]

An opposite thesis—the 'continuing divergence' hypothesis—emerges from sociological institutionalism. March and Olsen (1984, 1989), its main exponents, contest the view that institutions are always efficient and argue that organizations are likely to respond to external pressures by interpreting them in terms of pre-existing structures and values. From this perspective, existing differences between organizations are likely to be reproduced, even when they are placed in the same environment, since their adaptation to outside conditions is likely to be mediated by internally generated 'logics of appropriateness'. Applying this view to national coordination systems, Harmsen (1999) argues that a logic of divergence that is more likely to prevail.

National Coordination Systems

Detailed examination of the systems put in place by member states to respond to the demands and challenges of EU membership reveals a differentiated pattern of similarity and difference.

---

[7] See also Haas (1958), Derlien (2000), Kerremans (1996), and Lewis (1998).
[8] Olsen cites the work of Meyer and Rowan (1977), Thomas *et al.* (1987), DiMaggio and Powell (1991), Brunsson and Olsen (1993), and Scott and Meyer (1994).

Similarities Between National Systems

Several similarities emerge from the study of twelve member states (Kassim
et al. 2000; Kassim *et al.* 2001).[9] All have put in place specific arrangements
for coordinating EU policy making; the responsibilities of existing actors have
been adjusted and new ones created, coordination mechanisms have been
introduced or developed, and special processes and procedures established.
Seven further similarities are evident:

1. Heads of government have at their disposal the specialist expertise and
   institutional support necessary to enable them to carry out the increasingly
   routinized functions that they perform in EU decision making and, as the
   European Union has become a salient domestic issue, early warning and
   crisis management systems. Examples include the European Secretariat in
   the United Kingdom, the Chancellor's Office in Germany, and a special
   committee in Denmark.
2. Foreign affairs ministries continue to occupy a central role in national
   processes, but their position is being gradually eroded due to the increased
   involvement of prime ministers in EU matters, the direct involvement in
   EU policy making of subnational representatives and officials from the
   line ministries,[10] the expansion of EU competencies, which makes it less
   feasible for all communications from the national capital to be channelled
   through the foreign office, and the spread of new technology—fax
   machines and email—which puts domestic ministries into direct contact
   with their interlocutors in Brussels.
3. Interdepartmental coordination in EU matters is generally managed by
   mechanisms that have been specifically devised for the purpose, whether in
   the form of specialist administrative units—the Secrétariat général du
   comité interministeriel (SGCI) in France, the SSEU in Spain, the European
   Secretariat in the United Kingdom, the Department for the Coordination of
   European Community Policies in Italy, and the DGAC in Portugal—
   committees in Belgium, Germany, and Italy, or meetings in Austria.
4. Ministries have reorganized internal operation and structures, creating (with
   the exception of Spain) special units to coordinate European business and
   adjusting personnel policies to recruit officials with appropriate language

---

[9] Kassim, Peters, and Wright (2000) investigated the domestic coordination of EU policy in
ten member states: Austria, Belgium, Denmark, France, Germany, Greece, Italy, Portugal,
Spain, and the United Kingdom; Kassim *et al.* (2001) examined the coordination of EU policy
at the European level by eleven states: Austria, Belgium, France, Germany, Greece, Ireland,
Italy, the Netherlands, Portugal, Sweden, and the United Kingdom.

[10] The poignant remark of a Danish diplomat, quoted by Pedersen (2000), makes the point
well: 'we are no longer the only ones who read French'.

skills, introduce special training programmes (Maor and Stevens 1996), and support the 'recycling' of officials through Brussels.

5. 'Deparliamentarization' (Wessels and Rometsch 1996): national parliaments usually have a formal role in EU policy making, but are rarely influential (Norton 1996; Wessels and Rometsch 1996; Katz and Wessels 1999). Specialist committees and procedures have been put in place, but rarely do parliaments exercise a continuous influence on policy. Executive dominance, the volume of EU business and its technical character, and the speed at which business moves through the Council limit their ability to intervene.

6. Most member states have a junior minister for European affairs or the equivalent, but, with the exception of France, the office is not typically held by a political heavyweight.[11]

7. All member states have put in place a permanent representation on the front line in Brussels, which is the centrepiece of the national coordination effort at the European level. The mission is characteristically charged with 'upstream' functions, such as providing a 'postbox' (Spence 1995) for the national administration in general, providing an official point of contact between government and EU institutions and other member states (Wallace 1973: 57), and providing a base for national negotiators (Spence 1995), and 'downstream' responsibilities, including providing information for and advising the national capital. Permanent representations have flat hierarchies, officials enjoy considerable autonomy in their day-to-day work, and daily routines are marked by strong segmentation.

The Differences

Although not insignificant, the similarities between the coordination systems created by the member states are overshadowed by the differences that emerge from detailed inspection. These differences are apparent even with respect to the seven features identified above. Although charged with important tasks in all member states, for example, the status of the foreign ministry varies considerably. In some member states (e.g. Denmark, Portugal, and Spain), the foreign affairs ministry is the dominant actor. In others, responsibility is shared with the economics or finance ministry as in Germany and Greece, or the Prime Minister's department as in Italy, or the Cabinet

---

[11] Indeed, it seems to be widely thought that the creation of a 'proper' European ministry would lead either to the creation of a second foreign office or a super-ministry that reproduced internally the national administration, 'turning the coordination requirement from an interdepartmental one into an intradepartmental problem' (Derlien 2000).

Office as in the United Kingdom. In France it is the SGCI, responsible to the Hotel Matignon rather than the Quai d'Orsay, that sends instructions to the French Permanent Representation (FRANREP) (Menon 2001). The role of individual ministries in the overall process of coordination and the internal division of responsibilities provides a second example. In the United Kingdom, line ministries take the lead in EU policy. Each has a division responsible for internal coordination, which takes charge of horizontal issues, acts as troubleshooter, briefs ministers, offers specialist advice inside and outside the ministry, and mobilizes its networks in Whitehall and Brussels. By contrast, in Greece, coordination units tend to be 'conveyor belts rather than think tanks' (Spanou 2000) and EU policy is managed by the regular divisions.

Beyond these differences lie more systematic divergences. There are two fundamental dimensions along which national coordination systems vary. The first is coordination ambition. Some member states have far-reaching, strategic, and directive conceptions that are comprehensive in scope. They aim to construct an agreed position on virtually every issue across the full range of EU activities and competencies. Others have more modest ambitions and are selective in their approach. The second dimension concerns the extent to which coordination is centralized. In centralized systems, the aim is to define a negotiating stance at a relatively early stage of the EU policy process that is accepted by all interested parties, and to ensure the coherent presentation by all national representatives. The EU business is monitored by specialist structures at the centre of government, charged with overall responsibility for coordination and with the power to settle disputes that may arise between different departments. In decentralized systems, there is no single authoritative actor. In such systems, the machinery may exist to facilitate interdepartmental or intergovernmental consultation or bargaining, but no actor has the authority to impose solutions or to force a reconciliation of views.

Plotting the two dimensions produces four basic coordination types (see Figure 4.1): comprehensive centralizers; comprehensive decentralized; selective centralizers; and selective decentralized. Only the last is an empty cell. Four countries stand out as examples of comprehensive centralizers—France, the United Kingdom, Denmark, and Sweden (Menon 2000; Kassim 2000*a*; Pedersen 2000). The EU policy making in these states is characterized by an explicit and wide-ranging coordination ambition, and a highly centralized coordination system. The central body charged with ensuring that France's ambitious strategy is realized is the SGCI, a small elite unit of 150 officials, attached to the Prime Minister's Office—thereby, assuring its centrality and authority—which is admired for its efficiency and expertise (Lequesne 1993,

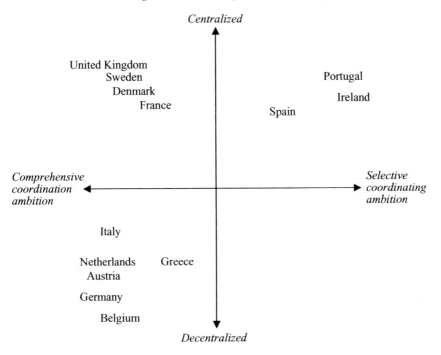

FIGURE 4.1. Systems for the coordination of EU policy by degree of centralization and coordinating ambition

Note: Figure shows the twelve member states for which data are available.

Source: Kassim *et al.* (2000, 2001).

1996; Guyomarch 1993).[12] The SGCI monitors developments within the European Union, 'receives and circulates EU documentation, disseminates information and invites preparatory studies on potential problems of harmonization with national law' (Wright 1996: 156). Since 1986, it has also been responsible for overseeing the transposition of EU directives into national law. On receipt of proposals from the Commission and in advance of the Council, the SGCI convenes interministerial meetings which all interested departments attend. In most cases, a position is agreed, but if agreement cannot be reached, the matter is referred by the SGCI to the political level where it is discussed by the cabinets of the ministers involved, or in rare cases by the ministers themselves. The SGCI alone is authorized to send instructions to France's Permanent Representation, even where only a single ministry is involved.

[12] 'French positions in all the institutions of the European Union must be expressed with clarity and the greatest possible coherence ... the unity of French positions is a necessary condition of the efficiency of our action ... [The] requirement of coherence in the French positions imposes the need for a strict respect of the procedures for interministerial concertation' (Prime Ministerial circular, cited in Menon 2000).

The United Kingdom has similar ambitions,[13] but its system is less central-ized. The principle of subsidiarity governs relations between actors at the cen-tre and individual ministries. The European Secretariat, with the Foreign and Commonwealth Office (FCO) and the UK Permanent Representation, form a *troika* at the centre of government that is responsible for EU policy coordina-tion. The European Secretariat, like the SGCI, is located close to the Prime Minister (in the Cabinet Office) and its mission is similarly defined, but is smaller (with a staff of about twenty) and less interventionist, taking action only where problems arise (Bender 1991).

Though also centralized, the Danish system is organized somewhat differ-ently. Coordination is managed through a pyramidal structure of committees, the base of which is formed by thirty-two specialist committees (Pedersen 2000). Discussion on Commission initiatives begins in these technical commit-tees that bring together both civil servants from interested departments and interest group representatives.[14] The committees are chaired by the lead depart-ment, which is responsible for preparing the position paper that provides the basis of discussion, and are always attended by a representative from the Foreign Ministry. Responsibility at the political level lies with two cabinet com-mittees, the EC Committee and the Foreign Policy Committee, both of which are chaired by the Ministry for Foreign Affairs. Although it has lost power in recent years to its senior partner—the Foreign Policy Committee—the EC Committee remains central (Pedersen 2000). The Foreign Policy Committee, which includes the Prime Minister, the Foreign Minister, and the eight ministers most involved with the European Union, meets (infrequently) to resolve highly sensitive political issues.

The Swedish system, reformed in 1999, similarly involves the Prime Minister's office and the Foreign Ministry. While the Coordination Group, located in the EU Department of the Foreign Ministry, ensures that 'Swedish standpoints are prepared for all items on upcoming Council agendas' (Mazey 2001: 263) and finalizes and transmits official instructions to Swedish repres-entatives, the content of those instructions is decided in the Fredagsgruppen, the weekly meeting of senior civil servants from the Prime Minister's Office, and the Ministries of Finance and Foreign Affairs. The meeting is chaired by

---

[13] The aim of coordination is defined as follows: 'for any EU activity or proposal ... agree-ment is reached on a UK policy in good time, taking account of identified UK interests and advancing or at least protecting those consistent with overall Government policy with realistic objectives taking account of the interests of other members of the European Union and that the policy agreed is followed through consistently during negotiation, and put into effect once deci-sions have been taken in Brussels' (cited in Kassim 2000*a*).

[14] These committees can be somewhat large. The committee for environmental affairs, for example, has seventy-five members (Pedersen 2000).

the State Secretary for EU Affairs, attached to the Prime Minister's Office, who heads a small unit responsible for developing long-term EU strategy and for resolving policy conflicts between ministries.

Selective centralizers include Ireland, Portugal, and Spain.[15] In the absence of a comprehensive ambition, coordination is focused on ensuring that national interests are effectively represented in sensitive policy areas. For all three countries, regional policy and fisheries are particularly salient. In addition, for Ireland and Portugal, managing the Council Presidency effectively has been an especially high priority. National coordination efforts in these states tend to be concentrated on these areas. Central coordinating structures and mechanisms vary, however, between the three states. In Portugal and Spain, the routine coordination of EU policy is the exclusive preserve of the foreign ministry. In Ireland, coordination is more informal. 'Interdepartmental coordination is assisted by a group of high ranking civil servants from the various Departments under the chairmanship of the Taoiseach's (Prime Minister's) Department' (Council 2001).

In comprehensive decentralized systems, found in Austria, Belgium, Germany, Greece, Italy, and the Netherlands, issue coverage is extensive, but no single actor, even the head of government, has the power routinely to impose solutions on the other players in technical policy fields. Coordination is led by the relevant technical ministry, which effectively decides the national standpoint, and tends to be minimal, compared to the positive, directive ambition that informs centralized systems. Although venues exist at the centre in all states that fall under this category—in Austria, Belgium, Germany, Italy, the Netherlands—or at the interstices between sectors, as in Belgium,[16] the function of these arenas is to allow participants to exchange views and information, and not usually to resolve conflict between departments. Although in Austria, for example, the country's negotiating stance is agreed at the weekly Tuesday meeting, policy making tends to be strictly sectoral. The lead department dominates decision making, producing in the Austrian case what Wolfgang Müller (2001) has described as 'ministerial government at the European level'. Germany, by contrast, has a 'twin-track system' (Derlien 2000), in which responsibility is shared between the foreign and finance ministries. While the first track, which links the foreign ministry with diplomats

---

[15] The inclusion of Spain in this category might appear surprising, in view of the role played by the autonomous communities. As Closa (forthcoming) argues, however, in practice subnational authorities are happy to allow the central government to be the dominant actor, not because of its neutrality necessarily, but to avoid potentially endless disagreement amongst themselves and the possibility that they might find themselves in a minority coalition. See also Molina (2000).

[16] The main committees are as follows: agriculture—the CIA; environment—CCPIE; energy—CIFE and CONCERE; research—CIS; and the economy—CEI (Council 2001).

in the Permanent Representation and other capitals, and which handles polity issues, is short, the second, running from the EU division in the finance ministry down to the *Länder* and up to the technical experts in the Permanent Representation, is longer and more complex. In practice, contacts along this second track are strongly departmentalized, encouraged by the principle of *Ressortsprinzip* (ministerial autonomy). These 'vertical brotherhood' (Derlien 2000) networks bring together like-minded experts with similar professional training, enabling domestic actors to negotiate the complexities of the multilevel game that confront the federal state,[17] bypassing the formal machinery and increasing the autonomy of ministerial departments vis-à-vis the central coordinators. In technical areas, German policy is formulated in sectoral networks, connecting specialists in Bonn, Brussels, and the *Länder*—hence, Derlien's description of it as 'semi-centralized'. Greece also has a dual system, but labour is shared somewhat differently. The Ministry of National Economy (formerly the Ministry of Coordination) coordinates EU-related economic policy and the technical ministries, and monitors adjustment of the economy to EC requirements, while the Ministry for Foreign Affairs is responsible for communication between individual ministries and the European Union, as well as the Permanent Representation. The first handles the internal aspects of EU policy, the latter external relations. As in Germany, sectoral differentiation is strongly pronounced.

In Italy, meanwhile, the Ministry of Foreign Affairs was historically the main coordinator, acting through its Directorates General for Economic Affairs and Political Affairs, but its influence has progressively diminished. Its decline began in 1980 with the creation of the Department for the Coordination of European Community Policies, headed by a Minister for European Policy who reports directly to the Prime Minister. In recent years, the Treasury has become increasingly influential, especially in financial matters, where it has taken control. Individual ministries have also assumed greater responsibility. Moreover, the influence of three parliamentary committees—the Foreign Affairs and EC Committee in the Chamber of Deputies, the Special Committee for EC policies, and the Senate's Foreign Affairs Committee and Giunta for EC Affairs—should not be overlooked.

In addition, in Belgium and Germany, and to a lesser extent Austria and Italy, the involvement of subnational authorities in coordination further

---

[17] Derlien (2000) uses a football metaphor to capture this complexity: 'bureaucratic professionals and (amateur) politicians are playing on three tiers these days: in the second division with sixteen teams (Lander), in the first division with fourteen teams (Bonn departments) and they join the European Cup competitions with fourteen other teams (Brussels), alternating between indoor and outdoor matches (interest groups, Bundestag and European Parliament)'.

disperses power. In the Belgian system, for example, European policy is decided by seven co-equal governments—the federal government, Wallonia, Flanders, and Brussels, and the French, Flemish, and German Communities—each of which has the power of veto. In Germany, the *Länder* not only participate in domestic coordination, but have developed their own 'foreign relations systems' (Derlien 2000), that connect *Land* ministries with their counterparts and the Economics Ministry in Bonn and feature representative offices in Brussels. The *Länder* also participate in coordination in Austria, even if the failure of a reform effort aimed at preserving their pre-accession position after 1995 has left them in a weak position (Müller 2000). In Italy, meanwhile, the Joint Standing Commission of the State and the Regions is the main arena where subnational interests are articulated.

Differences in member state organization in Brussels are often profound, despite the appearance of outward similarity. Although the permanent representation is important in the coordination systems of all member states, there are significant differences in organization and function. In terms of organization, missions vary in size, composition, personnel policy, and internal processes. The smallest is Luxembourg's with twenty officials, the largest is Germany's with sixty-eight.[18] Although the top official in all fifteen missions is invariably a diplomat, the deputy ambassador may come from the foreign service (France, Ireland, Portugal, and Sweden), the finance ministry (Germany), or the Treasury or the Department of Trade and Industry (the United Kingdom). In some missions (e.g. Austria), domestic political considerations have in the past led to the appointment of two deputies to ensure a balanced ticket between coalition partners (Müller 2000). Greece appoints an Economic Advisor at the same rank as Deputy to coordinate economic affairs. This arrangement reflects the domestic division of labour in EU policy coordination. Junior members of staff in the permanent representations have long ceased to be drawn exclusively from the diplomatic service, but there is significant variation in the ratio between foreign office officials and those from technical ministries. Hayes-Renshaw and Wallace (1997: 220) found a ratio of approximately 40:60 in favour of technical officials. Austria, Belgium, and Luxembourg, however, fall below the average, Greece and Italy above.[19]

---

[18] The source for these figures is the EU Committee of the American Chamber of Commerce in Belgium (2002).

[19] The proportion of diplomatic staff in the permanent representation does not, of course, provide the only measure of foreign office influence. Most missions are formally accountable to the foreign ministry. In addition, foreign office officials are often responsible for political and institutional affairs, administration, and media relations, and the Antici and the Mertens group members are usually diplomats.

Recruitment, career development, and staff development are organizational aspects of the permanent representation that also vary. In some member states, such as the United Kingdom, domestic ministries play a limited role in recruitment. Almost everywhere else, however, line ministries are active and influential. In Austria, Belgium, and Sweden, individual ministries have virtual autonomy over appointments in their area of functional responsibility. In others, including Ireland, Italy, and the Netherlands, ministries take staffing decisions, but the ambassador has a veto that is usually difficult to impose. In France, Greece, and the United Kingdom, appointments are made directly to the permanent representation and officials are responsible to the ambassador. This is true also of Ireland, though home departments continue to pay the salaries of their officials. In the Netherlands, officials are seconded to the Ministry of Foreign Affairs. This is also the case with Austria, though Müller notes that the authority of the Permanent Representative is only theoretical, since 'the Ministry for Foreign Affairs has no influence on recruitment of staff members, the length of their service in Brussels and much of their actual work' (2001). With respect to the internal functioning of the mission, though the organization of work is broadly similar, several member states have instituted formal mechanisms designed to overcome the effects of sectoralization. The Dutch Permanent Representation, for example, holds a daily meeting of all its personnel. The purpose of these 'morning prayers' (Wallace 1973: 63; Andeweg and Soetendorp 2001)—or 'thought for the day' (De Zwann 1995: 23)—is to exchange information about policy development among officials. Elsewhere, the missions of Germany, Ireland, Sweden, and the United Kingdom convene weekly meetings, which are also attended by all staff members.

More importantly, there are marked differences in the functions performed by permanent representations (see Table 4.1). The differences in upstream functions can be summarized as follows:

1. *Providing the main negotiators for meetings in Brussels* (Spence 1995): although most missions perform this function, some are too small, command insufficient human resources to ensure that all relevant meetings are covered—this is true of Austria and Ireland—or lack the domestic support necessary—the case with Greece—to participate in all meetings.
2. *Information gathering*: although the importance of this function is widely appreciated, the ambitions, methods used, and resources devoted by member states vary widely. The UK Permanent Representation (UKREP) pursues a maximalist strategy, with particular attention focused on Commission services and relations with the UK Commissioners and their *cabinets*, while officials in its Institutions Section of UKREP monitor 'what the EP is doing in its committees, in plenary, and in its corridors' (interview) and cultivate relations with MEPs in key positions (e.g. committee chairs

TABLE 4.1. *Functions of the permanent representations*

	Upstream functions				Downstream functions		
	Active lobbying of EU institutions	Attempt to set the EU policy agenda	Intersectoral coordination	Contact with private interests	Domestic interlocutors	Participates in domestic coordination	Status in domestic participation
Austria	No	No	No	Yes	Lead ministry	Not represented in coordination meetings	Medium
Belgium	No	No	No	Yes	Lead ministry and central coordinators	Yes	High
Denmark	n/a	n/a	n/a	n/a	Lead ministry	No specific role	n/a
Finland	n/a	n/a	n/a	n/a	Lead ministry	Yes	n/a
France	Yes	Yes	No	Yes	Lead ministry and central coordinators	At request of SGCI	Medium
Germany	Yes	Yes (high politics only)	No	Yes	Lead ministry	Yes	High
Greece	Yes, but limited	No	No	No	Lead ministry	Limited	Low, but coordinates on front-line in Brussels
Ireland	Yes, but limited	No	Yes	Limited	Lead ministry	Yes	High
Italy	No	No	No	Limited	Lead ministry	Limited	Low
Luxembourg	n/a	n/a	n/a	n/a	Lead ministry	Yes	High
Netherlands	Yes	No	Limited	Yes	Lead ministry and central coordinators	Yes	High
Portugal	Yes, but limited	No	No	No	Lead ministry and central coordinators	Yes	High
Spain	n/a	n/a	n/a	No	Lead ministry	n/a	High
Sweden	No	No	No	No	Lead ministry	Yes	High
United Kingdom	Yes	Yes	Yes	Yes	Lead ministry and central coordinators	Yes	High

Source: Kassim *et al.* (2000, 2001).

and *rapporteurs*). For some missions—that of Greece, for example—developing contacts is a personal matter that depends on the energies of individual officials (Spanou 2001), while for others with limited resources, including Ireland and Portugal's, other activities have greater priority.

3. *Sensitizing EU institutions to national policy stances* (Wright 1996), is a further function where there are differences in the energies expended by the member states and where, again, the United Kingdom has the most ambitious strategy. Recognizing that the best way to influence the content of policy is to intervene as early as possible, UKREP officials are encouraged to use their contacts with Commission officials to detect where policy initiatives are likely to emerge, so that they can alert the relevant domestic ministry to prepare a text (Hull 1993). Among other states, only France also has the ambition of influencing the EU policy agenda (Menon 2001).[20] Most member states lobby the Commission at a later stage of the process or restrict their actions to selected issues. Moreover, missions are also divided in their preparedness to use 'their' member(s) of the Commission. The United Kingdom is prepared to intervene at whichever level it deems appropriate to ensure that its views are known, but others, including Belgium and, until recently, the Netherlands, are more reluctant. Differences between permanent representations in levels of contact with the European Parliament, however, arise less because of scruples and more due to strategic considerations and the availability of resources. The European Parliament has generally attracted increasing attention from national governments, particularly in policy areas where codecision applies. Some, including France, the United Kingdom, Ireland, and the Netherlands, have designated liaison officers. Others, like Germany, regard the task as a routine responsibility of its desk officers.

4. *Providing a point of contact for nationals working in EU institutions* is a commitment undertaken by some, but by no means all, permanent representations. UKREP and FRANREP, for example, both provide career support services for their nationals (Kassim 2001; Menon 2001). Other missions, such as the Greece's Permanent Representation, take a more ad hoc approach or, as in the case of Belgium, make no particular effort.

5. *Interacting directly with the representatives of other member states* (Spence 1995) is a function where close convergence between national practices might have been anticipated. Beyond routine interaction, however, there are differences in the importance attributed to developing and maintaining a network of contacts and to building coalitions. Again, UKREP is

---

[20] This marks a recent change of approach. Until the 1990s, France made little attempt to intervene in the earlier technical stages of decision making and tended to leave it late and aim high (see Schmidt 1996; Menon 2001). This strategy was allegedly successful on occasion when Jacques Delors was Commission President.

particularly active. Officials enjoy institutional support in the form of a modest entertainment budget for socializing with colleagues from other states, leave a list of contacts for their successors, and are encouraged to spread their coalition-building efforts widely.
6. *Contact with private interests*: missions fall into three groups. Those in the first, such as Austria, take an inclusive approach, granting insider status to interest groups, such as the social partners. Members of the second, including Belgium, France, Germany, the Netherlands, and the United Kingdom, regard good relations with private interests as valuable, but have no similar structured relationship. Those in the third, including Greece and Portugal, have only very limited relations with interest groups.

There are also major differences in the 'downstream' functions that permanent representations perform. First, although all report back to the appropriate national bodies, UKREP is distinguished by the detail, quality, and frequency of its reports to the national capital and the fact that it monitors the full range of EU activity. Others limit their coverage to particular EU institutions (Greece, Portugal), track salient sectors only (Ireland), or focus on later phases of the policy process (Ireland). Belgium's Permanent Representation limits itself further by offering information only on the political–strategic aspects of dossiers, not their content (Kerremans and Beyers 2001). The most important difference, however, concerns the mission's role in domestic coordination processes (Wallace 1973: 57). This difference is structural and corresponds to a distinction between centralized and department-led coordination systems (Kassim and Peters 2001). In the former, where central coordinators have the power to broker interdepartmental agreements and impose solutions where necessary, the permanent representations:

(1) are in constant contact with the central coordinators (e.g. the SGCI in France, the European Secretariat in the United Kingdom) and officials in the line ministries;
(2) participate in central coordination and have direct involvement in decision making and arbitration;
(3) play a system-wide function in ensuring that national representatives negotiating in Brussels comply with the policy that has been interdepartmentally agreed.

In department-led systems, the Brussels-based mission:

(1) is less likely to be in regular contact with the prime minister's office or the foreign ministry;
(2) services the needs of the lead department rather than the system as a whole;
(3) has less influence at the centre, where the relevant line ministry takes the lead.

Explaining Member State Responses

Looking across systems of coordination, there is clearly no evidence of convergence around a single model. If the pressures towards convergence highlighted by rational choice institutionalism and the new institutionalism in organizational analysis are at work, their impact has been modest. The pattern that emerges is rather one of limited similarity combined with considerable divergence.

Explaining the similarities between national coordination systems is relatively straightforward. These derive principally from the rules, procedures, and routines of EU policy processes, which individual member states confront as takers. National governments conform to the rhythms imposed by, for example, the organization of work in the Council and the sequence of stages that comprise legislative procedures. Beyond the constraints imposed by the institutional structures of the Union, there is also a degree of mimicry (DiMaggio and Powell 1991), or 'lesson learning' (Rose 1991; Dolowitz and Marsh 1996), where, in the face of common problems, some states have copied features of the coordination systems of others that are considered successful. New entrants routinely examine how member states coordinate their input (Magone 2001), while many have attempted to emulate the British model, which is widely perceived as the most effective (see e.g. Lequesne 1993).

The differences in national strategies can be explained in terms of two factors: one historical–political, the other institutional. With respect to the first, the coordination ambitions of the member states reflect a preferred vision, and long-term policy aims in respect, of European integration. It is no accident that the countries that have the most comprehensive and centralized strategies—Denmark, France, Sweden, and the United Kingdom—are those that are most concerned about the protection of state sovereignty, preferring 'less Europe' to 'more Europe' and an intergovernmental over a federal model of integration. By contrast, states that desire ever closer union, such as Germany, have adopted a more relaxed attitude to day-to-day coordination, even if they mobilize resources when discussion turns to the future of the EU polity. Second, the institutions of coordination can be explained in terms of the impact of pre-existing domestic structures and values. Although falling a long way short of the institutional isomorphism anticipated by strict sociological institutionalists, the fundamental features that characterize the domestic polity are, indeed, reproduced in national coordination systems. March and Olsen (1984, 1989: 53–67), argue that institutions adapt to new circumstances by reproducing pre-existing forms, as well as 'more diffuse values concerning the correct distribution and exercise of public power' (Harmsen 1999: 85). Applied to the current topic, the pressures exerted by EU membership 'are necessarily mediated through the existing institutional structures and values which characterize each national politico-administrative system' (ibid.). The responses of the member states reflect the 'pre-existing balance of domestic institutional structures, as well as the broader matrices of values which define the nature of appropriate political forms in the case of each national polity' (Harmsen 1999: 81), producing a pattern of national differentiation. Recent empirical evidence suggests that three features of the domestic polity are particularly important: conception of coordination; the nature of the political opportunity structure; and the administrative opportunity structure (Kassim 2000*b*; Kassim and Peters 2001).

The most salient features of the political opportunity structure, such as the territorial organization of the state, the nature of the party system, the structure of the executive, the role of parliament, and the dominant form of interest intermediation, are perhaps the most important determinant. State structure has a pronounced impact. In historically unitary states—Denmark, France, Greece and, until 1998, the United Kingdom—coordination is the preserve of central government, while in the federal states—Austria, Belgium, Germany, and Spain—subnational authorities exercise varying degrees of influence. Amongst the latter, the status accorded to subnational level of government in EU policy typically reflects their domestic position. In Belgium and Germany, they are equal partners. In Spain, with its system of differentiated federalism, special status has been accorded to Catalonia and the Basque country (Molina 2000; Closa and Heywood forthcoming). The weak position of the *Länder* in Austria, meanwhile, is faithfully reflected in EU coordination. With respect to political factors, a majoritarian party system, for example, makes possible the pursuit of positive coordination, since it allows 'more hierarchical interministerial relations than does a coalition government' (Derlien 2000). The combination of single party government and party discipline in the United Kingdom, for example, is certainly consistent with the aim of policy coherence, though the Major years represent an exception. Coalition government may limit the set of feasible coordination options due to the fact that ministries are in the hands of different parties. In Austria, for example, the decision to share responsibility for coordination between the Chancellery and the Foreign Ministry was motivated by the concern of each of the parties in the 'grand coalition', the ÖVP and the SPÖ, to institute a permanent check on its governing partner. The structure of the executive is also influential. Where unified, as in the United Kingdom, the capacity for imposing decisions necessary for the operation of a strongly centralized system is likely to be present. Where divided or collegial, other coordination strategies may be necessary. In countries where the authority of the Prime Minister is limited (e.g. in Italy) or where ministerial autonomy is a key principle of government (e.g. in Austria and Germany), ministers can act with considerable independence in the European arena. France usually falls under the first category, but its split executive can permit the harmonious orchestration of EU policy to be disturbed (Menon 2000).

National administrative opportunity structures are also important. Three aspects stand out in particular. The first is degree to which the administration is integrated. Are there are sharp vertical or horizontal divisions? Where is the frontier between political appointments and permanent officials? Is there a cabinet system? Do officials belong to a single cadre or to distinct corps? The second is the type of administrative culture. The coordination system in the United Kingdom reflects the unity of the administration and traditional civil service norms such as information sharing, mutual support, and cooperation. In Austria, Greece, Italy, and the Netherlands, by contrast, the administration is more fragmented—a feature that is reflected in the system for EU policy coordination. The third is the conception of coordination that informs the administration. Conceptions of coordination differ cross-nationally (see Hayward and Wright 1998), ranging from the strongly directive view that government should 'speak with one voice' across all areas of activity to the belief that departments should keep each other informed of their actions or that coordination efforts should be selectively directed. These approaches are tied to other values, such as the need to construct consensus to legitimate policy choices. These differing conceptions are reflected in the national arrangements for managing EU policy. In the United Kingdom and France the emphasis on unity at the centre of government generates a strongly positive conception of coordination, which is embodied institutionally at the centre by the Cabinet Office and the Secrétariat Général du Gouvernement, and by long-standing norms, conventions, and administrative procedures, has been extended to EU policy making. The construction of consensus, a central feature of politics in Austria and Belgium, has been similarly transposed, as have more relaxed attitudes towards coordination taken in Germany, Greece, and Italy.[21]

Conclusion

Although it has become fashionable to argue that the impact of European integration on national administrations has been exaggerated, particularly in relation to other developments and trends, such as the new public management or privatization, the above discussion suggests that membership of the European Union has had important organizational consequences for government.

---

[21] An interesting exception is the Netherlands, where a cohesive approach to EU policy has emerged, even though departmental autonomy has been a long-pronounced feature of the Dutch administration (see Soetendorp and Andeweg 2001).

Responding both to the obligations of membership and the incentives to 'get things right in Brussels', all member states have put in place structures, procedures, and processes designed to manage their input into EU policy making. As Metcalfe (1994) has observed, international obligations require more, not less, of national administrative systems.

Although there are some similarities in the way that national administrations have been adapted, adjusted, or reformed in response to the challenges with which 'Europe' confronts them (e.g. in the development of institutional support for the heads of state and government, the role in polity issues played by foreign ministries, and the performance of core functions upstream by permanent representations), systematic investigation of national systems of EU policy coordination reveals marked differences in the arrangements put in place by the member states.[22] The two main lines of difference relate to the extent of the coordination ambition—comprehensive or selective?—and the degree to which coordination is centralized—centralized, where an interdepartmental position is defined and coherently presented, or decentralized, where line ministries are autonomous and/or subnational authorities are influential players. Three main types emerge: comprehensive centralizers; selective centralizers; and comprehensive decentralized systems.

The above analysis suggests, moreover, that these differences are deeply rooted in national political systems (see Table 4.2). The coordination ambition is linked tightly to the traditional aims of European policy and to national preferences concerning the nature of EU governance, with those states who favour an intergovernmental model pursuing a comprehensive strategy and more federally inclined states opting for a more relaxed and selective approach at least at the level of routine policy, while the national coordination system reflects closely, but not isomorphically, domestic political and administrative opportunity structures. The key institutional determinant appears to be the extent to which features of the domestic polity produce centralized or decentralized governance. That these characteristics are constitutional and structural suggests that the differences in national coordination arrangements are likely to persist, with all that that implies for the ease and effectiveness of EU decision making—particularly with enlargement imminent (see Presidency Conclusions of the Helsinki European Council 1999)—and the institutional complexity, capacity, and effectiveness of the European polity (Metcalfe 1994).

---

[22] That there should be significant variation is hardly surprising, since, to paraphrase Metcalfe (1994), national administrations were created to perform domestic functions and not to manage international policy making.

TABLE 4.2. *Type of EU coordination system, European policy, and structure of domestic polity*

	Type of EU coordination System	Traditional EU policy	Political opportunity structure[a]	Administrative opportunity structure
Austria	Comprehensive decentralized	Favours integration	Decentralized and non-majoritarian	Decentralized
Belgium	Comprehensive decentralized	Strongly favours deeper integration	Decentralized and non-majoritarian	Decentralized
Denmark	Comprehensive centralized	Prefers intergovernmental model	Centralized and majoritarian	Decentralized
France	Comprehensive centralized	Prefers intergovernmental model	Centralized and majoritarian	Centralized
Germany	Comprehensive decentralized	Strongly favours deeper integration	Decentralized and non-majoritarian	Decentralized
Greece	Comprehensive decentralized	Weakly favours integration	Centralized and majoritarian	Decentralized
Ireland	Selective centralized	Favours integration	Centralized and majoritarian	Centralized
Italy	Comprehensive decentralized	Strongly favours deeper integration	Decentralized and non-majoritarian	Decentralized
Netherlands	Comprehensive decentralized	Strongly favours deeper integration	Decentralized and non-majoritarian	Decentralized
Portugal	Selective centralized	Favours integration	Centralized and majoritarian	Centralized
Spain	Selective centralized	Strongly favours integration	Decentralized and majoritarian	Centralized
Sweden	Comprehensive centralized	Prefers intergovernmental model	Centralized and majoritarian	Centralized
United Kingdom	Comprehensive centralized	Prefers intergovernmental model	Centralized and majoritarian	Centralized

Note: [a] Non-majoritarian = weak coalition governments or strong ministerial autonomy; majoritarian = single-party government or well-disciplined coalitions and limited ministerial authority

REFERENCES

Abélès, M., Bellier, I., and McDonald, M. (1993). *Approche Anthropoloque de la Commission européenne*, unpublished report for the Commission.

Bender, B. (1991). 'Whitehall, Central Government and 1992', *Public Policy and Administration* 6(1): 13–20.

Brunsson, N. and Olsen, J. P. (1993). *The Reforming Organization* (London: Routledge).

Buitendijk, G., Van Schendelen, and Marinus P. C. M. (1995). 'Brussels Advisory Committees: A Channel of Influence'? *European Law Review* 20(1): 37–58.

Cini, M. (1997). 'Administrative Culture in the European Commission: The Cases of Competition and Environment', in N. Nugent (ed.), *The Heart of the Union: Studies of the European Commission* (Basingstoke: Macmillan).

Closa, C. and Heywood, P. (forthcoming). *Spain and the European Union* (Basingstoke: Palgrave).

Commission of the European Communities (1995). *Report On the Operation of the Treaty of European Union*, SEC (95) 731 Final, 10.5.95 (Luxembourg: Office for Official Publications of the European Communities).

de Bassompierre, G. (1990). *Changing the Guard in Brussels. An Insider's View of the Presidency* (New York: Praeger).

de Zwann, J. W. (1995). *The Permanent Representatives Committee: Its Role in European Union Decision-Making* (Amsterdam: Elsevier).

Derlien, Hans-Ulrich (2000). 'Germany: Failing Successfully'? in H. Kassim, B. G. Peters, and V. Wright (eds), *The National Co-ordination of EU Policy: The Domestic Level* (Oxford: Oxford University Press), 54–78.

DiMaggio, P. J. and Powell, W. W. (1991). *The New Institutionalism in Organizational Analysis* (Illinois: University of Chicago Press).

Dogan, Rhys (1997). 'Comitology: Little Procedures with Big Implications', *Western European Politics* 20(3): 31–60.

Dolowitz, D. and Marsh, D. (1996). 'Who Learns What From Whom: A Review of the Policy Transfer Literature', *Political Studies* XLIV: 343–57.

EU Committee of the American Chamber of Commerce in Belgium (2002). *EU Information Handbook* (Brussels: EU Committee of the American Chamber of Commerce in Belgium).

Falkner, G. and Nentwich, M. (2000). 'The Amsterdam Treaty: The Blueprint or the Future Institutional Balance?' in K. Neunreither and A. Wiener (eds), *European Integration After Amsterdam. Institutional Dynamics and Prospects for Democracy* (Oxford: Oxford University Press), 15–35.

Favell, A. (1998). 'The Europeanisation of Immigration Politics', European Integration On-line Papers (EioP), 2:10 at http://eiop.or.at/eiop/texte/1998-010a.htm

Garrett, G. (1995). 'From the Luxembourg Compromise to Codecision: Decision Making in the European Union', *Electoral Studies* 14(3): 289–308.

General Secretariat, Council of the European Union (1997). *Council Guide: Vol. I. Presidency Handbook* (Luxembourg: Office for Official Publications of the European Communities).

Greenwood, J. (1997). *Representing Interests in the European Union* (London: Routledge).

Greenwood, J. and Aspinwall, Mark (1997). *Collective Action in the European Union* (London: Routledge).

Guyomarch, A. (1993). 'The European Effect: Improving French Policy Co-ordination', *Staatswissenschaften und Staatspraxis* 4(3): 455–78.

Haas, E. B. (1958). *The Uniting of Europe* (Stanford, CA: Stanford University Press).

Hall, P. A. and Taylor, R. C. R. (1998). 'Political Science and the Three New Institutionalisms', *Political Studies* 44(4): 936–57.

Harmsen, R. (1999). 'The Europeanization of National Administrations: A Comparative Study of France and the Netherlands', *Governance*, 12(1): 81–113.

Hayes-Renshaw, F. and Wallace, H. (1997). *The Council of Ministers* (Basingstoke: Macmillan).

Hayward and Wright (1998). 'Policy Co-ordination in West European Core Executives', End of Award Report, unpublished mimeo.

Héritier, A., Knill, C., and Mingers, S. (1996). *Ringing the Changes in Europe. Regulatory Competition and Redefinition of the State. Britain, France, Germany* (Berlin: Walter de Gruyter).

Hix, S. (1999). *The Political System of the European Union* (Basingstoke: Macmillan).

Hoffmann, S. (1982). 'Reflections On the Nation State in Europe Today', *Journal of Common Market Studies* 21: 21–37.

Hull, Robert (1993). 'Lobbying Brussels: A View from Within', in S.Mazey and J. Richardson (eds), *Lobbying in the European Community* (Oxford: Oxford University Press), 82–92.

Kassim, H. (2000a). 'The United Kingdom', in H. Kassim, B. G. Peters, and V. Wright (eds), *The National Co-ordination of EU Policy: The Domestic Level* (Oxford: Oxford University Press), 22–53.

—— (2000b) 'Conclusion. The National Co-ordination of EU Policy: Confronting the Challenge', in H. Kassim, B. G. Peters, and V. Wright (eds), *The National Co-ordination of EU Policy: The Domestic Level* (Oxford: Oxford University Press), 235–64.

—— (2001). 'Representing the United Kingdom in Brussels: The Fine Art of Positive Co-ordination', in H. Kassim, A. Menon, B. G. Peters, and V. Wright (eds), *The National Co-ordination of EU Policy: The European Level* (Oxford: Oxford University Press), 47–76.

—— Menon, A., Peters, G., and Wright, V. (2001). *The National Co-ordination of EU Policy: The European Level* (Oxford: Oxford University Press).

—— and Peters, G. (2001). 'Conclusion: Co-ordinating National Action in Brussels—A Comparative Perspective', in H. Kassim, A. Menon, B. G. Peters, and V. Wright (eds), *The National Co-ordination of EU Policy: The European Level* (Oxford: Oxford University Press), 297–342.

—— Peters, B. G. and Wright, V. (2000a). 'Introduction', in H. Kassim, B. G. Peters and V. Wright (eds), *The National Co-ordination of EU Policy: The Domestic Level* (Oxford: Oxford University Press).

—— B. G. Peters, G. and V. Wright (2000b). *The National Co-ordination of EU Policy: The Domestic Level* (Oxford: Oxford University Press).

Katz, R. S. and Wessels, B. (1999). *The European Parliament, The National Parliaments and European Integration* (Oxford: Oxford University Press).

Kerremans, B. (1996). 'Do Institutions Make a Difference? Non-Institutionalism, Neo-Institutionalism and the Logic of Common Decision Making in the EU', *Governance* 9(2): 216–40.

—— (2000). 'Belgium', in H. Kassim, B. G. Peters and V. Wright (eds), *The National Co-ordination of EU Policy: The Domestic Level* (Oxford: Oxford University Press), 182–200.

—— and Beyers, J. (2001). 'The Belgian Permanent Representation to the European Union: Mailbox, Messenger or Representative'? in H. Kassim, A. Menon, B. G. Peters, and V. Wright (eds), *The National Co-ordination of EU Policy: The European Level* (Oxford: Oxford University Press), 191–210.

Kohler-Koch, B. and Eising, R. (1999). *The Transformation of Governance in the European Union* (London: Routledge).

Lenaerts, K. (1991). 'Some Reflections on the Separation of Powers in the European Community', *Common Market Law Review* 28(1): 11–35.

Lequesne, C. (1993). *Paris-Bruxelles: Comment se-fait la politique européenne de la France* (Paris: Presses de Fondation Nationale des Sciences Politiques).

—— (1996) 'French Central Government and the European Political System: Change and Adaptation Since the Single Act', in Y. Mény, P. Muller, and J-L. Quermonne (eds), *Adjusting to Europe* (London: Routledge).

Lewis, J. (1998). 'The Institutional Problem-Solving Capacities of the Council: The Committee of Permanent Representatives and the Methods of Community', Cologne: Max-Plank-Institut Für Gesellschaftsforschung, Discussion Paper 98/1.

Lowi, T. J. (1964). 'American Business, Public Policy, Case Studies and Political Theory', *World Politics* 16(4): 677–715.

Magone, J. (2000). 'Portugal', in H. Kassim, B. G. Peters, and V. Wright (eds), *The National Co-ordination of EU Policy: The Domestic Level* (Oxford: Oxford University Press).

—— (2001). 'The Portuguese Permanent Representation in Brussels: The Institutionalization of a simple system', in H. Rassim, A. Menon, B. G. Peters, and V. Wright (eds), *The National Coordination of EU Policy: The European Level* (Oxford: Oxford University Press).

Maor, M. and Stevens, H. (1996). 'Measuring The Impact of New Public Management and European Integration On Recruitment and Training in the UK Civil Service 1970–1995', European Institute, London School of Economics and Political Science.

March, J. and Olsen, J. (1984). 'The New Institutionalism: Organizational Facts in Political Life', *American Political Science Review* 78: 734–49.

—— —— (1989). *Rediscovering Institutions: The Organizational Basis of Politics* (New York: Free Press).

Marks, G. and McAdam, D. (1996). 'Social Movements and the Changing Structure of Political Opportunity in the European Union', in G. Marks, F. W. Scharpf, P. C. Schmitter, and W. Streeck (eds), *Governance in the European Union* (London: Sage), 95–120.

——, Hooghe, L., and Blank, K. (1996). 'European Integration From the 1980s', *Journal of Common Market Studies* 34(1): 341–78.

Maurer, A. and Wessels, W. (2001). 'The German Case: A Key Moderator in a Competitive Multi-Level Environment', in H. Kassim, A. Menon, B. G. Peters, and V. Wright (eds), *The National Co-ordination of EU Policy: The European Level* (Oxford: Oxford University Press), 101–28.

Mazey, S. (2001). 'The Swedish Permanent Representation to the European Union: Melding National and Collective Interests', in H. Kassim, A. Menon, B. G. Peters, and V. Wright (eds), *The National Co-ordination of EU Policy: The European Level* (Oxford: Oxford University Press).

—— and Richardson, J. (1993). *Lobbying in the European Community* (Oxford: Oxford University Press).

Menon (2001). 'The French Administration in Brussels', in H. Kassim, A. Menon, B. G. Peters, and V. Wright (eds), *The National Co-ordination of EU Policy: The European Level* (Oxford: Oxford University Press), 75–100.

—— (2000). 'France', in H. Kassim, B. G. Peters, and V. Wright (eds), *The National Co-ordination of EU Policy: The Domestic Level* (Oxford: Oxford University Press).

—— and Hayward, J. (1996). 'States, Industrial Policies and the European Union', in H. Kassim and A. Menon (eds), *The European Union and National Industrial Policy* (London: Routledge).

Metcalfe, L. (1994). 'International Policy Co-ordination and Public Management Reform', *International Review of Administrative Sciences* 60: 271–90.

Meyer, J. and Rowan, B. (1977). 'Institutionalized organizations: Formal Structure as Myth and Ceremony', *International Review of Administrative Sciences* 60: 271–90.

Molina, I. (2000). 'Spain', in H. Kassim, B. G. Peters, and V. Wright (eds), *The National Co-ordination of EU Policy* (Oxford: Oxford University Press).

Moravcsik, Andrew (1993). 'Preferences and Power in the European Community: A Liberal Intergovernmentalist Approach', *Journal of Common Market Studies* 31(4): 473–524.

—— (1994). 'Why the European Community Strengthens the State: Domestic Politics and International Cooperation', Center for European Studies, Working Paper Series, No. 52.

Müller (2001). 'Ministerial Government at the European Level: The Case of Austria', in H. Kassim, A. Menon, B. G. Peters, and V. Wright (eds), *The National Co-ordination of EU Policy: The European Level* (Oxford: Oxford University Press), 229–76.

Norton, P. (ed.) (1996). *National Parliaments and the European Union* (London: Frank Cass).

Olsen, Johan P. (1997) 'European Challenges to the Nation State', in B. Steunenberg and F. van Vught (eds), *Political Institutions and Public Policy* (Amsterdam: Kluwer Academic Publishers), 157–88.

O'Nuallain, Colm with Hocheit, Jean-Marc (1985). *The Presidency of the European Council of Ministers* (London: Croom Helm).

Page, E. C. (1997). *People Who Run Europe* (Oxford: Oxford University Press).

Pedersen, Thomas (2000). 'Denmark', in H. Kassim, B. Guy, and V. Wright (eds), *The National Co-ordination of EU Policy: The Domestic Level* (Oxford: Oxford University Press), 219–34.

Pedlar, J. H. and Van Schendelen, M. P. C. M. (1993). *Lobbying the European Union* (Aldershot: Dartmouth).

Peters, B. G. (1994). 'Agenda Setting in the EU', *Journal of European Public Policy* 1(1): 9–26.

Pollack, M. A. (1994). 'Creeping Competence: The Expanding Agenda of the European Community', *Journal of Public Policy* 14: 95–145.

Putnam, Robert D. (1988). 'Diplomacy and Domestic Politics: The logic of Two-level Games', *International Organization* 43(2): 427–60.

Richardson, J., Gustafsson, G., and Jordan, G. (1982). 'The Concept of Policy Style', in J. Richardson (ed.), *Policy Styles in Western Europe* (London: Allen and Unwin).

Rose, R. (1991). 'What Is Lesson Drawing'? *Journal of Public Policy* 11: 3–30.

Schmidt, V. A. (1996). *From State to Market? The Transformation of French Business and Government* (Cambridge: Cambridge University Press).

Scott, W. R. and Meyer, J. W., and Associates (1994). *Institutional Environments and Organzations* (Thousand Oaks, CA: Sage).

Scully, R. (1997). 'The EP and the Co-Decision Procedures: A Reassessment', *Journal of Legislative Studies* 3(3): 58–73.

Smith, M. P. (1997). 'The Commission Made Me Do It. The European Commission as a Strategic Asset in Domestic Politics', in Neill Nugent (ed.), *At the Heart of the Union: Studies of the European Commission* (Basingstoke: Macmillan), 167–86.

Soetendorp, B. and Andeweg, R. (2001). 'Dual Loyalties: The Dutch Permanent Representation to the European Union', in H. Kassim, A. Menon, B. G. Peters, and V. Wright (eds), *The National Co-ordination of EU Policy: The European Level* (Oxford: Oxford University Press).

Spanou, C. (2000). 'Greece', in H. Kassim, B. G. Peters, and V. Wright (eds), *The National Co-ordination of EU Policy: The Domestic Level* (Oxford: Oxford University Press).

Spence, D. (1995). 'The Co-ordination of European Policy by Member States', in M. Westlake (ed.), *The Council of the European Union* (London: Cartermill Publishing).

Thomas, G. M., Meyer, J., Ramirez, F., and Boli, J. (1987). *Institutional Structure: Constituting State, Society and the Individual* (Newbury Park, California: Sage).

Tsebelis, G. (1990). *Nested Games* (Berkeley: University of California Press).

Van Schendelen, M. C. P. M. (1996). '"The Council Decides": Does the Council Decide?', *Journal of Common Market Studies* 34(4): 531–48.

—— (1999). *EU Committees as Influential Policymakers* (Aldershot: Ashgate).

Wallace, H. (1973). *National Governments and the European Communities* (European Series No. 21, London: Chatham House).

Wessels, W. (1997). 'An Ever Closer Fusion? A Dynamic Macropolitical View On the Integration Process', *Journal of Common Market Studies* 4(1): 128–45.

—— and Rometsch, D. (1996). 'Conclusion: European Union and National Institutions', in D. Romestch and W. Wessels (eds), *The European Union and the Member States* (Manchester: Manchester University Press).

Westlake, M. (1995). *The Council of The European Union* (London: Cartermill Publishing).

Wright, V. (1996). 'The National Co-ordination of European Policy-Making Negotiating the Quagmire', in J. Richardson (ed.), *European Union. Policy and Policy-Making* (London: Routledge).

5

Variable Geometry, Multilevel Governance: European Integration and Subnational Government in the New Millennium

MIKE GOLDSMITH

Introduction

Variable geometry and multilevel governance are just two terms used to describe the changing nature of territorial politics within the European Union. The creation of the European Union, and the associated process of economic, political, and social integration which has accompanied it, has changed the nature of nation state and subnational politics as it had been known for at least two centuries.

This chapter seeks to evaluate some of the changes that have occurred, particularly over the last two decades, and which have resulted particularly in changing forms of subnational politics within the European Union. Most specifically it will examine the extent to which the essential distinction between Northern and Southern European styles of local politics (see *inter alia* Page and Goldsmith 1987; Goldsmith 2000; John 2001) is being undermined by the process of European integration and policy Europeanization to which Raedelli makes reference in this volume.[1] Last in this context it seeks to evaluate briefly current explanations offered of political integration within the European Union.

The chapter will suggest that key economic changes, some associated with globalization, others with the introduction of the Single Market, others with the process of deregulation that has taken place over the last twenty years,

---

[1] Some authors place considerable weight on the process of Europeanization of policy as a sign that a supranational form of governance is emerging within Europe—see for example, Sandholtz and Stone Sweet (1998). This author prefers to maintain a distinction between *formal* integration, as evidenced through the treaty processes and acceptance of European Court decisions, and a more *informal* process of integration through the Europeanization of public policy within the European Union, as well as other more informal social processes—travel, cultural, and educational which EU citizens increasingly enjoy.

have posed European cities and regions with a constantly changing and often different set of challenges, opportunities, and constraints as they seek to manage the turbulent environments in which they operate. Two examples illustrate this point. As the automotive industry has globalized, vehicle production has been relocated into the most economic sites. First, in the Netherlands, difficulties affecting DAF (as well as Phillips in another sector) posed severe problems for Eindhoven. In the United Kingdom, whilst Merseyside has benefited from Ford's decision to invest heavily in upmarket models (e.g. Jaguar), Dagenham has lost its plant, and in Luton Vauxhall has also cutback car production. Second, economic restructuring and deregulation also affected those regions heavily dependent on such old industries as coal and steel. Wallonia in Belgium; Nord Pas-de-Calais and Lorraine in France; South Yorkshire and the Scottish central belt in Britain all provide examples.

The chapter will also suggest that the political dynamic of the European Union, especially through the emergence of a strong regional policy, has encouraged forms of cooperative subnational politics which have subtly changed both national intergovernmental relationships and those between the European Union and nation states. Cross border cooperation through such programmes as INTEREG, cohesion policy requiring the adoption of the partnership principle, and pilot poverty programmes such as Poverty 1–3 and URBAN all provide examples where cities and regions have adapted as part of their attempts to win EU funding.

Whilst recent developments may have reasserted the primacy of the nation state within the EU political system, the chapter argues that further expansion of the EU means that the system of territorial politics in Europe remains unstable and continually subject to change, especially at the subnational level. In particular, whilst the old styles of Northern and Southern local politics remain, new cross-national networks of local and regional governments, reflecting the experience of regional policy, together with the way in which different cities and regions seek to be increasingly competitive in a global market, means that territorial politics within the European Union will remain unstable in the forseeable future.

The chapter will conclude by evaluating the extent to which ideas such as variable geometry and multilevel governance remain useful concepts in aiding our understanding of the processes of change through which EU territorial politics are currently passing.

Conceptualizing EU Integration

As a starting point it is useful to review the different ways in which EU integration has been conceptualized by observers over recent years.

Effectively there have been three main approaches. The first, dominant in the early life of the EU, and elements of which are important even today, perceives the process of European integration as an international regime, designed by sovereign states, who seek to regulate the development of economic and political interdependence through a process of international intergovernmental collaboration. Given that the EU is a treaty based organization—as distinct to a federal or confederal system such as the United States, Canada, Germany—it is first and foremost a *state centred* organization, in which the member states are at the centre of the decision-making process.[2] As a result change comes about incrementally, with the most significant changes brought about through a success of new Treaties such as those agreed in Maastricht (1992), Amsterdam (1995), and Nice (2000). Decisions on policies and program, finance and regulatory regimes are effectively ratified at the periodic meetings of the Council of Ministers, at which heads of state have frequently negotiated different terms to those originally proposed by the Commission, or have negotiated opt out arrangements (Social Charter), won specific deals (Thatcher and the budgetary rebate), or exercised a veto on proposals. For those (e.g. Hoffman 1982) who argue that the EU conforms to such a model, control remains vested in the nation states and changes depend on voluntary cooperation and bargaining between powerful member states. One possible example in which this process can be seen is the Nice agreement, under which it was the interest of the big states (e.g. Germany, France, and Britain) which dominated the final form the treaty took. As writers such as Hooghe (1996: 177) suggest, decision making under this model is effectively elitist, closed, opaque, and not readily accountable—giving rise to a form of institutional arrangements probably best characterized by de Gaulle's phrase a 'Europe de Patries' rather than some other form of arrangement.

Whilst such a characterization of the European Union might have been valid in its early years and up until the early 1980s, a number of factors have undermined the state-centred model more recently. First, there have been changes in the decision-making rules, with the introduction of Qualified Majority Voting on an increasing number of issue areas, thus negating the veto power of nation states in these areas. Second, the European Parliament now has a greater say in decision making than in the past, especially over the budget. Third, the emergence of the European Court as the arbiter on EU legal matters, in which its decisions are accepted by member states, means that nation states no longer have sovereignty over many areas formerly associated with state activities. Fourth, the growing process of 'government by regulation' through the

---

[2] Again it is important to distinguish this process from the emergence of a *supranational* set of institutions, as associated with authors such as Stone Sweet and Sandholtz (1998). The author returns to this question in the concluding section.

regulatory decisions of the Commission and of EU agencies again undermines the position of national governments. In other words, whilst nation states remain the most important actors at the centre of EU decision making, their position is less strong than it was twenty years ago.

The second model, often employed in more normative debates about the European Union, is essentially a federalist one, in which the European Union is a supranational state. It is usually described in the academic literature as a supranational model: in this model political decisions depend on the relationships between different levels of government (European Union, national, and subnational) and on how the powers and functions allocated to the different levels operate in practice in both formal and informal ways. Normatively this model comes closest to that propounded by the advocates of a federal Europe, or most often derided by Eurosceptics. Its strongest advocate could be found in Jacques Delors during his time as President of the Commission, who thought of the European Union as having a strong supranational core (i.e. the Commission) working with weakened nation states and a strengthened, but fragmented, regional periphery. This model is Delors's 'Europe of the Regions' writ large, giving rise to a contested hierarchy as regions compete amongst themselves and with the nation states over territorial representation, but with a powerful Commission at the centre acting effectively as the policy arbiter, given its key position as the policy initiator.

Such a view of the European Union was more prevalent in the late 1980s and early 1990s, during a period when regional policy and its associated expenditure levels were growing in importance. During this period the Commission—as the supranational body—tended to promote the regions and subnational government generally, seeking to mobilize them on a functional basis around a series of specific European-wide issues (Tommel 1998). And as regional policy grew in importance so did the development of widespread functional and territorial networks seeking to represent regional and local interests and to influence Commission policy—indeed some of these networks were specifically encouraged by the Commission itself in policy areas dealing with regional, environmental, innovation/technology transfer, and ITC issues (Cooke and Morgan 1998).

Development of an EU model along these lines would see a more pluralistic and competitive decision-making process, albeit one in which the Commission was central in what would otherwise be a highly fragmented process. More open and accessible than the state-centred model, it would be no more accountable, however, as decisions would still be taken behind closed doors and in the corridors of the Commission.

A third model emerged in the mid-1990s which characterized the EU as a system of multilevel governance, as developed in the writings of authors such as Gary Marks and Lisbet Hooghe (see e.g. Marks *et al.* 1996; Hooghe 1996, 1998;

Marks and Hooghe 2001). Hooghe characterized this system as a 'Europe with the Regions' as distinct from Delors's 'Europe of the Regions'. Here it is not only the Commission, European Parliament, the Court of Justice, EU agencies, and national governments who are involved, but also regional and other subnational levels as well. The result is a system of decision making in which there are multiple access points, multiple opportunities to exercise influence and pressure, and multiple places at which decisions are made. No predominant territorial principle guides decision-making, there is extensive subnational mobilization across all sectors (including the third or voluntary sector), and the different actors play a series of what are perhaps best thought of as grantsmanship games. Decision making in this case is described by Hooghe (1996) as 'pluralist with an elitist bias', in that only actors with valuable resources can participate—in other words the playing field is not a level one for all participants, and nation states can no longer act as gatekeepers able to close off the European policy agenda and political arena.

This multilevel governance model has attracted considerable attention in recent years (see *inter alia* Smith 1995, 1997; Benz 2000), as well as some criticism.

Conceptualizing Europeanization

Here it is easiest to follow Raedelli (this volume), even at the risk of simplification. First and foremost, Europeanization refers to the process by which increasing numbers of policy arenas have taken on a European dimension as the process of European integration has developed.[3] Such policy arenas are characterized by the presence of a wide variety of actors, be they the Commission and its directorates, national and subnational governments and agencies, and national and trans-national interest groups, brought together into a complex policy network. Regional policy, our focus here, was largely a national matter until the early to mid-1980s, but has been a major strand of EU policy since that time—one which brought subnational units and their representative bodies to Brussels in such large numbers. Agricultural policy has been Europeanized ever since the CAP came into being: when Britain joined, the National Farmers Union quickly transferred its attentions from Whitehall to Brussels. On the other hand, social policy has been somewhat marginalized at the European level, with more change probably being achieved through indirect regulation (e.g. in relation to the working hours directive) than direct intervention in processes of income redistribution or the provision of health care services. Both the latter remain by and large firmly

---

[3] The extent to which this process has developed is well brought out by Fligstein and McNichol (1998).

in the hands of national governments, though with some debate at the EU level and some work undertaken within the Commission.

Second, Europeanization can be used to describe the process of regulation by which a wide variety of policy areas are subject to regulations and direct-ives agreed in Brussels, largely at the behest of the Commission and accepted by member state governments—another form of policy making. This process has been well described by authors such as Majone (1996) and Cram (1997), and involves subnational governments in the implementation and/or enforce-ment of a growing number of such regulations across an increasing number of fields, ranging from health and safety through the environment to consumer standards and contracts.

Third, it is also clear that the Europeanization of policy arenas varies over time and with the agenda of the EU and its institutions. For example, the debate within the EU between widening and deepening during the 1990s has largely been resolved in favour of widening, by bringing in Central and East European countries at some future point. Given also decisions to limit the EU budget, or at least to set it within certain constraints, then changes in other areas of EU policy making are likely to follow. As we shall see regional pol-icy has already undergone some changes, and the area of ITC policy has moved from one of a concern with IT literacy in the early 1990s to one of communications regulation/deregulation today. Other policy areas likely to involve changing priorities are the Common Agricultural Policy, transport, and information technology and communications.

Subnational Government in the EU Context

Subnational government in the EU member countries has also changed markedly during the lifetime of the EEC/European Union. One can identify a number of pressures which have sought to bring about change, most being designed to bring about some form of decentralization within nation states. First, there has been pressure from below—what Loughlin (2000) and Keating and Loughlin (1997) would call regionalism, in which subnational territories, generally at the regional level, have pressured national governments to give such territories (usually claiming some nationalist status) a greater degree of autonomy. Two cases are readily apparent—the emergence of the autonomous communities in Spain, especially Catalonia and the Basque region, and the establishment of the Flemish and Wallonia regions in Belgium. In other cases this pressure has been a less direct cause of decentralization—as with devolu-tion to Scotland and Wales in Britain, or has met with less success—such as the pressure for recognition by Bretons in Brittany in France. This kind of meso development can be thought as a process of bottom up regionalism.

The second pressure has come from central governments themselves, generally in the form of a gradual transfer of functions from central to lower tier governments, and generally recognizing a strengthening of the intermediate or meso tier (Sharpe 1993). Scandinavian reforms, for example, have seen such functions as health and social welfare move down towards a strengthened county tier, and this move has also been accompanied by a reduction in the number of municipal or bottom tier governments (Albæk *et al.* 1997). In the early seventies Britain followed a similar path, though later moved in the opposite direction as under succesive Conservative governments the British political system became increasingly centralized, a trend reversed in part under the Blair Labour governments since 1997. France, with the decentralization reforms under Mitterrand, went down a similar path in the 1980s, with the establishment of a new (largely weak) regional tier, a strengthening of the departmental influence over the activities of the communes (especially encouraging the development of intercommunal cooperation), and generally strengthening the position of urban agglomerations and large cities (Michel 1999).

Third, pressure has been external to the nation state and reflects both increasing globalization and changes encouraged through the activities of the European Union, especially the development of regional policies by the Commission from the late 1980s onwards. It was this latter development which essentially gave rise to the multilevel governance model (Hooghe 1996), and it is a development which forms the substantive focus of this chapter.

However, even in this latter context, subnational governments found in the long-standing federal systems in the European Union have also undergone some change. Austria and Germany provide the examples. In both cases, it is the intermediate tier which is strong and often influential in negotiations on EU matters. In the case of Germany, for example, Hesse (1991) argues that intergovernmental relations within the then West Germany took the form of a cooperative federalism. Benz (2000) examining later experience in the mid-1990s highlights the extent to which the German *Länder* varied in the way in which they dealt with things European.

What has happened at the EU level to bring about what is effectively a fourth tier to the intergovernmental relationship? First, there has been the general trend towards a more globalized economy, with the resultant loosening of ties between place and capital, the rise of multinational companies, worldwide shifts in manufacturing activity and capacity, and changing technologies.[4] All of these place nation states and their subnational levels under pressure, as regions and cities compete to maintain their place in the overall

---

[4] The author is very aware that globalization is neither new nor complete—see, for example, Hirst and Thompson (1996). Nevertheless, these general trends are sufficiently forceful to encourage a process of adaptation at all territorial levels. For an example of how far territorial politics in Europe are indeed fragmented and changing, see Keating (1997*a,b*).

economic hierarchy, seek to become more innovative and to find ways in which they can compete in the global market place (Storper 1997; Cook and Morgan 1998). At the EU level, this process of change has resulted in the processes of European integration and Europeanization of policies gaining pace, especially in the years up to the Amsterdam Treaty. If that point in time brought about a slowing down of formal processes of deepening (integration) rather than widening or extending the European Union to the East, it has not stopped Europeanization completely, and in the years before, integration moved on quite rapidly. Four main sources of these processes are apparent, driven essentially by moves towards the introduction of the Single European Market, essentially the EU response to the economic globalization processes just discussed. First, there was acceptance of the principle of subsidiarity, adopted in the Maastricht Treaty, under which things are (supposedly) done at the lowest possible level of government within the European Union. Second, there has been an increase in the process of decision making by regulation within the European Union, under which the Commission has been able to issue a large number of directives which change the way in which a considerable number of policy actions are effectively determined—for example, in areas such as consumer protection, contracting, environmental control, employment law, and health and safety.

Third, in many cases these areas have been further Europeanized by decisions of the European Court of Justice (ECJ). As Hooghe and Marks (2001: 26–7) argue, the ECJ 'has transformed the European legal order in a supranational direction'. In so doing, it has promoted European integration by establishing that the Treaties on which the EU is based and its own decisions are legally superior to those of national courts, i.e. establishing the supremacy of European over national laws. These latter have also accepted Article 234 (ex. 77) of the Treaty of Rome which allows them to seek ECJ guidance on cases involving Community law, guidance which is rarely rejected. If such guidance is accepted, then other national courts usually accept the decision as a precedent, so that effectively ECJ rulings bind nation states. Yet the ECJ is not completely autonomous, since it depends on others—such as the Commission, lower courts, or other private actors bringing cases before it. Areas such as equal rights, employment, and consumer protection are all themes in which the ECJ has been active and with impacts, *inter alia*, affecting subnational governments.[5]

Last, but for our purposes a major point of focus, certain policy areas (regional, urban, innovation/exploitation) have had a predominantly sub-national focus, being implemented at regional or local levels. In the case of

---

[5] Whether this goes so far as to establish an EU constitution is debatable—see Shaw (1999) and references cited therein for a discussion of this point, which is outside the scope of this chapter.

regional policy, the involvement of subnational levels has been heightened through the adoption of the partnership principle, in which proposals for regional funding are developed on a partnership basis between the different levels of government and with cross-sector partnerships at the appropriate regional level, and where the implementation of the regional programme is largely undertaken at the regional level and monitored at both national and EU levels. The same policy focus has applied to some other policy arenas—IT, urban, and innovation policy being cases in point, though all of these have had a link to regional policy.

EU Regional Policy and Subnational Government

The last twenty years have seen the development of an extensive regional policy within the EU, largely designed to promote the cohesion of the union. What has been the key to this cohesion process has been the use of the EU's structural funds to aid the less developed/economically declining regions to help overcome their difficulties. That the more prosperous parts of the European Union have continued to grow, and that the gap between the richest and poorest regions has not necessarily narrowed, is to some extent irrelevant here—what is important is that EU regional policy and the structural funds have been of significant benefit to some parts of the EU (especially countries like Ireland, Spain, and Portugal) and have changed the relationship between different levels of government within the EU and within the member states generally (Tommel 1997). In some cases, arguably, the process has helped, whereas in others the impact has been marginal or even negative. What is also clear from a raft of research is that the reaction of different regions and localities has been different—in some cases regions, cities, and municipalities have taken advantage of regional policy to draw down significant funds and to heighten their political status within the national and European political systems, whereas in other cases almost the opposite has been true (Bullman 1994; Balme 1996; Rhodes 1995; Smith 1995; Desideri and Sanantonio 1996; Heinelt and Smith 1996; Goldsmith and Klaussen 1997; Jeffrey 1997; Le Galès and Lequesne 1997). Add to this the use of funds to promote cross border cooperation through the INTERREG programme, and one finds new spaces/territories beginning to emerge slowly.

This variable reaction is not simply because the Commission, in implementing regional policy, has defined eligibility criteria which exclude some subnational units whilst including others, a point to which we shall return. Rather has it to do with the way in which different countries have sought to operate the EU regional policy themselves and the different status which subnational units have in different countries, as well as their responsive capacity

(Goldsmith and Klaussen 1997). These persisting cultural differences are important in understanding the variable geometry of the European Union.

The Operation of EU Regional Policy

EU regional policy has operated in two different senses—formal, in terms of the definition and use of the structural funds, and informal, by which we refer to processes designed to amend the operation of regional policy, and ways in which the Commission in particular has sought to develop the regional level. First, however, we need to understand the Commission's interest in both these matters. As I have argued elsewhere (Goldsmith 1993), the Commission's interest in working with subnational governments derives not just from the formal objectives and imperatives of integration, but also from informal objectives and political processes. At one level the Commission works with subnational governments because it needs information on policy needs and processes as an *alternative* to that provided from national governments and from other interested parties. Indeed, different directorates of the Commission have themselves sponsored a large number of networks and activities which bring subnational governments into contact—with many of them being only too willing to take up these opportunities, giving rise to a form of clientelistic relationship at times. Not only do these networks provide an opportunity to exchange information, they provide an opportunity for the Commission to introduce new policy experiments.

Second, the Commission faces problems of implementation of its policies (Majone 2000). Despite cries and complaints about the Brussels bureaucracy, it remains small, and very dependent on others for implementation. Whilst implementation is often seen as the responsibility of national governments, in many cases detailed implementation is decentralized to lower levels of government or other agencies. Given that one major way through which both integration and policy development effectively takes place is through regulatory processes (Majone 1996; Wallace and Wallace 1996; Cram 1997; Young and Wallace 2000), then it is through the implementation of regulations and directives that such changes occur. Policy arenas such as environment, consumer protection and trading standards, contracting, and transport all provide examples of areas in which EU regulation has been important and where subnational governments have had the task of securing compliance with the new regulations.

Within this context, how has EU regional policy operated? The highpoint was during the Delors years, from the mid-1980s until the late 1990s. Using the structural funds, the Commission had been concerned from the mid-1980s onwards to reduce regional and social disparities within the European Union. Our concern here is with the use of two funds—the European Social Fund and the European Regional Development Fund,[6] since these were most applicable to subnational governments. Before 1988, these funds were largely used to fund nationally determined projects, though some Commission initiatives (INTERREG and the integrated developed projects, for example) were both more European wide and began to bring about a direct relationship between the Commission and subnational governments. Reform of these funds led to the introduction of coordinated multiannual programmes designed to promote economic development in the poorer areas of the European Union, using as a criteria for classifying such regions the standard NUTS scheme and taking as the poorest those with a GDP below a defined level for the European average (75 per cent in the first case). Different levels of funding were then attached to those areas who qualified under the classification for funding—those who were identified as Objective 1 regions receiving more funding than those in Objective 2 areas, who in turn received more than Objective 5 areas. The reform of the structural funds greatly increased the amount of EU funding going to support these elements of cohesion policy—doubling in the period 1987–93, and doubling again for the period 1994–99—or 32 per cent of the EU budget by the end of the second period.[7] Significant funds to play for, and as good grantsmanship players, those eligible quickly joined the game.

Furthermore, there were two further reforms or shifts in the policy. First, rather than supporting large-scale infrastructure development and investment incentives, the funds were designed to promote economic development, including significant funding for training and technology transfer. Second, there was an important change in the decision-making and implementation arrangements for the use of the funds. The new decision-making arrangements supported the idea of partnership between the different actors involved. In other words, rather than simply giving national governments what were effectively blank cheques to support nationally determined initiatives, the post-1989 use of the funds required proposals to come forward on the basis of an agreed strategy between national governments and the eligible regions, and at the regional level the funds also required partnerships between the public and private sectors along with the voluntary sector where appropriate.[8] Such changes meant that subnational governments (especially regional but also

[6] As Hooghe (1996: 3) rightly notes, three funds were involved—the Agricultural Fund underpinning the Common Agricultural Policy was the third. For discussion of the regional impact of the CAP see Dudek (2001).

[7] These figures do not take into account either a special cohesion fund designed to help the four poorest countries between 1994 and 1999, nor additional monies set aside to assist with the integration of Austria, Finland, and Sweden from 1995.

[8] For a detailed discussion of these changes and their operation until the mid-1990s, see especially Hooghe (1996).

city, county, and municipal) became legitimate actors in this game, a process reinforced by the adoption of the subsidiarity principle at Maastricht in 1992, which also recognized the importance of subnational governments in the process by offering them consultative status through the Committee of the Regions[9] (Tommel 1998).

Not surprisingly, in addition to those Objective 1 regions located in the poorest part of the European Union (Greece, Ireland, Portugal, Southern Italy, and Spain), significant other regions came to be included—especially as Objective 2 regions were to be found in those areas most heavily hit by the process of industrial restructuring associated with economic change in the early 1980s—mainly those regions linked to such industries as coal, steel, shipbuilding, and textile manufacturing in countries like Belgium, France, Italy, and the United Kingdom. After the reunification of Germany, former East European areas such as Sachsen Anhalt became eligible for funding, and post 1995, parts of Finland, Sweden, and Austria were also identified for funding. In addition, with the growing use of INTERREG arrangements, as well as funds for Objective 5, other areas found themselves playing on the European stage—and recognized the need to organize themselves to do so effectively.

Thus, early in the 1990s two developments were becoming apparent. At the national level, some regions were better at the game than others—thus, for example, in the United Kingdom it was Glasgow, Birmingham, later Manchester, and Liverpool, who were amongst the cities which learnt the new rules and appreciated the game quickest, whilst regionally Scotland and Wales were better at exploiting the funds available than were parts of England. Elsewhere, quickly on the scene were the 'Four Motors' (Rhônes-Alpes, Baden-Württemberg, Lombardy, and Catalonia) seeking to establish themselves at the economic heart of the new Europe (Kukawka 1996). Similarly Lille and Nord Pas-du-Calais took advantage of Objective 1 funding and of the INTERREG rules to link up with Kent in England to exploit the building of the Channel Tunnel, whilst Dutch municipalities on the border of the country also exploited INTERREG. Barcelona exploited its status as an Objective 1 area to secure extensive funding to assist the developments necessary to hold the Olympic Games in 1992 (Morata 1996). Wallonia in Belgium, together with coal mining areas in Britain and Lille in France, also benefited from their activities in the Coal Communities Campaign, which sought support successfully from the Commission to help regenerate the dying coalmining areas of Europe. Outside Objectives 1 and 2, it was areas like Cornwall in Britain which were to the fore in exploiting Commission funds, as well as those associated with the Atlantic Arc, the large number of regions and municipalities from Portugal to Ireland whose coastlines bordered the Atlantic, who,

---

[9] The impact of this new body is discussed briefly below.

although not eligible for large amounts of funding, recognized that by working together they could obtain support and recognition of their needs within the wider Union as early as 1989 (Guesnier 1993; Smith 1995; Brouard 1996). In all these cases, research suggests that two key factors helped decide whether or not regions and cities would become active: their eligibility for funding, and the quality of political and administrative leadership they possessed (Goldsmith and Klaussen 1997).

By the early 1990s, cross-EU subnational groupings were beginning to emerge, like EUROCITIES (a grouping of second cities across the European Union); the Association of European Municipalities and Regions, as well as more narrowly based bodies such as RETI (originally cities and regions based on traditional industries, but who now stress their technological and innovatory strengths), and MILAN (a motor industry network), were coming into being. And, like all good pressure groups, individually and collectively, they recognized that under Delors the Commission was where much of the action took place—and thus that Brussels was the place to be. The 1990s saw a rapid growth in the number of offices opened in Brussels by cities and regions across the European Union and by their associations. In 1985 there were only six regions with offices in Brussels: by 2000 there were over 160, covering all subnational systems within the European Union (John 2001: 86–7). The United Kingdom has the largest number of such offices (26), followed by Germany (21), and Spain (19). At the other extreme Portugal has only one such office, Ireland two, and Greece three. Such offices, which have full time representatives, act as a 'listening post' for local governments, and as a base from which they can carry out lobbying activities. They quickly developed a working relationship with the various Commission directorates—who themselves recognized the growing importance of the structural funds as possible resources for their own initiatives—so that they worked with those who were also seeking to exploit the funds for their own purposes. And these groups quickly realized that, if they could influence and shape the agenda rather than reacting to it or simply seeking early warning of new developments, then the opportunity arose for them to shape policy so that it suited *their* ends rather than those of others. In this sense such offices are the 'real and symbolic presence of subnational organisations outside the boundaries of their national state' (John 2001: 86).

Of course it is possible to overestimate the importance of these developments. Brussels, as the centre of EU activity, was and is a honeypot for those seeking to influence policy. In this respect the city has the same village like qualities as Washington, as groups exchange gossip, information and trade influence, and ideas. Subnational governments were only one such category of interest groups amongst many to be found there. And, as we have noted, the Commission and its directorates generally welcomed them, founding, linking, helping such networks to flourish.[10] Even so, especially in the unitary states where central government is relatively strong, as is the cases with the United Kingdom, Ireland, and Denmark, for example, local governemnts continue to recognize the dominance of the central government.

By the mid to late 1990s, this activity had reached its peak. People began to talk as if Delors' 'Europe of the Regions' was in place. The new Committee of the Regions had been established and was offering its opinions formally on a wide range of issues. Regions, countries, and cities across Europe were involved at the subnational level in developing a series of partnerships to exploit the structural funds, and national governments were having to recognize this change. And many such subnational governments were beginning to engage in what some authors have called 'paradiplomacy' (Aldecoa and Keating 1999; Palard 2000)—that is, establishing offices in Brussels and joining in bi- or multilateral discussions/relationships with their opposites across Europe, and joining European-wide bodies such as AERM and Eurocities. To the fore of this development were the Länder in Germany; Flanders and Wallonia in Brussels, as well as Catalonia in Spain. Scotland and Wales were also present. In the case of the German and Belgian regions, these were permitted to represent their country at Council of Ministers meetings (Jeffrey 1997; Kerremans 2000).[11] Cities—especially second cities—also joined the game as the creation of the Eurocities networks demonstrates. Nevertheless, change was afoot: Amsterdam in 1996 was the turning point.

Amsterdam resolved—at least in the mid-term—arguments amongst the member states about how the European Union should develop in future. First, if the creation of the Single European Market, the adoption of the subsidiarity principle, and regional policy had been about closer European integration (deepening the European Union), then the question of extending membership to countries in Central and East Europe was about widening the European Union. Second, member states were showing signs of concern about the increasing costs of financing the European Union, a problem not entirely resolved by the accession of three new members—Austria, Finland, and Sweden—in 1995. Third, the enlarged post-1995 Union was faced by continuing problems of decision making in the Council of Ministers and the need to extend the principle of qualified majority voting. Fourth, as the most expensive elements in the EU budget, both the CAP and regional policies were due for review. In the light of the Amsterdam decision to widen rather than deepen

---

[10] The author has some personal experience of this activity. In the mid-1990s he chaired a pan-EU network made up of universities, chambers of commerce, regional and city governments, and technology transfer/innovation centres under the RETI umbrella, which was able to benefit on several occasions from Commission largesse.

[11] Even in highly centralized Britain, following devolution Scotland has on occasion taken its place at the Council of Ministers (Foreign Office spokesman: 6 November 2001).

the European Union, and to do so at minimum cost to the EU budget, both these latter policies were likely to suffer financial cuts. Additionally, as the Commission's DG 16 in charge of regional policy gained more experience in the implementation of regional policy, it was beginning to change the rules of the game, tightening up the decision-making processes, setting tougher targets, and auditing programmes more carefully.

In such a context, it was perhaps inevitable that the post-1999 form of the structural funds would be different and that regional policy would be effectively downgraded amongst EU policy priorities, reflecting the fact that policy arenas rise and fall in importance. Although the Committee of the Regions and transnational organizations representing regional interests fought to retain regional policy funding levels, as did several national groupings, their success was limited (John and McAteer 1998). The Committee of the Regions had little impact and little influence (McCarthy 1997), specialist groups such as RETI perhaps a little more, since their efforts were at least partially encouraged by DG 16, itself seeking to retain its place in the sun. In the end, whilst regional policy remained in place, as did the Objective One areas (albeit with tougher criteria to meet), the post-1999 situation effectively redefined the boundaries of Objective 2 areas so that they covered larger territory, and with funding which was designed to aid their withdrawal symptoms over the next few years. Sutcliffe (2000) suggests that the geometry also changed a little—the Commission withdrawing in some areas (monitoring programmes and controlling finance) in favour of more central government intervention, but still deciding priorities and the rules of the game, and leaving a role for subnational governments by maintaining the partnership principle.

A variety of reasons can be advanced for these changes. First and foremost was the general weakness of subnational governments within EU policy and decision-making structures overall. Despite the appearance of influence and stature, they were always dependent on the support of national governments and their agendas, as well as on that of the Commission, which itself was enjoying an unprecedented role in EU decision-making in the late 1980s and early 1990s. In part the change was a step back from the new multilevel governance and a clearer recognition of the continuing dominant position of the nation state in EU decision making. The position of the Commission was not helped by the scandals which surrounded it in 1998 and the wholesale resignations of commissioners, the latter demanded and achieved by the European Parliament, which itself was seeking to test its own powers.

More simply perhaps was the fact that subnational governments themselves varied in their capacity to operate on the European level, singly and collectively. Not all regions, cities, and municipalities were equal to the task—either organizationally or in terms of their leadership and interest in things European (Goldsmith and Klaussen 1997; Bache and Jones 2000). Those generally well-known regions and cities which had adapted early to the game, and had benefited from the structural funds over time, still operate at the EU level—but for how long? If the money goes away, what would keep them as players at this level? And what do these changes mean for the nature of EU integration, Europeanized policy making and multilevel governance, and the future shape of territorial politics in Europe?

Some Concluding Remarks

At one level the answer to some of these questions is simple—not all that much. At another level, the answer is more complicated. To take the simple answer first, the processes of EU policy and decision making will continue, albeit in a context of a changing balance of power between the participating institutions and changing rules of the decision making game. What we have seen since Amsterdam is a reassertion of the dominant position of national governments in the EU decision-making processes and a change in their priorities at the Council of Ministers... widening rather than deepening is its simple expression. But the *routines* of policy and decision-making continue across the board—and not just for the major issues with which the Council of Ministers concerns itself. And at the very least, the European Union, through the Commission, seeks to establish common norms and standards through its regulatory procedures and activities.

In such a context, subnational governments continue to be involved, though perhaps not on the same scale as when cohesion policy was at its height. Most importantly, as the Commission and the ECJ continue to produce continuing directives, regulations, and decisions, the burden of implementation on subnational governments is likely to increase rather than diminish, and across a range of policy arenas. Similarly the arrival of new members of the European Union from Central and East Europe will, as several commentators have noted (Goldsmith 2000; John 2001: 91), provides new opportunities for the mobilization of subnational governments within the European Union—indeed expectation of such events has already produced some such developments, generally encouraged by the Commission.[12]

But at another level, the answer is more complicated. Even though it has moved towards being a more bounded political system, the European Union remains a weakly linked system by comparison with other (federal) systems in Europe and North America. In this context it shares more in

---

[12] Such activity is part of the preparation for future membership. Before Austria, Finland, and Sweden joined the European Union in 1995, they had been involved in a number of EU activities. Yet their degree of preparation was variable—Finland quickly active in Brussels and its networks, Austria and Sweden less so.

common with national federal systems in Europe in which it is the intermediate tier which remains relatively powerful—as is the case in Germany, Austria, and Switzerland. It is these national levels which determine the speed of formal political integration in Europe, whilst the process of Europeanizing public policy arenas brings about a process of informal integration—in the sense that differing elites become accustomed to the process of working together and learning from each other. For subnational governments, it may well be that the cross-national learning process is almost as important as the finance they receive, though undoubtedly the latter helps.

Such a process brings about the exchange of values and ideas about how politics works, challenging established orders and practices. Regions and localities face similar challenges across Europe in the face of increasing globalization. Political leaders and administrators increasingly meet and share ideas about solutions to problems and best practice. Transport provides a good example—to be a 'world city or region' one must have an international airport and rapid transit systems, notwithstanding all the accommodation, conference, cultural, and sporting facilities also expected. Opening up old waterfront areas has become commonplace from Oslo, through Hamburg, via Manchester, Bordeaux, Barcelona, Lisbon, and further South. Through exchange and partnership across the European Union, new policy paradigms appear, are shared and disseminated. For example, ideas about achieving greater public participation and involvement in planning and local decision making have also spread across the EU, largely as a result of regions and municipalities working together in cross-EU partnerships, whilst at the local level, such partnerships have encouraged the involvement of private and voluntary sector actors in local decision making. Such developments have also been particularly noticeable in the poverty and urban programmes adopted by the European Union (Bennington and Geddes 2000, 2001; Oberti 2000).

These changes are largely incremental and slow, and national characteristics and values remain predominant. At the subnational level, not all things are equal or the same, but the frame of reference within which a proactive region or city operates in Europe has been one set on a European and international scale, as such places seek to maintain or improve their position in the world economic hierarchy. Whilst some regions, cities, and municipalities choose to remain as they are or feel incompetent or impotent in the face of widespread change, others tackle change head on and in collaboration with others. What Balme and Le Galès (1997) called the 'bright stars' adapt and change and in so doing they bring about change in the way in which local politics operates in Europe. Others follow suit, albeit more slowly, so that old distinctions between North and South in terms of modes of operation (clientelistic versus non-clientelistic) may no longer be as valid as they were ten or twenty years ago (Goldsmith 2000; John 2001).

What is clear is that the experience of working within Europe for many cities and municipalities has changed the way they operate. Traditional cultural imperatives which led to the distinction between Northern and Southern political styles are no longer quite as important as they were: cross-national experience leads cities and municipalities to think about and do things differently. The examples of the Four Motors, the Atlantic Arc group, as well as the many INTERREG cooperations, simply mean that regional and local governments are increasingly aware of different ways of doing things. Notwithstanding the funding made available from the structural funds, the Commission and its directorates also encouraged extensive exchange of experience, distribution of best practice, and considerable cooperative working amongst subnational units on a trans-national basis (see *inter alia* Hingel 1993). Oversight of programmes at the EU level, together with its setting of targets and auditing of expenditures and programme implementation means that it becomes more difficult for clientelistic practices to be employed. The process may be slow, national paradigms may still be important, but working together in Europe, if only in terms of how to put the funding bids together, means that regions, cities and municipalities change the way they do things. Extending the European Union into Central and Eastern Europe simply brings more players into the game at all levels, complicating it still further, but also putting traditional values and methods under even greater pressure.

This is not to say that change is rapid or that old distinctions are no longer valid. What it does do is to suggest, as authors such as Keating (1997*a*), Goldsmith (2000), and John (2001) indicate, that territorial politics throughout Europe is in a state of flux. In other words, territorial politics within Europe and inside the European Union are unstable, changing, and likely to remain so for the forseeable future.

In the process of globalization and Europeanization, national governments, as well as those operating at subnational levels, have learnt that singly their influence is limited, and that they are largely dependent on collaboration with others to achieve change. The European Union is not about hierarchies, but about networks and interdependence in an ever-changing environment. Some of these networks are extremely formal, reflecting the operation of the formal institutions of the European Union, whilst others—especially in the policy areas—are often far less formal, and in many ways no less important. In this sense EU governance is supranational.

Explaining this European system of governance—giving it a theoretical basis—continues to challenge social scientists. The different models—state centred, supranational, multilevel governance—all have at least descriptive validity of the processes and relationships which they seek to explain. In so far as the European Union continues to be dominated by discussions amongst member states at the national level; in so far as the EU institutions such as the

Commission, Parliament, and the ECJ continue to be weak; and in so far as effective formal decision making depends on the acceptance of new treaties at the Council of Ministers, then the state-centred model remains valid. And in so far as policy and decision-making processes reflect hierarchical relationships between the Commission, national governments, and subnational units, involving a process of bargaining and negotiation between the different levels, then supranationalist approaches have validity. And in so far as these relationships involve informal networks crosscutting hierarchies and national boundaries, then the multilevel governance approach provides insights.

To describe the process as one involving variable geometric relationships is both insightful and arcane. It is insightful because the phrase captures the very essence of an almost constantly changing set of relationships over time.[13] It is arcane in that, because we do not fully know the rules and principles underlying the geometry, we lack a sound theoretical basis for understanding the European Union, its political insitutions, and its politics. In this context the need for new concepts and ideas remains imperative (Marks *et al.* 1996; Scharpf 1999; Rosamond 2000; Hooghe and Marks 2001).

REFERENCES

Albæk, E., Rose, L., Strómberg, L., and Ståhlberg, K. (1997). *Nordic Local Government Developmental Trends and Reforms in the Post-War Period* (Helsinki: Association of Finnish Local Authorities).

Aldecoa, F. and Keating, M. (eds) (1999). 'Paradiplomacy in Action', Special Issue, *Regional and Federal Studies* 9(1).

Bache, I. and Jones, R. (2000). 'Has EU Regional Policy Empowered the Regions? Spain and the UK', *Regional and Federal Studies* 10(3): 1–20.

Balme, R. (ed) (1996). *Les Politiques du Neo-Régionalisme* (Paris: Economica).

—— and Le Galès, P. (1997). 'Bright Stars and Black Holes', in Goldsmith and Klaussen (eds) *op. cit.*

Bennington, J. and Geddes, M. (2000). 'Exclusion sociale et partenariat local—la dimension europeenne', *Pôle Sud* 12: 79–84.

——(eds) (2001). *Local Partnership and Social Exclusion in the European Union* (London: Routledge).

Benz, A. (2000). 'Two Types of Multi-level Governance: Intergovernmental Relations in German and EU Regional Policy', *Regional and Federal Studies* 10(3): 21–44.

Brouard, S. (1996). 'L'Arc Atlantique comme enterprise politique: cooperation interrégionale et leadership politique', in Balme (ed.) *op cit.* pp. 69–90.

Bullman, U. (ed.) (1994). *Die Politik der dritten Ebene: Regionen im Europea der Union* (Baden-Baden: Nomos).

Chryssochou, D. (1997). 'New Challenges to the Study of European Integration', *Journal of Common Market Studies* 35(4): 521–42.

---

[13] For an interesting and stimulating discussion in this respect, see Chryssochoou (1997).

Cooke, P. and Morgan, K. (1998). *The Associational Economy* (Oxford: Oxford University Press).

Cram, L. (1997). *Policy-making in the EU* (London: Routledge).

Desideri, C. and Sanantonio, V. (1996). 'Building a Third Level in Europe; Prospects and Difficulties in Italy', *Regional and Federal Studies* 6(2): 96–116.

Dudek, C. (2001). 'The European Union's Effect Upon Regional Economic Development and Regional Government's Policy Making', *Regional and Federal Studies* 11(1): 101–25.

Fligstein, N. and McNichol, J. (1998). 'The Institutional Terrain of the European Union', in W. Sandholtz and A. Stone Sweet (eds), *European Integration and Supranational Governance* (Oxford: Oxford University Press), 59–91.

Goldsmith, M. (1993). 'The Europeanisation of Local Government', *Urban Studies* 30(4/5): 683–99.

——(2000). 'Local Politics in Europe', in R. Balme, A. Faure, and A. Mabileau (eds), *Les Nouvelles Politiques Locales*, Paris Presses de Sciences Po, pp. 149–68.

——and Klaussen, K. K. (eds) (1997). *European Integration and Local Government* (Cheltenham: Edward Elgar).

Guesnier, B. (1993). 'The Atlantic Arc: The Small and Medium Sized Enterprises and the Transfer of Technologies', in R. Cappelin and P. Batty (eds), *Regional Networks, Border Regions and European Integration* (London: Pion), 215–30.

Heinelt, H. and Smith, R. (1996). *Policy Networks and European Structural Funds* (Aldershot: Avebury).

Hingel, A. J. (1993). 'The Prime Role of Regional Cooperation in European Integration', in R. Cappelin and P. Batty (eds), *Regional Networks, Border Regions and European Integration* (London: Pion), 21–30.

Hesse, J. (1991). 'Local Government in a Federal State: The Cases of West Germany', in J. Hesse (ed.), *Local Government and Urban Affairs in International Perspective* (Baden-Baden: Nomos Verlagsgesellschaft), 353–86.

Hirst, P. and Thompson, G. (1996). *Globalization in Question* (London: Polity Press).

Hoffman, S. (1982). 'Reflections on the Nation State in Europe Today', *Journal of Common Market Studies* 20: 21–37.

Hooghe, Liesbet (ed.) (1996). *Cohesion Policy and European Integration* (Oxford: Clarendon Press).

——(1998). 'EU Cohesion Policy and Competing Models of European Capitalism', *Journal of Common Market Studies* 36: 457–47.

——and Marks, G. (2001). *Multi-Level Governance and European Integration* (Oxford: Rowman and Littlefield).

Jeffery, C. (ed.) (1997). *The Regional Dimension of the European Union: Towards a Third Level in Europe* (London: Frank Cass).

John, P. (2001). *Local Governance in Europe* (London: Sage).

——and McAteer, M. (1998). 'Sub-national Institutions and the New European Governance: UK Local Authority Lobbying Strategies for the IGC', *Regional and Federal Studies* 8(3): 104–24.

Keating, M. (1997*a*). *The New Regionalism in Western Europe* (Cheltenham: Edward Elgar).

——(1997*b*). 'States, Europe and Regions', Occasional Paper, EUI.

Keating, M. and Loughlin, J. (eds) (1997). *The Political Economy of Regionalism* (London: Frank Cass).

Kerremans, B. (2000). 'Determining a European Policy in a Multi-level Setting', *Regional and Federal Studies* 10(1): 36–61.

Kukawka, P. (1996). 'Le Quadrige européen ou l'Europe par les régions', in Balme (ed.) *op cit.* pp. 91–106.

LeGales, P. and Lequesne, C. (eds) (1997). *Les Paradoxes des Régions en Europe* (Paris: La Decouverte).

Loughlin, J. (2000). 'Regional Autonomy and State Paradigm Shifts', *Regional and Federal Studies* 10(2): 10–34.

McCarthy, R. (1997). 'The Committee of the Regions: An Advisory's Body's Tortuous Path to Influence', *Journal of European Public Policy* 4(3): 439–54.

Majone, G. (1996). *Regulating Europe* (London: Routledge).

——(2000). 'The Credibility Crisis of Community Regulation', *Journal of Common Market Studies* 38(2): 273–302.

Marks, G., Scharpf, F., Schmitter, P., and Streek, W. (1996). *Governance in the European Union* (London: Sage).

Michel, H. (1998). 'Government or Governance? The Case of the French Local Political System', *West European Politics* 21(3): 146–69.

Morata, F. (1996).' Barcelone et la Catogne dans l'arene europeenne', in Balme *et al.* (eds). *op cit.* pp. 109–33.

Oberti, M. (2000). 'Local Forms of Urban Anti-poverty Strategies in Europe', *International Journal of Urban and Regional Research* 24(3): 536–53.

Page, E. C. and Goldsmith, M. (1987). *Central and Local Government Relations* (London: Sage).

Palard, J. (ed.) (1999). 'Les Relations Internationales des Régions en Europe', Special issue *Études Internationales* 30(4).

Rhodes, M. (ed.) (1995). *The Regions and the New Europe* (Manchester: Manchester University Press).

Rosamond, B. (2000). *Theories of European Integration* (Basingstoke: Palgrave).

Sandholtz, W. and Stone Sweet, A. (eds) (1998). *European Integration and Supranational Governance* (Oxford: Oxford University Press).

Scharpf, F. (1999). *Governing in Europe, Effective and Democratic?* (Oxford: OUP).

Sharpe, L. J. (1993). *The Rise of the Meso* (London: Sage).

Shaw, J. (1999). 'Postnational Constitutionalism in the European Union', *Journal of European Public Policy* 6(4): 579–97.

Smith, A. (1995). *L'Europe Politique Au Miroir Du Local* (Paris: L'Harmattan).

——(1997). 'Studying Multi-level Governance: Examples from French Translations of the Structural Funds', *Public Administration* 75: 711–29.

Storper, M. (1997). *The Regional World: Territorial Development in a Global Economy* (London: The Guilford Press).

Sutcliffe, J. (2000). 'The 1999 Reform of the Structural Fund Regulations: Multi-level Governance or Renationalization'? *Journal of European Public Policy* 7(2): 290–309.

Tommel, I. (1997). 'The EU and the Regions: Towards a Three Tier System or New Modes of Regulation'? *Government and Policy* 15.

—— (1998). 'Transformation of Governance: The European Commission's Strategy for Creating a "Europe of the Regions"', *Regional and Federal Studies* 8(2): 52–80.

Wallace, H. and Wallace, W. (eds) (1996). *Policy Making in the European Union*, 4th Edition (Oxford: Oxford University Press).

Young, A. and Wallace, H. (2000). *Regulatory Politics in the Enlarging European Union* (Manchester: Manchester University Press).

6

Europeanization in Comparative Perspective: Institutional Fit and National Adaptation

MARCO GIULIANI

Introduction

This chapter addresses the issue of whether the domestic institutional architectures of the fifteen member states affect the way in which they react to the challenges of European governance. More specifically, it will empirically test different models in order to assess if macroinstitutional features are systematically correlated to their degree of adaptation to the European Union (EU).

This research question is strictly connected to the issue of Europeanization, either in its bottom-up or top-down meaning (Börzel 2002). On the one hand, if we conceptualize it as 'the emergence and development at the European level of distinct structures of governance' (Risse *et al.* 2001: 3), there will be member states more or less capable of keeping the pace with this process, thus showing fewer or greater problems of adaptation. On the other, if Europeanization is conceived as 'change in member states' policies, practices, and politics' (Schmidt 2001), the question of how domestic institutional structures impact on member states capacity of adjusting their governance mechanisms rests on the forefront (Ladrech 1994).

The present volume testifies to how the debate over a more precise definition of the concept is far from settled.[1] Nonetheless, for the purposes of the present analysis and as starting point for a purely empirical study, we may assume that Europeanization refers to a process whereby the European institutional political arena becomes autonomous in respect to the constraints, preferences,

I would like to thank Tanja Börzel, Kevin Featherstone, Fabio Franchino, and Claudio Radaelli for their comments. Many thanks even to Arend Lijphart for his original data and suggestions and to George Tsebelis for his views on the updating/completion of his database on veto players.

[1] See particularly the chapters written by Featherstone, Radaelli, Börzel and Risse, and Kohler-Koch, but even the work of Olsen (1995, 2002).

and governance habits of the member states, while, at the same time, the latter have to adapt themselves to the structures, policies, formal rules, and practices that have been consolidated at the EU level.

This definition does not deal with the most problematic junctures of the current debate, although it implicitly assumes that Europeanization (and thus adaptation) '[is] a matter of degree' (Featherstone, this volume, Chapter 1).[2] In other words, some national political systems are better than others at dealing with the challenges put forward by the recent evolution of governance within the European Union. In the present chapter we will try to assess if, and possibly to what extent, this disparity is accounted for by domestic institutional factors.

A part from the analyses presented in this volume, a considerable number of studies have tried to address this problem (e.g. Schmidt 1997, 1999; Conzelmann 1998; Börzel 1999; Knill and Lehmkuhl 1999; Cowles *et al.* 2001; Falkner 2001). However, the present work differs from these previous studies in at least three ways.

First, it proposes a comparative analysis of all fifteen member states, rather than the more usual comparison between a pair of countries or a limited number of them. Second, it specifically tests a series of alternative hypotheses in a macro fashion, involving a whole series of policy sectors in which the European Union is active, rather than carrying out an in-depth reconstruction of individual public policies. Finally, it uses medium-range institutional models that have been elaborated within comparative politics, rather than applying interpretative frameworks that have been specifically developed from research into the European Union, in order to reveal the interaction between European institutions and member states.

More specifically, we will test if a consensual rather than a majoritarian institutional architecture (Lijphart 1999) represents a favourable precondition for a member state's adaptation to EU politics. Additionally, we will verify if the number of formal veto players (VPS; Tsebelis 2002) affects the domestic process of Europeanization.

Rival Hypotheses

The EU member countries constitute a virtually ideal research field for the application of the comparative method (Lijphart 1971; Collier 1993). They are all consolidated democracies of more than twenty years standing, they all belong to the same geopolitical area, and they offer the possibility to use historical series of standard figures. However, they differ as to certain crucially

---

[2] At our level of analysis, these concepts avoid the methodological risks pointed out by Radaelli in his chapter and can be correctly considered in terms of *continua*.

important institutional variables—plurality vs. proportional elections, parliamentary governments vs. presidential ones, two-party vs. multiparty systems, and so on (Weaver and Rockman 1993). But rather than simply proceeding by way of pair comparisons and using dummy variables, we will elaborate upon two of the most firmly established models advanced in comparative politics.

On one side, Lijphart (1999), draws the distinction between the majority and consensus models of democracy through an accurate operationalization of ten variables clustered around two independent dimensions, the executives-parties and the federal-unitary ones. Moreover, in his analysis he claims that the European Union itself—because of its coalition executive (the Commission), its bicameralism (the European Parliament and the Council of Ministers), its proportionally elected multiparty system, its federal structure protected by rigid treaties and a supreme court, and its independent central bank—displays the typical features of a consensual system.

Thus, extending Lijphart's reasoning, we have at least one good theoretical reason in order to expect *consensus democracies performing better than majoritarian ones at the EU level*: institutional isomorphism. Even without subscribing the idea of some sort of Pareto supremacy of consensualism, it is possible to argue that those internal institutional structures that are more in keeping with the political reality of the European Union will have fewer problems in adapting to the latter. The interaction between the national and supranational levels is lubricated by the common familiarity with power-sharing arenas, the similar consensual policy style, and the joint attitude toward positive-sum games.

Katzenstein used the same argument in order to explain why Germany and the smaller member countries find themselves at home in the European political arenas. The 'structural congruence' that exists between the national and EU levels in these countries, guaranteed by 'similar institutions and practices', facilitates a softer passage towards integration, whereas 'other political systems mesh less well with the European polity' (Katzenstein 1997: 40–1). Likewise, Bulmer (1997: 76) highlights the positive results of the 'strikingly good fit' of such systems 'with the character of the European Union'.

On the other hand, the work of Tsebelis (1995, 2002), starting from the traditional assumptions of methodological individualism, turns around the concept of VPS, defined as those actors whose consent is needed in order to produce any policy change.[3] He demonstrates that the number of VPS should be negatively related to the potential for policy innovation in the diverse political systems, and to their capacity of actively responding to external challenges and of 'adapt[ing] to exogenous shocks' (Tsebelis 1999: 591).

---

[3] VPS include, first and foremost, all those parties making up the executive, together with those institutional players capable of impeding the adoption of legislative measures—such as a president granted veto powers in the case of divided government, or a powerful second chamber with a different majority from that within the executive.

Europeanization can be seen as a challenge to national political systems and to their governance capacity, having much to do with the adaptation to supranational political dynamics that are not fully controlled by national policy makers. Thus, following Tsebelis, and elaborating upon the qualitative results of several scholars (e.g. Haverland 2000; Héritier 2001), we could argue that *member states characterized by a low number of VPS can promptly adapt themselves to the formal and informal requirements of Europeanization.*

Although the proposed generalizations result from diverse assumptions, and are thus analytically independent from each other, they in fact advance opposing forecasts. Consensual democracies, in as far as they are characterized by multiparty systems, wide coalition-style executives, and a strong two-chamber system, naturally feature among those regimes with a considerable number of VPS. Vice versa, the most promising systems in Tsebelis' view are likely to be classified by Lijphart among the majoritarian democracies. Thus, the propositions advanced can be considered to be rival, opposing hypotheses, and it is up to us to prove one of the two wrong, or to assert the irrelevance of internal institutional structure to the question of Europeanization.

The Dataset

In order to test and control our rival hypotheses we have first collected institutional data regarding the fifteen EU member states for the period 1986–2000, strictly following the original operationalization of the two models.[4] The degree of consensual democracy on both Lijphart's dimensions, and the number of VPS thus represent our independent variables.

On the dependent side, we have calculated a standardized index of national adaptation based upon four different measures of responsiveness to the challenges of EU policy making: the rate of prompt transposition of directives, and the national quota of letters of formal notice, reasoned opinions, and references to the European Court of Justice.[5] Europeanization, adaptation, and goodness of fit between the domestic and the EU level are usually studied with a policy approach that identifies sector-specific indicators. But here we need to provide a synthetic overview of the type of relations that exist between the European Union and national institutions, and assessing the way in which member countries respond to the legal duties deriving from their European membership seems the most straightforward and consistent strategy of investigation.

---

[4] See the appendix for a complete list of the variables, and for further specifications.
[5] We acknowledge the fact that EU statistics should be used with due caution (Giuliani 1996; Mendrinou 1996), but our comparative approach mostly avoids the problems pointed out by Börzel (2001).

Figure 6.1 provides a purely descriptive picture of the trend of our adaptation index for each of the fifteen member countries. Given its average value of zero, it is extremely easy to see which countries deserve the title of 'leaders, or in the laggards' European Union. Similarly, if we ignore short-term oscillations,

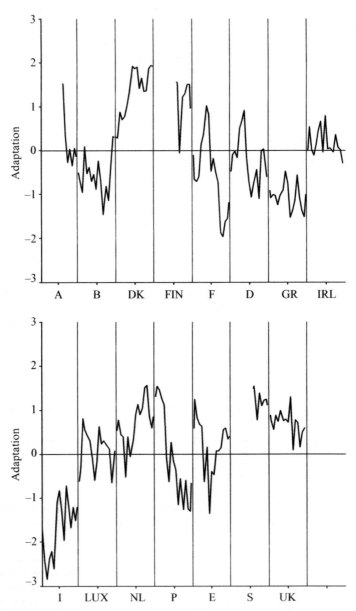

FIGURE 6.1. National adaptation to the EU (1986–2000)

it is just as simple to recognize the presence of any trends towards improvement or degeneration in national performance, or the gap separating an individual country from the average level of adaptation to European Union.

As well as independent and dependent variables, we have also included in the database a number of control variables regarding, for example, the size, the political influence, the economic weight, the legislative prerogatives of governments, and the length of EU membership of the different countries. These variables are mainly used in order to identify the existence of spurious relations, rather than to construct heterogeneous, computer-induced models whose only value appears to be that of guaranteeing a higher squared R.[6] It goes without saying that there are innumerable other sector variables, or even policy-specific variables, which influence the processes of Europeanization at the micro level, as proven by the case studies presented in this volume. Nonetheless we have to underline that, in spite of the fact that the amount of variance explained by the macro-institutional variables will probably be very small, simply demonstrating a (statistically) significant effect of domestic institutions on the degree of Europeanization would be an interesting research result.

This work, as it will now be clear, explicitly challenges Olsen's position postulating that the study of Europeanization does not fit easily 'the language of dependent and independent variables and the logic of regression analysis' (1996: 271; quoted by Featherstone in the introductory chapter). But our quantitative perspective does not question the fact that the dynamics we are trying to investigate are complex processes which depend from a multiplicity of factors, and which deserve the application of all the tools of political scientists.

The Empirical Test

The registration of the quoted variables by means of annual observations covering the period 1986–2000 for the fifteen member countries has enabled us to assemble a time series—cross section dataset composed of 198 independent observations.[7] A summary of average values and figures for the range

---

[6] See, for example, Lampinen and Uusiklyä (1998) or Mbaye (2001). Their most 'parsimonious' models include a mixture of corruption indices and surveys regarding the support of public opinion, national dummies and economic power, additional indices of regional autonomy, and alleged measures of bureaucratic efficiency. Otherwise, we are often presented with over thirty variables of various different kinds, utilized to produce regressions for just fifteen cases.

[7] As specified in the appendix, the construction of the dataset avoids the more usual problems of self-correlation and heteroscedasticity that normally afflict pooled time series analyses (Beck and Katz 1995; Kittel 1999), while, at the same time, preserving variation both for the independent and dependent variables. In order to make use of the standard statistical methods for quantitative data (e.g. OLS regression), we further need to satisfy the prerequisite of linearity. Those studies which use average figures calculated over the long term often have to deal

registered over this time period for each country regarding the main independent and dependent variables is shown in Table 6.1.

As regards Lijphart's characteristic variables (Columns 2 and 3), positive values show higher levels of consensualism, whereas negative values characterize Westminster democracies. Less than half of member states can be defined as purely consensual (Belgium and Holland) or purely majoritarian (the United Kingdom, Luxembourg, Greece, and Sweden). A mixed combination is just as common: the most striking example of this is Germany, with an extremely high consensual value as regards the federal–unitary dimension, but clearly 'Westminster' when it comes to the executives–parties dimension.

Column 4 shows the average number of veto players. The three countries with the lowest figures are those with one-party governments for the entire period in question—that is, the United Kingdom, Spain, and Sweden; whereas those characterized by the highest figures are Finland, Italy and Belgium. As we mention in the appendix, Germany and Portugal are the only countries who see a rise in the number of their VPS due to the presence at certain times of relevant institutional actors, the Bundesrat and the President, respectively.

As far as the dependent variables are concerned, Figure 6.1 has already provided us with an overview of the oscillations of the 'adaptation index', and thus Table 6.1 only presents the absolute values of the original four variables: the percentage of transpositions and the respective shares of infringements at the various stages of the procedure. In the first of these (Column 5), higher values denote a better degree of adaptation to EU policy, while the exact opposite is true in the other three cases (Columns 6–8).

It is easy to detect the existence of an inverse relationship between promptness in implementing directives and infringement proceedings, at least in the case of those countries with longer EU membership. Nevertheless, it is more interesting to observe how some countries systematically tend to present an increasingly worrying picture as the gravity of the infringement rises. These countries, not surprisingly, include Italy, Belgium, and Greece, traditionally considered the laggards of the European Union. On the other hand, there are some governments that manage to solve infringement problems before the Commission sets out to investigate matters, or at least before they run the risk of a European Court ruling condemning their conduct. This group

with an excessively small N and with problems of distribution. Having gathered annual figures avoids both problems. The F tests of the linearity of the adaptation index with respect to each of the independent variables, together with the plots of residues, are perfectly reassuring; likewise, the individual DfBetas measurements would seem to indicate that there are no outliers capable of disproportionately influencing the inclination of the regression lines. This means that there is little point in invoking some form of national exception—as is nearly always done for countries like Italy or Greece—in order to explain their low degree of adaptation to European legislation.

TABLE 6.1. *Mean and range values of main independent and dependent variables*

	Executives–parties dimension	Federal–unitary dimension	Veto players	% prompt transposition new directives	% letters of formal notice	% reasoned opinions	% references to the ECJ
A							
Mean	−0.67	1.05	2.00	53.84	6.78	5.45	2.34
Range	0.84	0.00	0.00	21.54	11.17	11.38	5.06
B							
Mean	0.94	1.01	4.45	74.82	8.20	10.39	13.26
Range	1.16	0.39	2.00	50.47	4.55	8.72	18.83
D							
Mean	−0.62	2.55	2.65	76.55	8.21	8.68	7.88
Range	0.74	0.00	1.00	51.41	5.93	9.86	14.16
DK							
Mean	0.95	−0.47	2.70	84.02	4.60	1.47	0.89
Range	1.12	0.00	1.87	42.64	4.37	3.05	4.11
E							
Mean	−0.41	0.61	1.00	79.81	7.57	6.52	5.45
Range	1.45	0.00	0.00	39.33	7.59	15.73	11.36
F							
Mean	−0.71	0.13	2.36	75.38	9.41	10.69	10.81
Range	1.56	0.00	4.00	52.86	7.04	14.64	18.10
FIN							
Mean	0.71	−0.64	4.91	66.00	7.42	1.48	0.52
Range	0.24	0.00	0.57	18.04	25.20	3.04	2.33
GR							
Mean	−0.48	−1.07	1.32	71.43	10.60	12.13	16.24
Range	1.33	0.00	1.27	60.00	15.46	12.83	45.83

TABLE 6.1. *Continued*

	Executives–parties dimension	Federal–unitary dimension	Veto players	% prompt transposition new directives	% letters of formal notice	% reasoned opinions	% references to the ECJ
I							
Mean	1.97	−0.04	4.94	74.20	11.25	16.39	21.57
Range	0.90	0.10	3.52	57.80	12.24	20.53	27.14
IRL							
Mean	0.56	−0.50	2.01	76.34	6.67	6.36	6.72
Range	0.84	0.00	2.00	48.67	4.76	10.62	14.06
LUX							
Mean	−0.95	−0.74	2.00	75.81	6.14	6.41	8.42
Range	1.64	0.00	0.00	52.63	4.92	5.17	22.26
NL							
Mean	0.25	0.55	2.42	81.08	5.95	4.59	4.50
Range	1.09	0.00	1.00	40.05	6.04	5.10	11.36
P							
Mean	0.19	−0.78	1.65	69.80	7.74	8.22	3.65
Range	1.77	0.00	1.00	64.91	18.12	20.44	11.57
S							
Mean	−0.20	−0.72	1.00	63.60	4.51	1.65	0.52
Range	0.22	0.00	0.00	21.38	5.85	3.04	1.74
UK							
Mean	−1.62	−1.14	1.00	78.39	6.45	4.72	2.04
Range	0.78	0.00	0.00	59.45	3.99	5.66	5.21
EU							
Mean	0.00	0.00	2.40	75.30	7.60	7.58	7.79
Range	4.44	3.68	6.00	66.52	25.20	29.44	52.08

TABLE 6.2. *Institutional variables and national adaptation (correlation coefficients)*

		Adaptation	Transposition	Formal notice	Reasoned opinion	Reference to ECJ
Veto players	Pearson *r*	−0.291**	−0.127*	0.198**	0.275**	0.360**
	Sig.	0.000	0.039	0.003	0.000	0.000
Executive–parties dimension	Pearson *r*	−0.163*	−0.057	0.067	0.168**	0.253**
	Sig.	0.011	0.216	0.175	0.009	0.000
Federal–unitary dimension	Pearson *r*	−0.116	−0.038	0.107	0.133*	0.103
	Sig.	0.052	0.300	0.066	0.031	0.075

**$p < 0.01$ (A-tail).
*$p < 0.05$ (1-tail).

includes Denmark, the United Kingdom, and for somewhat different reasons, Austria, Sweden, and Finland.[8]

The last line in the table provides a comparison with the average figure for the European Union as a whole in the case of each variable taken into consideration. This enables us to evaluate the position of each country in terms of both institutional architecture and EU performance.

Turning to the first results of the bivariate analysis, Table 6.2 presents the correlation coefficients for all the independent and dependent variables.

The main finding of this basic elaboration is that institutions do matter for Europeanization, but not every institutional dimension is equally relevant and we do not find support for all of the hypotheses advanced in the previous paragraphs.

The correlation between the number of VPS and the degree of national adaptation is negative, as expected, and statistically highly significant ($r = -0.291$). The same variable is also significantly correlated to each of the original components of adaptation, and also displays an increasing explicatory value as the member country's infringement status worsens. If the number of veto players reveals a Pearson correlation of -0.127 with the levels of annual transposition of new directives, this value rises to 0.198 with the opening of

---

[8] Given the 'technical' time required for completion of the bureaucratic procedures in the case of infringement, during the initial years all the 'new entry' countries are called in front of the court much less than the others, and certainly less frequently than those member states displaying the same degree of transposition. Generally speaking, because of the unavoidable difficulties in getting used to the European Union, new entries have percentages of prompt transposition of new directives which stand out against their reputation as zealous Europeanists.

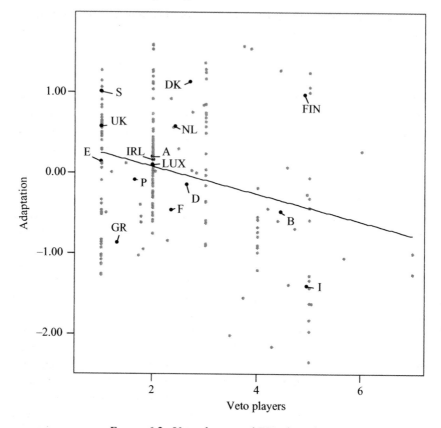

FIGURE 6.2. Veto players and EU adaptation

infringement proceedings, to 0.275 with the giving of reasoned opinion, and to 0.360 with the references to the European Court of Justice.

VPS is, among the three institutional variables, the one that performs best, and the OLS regression portrayed in Figure 6.2 helps in understanding its relationship with the adaptation index. An increase in the number of VPS corresponds to a greater misfit of national systems when faced with the process of Europeanization. The (grey) points represent each single country-year observation, whereas the average national values have been added (black points) in order to provide an overall idea of the EU performance of the different member states. Some of them, like Denmark or Finland, show a degree of adaptation which is clearly higher that the one predicted on the basis of VPS, while others, such as Greece or Italy, underperform in respect to their institutional pattern.

The role of VPS can be further intuitively appreciated if we consider the 'predictable' effect due to this variable on the EU performance of the extreme cases: the United Kingdom (or Spain or Sweden) with one veto player on one side, and Italy with almost five veto players on the other. Due to VPS, Italy has, 'on average' and each year, 4 per cent fewer transpositions, 1.5 per cent more letters of formal notice, 4 per cent more reasoned opinions, and 7.5 per cent more references to the European Court of Justice than the United Kingdom.

While the hypothesis regarding the dynamics of Europeanization generated by the application of Tsebelis' model has been confirmed, the same cannot be said of the propositions formulated on the basis of Lijphart's thinking. Actually, returning to the data presented in Table 6.2, consensual democracies appear *inversely* correlated to the degree of adaptation as far as the executives–parties dimension is concerned, and devoid of any statistically significant relation as for the federal–unitary dimension.

We have already noticed that the propositions formulated on the basis of the work of Tsebelis and Lijphart could be seen as rival hypotheses, thus it is no real surprise to see that consensual democracies display a significantly poorer performance than Westminster systems. The correlation between the executives–parties dimension and the adaptation index is -0.163 which, beyond having the wrong sign, is much lower than that recorded for VPS and even displays a slightly poorer level of significance.

Pearson correlations computed with respect to the shares of transposition and to the three stages of infringement procedures help to complete the overall picture. The consensual/majoritarian nature of a country's institutions does not seem to affect either its capacity to implement new directives in good time, or its skill in avoiding letters of formal notice. In the case of both of these variables, emphasis should be placed on the fact that the relation does not even satisfy the loosest of requirements of statistical significance, rather than on the correlation coefficient. This significance is achieved in the case of the last two of the original dependent variables, but the sign is always opposite to that initially forecast.

An even clearer argument could be submitted regarding Lijphart's second dimension. As far as the consensual institutional structures on the federal–unitary level are concerned, we can simply affirm the validity of the null hypothesis concerning the lack of influence of these structures upon the degree of national adaptation to the European Union. The last line of Table 6.2 clearly points to the fact that practically no correlation furnishes a sufficient guarantee of significance, thus implying that nothing can be said regarding the actual weight of such institutional variables.

To sum up then, the hypothesis whereby the consensual countries, due either to their intrinsic qualities or to a greater similarity to the Community's power-sharing structure, would appear to have some form of relative advantage, is to be considered disproved. With regard to the first dimension of consensualism, the majoritarian democracies perform better—and we are going to take a closer look at this now—whereas no significant effects can be seen on the second dimension.

Controlling the Hypotheses

In order that the relations we have just tested be considered sufficiently trustworthy, we need to check for the existence of spurious relations. Should the introduction of relevant control variables fail to modify the significance of the effect produced by the number of VPS or, at this point, by the majoritarian structure on EU adaptation, then we should consider their inclusion in a multivariate model.

One factor that could initially interfere with our institutional models is country size. This variable is important both from the political point of view, in terms of the weight a country may have in EU-level negotiations, and from the socio-economic point of view, given the greater difficulty in implementing Community policies in a large-scale, heterogeneous, and more complex context than would be the case in smaller countries.

In order to fully understand the multifaceted nature of this analytical dimension, a wide range of different indicators have been adopted. However, despite their only partially overlapping semantic character, they have all emerged as being inversely correlated in a statistically significant manner ($p < 0.01$) to the 'adaptation' index: with an increase in population ($r = -0.267$), in GNP ($r = -0.239$), in the percentage of votes in the Council ($r = -0.330$), in the percentage of MEPs ($r = -0.290$), and in Shapley's power index ($r = -0.310$), the fit with Community governance diminishes. Clearly, internal causes during the implementation phase are stronger than those associated with greater influence during the upward phase of decision making in determining a country's degree of adaptation to the challenge of Europeanization.

Even recent membership of the European Union can be seen to play a certain role in determining Community fit, and as such should not be underestimated. In theory, during the period covered by the present analysis, the countries that should have experienced significant problems of acclimatization are Spain and Portugal (during the years after 1986), together with Austria, Sweden, and Finland (after 1995). However, there are political and technical reasons why both length of EU membership ($r = -0.302$) and the dummy variable built upon it in order to distinguish the older member countries from the more recent ones ($r = -0.318$), are negatively correlated to the degree of adaptation to the Union ($p < 0.01$). In fact, for the above-mentioned group of countries, the early years of membership proved to be relatively unproblematic, whereas the older members were the ones who experienced greater difficulty.

Recently, the prerequisites required of new entrants have been raised, and the last wave of new entries was constituted by countries who, as a result of their prior existence within the European economic space, already largely reflected the *acquis communautaire*. On the one hand, national governments had prepared beforehand for entry to the European Union in order to respect their new institutional obligations, and on the other hand, they wished to behave correctly from the very outset in order to demonstrate their right to belong to the 'European Club'. Moreover, the Commission itself often grants a form of transition period to countries coming into the European Union for the first time (Börzel 2001), thus acknowledging their initial difficulty in getting used to the new setting. Then, as we have already mentioned, there are certain technical terms for carrying out the various stages of infringement procedures, which similarly help to improve the statistical performance of the various countries during their first years of membership.[9]

Finally, we need to check our institutional hypotheses for two other variables which came to light during an earlier exploratory analysis: the effective number of political parties, and government's control over agenda setting. The first of these two is already included in the calculation of the first dimension of consensual democracy as proposed by Lijphart, but there is an important logical reason for checking it nonetheless. We could hypothesize, in fact, that the inverse relationship between the number of VPS and adaptation results from the considerable number of political parties present in parliament, without the variable regarding government or institutional actors with veto powers having any separate explicatory value. In fact, the actual number of parties is closely linked to all the independent variables we have used here ($r = 0.795$ with VPS, $r = 0.734$ with Lijphart's executives–parties dimension), this increasing the risk of spurious relations.

The second variable, measured by Döring (1995) using a special index,[10] also exhibits a close relationship with the proposed institutional models ($r = 0.334$ with VPS, $r = 0.398$ with Lijphart's first dimension), and is significantly associated with all measurements of adaptation. The idea underlying its inclusion is that the fit with European politics depends not so much on the majoritarian character of a democracy, nor on the number of political parties in government, but on the autonomy and strength of the latter in getting parliament

---

[9] In truth, if we break down the adaptation index into its original components, recent entry can be seen to be inversely correlated to the percentage of transposed directives, thus suggesting the existence of above-average delays for the new-entry nations. Such delays do not result, however, in a proportionately high share of infringement proceedings, given both the technical delays we have mentioned, and the capacity of the countries themselves to recoup their initial failings before they become of judicial interest to the European Commission.

[10] See the appendix for further specifications.

TABLE 6.3. *Partial correlations: national adaptation and institutional variables*

		Adaptation	Transposition	Formal notice	Reasoned opinion	Reference to ECJ
Veto players	Partial r	−0.341**	−0.172**	0.344**	0.320**	0.281**
	Sig.	0.000	0.009	0.000	0.000	0.000
Executive-parties dimension	Partial r	−0.224**	−0.077	0.221**	0.252**	0.198**
	Sig.	0.001	0.146	0.001	0.000	0.003

Controlling for recent entry, Shapley index, effective number of parties, and agenda-setting power.
**$p < 0.01$ (1-tail).

to accept its own priorities and agenda, both of which are defined in part as a result of agreements signed within the EU arena.

Table 6.3 shows the partial correlations between the adaptation index and the institutional variables defined by the two opposing models, controlling for the effect of all the above-mentioned factors: recent entry to the European Union, the size of a country in the form of Shapley's index of power, the effective number of political parties, and the agenda-setting power of the government. None of the original correlation coefficients has been affected to any degree by such checks, thus reassuring us about the reliability of the research results that have emerged so far, the absence of any spurious relations, and the validity of our institutional explanation. Those democracies with few VPS have adapted better to the European political arena ($r = -0.341$), whereas, once again, it is the majoritarian democracies rather than the consensual ones who are seen to perform better ($r = -0.224$ with regard to Lijphart's first dimension).

The picture does not change if we use, as dependent variables, the original measures concerning implementation of new directives and national shares of infringement recorded at various stages of proceedings. However, we can see that the number of VPS systematically provides a better explanation than the Westminster character of a political system, and the correlation between the latter and the percentage of new directives transposed is not statistically significant ($p > 0.05$).

Despite this, we cannot be sure at present which of the two institutional models—veto players or majoritarian democracy—works better. The only way to resolve this conundrum is to check whether, given a certain effect of one variable, the other variable becomes less significant or not. In other words, we need to carry out a further, parallel check by means of partial correlations.

TABLE 6.4. *Partial correlations: veto players or majoritarian democracy?*

		Adaptation
Veto players[a]	Partial *r*	−0.249**
	Sig.	0.000
Executive–parties dimension[b]	Partial *r*	0.052
	Sig.	0.235

[a] Controlling for executive–parties dimension.
[b] Controlling for veto players.
**$p < 0.01$ (1-tail).

Table 6.4 does just this. While the majoritarian nature of a democracy is incapable of significantly reducing the separate effect of the number of VPS on EU adaptation and, more importantly, it does not affect the statistical significance of the correlation at all, the exact opposite is true when the latter variable controls the explicatory potential of Lijphart's executives-parties dimension. In this case, the correlation approximates to zero, and the values of *p* rise well above acceptable levels. In other words, our figures enable us to further discriminate between two, albeit congruent, hypotheses, thus showing the explicatory superiority in this field of the concept of veto player over that of the majoritarian character of a political system.

To What Degree do Institutions Count?

Having positively answered the question regarding the role of institutions, it is now possible to bring our analysis one step further and propose a parsimonious model aimed at investigating *to what extent*—and not just *whether*—institutional variables count. We then built a stepwise multiple regression designed to illustrate the degree of adaptation starting from those factors that have been the most promising so far: that is, the number of veto players, the effective number of political parties, Shapley's power index, the index of control over agenda setting exercised by the executive, and recent entry into the European Union.

It is important to stress the fact that, apart from the year of entry, the whole model rests upon institutional variables, since our aim here is not that of explaining adaptation per se, but the importance of institutions in it.

Table 6.5 shows the main results of this elaboration, with, following the rows, the five models incrementally generated by adding the variable with the greatest explicatory value and, in the columns, the respective standardized

TABLE 6.5. *An institutional model (stepwise regression)*

Model	Variables	Stand. coefficients (beta)	Sig. t	Adjusted R^2
1	Recent entry	0.318	0.000	0.096
2	Recent entry	0.301	0.000	0.166
	Veto players	−0.272	0.000	
3	Recent entry	0.292	0.000	0.233
	Veto players	−0.621	0.000	
	Effective n of parties	0.438	0.000	
4	Recent entry	0.264	0.000	0.267
	Veto players	−0.541	0.000	
	Effective n of parties	0.341	0.001	
	Shapley index	−0.202	0.002	
5	Recent entry	0.235	0.000	0.295
	Veto players	−0.515	0.000	
	Effective n of parties	0.222	0.047	
	Shapley index	−0.203	0.002	
	Agenda-setting power	0.204	0.004	

regression coefficients (beta), the estimators' values of significance (Sig. t), and the explained variance of the model (adjusted R^2).

None of the models features variables with any problems of significance. Apart from the actual number of political parties in the last model, the stringent $p < 0.01$ standard is always adhered to. The first variable to be included by the stepwise regression is recent entry to the European Union. This choice is mainly due to the technical reasons we explained in the previous section, although the separate explicatory potential of this variable is partially reabsorbed into subsequent models. The number of VPS comes to the fore at once as a pivotal factor within this multivariate analysis. It is already present in model 2, where it immediately takes on a central role, and is also seen to be the variable that most affects the degree of adaptation in the full model. In fact, with the inclusion of the number of parties as well, its Beta value rises considerably, and in the end stands at double the standardized coefficients for all the other variables. The signs of the latter are those mentioned in the previous pages: adaptation decreases with an increase in the number of VPS and in the size of the country, whereas it rises with recent entry into the European Union, with the executive's control over agenda setting, and, surprisingly enough, with the actual number of parties. Evidently, once having purged the concept of consensual democracy of those factors pertaining to the nature and domination of the executive, party pluralism itself does not either hinder or slow the process of Europeanization.

As far as the explained variance is concerned, the full model uses just five variables—only three of which are the result of an explicit internal choice as such—to explain about 30 per cent of the empirically observed adaptation (adjusted $R^2 = 0.295$). While it may be true that even more parsimonious models also offer comforting results in terms of explained variance, the significance of the coefficients of all variables, as well as the worth of the full model when also applied to individual original dependent variables—that is, the levels of transposition rather than reasoned opinion or appeals to the European Court of Justice[11]—would suggest that it is not worth sacrificing three points of variance in order to improve the parsimonious style of the causal links.

An R^2 equal to the one we found may be a lot or little, according to the point of view. For an analysis which has been purposely limited to macro-institutional variables, we think it is a fairly good result. If, on the other hand, one looks at things from a prescriptive point of view, then things are very different. It is of course true that the degree of adaptation to the European Union may be influenced by constitutional or para-constitutional modifications designed to reduce the number of veto players, but this does not appear to be the easiest route to take. On the one hand, it would involve complicated reforms that prove difficult to adopt, and the outcome of which cannot always be kept under perfect control by institutional engineering. On the other hand, a large share of variance still remains unexplained and, at the same time, a similar share of adaptation to the European Union could be produced following other reform strategies. Those countries that invariably lie below the regression line could rise above it thanks to small-scale organizational and policy reforms, rather than counting on improving their degree of domestic Europeanization as a result of shifts along the axes guaranteed by complicated large-scale constitutional reforms.

In our opinion, the organizational and micro-institutional approach is the right one to adopt, even in order to increase the forecasting capacity of this kind of analysis. Without blindly pursuing the idea of an absolute best fit, frantically collecting political, socio-economic, demographic, and other variables, it is possible to extend our type of investigation to a new set of institutional variables linked not to the general characteristics of national political systems as has been done so far, but to those structures specifically designed for the administration of a nation's European affairs (Kassim *et al.* 2000, 2001). For example, structures such as those present within government (an ad hoc

---

[11] The multiple regressions elaborated in order to explain the national quota of infringements at the different steps are always statistically consistent ($p < 0.01$), and VPS is constantly the pivotal variable. The amount of explained variance is 25.0% for the letters of formal notice, 30.4% for the reasoned opinions, and 29.2% for the referrals to the European Court of Justice. Retaining the role of VPS, the only model which has a slightly poorer level of statistical consistency ($p < 0.05$) is the one explaining the more hectic level of yearly transpositions, in which the variables other than VPS loose some significance.

EU Ministry vs. special offices in each department); the role of parliament and parliamentary commissions during the ascendant and descendent stages of EU decision-making processes (democratic ties binding the executive vs. the greatest possible freedom for government); the organization and equipping of permanent representatives in Brussels; the integration of subnational levels, and so forth. This appears to be the way forward if we wish to increase the explicatory potential of institutional models, and to pave the way for medium-term reforms: more concrete, specific, and feasible policies devoid of potentially undesirable side effects.

Conclusions

Our analysis has demonstrated that domestic institutions influence the way in which national political systems relate themselves to the European Union and adapt their normative framework to the process of Europeanization. A low number of veto points (Immergut 1992) facilitates this process, by reducing the internal decision-making costs and favouring the flexibility and promptness of the policy-making system. On the other hand, institutional isomorphism and consensual style do not facilitate the interaction between the national and the European level.

The comparative analysis helped us to further discriminate between different types of 'hard-headed' democracies, recognizing the explicative potential of the concept of VPS vis-à-vis that of a majoritarian political system.

If institutions do count, they don't necessarily make a lot of difference. It is possible to conceive a whole series of variables that affect the way in which a member state participates and adapts to EU governance. For instance, we should not forget the potential existence of informal VPS,[12] like trade unions, entrepreneurial associations, regional governments, and courts, whose preferences and traditional rules of behaviour may conflict with the process of Europeanization and aggravate the political misfit of a member state. Even the organization and factual implementation of foreign policy, as well as the European commitment of a national government, impact on these matters, and the case studies presented in this volume offer a clear picture of the effect of policy-specific factors.

However, these explanations, once acknowledged their systematic contribution, are not rival hypotheses, but contribute to a better understanding of the Europeanization process.

---

[12] Birchfield and Crepaz (1998), in order to conjugate empirical findings from the consensual and VPS tradition, posit a difference between collective and competitive veto players.

Appendix

The pooled dataset contains annual independent observations for the fifteen EU member states in the 1986–2000 period. In order to elaborate Lijphart's indexes of consensualism, we have collected, standardized, and, if necessary, weighted for shorter time spans, data regarding the effective number of parties (with the usual Laakso and Taagepera index), the percentage of time during which one-party or minimum-winning governments have ruled, the duration of the executives, the electoral disproportionality (using Gallagher index), the degree of pluralism in the representation of interests (according to Siaroff 1999), the indexes of federalism, bicameralism, constitutional rigidity, judicial review, and central banks' independence (Lijphart 1999). At the same time we have calculated the number of partisan and institutional VPS according to the rules proposed by Tsebelis (2002): apart from the parties belonging to the government coalition we had to include, in the case of Germany, the Bundesrat when it was ruled by a different majority from that supporting the executive and, for Portugal, the President when he/she did not belong to the governing parliamentary majority.

The adaptation index has been computed starting from the standardized and deseasonalized national quota of infringement proceedings at the three levels, and from the percentage of transpositions calculated exclusively from the total amount of directives expiring each year. In this manner, it has been possible to avoid from the start the problems of self-correlation which are typical of pooled time series.

As for control variables, we have tested different social, economic, and political indices related to the 'size' of a country: its population, Gross National Product, percentage of Euro-MPs, number of Council votes in case of qualified majority, and the Shapley-Shubik index of power calculated from the weighting of votes in the Council (Nurmi and Meskanen 1999). We have used the index of executive control of the agenda-setting proposed by Döring (1995), elaborated upon several dimensions pertaining to the statutory instruments in the hand of governments vis-à-vis the parliament, in order to control for its predominance over the legislature in the policy making. Finally we have introduced the length of EU membership, subsequently recoded as a dichotomic variable (more or less than five years), given the likely difficulties of newcomers in becoming familiar with the rules and routines of the European Union.

REFERENCES

Beck, N. and Katz, J. (1995). 'What to do (and not to do) with Time-Series Cross-Section Data', *The American Political Science Review* 89(3): 634–47.

Birchfield, V. and Crepaz, M. (1998). 'The Impact of Constitutional Structures and Collective and Competitive Veto Points on Income Inequality in Industrialized Democracies', *European Journal of Political Research* 34: 175–200.

Börzel, T. (1999). 'Towards Convergence in Europe? Institutional Adaptation to Europeanization in Germany and Spain', *Journal of Common Market Studies* 37(4): 573–96.

Börzel, T. (2001). 'Non-compliance in the European Union: Pathology or Statistical Artifact?', *Journal of European Public Policy* 8(5): 803–24.

—— (2002). 'Member State Responses to Europeanization', *Journal of Common Market Studies* 40(2): 193–214.

Bulmer, S. (1997). 'Shaping the Rules? The Constitutive Politics of the European Union and German Power', in P. J. Katzenstein (ed.), *Tamed Power. Germany in Europe* (Ithaca: Cornell U.P.), 49–79.

Collier, D. (1993). 'The Comparative Method', in A. W. Finifter (ed.), *Political Science: The State of the Discipline* (Washington: The American Political Science Association).

Conzelmann, T. (1998). 'Europeanization of Regional Development Policies? Linking the Multi-level Governance Approach with Theories of Policy Learning and Policy Change', *EIOP Paper* 2(4).

Cowles, M. G., Caporaso, J., and Risse, T. (2001). *Transforming Europe. Europeanization and Domestic Change* (Ithaca: Cornell University Press).

Döring, H. (ed.) (1995). *Parliaments and Majority Rule in Western Europe* (New York: St. Martin Press).

Falkner, G. (2001). 'Policy Networks in a Multi-Level System: Convergence Towards Moderate Diversity?', in K. H. Goetz and S. Hix (eds), *Europeanised Politics? European Integration and National Political Systems* (London: Frank Cass), 94–120.

Giuliani, M. (1996). 'Italy', in D. Rometsch and W. Wessels (eds), *The European Union and Member States. Towards Institutional Fusion?* (Manchester: Manchester University Press), 105–33.

Haverland, M. (2000). 'National Adaptation to European Integration: The Importance of Institutional Veto Points', *Journal of Public Policy* 20(1): 83–103.

Héritier, A. (2001). 'Differential Europe: National Administrative Responses to Community Policy', in Cowles, Caporaso, and Risse (eds), (2001: 44–59).

Immergut, E. (1992). 'The Rules of the Game: The Logic of the Health Policy-making in France, Switzerland, and Sweden', in S. Steinmo *et al.* (eds), *Structuring Politics. Historical Institutionalism in Comparative Analysis* (Cambridge: Cambridge University Press), 57–89.

Kassim, H. *et al.* (eds) (2000). *The National Coordination of EU Policy: The Domestic Level* (Oxford: Oxford University Press).

—— (eds) (2001). *The National Coordination of EU Policy: The European Level* (Oxford: Oxford University Press).

Katzenstein, P. J. (1997). 'United Germany in an Integrating Europe', in P. J. Katzenstein (ed.), *Tamed Power. Germany in Europe* (Ithaca: Cornell University Press), 1–48.

Kittel, B. (1999). 'Sense and Sensitivity in Pooled Analysis of Political Data', *European Journal of Political Research* 35: 225–53.

Knill, C. and Lehmkuhl, D. (1999). 'How Europe Matters. Different Mechanism of Europeanization', *EIOP Paper* 3(7).

Ladrech, R. (1994). 'Europeanization of Domestic Politics and Institutions. The Case of France', *Journal of Common Market Studies* 32(1): 69–88.

Lampinen, R. and Uusikylä, P. (1998). 'Implementation Deficit. Why Member States do non Comply with EU Directives?', *Scandinavian Political Studies* 21(3): 231–51.

Lijphart, A. (1971). 'Comparative Politics and Comparative Method', *American Political Science Review* 65: 682–93.

——(1999). *Patterns of Democracy. Government Forms and Performance in Thirty-Six Countries* (New Haven: Yale University Press).

Mbaye, H. A. D. (2001). 'Why National States Comply with Supranational Law', *European Union Politics* 2(3): 259–81.

Mendrinou, M. (1996). 'Non-compliance and the European Commission's Role in Integration', *Journal of European Public Policy* 3(1): 1–22.

Nurmi, H. and Meskanen, T. (1999). 'A Priori Power Measures and the Institutions of the European Union', *European Journal of Political Research* 35: 161–79.

Olsen, J. (1995). 'European Challenges of the Nation-State', *ARENA Working Paper* 14.

——(1996). 'Europeanization and Nation-State Dynamics', in S. Gustavsson and L. Levin (eds), *The Future of the Nation-State* (Stockholm: Nerenius and Santérus Publishers).

——(2002). 'The Many Faces of Europeanization', *ARENA Working Paper* 2.

Schmidt, V. (1997). 'European Integration and Democracy: The Differences Among Member States', *Journal of European Public Policy* 4(1): 128–45.

——(1999). 'National Patterns of Governance Under Siege: The Impact of European Integration', in B. Kohler-Koch and R. Eising (eds), *The Transformation of Governance in the European Union* (London: Routledge), 155–72.

——(2001). 'Europeanization and the Mechanics of Economic Policy Adjustment', *EIOP Paper* 5(6).

Siaroff, A. (1999). 'Corporatism in 24 Industrial Democracies', *European Journal of Political Research* 36: 175–205.

Tsebelis, G. (1995). 'Veto Players and Law Production in Parliamentary Democracies', in H. Döring (ed.) (1995: 83–111).

——(1999). 'Veto Payers and Law Production in Parliamentary Democracies: An Empirical Analysis', *American Political Science Review* 93(3): 591–607.

——(2002). *Veto Players: How Political Institutions Work* (Princeton: Princeton University Press).

Weaver, R. K. and Rockman, B. A. (eds) (1993). *Do Institutions Matter? Government Capabilities in the United States and Abroad* (Washington: The Brookings Institution).

III

Europeanization and Policy Analysis

7

Europeanization as Interpretation, Translation, and Editing of Public Policies

ULRIKA MÖRTH

Introduction

In this chapter it is argued that *Europeanization* is a process of institutionalization in which new rules and new ways of thinking evolve. Within these new institutional and ideational structures a policy will change and take new forms. As Risse and Börzel write in their chapter on sociological institutionalism, 'Collective understandings and intersubjective meaning structures strongly influence the way actors define their goals and what they perceive as rational action'. By arguing that *Europeanization* is a process of institutionalization I have brought the concept to 'normal' political science as Radaelli discusses in his chapter. *Europeanization* can thus be studied as the emergence of new rules of the game that will structure the policy processes at the European level and the domestic level. A more relevant term than *Europeanization* is perhaps EU-ization since most of our empirical studies on *Europeanization* concern politics within the European Union. It is, however, difficult to imagine that there are European political processes and issues that cannot be linked to the European Union.

The multilevel governance of the European Union and the federal components of the political system suggest that the EU level and national levels are interlinked (cf. Nicolaides and Howse 2001). In the sociological institutionalist literature, however, we do not get any guidance on how political processes and levels interact. We need, therefore, to combine the sociological institutionalist notion of the emergence of rules and norms with the international relations (IR) literature on the relationship between the state and its external environment. Three analytical perspectives can be discerned in that literature. The first perspective is the realist tradition that suggests that a state's domestic policy is affected by events in the international system (Waltz 1979). A reversed causal relationship has been suggested by the second analytical perspective—the second image reversed literature (Gourevitch 1986). These two perspectives entail an analytical separation between what goes on inside a state and what goes on outside the state. This notion has been criticized by the literature of the third perspective that proposes that states are porous in a globalized world and that the borders between the internal and external processes of the state are diffuse (Rosenau 1990; Ruggie 1993, 1998a; see also Walker 1993).

This IR-oriented debate has now become part of the European Union and European-oriented literature in the shape of the concept of *Europeanization*. The overall question in this literature is how we should analyse the relationship between the European Union and its member states. Is it feasible to make an analytical distinction between what goes on at the EU level, on the one hand, and what goes on in the member states, on the other hand? Or should these two processes be linked to each other in an effort to present an analytical framework that takes into account the interactions between the two processes? I believe that we have very little to gain in our effort to study *Europeanization* if we do not allow our analytical tools to comprise the empirical complexity that exists between the European Union and the member states.

According to a sociological institutionalist perspective, combined with the IR notion of a porous state, *Europeanization* entails that states take part in the formation of new norms and rules at the EU level. States participate in the informal and formal EU policy-making processes and in the legalization processes from its early start in the Commission, through the decisions in the Council and the specifications within the comitology. Héritier argues that the national and European policy processes can be studied as parallel processes that sometimes cross each other (Héritier 2001). How they are linked to each other is an empirical question, and by studying various types of cases of *Europeanization* we can develop a theoretical framework on how the two levels interact.

A perspective that focuses on a close interaction between the EU level and the domestic level means that the source of change cannot easily be determined. I agree with Kohler-Koch's argument that impact studies on *Europeanization* may miss important transformative processes since these studies define the dependent variable in very narrow terms. Another problem with impact studies is the fact that hard law is seldom clear and without multiple interpretations. This does not necessarily mean that there are no pressures for domestic change (Green Cowles *et al.* 2001), but that it is often unclear what kind of changes are regarded as necessary to adjust to the European Union. EU policies and legalizations do not travel as ready-made packages. This is even more so in cases of 'horizontal' *Europeanization*, that is, framework directives and soft law that seem to have increased in importance in the European Union during recent years. European authority is not exclusively based on hierarchical supranational decision making and upon coercive rules within the community pillar. It can also consist of less binding rules and other loose intergovernmental agreements. Soft law is often defined in terms of the legal form of the rule, that is the non-binding rule. Soft law can also be defined in terms of content, that is a rule that is legally binding but loose in content (Shelton 2001). The empirical illustrations in this chapter are based on the ongoing formation of European cooperation on defence equipment. The analysis focuses on the institutionalization of the rules for the European cooperation on defence equipment and how these rules are edited at the domestic level. Students of European integration seldom analyse *Europeanization* in other policy areas than those that belong to the first pillar of the European Union in which hard law dominates. This is unfortunate since *this process* takes place within other policy areas within the second pillar and within policy areas that are more loosely linked to the European Union and its legal framework. The next section elaborates on the concept of institutionalization and how it can be useful in empirical research on *Europeanization*.

Institutionalization

According to the neoinstitutionalist turn in political science during the last decade, institutions are social phenomena that can create stable patterns of collective and individual behaviour (Premfors 2001; see also Peters 1999). Rules, procedures, and certain structures can constrain and/or facilitate actors' behaviour, but they can also form actors' preferences and interests. There is thus a wide array of social phenomena that can be called institutions and they can have different impacts on collective and individual behaviour. In the sociological institutionalism approach institutions take on a rule-like status in social thought and action (March and Olsen 1989; Meyer and Rowan 1991; Powell and DiMaggio 1991). Other approaches, such as rational-choice institutionalism and historical institutionalism, do not require a taken for granted status in order to define something as an institution (Shepsle 1989; North 1990; Thelen and Steinmo 1992). In the political world there are very few institutions that can be regarded as taken for granted in the sense that they are not contested. However, there are rules that are less contested than others and which therefore to a large extent influence individual and collective behaviour. How these rules become more or less taken for granted is a process that can vary over time. We should therefore search for processes of institutionalization instead of trying to identify fixed static institutions. In the context of EU politics these processes of institutionalization can be regarded as processes of *Europeanization* (cf. Stone Sweet *et al.* 2001).

I make a distinction between regulative rules—legal and other concrete rules—and constitutive rules which 'define the set of practices that make up a particular class of consciously organized social activity—that is, to say, they specify what counts as that activity' (Ruggie 1998*b*: 871; cf. Searle 1995; Ruggie 1998*a*). This kind of identity meta rule making can thus be defined as the construction of constitutive rules without which the regulative rules cannot take effect. Regulative rules are rather easily identified since they concern legal rules, for instance the treaties and other legal rules. They can also be non-coercive rules, soft law, that is, rules that have no legally binding force but that can have practical effects (Shaw 1996). By constitutive rules I mean rules that in a fundamental way determine how an issue is to be interpreted. Such rules are of course not easily separated from regulative rules, but various legal articles in the EU treaties are based on different ideas of the European Union as a would-be polity. Hence, different rules—regulative and constitutive— determine how an issue is labelled and framed. Frame competition implies that the contending parties hold different ideas of the integration process. A fundamental ideational division in European politics is, for instance, if issues should be handled according to the Community method (supranational decision making) or if they should be decided with unanimity (intergovernmental decision making).

According to a sociological institutional perspective, actors follow rules. I would also argue that actors influence the rules of the game. *Europeanization* takes shape in a process in which the actors determine what counts as activity. The two rationalitities and logics—the logic of consequentialism and the logic of appropriateness—are both relevant in order to study the process of *Europeanization* (cf. Green Cowles *et al.* 2001). Thus, 'actors both calculate consequences and follow rules' (cf. March and Olsen 1998; Fierke and Wiener 1999; Laegreid and Roness 1999: 308; Marcussen *et al.* 1999).

What then are the possible outcomes of a process of *Europeanization*? According to my sociological institutionalist approach I would expect to find the construction of rules of the game, especially constitutive rules. Since these rules are wide in scope, especially the constitutive rules, they are interpreted and edited by national actors so that they fit into the domestic political context. Drawing from a literature on organizational change and reform, it is argued that states and other organizations follow and imitate each other but that there is room for domestic interpretation, editing, and translation. Institutional isomorphism does not necessarily result in similarity in every aspect of policy, legal, organizational changes, etc. The mechanical transfer model has been questioned by students of organizational studies who have analysed the diffusion process of organizational reforms (Brunsson and Olsen 1993; Strang and Meyer 1994; Czarniawska and Sevon 1996). These studies have found that the ideas on organizational reforms are part of a continuous editing process. What is to be imitated is not a given phenomenon. 'I will see imitation as a process in which something is created and transformed by chains of translators' (Sevon 1996: 51). Projects initiated at the European level create a negotiation space and interpretative flexibility that are negotiated at the domestic level (cf. Law and Callon 1992). The governments need room for manoeuvre in order to get legitimacy in the domestic political process for the decisions made at the EU level. The trick is to maintain some ambiguity in the agreements, laws, etc. at the EU level, while at the same time being able to move forward in the integration process (Mörth 2000).

The crucial question is of course what we mean by similarity and differences, when students of *Europeanization* argue that Europe matters differently in the various EU member states (Green Cowles *et al.* 2001; Héritier *et al.* 2001). We have to decide whether the reforms in a country implement an EU directive or a guideline in a way that is similar to or different from other countries and if the implementation is in line with the EU policy and legalization. This can be decided from a legal point of view or based on a criterion that takes into account a process of domestic editing. A legal criterion would then be that the reforms are more or less identical in terms of the legal framework. Similarity thus means that countries must establish the same legal framework to conduct and implement a similar policy. A criterion built on domestic editing suggests that if rules, especially constitutive, are translated into a domestic context in different EU member states, we have a case of similarity. An important methodological question is of course how we can identify the constitutive rules that are edited at the domestic level. The answer to that problem is that we need to analyse the rule-making activities at the European Union and European level. We should, however, be aware that constitutive rules are not necessarily constructed in a sequential fashion. One important feature in EU politics is that political processes at the European Union and domestic levels have a tendency to occur at the same time (Ekengren 1999). It is therefore essential to study the two levels simultaneously and to establish to what extent the rules are constructed between the European Union/European and the domestic levels. One hypothesis is that the more the government and other domestic actors are involved in the rule making process at the European Union/European level, the less effort they have to put into the domestic editing.

The criterion on domestic editing does not necessarily explain why Europe matters differently in various states. However, it can help us to identify the mechanisms behind various forms that *Europeanization* takes in different countries within the same policy area. An operationalization of the concept of *Europeanization* that focuses on the construction of constitutive rules and domestic editing of these rules can discover important processes of ideational similarity between countries, even though they adapt very differently to the European Union. Governments take part in EU decision making on general rules that will guide them in the domestic editing process. Directives on market deregulations and other politically sensitive issues often leave room for domestic interpretation of how to realize the legislation (Héritier 1999).

The following section discusses how new rules of the game have evolved on how to cooperate in Europe on defence equipment. We then move on to study in what ways these rules have been edited to fit into the domestic contexts of Sweden, France, and the United Kingdom.

Europeanization and Defence Equipment

Two Projects and One Issue

Defence equipment is a cross-pillar issue since it concerns both an important building block in the process towards a European defence policy and a crucial power instrument in the race for technological competitiveness in relation to the United States. The process of *Europeanization*, to decide on the rules of the game for this cooperation, has therefore involved multiple actors from different paths in the European integration process. Indeed, the issue of defence equipment has been handled and conceptualized within the political economy project developed through the European Union, and the defence and security project, organized through NATO and the WEU, and recently through the European Union. Various actors within the first and second pillars of the European Union have claimed right of definition and categorization of the issue of defence equipment. Parts of the Commission have argued that the issue of defence equipment belongs to the Community pillar whereas the EU governments have argued that the issue is a building block in the EU's emerging defence policy within its second pillar. Important questions are at stake that explain a situation with competing conceptualizations on the issue of defence equipment. Should European cooperation on defence equipment be designed from a market and competition perspective, or is it the needs and policy formulations on the formation of a European defence policy that should determine such a cooperation?

The issue of defence equipment activates different questions and actors. The Commission is a strong actor in the first pillar, whereas the European Council and the Council are the crucial actors in the second pillar. This is so because the issue belongs to different political and ideational contexts in European politics. The regulative rules within the first pillar concern market-making activities, for instance competition and state aid rules. An important and contested regulative rule is Article 296 (formerly Article 223) in the Treaty of European Union. It allows governments to exempt defence firms from EU rules on mergers, monopolies, and procurement. According to the Commission, some member states have interpreted this Article broadly with the result that the EU industry has lost ground to the US industry. It has therefore proposed a stricter interpretation of the Article. Some parts of the Commission have even argued that the defence industry sector should gradually be incorporated into the EU's competition policy and state-aid regulations (Mörth 2001). Communications from the Commission in the early and mid-1990s show that it sees a clear tension and competition between a market-making perspective and a security-oriented perspective on the issue of defence equipment (see, for instance, European Commission 1996, COM (96), 10). The constitutive rule in the market project is that issues within the first pillar should be handled according to a supranational decision-making process, since these issues concern Europe's economic and technological competitiveness vis-à-vis the United States. The underlying logic behind this rule is the increasing economic and technological interdependence between states that necessitates a European strategy towards the United States. The dynamics behind the need to form strong European defence companies, and to create a European defence equipment market, is thus to be found in the ongoing technological and industrial internationalization of technology. The prime issue within the market project and the first pillar is to strengthen Europe's technological and economic capacity.

An important regulative rule in the second pillar is Article 17 (formerly J.7) of the Amsterdam Treaty, which declares that the 'progressive framing of a common defence policy will be supported, as Member States consider appropriate, by cooperation between them in the field of armaments' (Article 17.1). Thus, an intergovernmental way (i.e. within the second pillar) of handling the issue of defence equipment is emphasized. There is a political reluctance from the European Council and the Council of Ministers to give the European Commission and the community pillar a strong role on the issue of defence equipment. The constitutive rule in the defence project is the general notion that defence issues should be dealt with in an intergovernmental way since these issues concern national sovereignty. Traditional security, that is, security expressed in terms of military threats and power, is based on the logic of anarchy, which necessitates that states control defence issues. The political ambition to create a European capacity to handle military crises—and to create a European actorness on defence—is combined with an intergovernmental decision-making process. The driving force behind the need to form such an actor capacity is the changing security situation after the end of the Cold War.

New Rules of the Game

In November 1997 the European Commission presented a new way to conceptualize the issue of defence equipment and how a more complex frame could be handled in practice. The communication (COM (97), 583 final)—'The European Aerospace Industry: Meeting the Global Challenge'—was related to the communication in 1996 on the restructuring of the defence industry (COM (96), 10, see also COM (90) 556 final and COM (92) 164 final). A memorandum with the same title had been presented earlier, in October 1997, by the two commissioners, Hans van den Broek (external relations) and Martin Bangemann (industrial affairs). The memorandum and communication from 1997 are very clear on the dual nature of the defence industry and do not pursue one perspective as previous communications did. They discuss a combined community and CFSP perspective on the issue of defence equipment. 'An integrated European market for defence products must be set up using a combination of all the instruments at the Union's disposal: Community and Common Foreign and Security Policy, legislative and non-legislative instruments' (Com (96) 10: 2). The defence industry is both a 'major means of production and essential to foreign and security policy. Any action by the European Union has to take this dual nature into account, if necessary by adapting the resources within the Community's jurisdiction' (ibid.: 5). The Commission suggests that Article 296 should be interpreted restrictively and that materials for the defence sector should be divided into three categories. This would mean that only sensitive goods—'highly sensitive goods' (such as nuclear)—would be covered by Article 296 (ibid.).

The earlier tension between a market and a defence frame in the communication from January 1996 is clearly toned down. The two DGs, III (Enterprise) and DG IA (Foreign and security policy), seem to have divided the issue in a more constructive work-sharing arrangement than was the case in the earlier communications (Mörth 2000). The new communication from November 1997 consists of two parts. The first part discusses a proposal for a common position on drawing up a European defence equipment policy with special emphasis on the creation of intracommunity transfers, public procurement, and common customs arrangements. The legal basis for this common proposition is Article J.2 in the Treaty on European Union (second pillar of the EU).[1]

The second part presents an action plan for defence-related industries, that is, what the Commission considers to be necessary measures 'to ensure progress towards a true European market for defence products' (COM (97) 583: 5). Fourteen actions are presented: intracommunity transfers, a European company statute, public procurement, RTD, standardization, customs duties, innovation-transfer of technology and SMEs, competition policy, exports-dual-use goods and conventional armaments, structural funds, indirect taxation-direct taxation, principles for market access, benchmarking, enlargement. The communication clearly entails a combination of the first- and second-pillar instruments. A European defence equipment policy would be linked to Community policies (industry, trade, customs, the regions, competition, innovation, and research) and CFSP measures—it would be a 'pillar one and a half'.

---

[1] The new number is 12 in the consolidated Amsterdam Treaty.

The Council has been reluctant to discuss the communications on the restructuration of the European defence industry and the question of how to create a European defence equipment market (Mörth 2001). The political handling has instead taken place between a limited number of governments in a cooperative arrangement formally outside the European Union. In a statement issued by six European governments in 1998 it was declared that the 'Ministers consider that a strong, competitive, and efficient defence industry is a key element of European security and identity as well as of the European scientific and technological base . . . Participation in the European armaments base should be balanced and should reflect the principle of interdependence' (Joint Statement of 20 April 1998 by the six LoI defence ministers). The political initiative was an important part of the so-called Letter of Intent (LoI) that was signed in the summer of 1998, which aimed to enhance the creation of Transnational Defence Companies. The founding governments of the LoI, France, Germany, and the United Kingdom, made it clear in a statement in November 1997 that they wanted to launch various measures to enhance transnational industrial collaboration. They urged the national defence industries—the national champions—to present a plan and timetable for industrial restructuring and integration (Schmitt 2000). Already in 1996 the Joint Armaments Cooperation Organization, OCCAR (Organisme conjoint de coopération en matière d'armement), had been created to act as a joint programme office on behalf of France, Germany, the United Kingdom, and Italy.

The overall ambition of the LoI is to enhance the conditions for the defence companies and to create closer political cooperation in an issue area that concerns economic as well as security aspects. The aim is thus to create a regulatory framework for the defence industry at the European level. Although the US is hardly mentioned in the political statements, it is obvious that 'the Other' is omnipresent and that the American consolidation of its defence industry was an important driving force for the European political process (Interview with Swedish defence minister Björn von Sydow 2000). The LoI process is thus a clear European political process that aims to strengthen the European defence industrial capacity in relation to the US.

The work within LoI has been organized horizontally in the way that the countries have established six working groups that address different aspects of a closer European cooperation on defence equipment (Security of Supply, Export Procedures, Security of Information, Technical Information, RTD, Harmonization of Military Requirements), consisting of officials from the six governments.[2] The working groups have been responsible for providing 'policy advice to, or undertaking specific tasks for, the Executive Committee'

---

[2] Representatives from the industry have participated on various occasions but have not been formally part of the working groups.

(LoI 1998: 8).[3] Thus, in the early LoI process, the governments identified six major areas in which there were perceived obstacles to industrial restructuring at the European level. The six reports have been discussed within each country and functioned as an important phase in the political process, which in July 2000 resulted in a general Framework agreement that was signed by the six governments—the so-called Farnborough agreement. The national parliaments will ratify the agreement, which indicates that it has a rather strong legal status. Time-consuming national ratification can be avoided since two countries can proceed with their cooperation once they have ratified the agreement (Article 55 in the Framework agreement). So, in contrast to the LoI in July 1998, the Framework agreement is a legally binding document. The agreement from July 2000 reinforces and confirms the earlier joint statements and working group reports of LoI. On some points the agreement is clearer and more elaborated than in earlier documents. The Executive Committee is given a more permanent status. It will exercise 'executive-level oversight of this Agreement, monitoring its effectiveness, and providing an annual status report to the Parties' (LoI, Framework Agreement, July 2000, Article 3). The Committee shall meet 'as frequently as necessary for the efficient fulfilment of its responsibilities…' (ibid.). The Framework agreement explicitly mentions the EU's code of conduct for arms in connection to the issue of transfers and export procedures with countries outside the LoI circle. This has been interpreted as the important legitimation base for the entire LoI agreement (Interview with Swedish Defence minister Björn von Sydow 2000). The six governments thereby guarantee that they will not pursue an export policy different from that which is decided within the European Union. The objective of the agreement is to 'bring closer, simplify, and reduce, where appropriate, national export control procedures for Transfers and Exports of Military goods and technologies' (LoI, Framework Agreement, Article 1).

The rather loose Articles in the Framework agreement raise the question what kind of specific agreements will follow from the general agreement. It is thus rather unclear what kinds of domestic change will follow from the general agreement when it comes to procurement, export, and other aspects of a defence equipment and industrial policy. The room for domestic interpretation is thus wide. Another issue is whether these changes should be based on legally binding documents and agreements. Legally binding agreements could be politically sensitive, since they would entail perceived losses of national sovereignty. Less binding agreements are also problematic since they would be easier for countries to break, for instance in the case of security of supply. Furthermore, the governments have clearly stated that by accepting mutual interdependence they will abandon domestic industrial capacity. The

---

[3] The Executive Committee of LoI consists of high officials from each country.

LoI governments have argued all along that the cooperation must be based on consultation and communication, that is, on mutual interdependence and trust. The commercial principles in the European cooperation are crucial in the Farnborough agreement. This means that the governments will not be allowed to have direct influence on a Transnational Defence Company (TDC) (LoI 1998). The companies will be run on a commercial basis, have private capital markets, and be listed on the Stock Exchange.

It is quite obvious that the LoI initiative—as shown by the documents from the ministers and working groups—tries to handle a tension between the two aspects on defence equipment. The end of the Cold War has put the European governments in a dilemma—a dilemma that placed them between an emphasis on national security interests, on the one hand, and the internationalization of economy and technology, on the other. A closer relationship between civilian and defence-related industry is needed for reasons of economic competitiveness, but a strong European defence industry is also an important foundation for a European defence identity and capacity.

To sum up, a new understanding of the issue of defence equipment has emerged in the sense that the European Commission, that started the process towards a closer European cooperation on defence equipment, and the six LoI governments have expressed the view that the issue is complex and consists of both market and defence components. This is especially salient within the Commission, which has argued that the issue of defence equipment belongs to the first and second pillars of the European Union and that the legal (regulative) rules from these two pillars should be combined. The LoI countries have, however, chosen a looser intergovernmental set-up that is formally outside the European Union. The Farnborough agreement combines security and market aspects, something that the European governments rejected in the EU context. The two projects of the European integration process are thus not seen as competitive projects. The constitutive rules of the market project, a European technological competitiveness towards the United States, and the constitutive rule of the defence project, the preservation of national security, are part of the same agreement. The Farnbourogh agreement adds a new constitutive rule on how to cooperate on defence equipment—that of mutual interdependence. How have these rules been handled by the various governments? In what ways can France, with its strong state presence in the defence industrial sector, and the United Kingdom, with its market-oriented policy, be part of the same political cooperation and agreement?

Domestic Editing

The political commitments in the Farnborough agreement are extensive. The governments explicitly recognize that they can no longer be self-sufficient in defence equipment and that they must establish common procurement procedures. Common export control rules will also be needed if these countries are to be able to establish a common market on defence equipment. The agreement stresses the importance of transnational defence companies. The new companies should be run on commercial grounds and governments will have no direct influence on how they are run. National champions are not considered to be enough in a world of technological and economic globalization. A common framework for cooperation is also needed from a European security and defence perspective.

As in other intergovernmental agreements, even though it is legally binding the document lacks precision on how these political commitments will be transformed into the national and domestic context. What are the pressures for domestic change followed by the Farnborough agreement? How have the new rules of the game—regulative and constitutive—been edited and interpreted by the governments?

The traditional Swedish neutrality policy has entailed that international interdependence on strategic technology has been regarded as a threat to national autonomy. The gradual change of Sweden's security policy, due to the end of the Cold War, has changed this perspective in a fundamental way. In the mid-1990s the Swedish Government presented a view of the increasing cooperation within the defence equipment sector and national defence and security policy. International cooperation within defence equipment was not presented as a threat but as an opportunity. The Government went even further and argued that the international defence equipment cooperation was a prerequisite for the survival of the Swedish national defence and the national defence industry (Mörth 2000b). In line with the Swedish general intergovernmental policy towards the European Union, it has toned down every supranational aspect of the Farnborough agreement. It has instead welcomed a more intergovernmental and loose cooperative structure. Furthermore, the Farnborough agreement is not interpreted by the Swedish government as a problem in connection with its close transatlantic relationship on defence equipment. Swedish decision-makers have repeatedly argued that there is no contradiction between the notion of building a stronger European defence industrial base and the fact that the United States is a major player within this policy field. In the defence bill from spring 1999 it is stated that 'European cooperation within defence industry should be fashioned in such a way as not to negatively affect transatlantic relations within this area' (Swedish Government Bill, 1998/99: 74: 125).

This Swedish notion of the end of national self-sufficiency has not only prevailed at the level of rhetoric. Major changes in the Swedish defence industrial landscape have taken place during the 1990s. The industry is privatized and the Swedish state is no part of its structure of ownership. The defence industry is also transnational in the sense that British and other foreign companies own part of it. This restructuring process has gone rather smoothly and without any debate on 'hollowing out' the Swedish defence industrial base (Britz 2000*a*). The traditionally close relationship between state and industry in this sector has not been an issue. This is not surprising considering the weak corporatist tradition in Sweden in the 1990s and early 2000s.

The shift in the Swedish defence equipment policy from self-sufficiency to mutual interdependence is also evident in Great Britain and France (Britz and Eriksson 2000). Another common feature in these countries' defence equipment policies is the emphasis on how economic considerations to a larger extent have to determine the future of the defence industry.

The British government has followed the most marked market-oriented policy towards the restructuring of the defence industry. As in the case of the Swedish government it has been in favour of private or transnational companies. The process of privatizing the industry had started in the 1980s and by the 1990s all defence industrial companies were private. 'When it comes to the British restructuring process, British governments have mainly let money talk. They have pushed for a restructuring process to take place, but have not really tried to steer how this has been done' (ibid.: 235). The British government has thus interpreted the European-level process as a market process with a weak presence of the state. The British government has also recognized that consolidation of the defence industry 'may involve the loss of some domestic industrial capacity in order to preserve other capabilities. This is leading to more mutual interdependence between nations and companies alike. Governments need an assurance of security of supply, just as companies need to know the procurement plans of governments to construct viable business structure' (White Paper 1999, paragraph 99, Ministry of Defence, United Kingdom). The LoI initiative is therefore welcomed by the British government (ibid.). Britain's special relationship with the United States has also entailed that the governments has interpreted the LoI process as open for transatlantic links (Britz and Eriksson 2000).

The French government, which traditionally has been a strong owner in the defence sector, has more reluctantly given up its control over the industry. The European dimension of the defence industrial policy is present in the Defence White Paper in 1994. In the paper it is stated that the European states should 'manifest their solidarity with each other, through a European preference' (Britz 2000*b*). The French government emphasized, as in its general European Union and European political approach, the importance of intergovernmental cooperation on defence equipment. As the French Prime Minister stated in a speech given in September 1998, 'Our conviction is that the creation of an industrial and technological defence industry base, constituted by strong units, which primarily lean upon a market constituting the whole of Europe, is a necessary condition for the creation of a true common European defence industry'. (Discours à L'institut des Hautes Etudes de Défense Nationale à Paris, September 3, 1998. Translation by the author.)[4]

Due to domestic opposition against a more private industry, especially from the unions, the privatization of the defence industry started rather late in the 1990s. It was also conducted in a very French way. In 1999 the French state agreed to privatize Aérospatiale 'and then only if it could hold a golden share' (Britz 2000*b*: 236). In parallel to this development the French government has launched major changes of its defence policy. The 'anti-American' components of its security policy have entailed that the LoI process has been interpreted in exclusively European terms. As French Defence Minister Alain Richard put it in a speech on 1 July 2000, '[European defence industry] won't reach its potential unless European governments decide to give an impulse to industry research and to acquire the defence equipment in a harmonized manner, in a fashion that is directed toward future developments' (Seminaire vers un culture européénne de defence et de securité;[5] see also Britz and Eriksson 2000).

To sum up, in parallel with the European-level process there have been major domestic changes in the defence industrial policy sector. In fact, these processes at the two levels have crossed each other and it is difficult to separate them. The governments in Sweden, the United Kingdom, and France have all changed their security and defence policies due to the end of the Cold War. A more international and European-oriented security policy replaced a national-oriented policy. The new policy paved the way for a more open political attitude towards European cooperation on defence equipment and its implications on national autonomy and of state control over the defence industry. In the defence industrial sector, the privatization processes in the countries have led to the creation of two European companies in the aerospace sector: BAE Systems (formerly BAE) and EADS Aérospatiale/DASA/CASA and Finmeccanica Alenia (Mörth 2001).

Furthermore, the domestic context in the three countries varied. By participating in the rule-making activities at the European level, the governments in Sweden, France, and the United Kingdom created room for domestic editing and interpretation so that the agreement fitted into the specific domestic political conditions. The main explanation for the various processes of editing seems to be different state traditions regarding both security policy and the general relationship between state and markets (cf. Dyson 1980).

---

[4] www.premier-ministre.gouv.fr/fr/p.cfm?ref=4235&d=361.
[5] www.defense.gouv.fr/actualites/communiques/d100700/100700.htm

Conclusion

According to a sociological institutionalist approach, *Europeanization* is here defined as a process of institutionalization in which new rules of the game are constructed, especially constitutive rules. Since these rules are wide in scope, they are interpreted and edited by national actors so that they fit into the domestic political context. The Farnborough agreement on closer cooperation on defence equipment was quite elastic and created room for domestic interpretation and editing. The constitutive rules that were agreed on the European level were also important in the domestic political process, for instance concerning the close interlinkage between defence and market aspects of the issue of defence equipment. Another constitutive rule that could be found at the European and the domestic political levels was that there was no perceived contradiction between national sovereignty and a European capacity on defence equipment. The processes at the European and domestic levels were interlinked. Indeed, the Farnborough agreement was the result of extensive contacts and negotiations by politicians as well as officials from the six governments. The organization of the LoI working groups was transnational and horizontal.

As suggested by Radaelli in his introductory chapter, the impact of EU public policy is contingent on whether a country is already involved in a process of reform or not. The end of the Cold War started a process of change in the countries that entailed that there was a domestic susceptibility for closer European cooperation on defence equipment. The rules agreed at the European Union and European level can of course strengthen the ongoing domestic process by providing additional legitimacy to domestic reformers in search of justifications for various reforms. The Swedish government has, for instance, often emphasized the need for domestic reforms in the defence sector in order to fit into the new European security and defence capacity. This means that changes at the European level can prepare the ground for major domestic policy change. It is, however, important to bear in mind that demands from the European Union are often ambiguous and unclear, which leaves openings for domestic editing and translations. There are also 'frequently conflicts and opposing views about how the strategy for adaptation to the European Union should be organized and what its content should be' (Jacobsson *et al.* 2001: 28).

The empirical findings in the case of defence equipment make it difficult to assess the contribution of a single independent EU variable to the process of domestic policy change. I argue that the empirical evidence points in another direction and that it is misleading to think that we can always establish the EU's impact on the domestic political process. I would even argue that the processes at the European and domestic levels are mutually constitutive and that they cannot be studied as separate processes. States do not exist outside the European Union. The case of defence equipment illustrates that the states are part of the process at the European Union and European level and that they are not 'hit' by the European Union. *Europeanization* is a process of institutionalization in which constitutive and regulative rules are constructed.

This does not mean that there were no adaptational pressures for domestic change. The process towards institutional isomorphism consisted of socialization and imitation rather than coercion. The multiple actors at the national and European levels formed a transnational political community in which the new rules of the game were formed. The rationale for establishing European cooperation on defence equipment was the notion of an American threat, and that Europe must build up a strong regulatory framework and policy within the defence industrial sector.

Furthermore, if *Europeanization* is a process, it could be difficult to distinguish between the process leading to the formation of a certain policy and the reverberation of that policy in the national arenas, as suggested by Radaelli in this volume. In my usage and definition of *Europeanization*, it is a process in which new rules of the game are constructed. Policy formation and policy change take place within these new structural conditions.

How can we then analyse *Europeanization* as processes of institutionalizations in which the European and national levels are mutually constitutive? It is easy to argue that the state's embeddedness in the European Union makes it difficult to be more specific in the analysis. The challenge is to study empirical complexity without losing analytical clarity. One could of course argue that it is an empirical question if states are embedded in the European Union. However, concepts and theories guide empirical analysis and you often 'find what you seek'. The traditional Weberian state concept that dominates the analysis of the European integration process is focused on how states use the European Union as an arena for intergovernmental bargaining. It is, therefore, most likely that the approach limits the empirical analysis in the sense that it is difficult to study a more sociological institutionalist approach on how new preferences and policies evolve. Another state concept is needed in order to study that process. Drawing on Ruggie's notion of the European Union as a 'multiperspectival polity' (1993), it can be argued that states cannot be treated as external actors in the European Union. In contrast to the Westphalian state, states can be regarded as disjointed and fragmented. 'Process and activity become more important than structure and fixed institutions. The state becomes not so much a thing...as a set of spatially detached activities, diffused across the Member States...' (Caporaso 1996: 45; see also Smith 1996). According to this reasoning, states are embedded in the European Union. The analysis covers new types of state activities, and how new forms of European authority structures can change the domestic political process. Helen and William Wallace (2000) have suggested the term 'intense transgovernmentalism' in order to analyse extensive engagements by governments that are not necessarily based on a hierarchical supranational decision making or upon coercive rules. The term 'intense transgovernmentalism' can capture a more governance-like authority structure, that is, of soft law, networks, competition, and knowledge (cf. Boli and George 1999). This chapter has shown that the state is more embedded than is implied by the term 'intergovernmentalism', without going as far as formal delegation of sovereignty.

REFERENCES

Boli, J. and George, M. (eds) (1999). *Constructing World Culture* (Stanford: Stanford University Press).

Britz, Malena (2000*a*). 'The Development of Swedish and French Defence Industrial Companies 1994–1999—A Comparative Study', *SCORE Working Paper 6*.

——(2000*b*). 'A Comparative Analysis', in *British, German and French Defence Industrial Policy in the 1990s*. Swedish Research Defence Establishment.

——and Eriksson, Arita (2000). *British, German and French Defence Industrial Policy in the 1990s*. Swedish Defence Research Establishment.

Brunsson, Nils and Olsen, Johan P. (1993). *The Reforming Organization* (London: Routledge).

Caporaso, James A. (1996). 'The European Union and Forms of State. Westphalian, Regulatory or Post-Modern'? *Journal of Common Market Studies* 34: 29–51.

Czarniawska, Barbara and Sevon, Guje (eds) (1996). *Translating Organizational Change* (New York/Berlin: de Gruyter).

DiMaggio, Paul J. and Powell, Walter W. (1991). 'The Iron Cage Revisited: Institutional Isomorphism and Collective Rationality in Organizational Fields', in Walter W. Powell and Paul J. DiMaggio (eds), *The New Institutionalism in Organizational Analysis* (Chicago/London: The University of Chicago Press), 63–82.

Dyson, Kenneth (1980). *The State Tradition in Western Europe: A Study of an Idea and Institution* (New York: Oxford University Press).

Ekengren, Magnus (1999). *Time and European Governance. The Empirical Value of Three Reflective Approaches*. Stockholm Studies in Politics, 63, The Department of Political Science, Stockholm University.

European Commission (1990). 'Industrial Policy in an Open and Competitive Environment: Guidelines for a Community Approach' (COM (90) 556 final).

——(1992). 'The European Aircraft Industry—First Assessment and Possible Community Actions' (COM (92) 164 final).

——(1996). 'The Challenges Facing the European Defence-Related Industry, A Contribution for Action at European Level' (COM (96) 10 final).

European Commission (1997). 'Implementing European Union Strategy on Defence-Related Industries' (COM (97) 583 final).

Fierke, Karin and Wiener, Antje (1999). 'Constructing Institutional Interests: EU and NATO Enlargment', *Journal of European Public Policy* 6: 721–42.

Framework Agreement Between the French Republic, the Federal Republic of Germany, the Italian Republic, the Kingdom of Spain, the Kingdom of Sweden, and the United Kingdom of Great Britain and Northern Ireland Concerning Measures to Facilitate the Restructuring and Operation of the European Defence Industry, Farnborough, July 2000.

Gourevitch, Peter (1986). *Politics in Hard Times—Comparative Responses to International Economic Crises* (Ithaca/London: Cornell University Press).

Green Cowles, Maria, Caporaso, James, and Risse, Thomas (eds) (2001). *Transforming Europe. Europeanization and Domestic Change* (Ithaca: Cornell University Press).

Héritier, Adrienne (1999). *Policy-Making and Diversity in Europe Escape from Deadlock* (Cambridge: Cambridge University Press), 1–21.

——*et al.* (2001). 'Differential Europe: The European Union Impact on National Policymaking', in Adrienne Héritier, Dieter Kerwer, Christopher Knill, Dirk Lehmkuhl, Michael Teutsch, and Anne-Cécile Douillet (eds), *Differential Europe— The European Union Impact on National Policymaking* (Lanham, MD: Rowman and Littlefield).

Jacobsson, Bengt, Laegreid, Per, and Pedersen, Ove K. (2001). 'Transforming States', *SCORE Working Paper 4*.

Laegreid, Per and Roness, Paul G. (1999). 'Administrative Reform as Organized Attention', in Morten Egeberg and Per Laegreid (eds), *Organizing Political Institutions* (Oslo: Scandinavian University Press), 301–30.

Law, John and Callon, Michael (1992). 'The Life and Death of an Aircraft: A Network Analysis of Technical Change', in Wiebe E. Bijker and John Law (eds), *Shaping Technology/Building Society: Studies in Sociotechnical Change* (Cambridge, MA: MIT Press), 21–52.

'Letter of Intent (LoI) between Ministers of Defence from France, Germany, Italy, Spain and Sweden Concerning measures to facilitate the restructuring of European defence industry', July 1998.

March, James and Olsen, Johan P. (1989). *Rediscovering Institutions* (New York: Free Press).

——(1998). 'The Institutional Dynamics of International Political Orders', *International Organization* 52(4): 943–70.

Marcussen, Marcus, Risse, Thomas, Engelmann-Martin, Daniela, Knopf, Hans Joachim, and Roscher, Klaus (1999). 'Constructing Europe? The Evolution of French, British and German Nation State Identities', *Journal of European Public Policy* 6: 614–33.

Meyer, John and Rowan, Brian (1977/91). 'Institutionalized Organizations: Formal Structures as Myth and Ceremony', in Walter W. Powell and Paul DiMaggio (eds), *The New Institutionalism in Organizational Analysis* (Chicago: University of Chicago Press), 41–82.

Mörth, Ulrika (2000a). 'Competing Frames in the European Commission—the Case of the Defence Industry and Equipment Issue', *Journal of European Public Policy* 7(2): 173–89.

—— (2000*b*). 'Swedish Industrial Policy and Research and Technological Development: The Case of European Defence Equipment', in Lee Miles (ed.), *Sweden and the EU Evaluated* (London: Continuum), 127–45.

—— (2001). 'The Building of Europe—the Organising of European Armaments Co-operation', manuscript.

Nicolaidis, Kalypso and Howse, Robert (eds) (2001). *The Federal Vision—Legitimacy and Levels of Governance in the United States and the European Union* (Oxford: Oxford University Press).

North, Douglas (1990). *Institutions, Institutional Change and Economic Performance* (Cambridge: Cambridge University Press).

Peters, Guy (1999). *Institutional Theory in Political Science* (London/New York: Pinter).

Premfors, Rune (2001). 'Democracy in Sweden: A Historical and Comparative Perspective manuscript'.

Rosenau, James (1990). *Turbulence in World Politics* (New York: Harvester Wheatsheaf).

Ruggie, John Gerard (1993). 'Territoriality and Beyond. Problematizing Modernity in International Relations', *International Organization* 47: 139–73.

—— (1998*a*). 'What Makes the World Hang Together? Neo-utilitarianism and the Social Constructivist Challenge', *International Organization* 52(4): 855–85.

—— (1998*b*). *Constructing the World Polity* (London/New York: Routledge).

Schmitt, Burkardt (2000). 'From Cooperation to Integration: Defence and Aerospace Industries in Europe', *Chaillot Papers 40* (Paris: Institute for Security Studies, Western European Union).

Searle, John R. (1995). *The Construction of Social Reality* (New York: Free Press).

Sevón, Guje (1996). 'Organizational Imitation in Identity Transformation', in Barbara Czarniawska and Guje Sevón (eds), *Translating Organizational Change* (New York/Berlin: de Gruyter), 49–67.

Shaw, Jo. (1996). *Law of the European Union* (London: Macmillan).

Shelton, Dinah (2001). *Commitment and Compliance—The Role of Non-Binding Norms in the International Legal System* (Oxford: Oxford University Press).

Shepsle, K. A. (1989). 'Studying Institutions: Lessons from the Rational Choice Approach', *Journal of Theoretical Politics* 1: 131–47.

Smith, Michael (1996). 'The European Union and a Changing Europe: Establishing the Boundaries of Order', *Journal of Common Market Studies* 34: 5–28.

Stone Sweet A., Sandholtz, W., and Fligstein, Neil (2001). 'The Instutionalization of European Space', in Alec Stone Sweet, Wayne Sandholtz, and Neil Fligstein (eds), *The Institutionalization of Europe* (Oxford: Oxford University Press), 1–28.

Strang, D. and Meyer, John (1994). 'Institutional Conditions for Diffusion', in W. Richard Scott and John W. Meyer (eds), *Institutional Environments and Organizations* (London: Sage).

Swedish Government Bill 1998/1999: 74.

Thelen, Kathleen and Steinmo, Svein (1992). 'Historical Institutionalism in comparative politics', in Svein Steinmo, Kathleen Thelen, and Frank Longstreth (eds), *Structuring Politics. Historical Institutionalism in Comparative Analysis* (Cambridge: Cambridge University Press).

Von Sydow, Björn (2000). Swedish Defence Minister, Inteview, October.

Walker, R. B. J. (1993). *Inside/outside: International Relations as Political Theory* (Cambridge: Cambridge University Press).

Wallace, Helen and Wallace, William (2000). *Policy Making in the European Union* (Oxford: Oxford University Press).

Waltz, Kenneth (1979). *Theory of International Relations* (Reading, MA: Addison-Wesley).

8

Europeanization as Convergence: The Regulation of Media Markets in the European Union

Introduction

One of the challenges of Europeanization as an innovative research agenda is the identification of mechanisms through which domestic public policy is 'Europeanized'. In his chapter, Radaelli identified two types of mechanisms: vertical and horizontal. This chapter elaborates these mechanisms by considering the case of media market regulation in the European Union (EU). It is argued that Europeanization of this policy area can be understood by looking at the *interplay* between the two mechanisms. The first vertical mechanism consists of direct mandates from the European institutions in the form of directives, competition decisions, and European Court of Justice (ECJ) decisions. The second mechanism is horizontal. Whereas Radaelli's chapter illustrated a horizontal framing mechanism with the example of the open method of coordination (OMC), this chapter will provide evidence of the horizontal mechanism through the observation of forum politics (see also Coen and Dannreuther, this volume, on policy fora). This takes place when policy instruments are diffused through high level working groups, committees, platforms of regulators, and other EU-level forums. Although these fora are not institutionalized, as is the open method of coordination, they have produced substantial convergence in the choice of policy instruments used to regulate media markets at national levels. Therefore the two mechanisms, horizontal and vertical, have a compound effect in that the overall result—produced by the different EU institutions (Commission, EC competition authority, and the 'community of courts') and fora (working groups, platforms, and other forums)—is one of a Europeanization of national policy arenas.

One finding of this approach is that Europeanization is a multiinstitutional, multiactor, and multiprocess phenomenon. It is only by considering the interaction and the overall cumulative effect of vertical and horizontal mechanisms that one can make sense of the real impact of the European Union in media market regulation. This approach is consistent with a research agenda that puts emphasis on compound effects and ultimately aims at measuring the impact of EU public policy (see Radaelli and Giuliani in this volume). This chapter detects convergence in policy paradigms, domestic laws, and policy instruments. This does not necessarily mean that all aspects of media market regulation in the European Union are converging. However, convergence in this area has gone well beyond the formation of 'communities of discourse' and shared beliefs. It has penetrated the fabric of law and the toolbox used by domestic policy makers. There is no doubt that Europeanization has produced substantial convergence at national levels.

From the advent of the Single Market, a gradual convergence in member state media regulation can be observed. Europeanization of this policy domain began during the 1970s with the first ECJ decisions, following which the latter has made over fifty media market decisions. These have provided the European Commission (EC) with a basis for a number of initiatives during 1980s which affected the media market, most significant of which is the 1989 *Television Without Frontiers* (*TWF*) directive.[1]

Following TWF, the EC sought to advance policy making in the media field with two initiatives: *media ownership* and *convergence*.[2] Both initiatives presented significant political impasses to the EC due to the lack of legal bases in the treaties. The Commission has since found other ways of governing media markets: through the suggestion of best practice, models and solutions to domestic policy problems, effecting national policies through the use of competition law, and the initiation of European level forums (e.g. EPRA, ISPO, JRC).[3] European level fora served to promote regulatory instruments suggested

---

[1] Council Directive 92/38/EEC of 11 May 1992 on the adoption of standards for satellite broadcasting of television signals; Council resolution of 22 July 1993 on the development of technology and standards in the field of advanced television services; Council resolution of 27 June 1994 on a framework for Community policy on digital video broadcasting; *Television Without Frontiers* Commission Directive 89/552/EEC. Television Without Frontiers Directive 97/36/EC of 30 June 1997; Council Decision 1999/297/CE, of 26 April 1999, establishing a Community statistical information infrastructure relating to the industry and markets of the audio–visual and related sectors; Communication of 14 December 1999 from the Commission to the Council, the European Parliament, the Economic and Social Committee, and the Committee of the Regions: Principles and guidelines for the Community's audio–visual policy in the digital age.

[2] Green Paper on *Pluralism and Media Concentration in the Internal Market* COMM (92) 480, 23.12.92; Green Paper relating to the Consultation *Process Relating to the Green Paper* on *'Pluralism and Media Concentration in the Internal Market—an Assessment of the Need for Community Action*, COM (94) 353 final, 05.10.1994; EC *Green Paper on the Convergence of the Telecommunications, Media and Information Technology Sectors, and the Implications for Regulation* COM (97) 623, 3 December 1997.

[3] European Platform of Regulatory Authorities (EPRA); Institute for Prospective Technological Studies (JRC); Information Society Project (ISPO).

in Commission reports, green papers, and draft directives. Consultation with national experts and interest groups enabled the dissemination of suggested policy instruments to national levels. In parallel, the EC competition directorate has taken an increasingly active role in determining the development of media markets in Europe. The EC Merger Task Force (MTF) has taken an increasingly hands-on approach to governing media mergers and acquisitions, even domestic market cases. In many cases, MTF decision making has run roughshod over political choices made at the domestic level regardless of national cries of subsidiarity (even, in cases, those of national ministers and heads of state).

In order to observe the process of Europeanization, the chapter first examines vertical mechanisms (EC directives, ECJ decisions, EC competition decisions) and, second, horizontal mechanisms (suggestion of best practice through European level policy forums). Sections 'The Impact of ECJ Decisions on National Regulation' and 'Vertical Europeanization via EC Merger Policy' will provide an overview of ECJ and competition decisions. Section 'The Commission and New Modes of Governance' will overview how policy ideas travel through European-level forums. Section 'Conclusion' will draw conclusions on how Europeanization has driven convergence of national media policies.

The Impact of ECJ Decisions on National Regulation

The establishment and evolvement of the European Union into its present state has largely been determined by the ECJ. Snyder summarizes the ECJ's role as an EU institution by stating 'the ECJ...has a central role in the creation of the EC and of its internal market, for the ECJ is a major creative force in Community law making, policy making, and politics' (1990: 26). The ECJ has taken many decisions relating to the media industry. These decisions in turn are influencing are fuelling Europeanization. As it is adjudging an industry affecting national culture and democratic outcome, many of the ECJ's media decisions have had political significance. Indeed, the ECJ was the first European institution to tackle the tricky and controversial question of whether media policy should be considered as coming under national cultural policy, and therefore be exempted from EU competition rules, or be considered as an EU single market issue. This has enabled other EU institutions to take an increasingly active policy approach towards governing media markets. In the 1990s, the ECJ considered the status of public service broadcasters.

The first significant ECJ case dealing with the broadcasting is the *Sacchi case*.[4] In 1974, the Tribunal Court of Biella, Italy asked the ECJ whether the

---

[4] *Case 155/73 Tribunale civile e penale di Biella* [30.04.74, ECR 0409–0433].

movement of services within the common market applied to television signals. The ECJ ruled that 'in the absence of express provision to the contrary
in the treaty, a television signal must, by reason of its nature, be regarded a
provision of services'. The Court further established in the 1980 *Debauve
case*[5] that any discrimination by a member state against a broadcasting signal
due to national origin is illegal. The ruling related to three cable broadcasters
of foreign origin which were transmitting advertising to cable subscribers in
Belgium. Belgian legislation at the time banned the transmission of commercial advertising.[6]

The *Sacchi* and *Debauve* rulings were extremely significant for the future
development of EU media policy. The *Sacchi* case declared that broadcasting
be considered a tradable service. Therewith the sector was established as ripe
for the single market policy making. The *Debauve* case further eroded the
national domain for broadcasting policy by permitting broadcasts from
abroad. Both *Sacchi* and *Debauve* provided a legal basis for the EC 1989
Television without Frontiers.

The next ECJ dealing with cross-national broadcasting was the *Coditel* case.[7]
In 1980 an exclusive licence for showing the film 'La Boucher' was granted to
Cinévog, a Belgian company, for use in Belgium and Luxembourg. The film
could be shown on television only after forty months of its cinema release.
However, the cable company, Coditel, had bought rights to the film from a
German company which could show the film (in Germany) after only twelve
months of general release. As Coditel also showed the film to its subscribers in
Belgium and Luxembourg it was ruled to be infringing upon Cinévog's exclusive rights. The court ruled in favour of Cinévog, but added that each exclusive
rights case must be examined in the context of the relevant market.

In contrast to the Cinévog ruling, in its next case on exclusive rights, the
ECJ ruled that an infringement of European law occurred. This was the first
of the *Magill* cases which handled the appeal for annulment of a decision
made in the EC by ITP (Independent Television Publications of ITV). The
case dealt with the public service broadcasters BBC, ITP, and RTE in Ireland
and Northern Ireland, which owned exclusive rights to publish their programming schedules, and Magill TV Guide Limited, which wished to publish a
programming guide. Magill had started publishing the guide including all
programming schedules in 1985 but was prevented from doing so by an Irish
court injunction in 1986 (a case brought about by the BBC, ITP, and RTE).
The decision was overturned by an Irish high court. It was then taken up by
the EC competition authority which determined in separate rulings that the

[5] *Procureur du Roi V. Marc J.V.C. Debauve and others.* Case 52/79 [1980] ECR 0833,
18 March 1980.
[6] Article 21 of the Royal Decree of 24 December 1966 (Moniteur Belge of 24 January 1967).
[7] *Coditel SA V. Cinévog Films SA* Case 62/79 [1980] ECR 881.

exclusive licences infringed Article 86 of the treaty determining dominant market position. An annulment of the Commission decision was sought by the BBC, ITP, and RTE at the European Court of First Instance (CFI). The CFI in three separate rulings decided against the BBC, ITP, and RTE in support of the EC decisions.[8] It stated that ITV had used 'the copyright in its weekly programme listings under national law to reserve the exclusive right to publish those listings, thus preventing the emergence on the ancillary market of television magazines, where it enjoys a monopoly, of a new product containing the programmes of all the broadcasting stations capable of being received by television viewers, for which there is potential consumer demand'. RTE and ITP appealed to the ECJ which in a final ruling in 1994 upheld the three CFI *Magill* decisions.[9] These rulings had consequences for all EU Member States. PSBs could no longer enjoy exclusive rights to programming guides.

In the meantime, the European Union passed its 1989 *TWF* broadcasting directive which established a legal framework for the creation of a single audio–visual market. The EC was successful in TWF in adding requirements that dealt with issues that went beyond market regulation. TWF required: a majority proportion of transmission time be reserved for European works; 10 per cent of transmission time or 10 per cent of programming budget for European works created by independent producers; interruption of films by advertising limited to once every 45 min; exclusion of advertising during news, current affairs programmes, documentaries, religious programmes, and children's programmes; prohibition of advertising cigarettes, prescription medicines, and medical treatment; a limit of advertising time to 20 per cent of the daily transmission time and 20 per cent within a given clock hour; the protection of minors; and prohibition of incitement to hatred on grounds of race, sex, religion, or nationality.

Following the 1989 Television Without Frontiers directive, there was a dramatic increase in ECJ court cases dealing with media markets (see Figure 8.1) which challenged the domain of media policy (as cultural policy) as belonging exclusively to the member state. The first of these was the *Commission of the European Communities V. Kingdom of the Netherlands* case of 1991.[10] When the first case was brought to the ECJ in 1989, under Dutch cable law companies were prohibited from 'transmitting programs offered by foreign

---

[8] Case T-76/89 *Independent Television Publications Ltd V. Commission of the European Communities* [OJC 10.07.91 ECR II-0575] Court of First Instance (Second Chamber); and Case T-70/89 *The British Broadcasting Corporation and BBC Enterprises Limited V. Commission of the European Communities* [OJC 201/13, 10.07.91, ECR II-0535].

[9] Joined cases C-241/91 P AND C-242/91 P *Radio Telefos Eireann (RTE) and Independent Television Publications Ltd V. Commission of the European Communities* [ECR I-0743, 06.04.95].

[10] Two previous cases dealing with the foreign transmission of advertising also ruled against Dutch cable law: Case-352/85 *Bond van Adverteerders* [ECR 2085, 1988] and Case C-288/89 *Collectieve Antennevoorziening Gouda* [ECR I 4007, 1991].

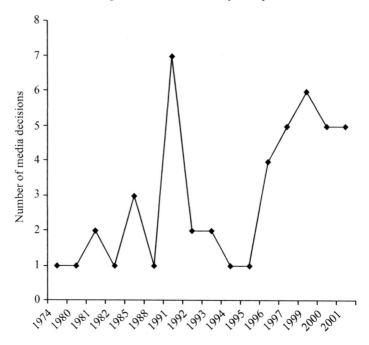

FIGURE 8.1. Number of ECJ media decisions 1974–2001
Source: Compiled by author.

broadcasting organizations and broadcasters in foreign countries were pro-
hibited from broadcasting programmes with Dutch advertisements to the
Dutch audience' (Korthals Altes 1993: 32). The Court ruled against the
Netherlands, claiming that:

> Even if such a restriction forms part of a cultural policy intended to safeguard the
> freedom of expression of the various social, cultural, religious and philosophical com-
> ponents of society by ensuring the survival of an undertaking which provides them
> with technical resources, it goes beyond the objective pursued, since pluralism in the
> audio–visual sector of a Member State cannot be affected in any way by allowing the
> national bodies operating in that sector to make use of providers of services estab-
> lished in other Member States.

Among other things, the Court's decision meant that domestic companies
were no longer obligated to purchase content material solely from Dutch
providers. The Netherlands subsequently had to make changes to its national
Media Act of 18 December 1991, which provoked a greater sector liberalization than had been envisioned by the Dutch authorities. As Korthals Altes
states 'it is European law that opened the Dutch broadcasting system' (1993:
329). The 1991 Dutch Act still represented a relatively strict regulatory

regime. As all terrestrial frequencies were reserved for the public stations, private television (national or transitional) were constrained to the local cable networks. However, the simultaneous enactment of the EC *Television Without Frontiers* in other countries rendered the Dutch Media Act useless in this respect. As a small country with many bordering countries, the Netherlands had the unique problem of a high level of cross-border transmissions (often in the Dutch language). At present, 40 per cent of audience share in the Netherlands comes from foreign broadcasts (CIT 2001). A large proportion of which goes to the Luxembourg-based channels, RTL 4 and 5.

Another case, decided only six days later, further chiselled away at the member state jurisdiction for broadcasting policy. The Greek *Elliniki Radiophonia Tilorassi-Anonimi Etairia V. Dimotiki Etairia Pliroforissis and Sotirios Kouvelas* case was concerned with the Greek Law No. 1730/1987 which banned commercial broadcasters and, in the ECJ's view, established a 'public television monopoly'. In 1988, the Mayor of Thessaloniki set up a television station and began to broadcast. A Greek court injunction was issued to restrain transmission and order seizure of station equipment. The case was taken to a national court, which referred the case to the ECJ. Although this presented a case of sensitive national policy, the ECJ choose to intervene. It decided that the Greek public broadcaster monopolized not only *transmission* but also *exclusive rights*. In this respect, the Court ruled that the establishment of a public broadcasting monopoly 'must be regarded as an ostensibly illegal measure by virtue of the combined provisions of Articles 90 and 86, which cannot be justified by virtue of Article 90(2)'. By this time, perhaps in anticipation of the ECJ ruling, the Greek government had passed a new media Law No. 1866/1989 allowing for commercial television stations at the local level.

This determination on behalf of the ECJ to intervene in national media policy (often encompassing cultural policy aims) continued in 1992, when the ECJ ruled against the Belgian state in *European Communities V. Kingdom of Belgium*. It decided that Belgium had failed to fulfil its obligations under Articles 52, 59, 60, and 221 of the EEC Treaty on four accounts: by prohibiting cable programmes from other member states where the programme was not in the language stipulated by Belgian law; by subjecting cable commercial broadcasters from other member states to prior authorization, to which conditions might have been attached; by reserving 51 per cent of the capital of the Flemish commercial broadcaster for publishers of Dutch-language daily and weekly newspapers; and by compelling commercial broadcasters to constitute a compulsory part of their programming to cultural interest.

Two years later, another case was brought to challenge national broadcasting law. In 1994, the ECJ ruled that the United Kingdom had failed to adequately implement the *Television Without Frontiers (TWF)* directive in the *Commission of the European Communities V. United Kingdom of Great Britain and Northern Ireland* case. The Commission informed the United Kingdom that it had failed to correctly transpose several articles of the *TWF* directive into its UK Broadcasting Act 1990. This because the UK Broadcasting Act treated domestic satellite services differently than non-domestic satellite services (in Section 43) and because it continued to exercise control over foreign broadcasts. The United Kingdom therewith maintained jurisdiction over Sky Television, which was broadcasting from Luxembourg. The ECJ ruled in favour of the Commission and suggested a rewording of the 1990 Broadcasting Act, by which time the 1996 Broadcasting Act was almost in place.

This case was followed by the 1996 *Eurovision* case. The case dealt with programming rights acquired by the European Broadcasting Union (EBU) which were for exclusive use of its PSB members.[11] The European Commission had exempted the EBU from EU competition rules under Article 85 (3) (now Article 81 EC) to enable it to share exclusive rights in view of the EBU members' public service role.[12] Although the French commercial broadcasters Canal Plus and TF1 had been granted membership by the EBU in 1984 and in 1986 (while they were still public but were soon afterwards privatized), three private groups, La Cinq, M6, and Antena 3, were later refused membership. La Cinq, M6, Antena, RTI, and Telecinco took the case to the CFI. In two cases (one jointly decided), the CFI ruled against the Commission's decision to exempt the EBU from competition rules. In 1994, Métropole Télévision was again denied EBU membership, and asked the Commission to investigate under state aid rules. The Commission refused (Commission decision of 29 June 1999). Métropole Télévision took the case the ECJ in 1999. The Court decided in March 2001 that the Commission should have investigated the case. This means that the Commission will most likely be required to decide on PSB exclusive rights agreements in the future.

A case dealing with Flemish media regulation emerged in 1997 with *VT4 Ltd V. Vlaamse Gemeenschap*. According to Belgian law, the Flemish Executive can license only one commercial television broadcaster at a time. In 1987 this licence was granted to Vlaamse Televisie Maatschappij NV ('VTM') to broadcast its station VT4 for a term of eighteen years. Under the same provisions, only one broadcaster (radio or television) for the Flemish Community may be licensed to transmit advertising. This licence was also issued to VT4 for a term of eighteen years in 1987. In Flanders, VTM therefore holds a legal monopoly in commercial television and television advertising. With the eighteen year licence intact, VTM was bought by Scandinavian Broadcasting SA (registered

---

[11] From 1988, the EBU membership was restricted to public service broadcasters.

[12] Commission Decision 93/403/EEC of 11 June 1993 relating to a proceeding pursuant to Article 85 of the EEC Treaty (OJ 1993 L 179, p. 23), whereby it granted an exemption under Article 85(3) ('the exemption' decision).

in Luxembourg) and VT4's broadcasting headquarters relocated to London. VT4 secured a non-domestic satellite service licence from the United Kingdom permitting it to broadcast to Flanders under UK regulation (pertaining to non-satellite broadcasts). In reaction to this evasion of Flemish media law, the Flemish Minister of Culture and Brussels Affairs prohibited the retransmission of VT4 programming by cable network operators in Flanders from 16 January 1995. This decision, by the Flemish minister, was overturned by the ECJ, which found it to be in conflict with *TWF*. This ECJ ruling enables media companies to bypass national laws by moving their headquarters abroad.

A similar case was ruled on the same day against Belgium, again uphold-ing *TWF*. The United Kingdom had this time issued a non-domestic satellite service licence for UK Turner Entertainment Network International Limited (subsidiary of the US American Turner Group), which owns The Cartoon Network Limited, and Turner Network Television Limited, which broadcast programmes via the Astra satellite. On 17 September 1993 Turner International Network Sales Limited concluded an agreement with Coditel, the German cable television company, to distribute Turner programming to Brussels. As there was no legislation at that time governing cable television in Brussels, a Royal Decree was issued the day before the agreement (on 16 September 1993) designed to stop the cable company from taking advan-tage of the lack of legislation. Coditel was prohibited from distributing 'TNT' and 'Cartoon Network'. Turner International Network Sales Ltd took the case to the Tribunal de Commerce in Brussels for an interim order allowing Coditel to carry out its contract. The order was granted by the tribunal on 26 October 1993 and Coditel began broadcasting. In June 1994 the Belgian state brought third-party proceedings against the interim order (of 26 October). In November 1994, the Tribunal de Commerce referred the case to the ECJ and banned Coditel from broadcasting until a decision had been made. This decision was reversed in April 1995 by the Belgian Cour d'Appel, which withdrew the case from the ECJ. Meanwhile, the Belgian state began separate criminal proceedings against Paul Denuit, the managing director of Coditel, for ignoring the Ministerial Decree of 17 September 1993. The Tribunal de Première Instance referred the case to the ECJ, which ruled in favour of Denuit in 1997 and upheld *TWF*. Again, as in the VTM satellite case, the ECJ ruling enables cable companies to circum-vent national legislation by broadcasting from abroad.

The issue of cross-national broadcasting resurfaced in 1997 with the *Tiercé Ladbroke SA V. Commission of the European Communities* case. Tiercé Ladbroke SA asked the ECJ for an annulment of the EC Decision of 24 June 1993. The EC had rejected a complaint lodged by Tiercé Ladbroke SA against Pari Mutuel Urbain (PMU) and Pari Mutuel International (PMI), the principal French sociétes de courses (horseracing associations). PMI had granted Deutscher Sportverlag Kurt Stoof GmbH & Co. ('DSV') exclusive rights to

French horseracing broadcasts in Germany and Austria. In September 1989, Ladbroke asked DSV to grant it the right to retransmit the broadcasts in Belgium. DSV refused in October 1989 on the grounds that its contract with PMI prevented it from retransmitting the French sound and pictures outside the licensed territory. However, PMI runs a service called 'Courses en direct' that enables horse races in France to be viewed live by satellite. PMI was prepared to licence this service to three Belgian companies: Pari Mutuel Unifié Belge, Tiercé Franco-Belge, and Dumoulin—but not to Ladbroke. The EC rejected the complaint by Ladbroke. The Court upheld the Commission's decision.

In three recent decisions, the ECJ has been asked to decide whether the European Commission should rule on whether the public service television should be prohibited from raising funding through advertising (as a digression of state aid rules). The Commission has thus far viewed this matter as one of national concern. In the three decisions raised by private companies in France and Portugal, the ECJ has ruled that the Commission should *indeed* be obliged to judge on this issue in the future (Télévision Française V. European Commission (1999), SIC V. Commission (2000), and Commission V. TF1 (2001)). The EC Directorate for competition subsequently came out with its 2001 *Communication on the application of State aid rules to public service broadcasting*[13] in which it recognizes PSB importance for maintaining pluralism. The Communication refers to the 'public service' Protocol of the 1997 Treaty of Amsterdam and quotes the 2000 EC *Communication on Services of General Interest in Europe*,[14] which states: 'the choice of the financing scheme falls within the competence of the Member State, and there can be no objection in principle to the choice of a dual financing scheme (combining public funds and advertising revenues) rather than a single funding scheme (solely public funds) as long as competition in the relevant markets (e.g. advertising, acquisition and/or sale of programmes) is not affected to an extent which is contrary to the Community interest'. With this as a general rule, future advertising and funding complaints are to be decided on a case by case basis.

Most cases from this period onwards have dealt with the correct implementation of EC Directives. Four cases were brought to the ECJ by the Commission in 2000 and 2001 against France, Italy, Luxembourg, and Spain. The ECJ ruled that France had failed to implement Directive 95/47/EC.[15] Italy was found to have failed to implement the 1997 TWF Directive, particularly the provisions relating to advertising.[16] Spain (again in dispute with

---

[13] Communication from the Commission on the application of State aid rules to public service broadcasting. *OJ C 320, 15.11.2001*, pp. 5–11 and Commission clarifies application of State aid rules to Public Service Broadcasting Press Release—IP/01/1429—17.10.2001.

[14] *Communication on Services of General Interest in Europe* COM(2000) 580 final, p. 35.

[15] Case C-319/99 *Commission v. France* 2000 23.11.00.

[16] Case C-207/00 *Commission v. Italy* 2001 14.06.01 Failure to transpose Directive 97/36/EC.

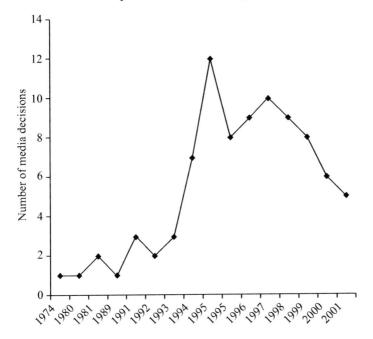

FIGURE 8.2. Number of MTF media decisions 1989–2001
Source: Compiled by author.

Canal Plus) was found to have incorrectly transposed Directive 95/47/EC (standards for the transmission of television signals) by requiring registration of digital television operators as a condition for licensing.[17] Luxembourg was found to have failed to implement the 1997 TWF.[18]

Vertical Europeanization via EC Merger Policy

Competition policy has long been recognized as a key policy area of the Commission (Wilks and McGowan 1995; Cini and McGowan 1997). Within the Commission, DG Competition has responsibility for competition decisions and, since 1995, has housed the Merger Task Force (MTF). EC merger law has been utilized in a great number of decisions concerning media markets (Figure 8.2), which has promoted Europeanization in the regulation of national media markets, particularly in digital television.

[17] *Canal Satélite Digital* SL v. *Administración General del Estado* 2001 08.03.01 Ruling on technical standards and registration rules set by the Spanish government.
[18] Case C-119/00 *Commission* v *Luxembourg* 2001 21.06.01 Failure to implement Directive 97/36/EC.

EC competition law is applicable to European markets when agreements between companies are seen to come into conflict with the creation of a Single Market or there is generally a perceived threat to competition through cartels, monopolies, or mergers. However, Cini and McGowan highlight that a key objective of competition policy is the protection of the consumer, as has been a tradition of the United States, United Kingdom, and many other national competition regimes. This entails 'the defence of the individual against big business, usually for moral or political reasons' (Cini and McGowan 1997: 4).[19] At the national level, this is where extra constraints on media markets have come in to play. For instance, in the United Kingdom, the application of competition law has been balanced by the use of the public interest test in the media sector. The same *political* considerations effect competition policy at the European level. These considerations have manifested themselves in various ways. Mostly political concerns are dealt with informally, within the *cabinet* of the competition Commissioner, where a final decision on all competition cases is taken.

Following the 1989 *TWF* Directive and the 1989 Merger Regulation, there was a dramatic increase in the number of media market decisions (see Figure 8.2). Between 1989–99, the EC made over fifty formal decisions in the media sector. The majority of decisions were decided positively in favour of market concentration. However, eight of the decisions resulted in negative decisions. This is significant, as within the period 1990–99 only ten of 1,104 merger decisions made by the EC were negative.[20] No less than six of these ten negative decisions dealt with the media sector.[21] A further two negative decisions were taken in the media sector under Article 85 of the Treaty of Rome during the same period.[22] This brings the total of formal negative decisions taken by the EC in the media sector to eight in a ten-year period. If informal decisions[23] are included, the total number of negative decisions made against media market concentrations amounts to nine. This occurred when the EC informally suggested that BSkyB

[19] Cini and McGowan state that when the competition authority was set up, 'an identifiable consumer culture provided evidence of a public interest dimension within the policy' (1997: 24). At the time, consumer policy was situated within the same Directorate General.

[20] Cini and McGowan also note the high occurrence of negative decisions in the media sector, amounting to 4 out of 7 by 1996 (1997: 130). Other authors have also commented upon this phenomenon (Kon 1996). Since this time (1999–2002), have been a further 865 decisions taken—meaning a total of 1,969 have been made by the MTF between 1995–2002, eighteen of which were prohibitions. See EC competition Statistics on European Merger Control: http://europa.eu.int/comm/competition/mergers/cases/stats.html.

[21] These are MSG Media Service Case No. IV/M.469 1994 [OJL 364, 09.11.94]; Nordic Satellite Distribution Case No. IV/M.490 1995 [OJL 53, 19.07.95]; RTL/Veronica/Endemol Case No. IV/M.553 1995 [OJL 294, 19.11.96]; Telefónica/Canal Plus/Cablevisión Case No. IV/M.0709 1996 [OJC 228/05, 07.08.96]; Deutsche Telekom/Betaresearch Case No. IV/M.1027 1998 [27.05.98]; and DF1/Premiere Case No. IV/M.993 1998 [01.06.98].

[22] Screensport/EBU Case No. IV/32.524 1991 [OJL 063/32, 09.03.91]; Tiercé Ladbroke SA Case No. IV/33 1993 [OJC 699, 24.06.93].

[23] Many of these are decided in letters although there is a problem with this as letters have no legal validity. For discussion see Emma Tucker, 'Europe's Paper Mountain' *Financial Times* 11.02.98.

be excluded from British Digital Broadcasting (BDB) when the United Kingdom issued digital licences in 1997. Informal negotiations were also attempted to deal with the Premiere/DF1 digital platform, until the case was officially registered with the European Commission in December 1997.

Following the *TWF*, the first negative decision concerning media markets was the 1991 Screensport/EBU decision.[24] The MTF determined that a joint venture between the EBU and News International presented a dominant market position. In 1988, the satellite sports company, Screensport, had filed two complaints with the MTF. The first related to its inability to access Eurosport exclusive rights. In its second complaint, Screensport claimed that Satellite Sport Services Ltd, a joint venture between the EBU and News International, occupied an unduly dominant position in the European market for sports broadcasting. The MTF decided to split the case in two, firstly tackling the legitimacy of Satellite Sport Services Ltd. In May 1988, seventeen members of the European Broadcasting Union (EBU), which is made up of public service broadcasters (PSBs), had signed an exclusive rights agreement (the Eurosport Consortium Agreement) to share sporting broadcasts. Later that year, in December, the EBU set up the joint venture Satellite Sport Services Ltd, with News International, to provide sports programming. The EBU and News International then signed two exclusive rights agreements with the joint venture company: a Services Agreement and a Facilities Agreement. An additional Guarantee was signed between News International and Eurosport. The MTF ruled in favour of Screensport, and against the EBU/News International joint venture, determining an infringement of Article 85(1) as the joint venture excluded third parties' access. The complaint against the EBU's exclusive rights agreement was decided later in 1993. In this case, the European Commission exempted the EBU from EU competition rules and permitted the EBU to hold exclusive rights to broadcast sports events (based upon the Eurovision system).[25] This decision was later challenged in the ECJ (as detailed in Section 'The Impact of ECJ Decisions on National Regulation').

The next case of significance was the 1991 *ABC/Generale des Eaux/Canal+/WHSmith* decision.[26] The proposed joint venture dealt with an agreement between ESPN Inc. (a subsidiary of Capital Cities/ABC), Générale d'Images (GdI) (a subsidiary of Compagnie Générale des Eaux), and Canal Plus to acquire the television interests of W.H. Smith. Capital Cities/ABC is a US communications group, with a particular interest in selling sports programmes (baseball and American football) to European pay television channels. Canal Plus is the French pay television channel. The three groups acquired WHSTV, which belonged to W.H. Smith. WHSTV owns TESN, the

---

[24] 91/130/EEC: Commission Decision of 19 February 1991 relating to a proceeding pursuant to Article 85 of the EEC Treaty (IV/32.524 – Screensport/EBU members).
[25] EBU/Eurovision Decision Case No. IV/32.150 [OJL 179/06, 22.07.93].
[26] ABC/Generale des Eaux/Canalt/WH Smith [IV/M.110, 10.09.91].

European Sports Network (ESPN)[27] (formerly Screensport), LifeStyle TV, Kindernet, Cable Jukebox, and the Molinare Group. (WHSTV also owned Yorkshire TV, but this was not included in the acquisition). The joint venture between the three companies was eventually permitted to go ahead. However, it is significant that the MTF used this case to more narrowly define the product market in broadcasting. It determined in its decision that pay television and commercial free access television constituted separate product markets. The case is also interesting because it again dealt with sports broadcasting, which was deemed by the MTF to be 'particularly amenable for transnational broadcasting as (it) transcend(s) national, cultural, and linguistic barriers'. This is significant for future decisions as sports broadcasting is no longer considered to be restricted to national (geographical) markets, but is now a 'European' issue.

MTF investigations of concentrations taking place between the largest German media groups are numerous. Between 1994 and 1999, the MTF investigated no less than fourteen joint ventures involving German media groups. Nine investigations handled joint ventures taking place solely between German companies, within the national German market.[28] Six investigations dealt with German groups seeking joint ventures externally to Germany.[29] In 1994, the MTF decided the first two of these cases, which dealt with cross-border acquisitions: the Kirch/Richemont/Telepiù case and the Bertelsmann/News International/Vox case.[30] The cases were decided positively, but the MTF, as in the *ABC/Generale des Eaux/Canal + /WHSmith* case, narrows the definition of pay and commercial free access television.

The definition of broadcasting markets was narrowed further in the 1994 Kirch/Richemont/Telepiù case (No. IV/M.410). In this case, Kirch and Richemont acquired joint control of the Italian television group Telepiù S.r.1 (owned at the time by Berlusconi). The Commission decided positively as the Italian language market presented a new market for the companies involved. On 27 June 1994, Richemont (through its subsidiary, Ichor) acquired CIT (which

---

[27] European Sports Network runs TV Sport, Sportkanal, and Sportnet.

[28] MSG Media Service (Case No. IV/M.469, OJL 364, 09.11.94); N-TV (Case No IV/M.810, OJC 366/05, 05.12.96); Bertelsmann/Burda/Springer Hos MM (Case No IV/M.972, 15.09.97); Bertelsmann/Burda Hos Lifeline (Case No IV/M.973, 15.09.97); Deutsche Telekom/Betaresearch (Case No. IV/M.1027, 27.95.98); DF1/Premiere (Case No. IV/M.993, 01.06.98); Bertelsmann/Burda/Futurekids (Case No . IV/M. 1072, 29.01.98). Havas/Bertelsmann/Doyma (Case No. IV/M.800, 27.08.98).

[29] Kirch/Richemont/Telepiù Decision (Case No. IV/M.410, OJC 225/04, 13.08.94); Bertelsmann/News International/Vox Decision (Case No. IV/M.489, OJ C 274/06, 01.10.94); Vox (II) (Case No. IV/M.525, OJ C 57/06, 07.03.95); Kirch/Richemont/Multichoice/Telepiù (Case No. IV/M.584, OJC 129/07, 16.06.95); Bertelsmann/CLT (Ufa), Case No. IV/M.0779, OJC 364/05, 04.12.96); Deutsch Telekom/Betaresearch Case No. IV/M.1027.

[30] The Kirch/Richemont/Telepiù Decision Case No. IV/M.410 1994 [OJC 225/04, 13.08.94] and the Bertelsmann/News International/Vox Decision Case No. IV/M.489 1994 [OJ C 274/06, 01.10.94].

held 25 per cent of Telepiù) and Kirch (through its subsidiary Beteiligungs-
GmbH) upped its stake in Telepiù from 34.72 to 40.73 per cent. The remaining
shareholders in Telepiù were the Della Valle Group (23.39 per cent) and
Fininvest (10 per cent). It was agreed that the President of the Board would represent Kirch. The Commission decided in this case that Kirch and Richemont's
joint control of Telepiù did not present a problem of coordination of competitive
behaviour because Richemont and Kirch operated in separate pay-television
television markets according to geographic criteria. This opened the Italian
market for the first time to foreign competition.

This dividing of free access as opposed to pay-access markets was confirmed in a different media decision made by the MTF in the same year. In the
1994 Bertelsmann/News International/Vox case (Case No. IV/M.489), News
International bought a 49.9 per cent stake in Vox, a German free-to-air television channel. Vox was 24.9 per cent owned by Bertelsmann. Because media
markets are divided linguistically by the MTF, it was considered whether the
acquisition strengthened either of the companies' dominant positions in the
German television market. Up until this point, News International had entered
the German language market some years before through a joint venture with
Selco (50 per cent owned by Kirch's Pro 7). The Commission decided again
that free access channels and pay channels constituted separated markets.
Therefore, because Vox was a free-to-air channel, the MTF did not consider
News International to be increasing its dominance in the German language
market, since the company was present in two separate markets: free-to-air
and pay television. The MTF also considered the potential for Bertelsmann
and News International to trade film rights. It was concluded that this did not
at that point in time present a problem for the German market. However, this
could again be an issue, now that Kirch is bankrupt and selling off its assets.

In 1994, the Commission made the first of what could be labelled four highly
controversial negative decisions on joint ventures in the German market.[31] In its
1994 MSG Media Service decision, the Commission ruled against a German
joint venture for pay television Media Service GmbH (MSG) between
Bertelsmann, Kirch, and Deutsche Telekom (DT).[32] The proposal was a joint
pay-television venture between Bertelsmann AG, Taurus Beteiligungs GmbH
(belonging to Kirch), and Deutsche Bundespost Telekom (the public telecommunications group). The MTF found the joint venture to be incompatible with
the common market as it would have created a dominant position in three

---

[31] MSG Media Service (Case No. IV/M.469, OJL 364, 09.11.94), Deutsche
Telekom/Betaresearch (Case No. IV/M.1027, 27.95.98), DF1/Premiere (Case No. IV/M.993,
01.06.98.), Betaresearch *et al.* (1998), and Deutsch Telekom/Betaresearch Case No. IV/M.1027.
[32] 94/922/EC: Commission Decision of 9 November 1994 relating to a proceeding pursuant
to Council Regulation (EEC) No 4064/89 (IV/M.469—MSG Media Service) *Official journal
NO. L 364, 31/12/1994 P. 0001–0021*].

markets: technical services (MSG), pay television (Kirch and Bertlesmann through Premiere), and cable distribution (DT). The Commission also considered that MSG was likely to gain a lasting dominant position in new media markets (of the future), particularly for digital television where it would foreclose the market to new entrants. Even though these were economic rationales for preventing the joint venture, it is plain to see that such a joint venture had serious implications for cultural (and political) representation in Germany.

The next media concentration to be prohibited by the MTF was Nordic Satellite Distribution (NSD) in 1995.[33] This related to the capacity of a satellite television responder. The MTF found that NSD (a joint venture between Norsk Telecomm, Tele Denmark, and Kinnevik) would acquire a dominant position in the market for satellite television transponder services targeted towards Nordic viewers. This would in turn strengthen Tele Denmark's dominant position in the Danish cable television market. The vertical integration of NSD meant that the companies' respective positions in their national markets would reinforce each other. In addition, the Commission reasoned that the NSD would lead to the dominance of Viasat (Kinnevik's subsidiary) in the specific market of pay-television distribution (to direct-to-home households). The MTF expressed in this case that it wished to ensure that the Scandinavian markets, which were in a stage of liberalization, were not foreclosed to third parties (Butterworth's Merger Control Review 1995).

Soon afterwards, the Commission ruled against the 1995 *Holland Media Group (HMG)* joint venture.[34] The *Holland Media Group* had proposed a joint venture in commercial television in the Netherlands between RTL4 S.A., Vereniging Veronica Omroeperganisatie, and Endemol Entertainment Holding BV. The Dutch government had requested a ruling on the case under Article 22(3) of the Merger Regulation. Had the Dutch government not referred the case, the Commission would have had no jurisdiction to judge it as the turnover thresholds were below those required by the Merger Regulation.[35] The MTF ruled the agreement would lead to the creation of a dominant position in the Dutch advertising market and strengthen Endemol's dominant position in the market for independent Dutch-language television production. Clearly, as this case dealt with a purely national case and a venture with a comparatively low turnover, the Commission's concerns in this case overstepped those of ensuring a

[33] Commission Decision of 19 July 1995 declaring a concentration to be incompatible with the common market and the functioning of the EEA Agreement (Case No IV/M.490—Nordic Satellite Distribution) (96/177/EC).

[34] 96/346/EC: Commission Decision of 20 September 1995 relating to a proceeding pursuant to Council Regulation (EEC) No 4064/89 (IV/M.553–RTL/Veronica/Endemol). Official journal NO. L 134 , 05/06/1996 P. 0032–0052.

[35] If a case is referred to the European Commission under Article 22(3) of the Merger Regulation, the companies are permitted to go ahead with their proposed concentration while the case is being examined.

competition market. When commenting on the case, Commissioner Van Miert stated that 'the strict application of the competition rules can also contribute to maintaining plurality in this sensitive sector' (Lang 1997: 42). Later in July 1996, the Commission approved the joint venture following the withdrawal of Endemol from the project. Endemol challenged the MTF over the ruling at the CFI and lost.

In 1997, five decisions were made on joint ventures within the German media market, which is showing an increasingly high degree of market concentration. The two joint ventures between the large press groups Bertelsmann and Burda,[36] and Bertelsmann, Burda, and Springer[37] were examined and approved. In the three broadcasting cases, the MTF reached *negative* decisions. The broadcasting cases dealt with the proposed acquisition and joint control of the German pay-TV operator Premiere and BetaResearch by Bertelsmann and Kirch. Bertelsmann and Kirch owned Premiere and DF1 respectively, which represented the only pay-television packages in Germany. The plan was to launch a joint digital platform. Together, the two companies also controlled the standard digital set top box and had extensive programming rights. In the first decision, the Commission pronounced the joint venture as incompatible with the common market, as it represented a concentration in the 'European German-speaking market'. The Commission had initially put informal pressure on the German government and the Bundeskartellamt (the German Cartel Office) to decide the case at the national level. When the German government decided to approve the joint venture (against the wishes of the 6 SPD German *Länder* which refused to license the service), the European Commission warned the three companies that they risked a fine of a maximum of 10 per cent of their combined turnovers if they proceeded with plans to launch the digital service without notifying the European Commission. The MTF opened an investigation. Under Kohl's leadership, the German government expressed opposition to a negative ruling on behalf of the Commission. ('Freund Kohl in geheimer Mission', *Süddeutsche Zeitung*, 17.12.97). Despite this political resistance, the Commission prevented the joint venture under EU Merger Regulation.[38]

The second case (which was filed at the same time as DF1/Premiere) was Deutsche Telekom/Betaresearch.[39] This second case related to the joint control of the D-Box decoder by Bertelsmann, Kirch, and Deutsche Telekom. A negative decision was adopted by the Commission on 27.5.1998. Shortly

---

[36] Case No IV/M.973 Bertelsmann/Burda Hos Lifeline [15.09.97].

[37] Case No IV/M.972 Bertelsmann/Burda/Springer Hos MM [15.09.97].

[38] It was only possible for the Commission to intervene in the German market because the MTF could argue that domestic media concentration effected linguistic markets external to Germany–Austria and the German speaking minorities in the Netherlands and Belgium.

[39] Deutsche Telekom/Betaresearch Case No. IV/M.1027.

afterwards, the President of the Bundeskartellamt, Dieter Wolf, stated 'the majority of national states lacked both the strength and the courage to do anything about their respective monopolies. A higher political level was called upon to do so, and this is where the European Commission came in.'[40] This statement indicates that increasing media concentration renders national governments powerless to stand up to large media groups. The Dutch *HMG*, German *Bertelsmann/Kirch/Premiere*, and British *BDB* (below) cases clearly demonstrate this.

As in Germany, the UK's media market has also come under scrutiny from the MTF which has investigated four cases of dominant position within the British domestic market.[41] In one case, the British Telecom/MCI (1993), the MTF prevented a market concentration. The second case dealt with BSkyB's involvement in British Digital Broadcasting (BDB). The DTI had approved BSkyB's participation in the creation of British Digital Broadcasting (BDB, later known as ONdigital). The Commission launched a series of informal discussions with UK regulatory bodies (Snoddy (1997) claims that these talks were initiated by the ITC). The Commission argued that the joint venture BDB would strengthen BSkyB's dominant position in the UK pay-television market and encourage cooperation (rather than competition) between BDB and BSkyB. In particular, the MTF stated that granting a licence to the joint venture as it stood would strengthen the dominant position of BSkyB, which would be contrary to a principle ruled in by the ECJ in *Ahmed Saeed Flugreisen*[42] (Lang 1997: 32). The UK government, referring to EC advice, decided that BSkyB should not join the joint venture.

Again the issue of national media concentration came to the fore, this time in Spain. A case decided negatively in 1996 concerned the acquisition of Cablevisión by Telefónica de España and Sogecable SA, a subsidiary of Canal Plus España.[43] The MTF found that the venture affected the supply of services to cable television operators and prevented new entrants to markets for pay and cable television. Originally, the companies had notified the acquisition to the Spanish Competition Defence Tribunal (TDC), which vetoed the joint venture, but it was overruled by the Spanish government. After this, the Commission wrote to Canal Plus España requesting notification to the Commission (indeed,

---

[40] Wolf, Diete (1997). Position on the subject of 'Commission and National Competence—A Debate'. Paper presented at the Future of Merger Control in Europe conference, European University Institute, Florence, 26.09.97 by Committee C (Antitrust and Trade Law) of the International Bar Association.

[41] 1993 BBC/BSkyB/Football Association Case No. IV/33.145 and IV/33.245 [OJC 94/6, 03.04.93]; 1993 British Telecom/MCI Case IV/M.353 [OJC 259/03, 27.08.93]; 1997 British Telecom/MCI (II) Case No IV/M.856 [14.05.97]; 1997 BSkyB/British Digital Broadcasting Case IV/M. 300.

[42] Case 66/86, *Ahmed Saeed Flugreisen* ECR 802. The principle is based on Article 5 of the treaties.   [43] 1996 Case No. IV/M.0709 [OJC 228/05, 07.08.96].

informally the Commission had to put up a considerable fight to wrench the decision away from the Spanish government). Following a negative decision by the MTF, Sogecable sought an annulment in the CFI and a suspension of the Commission's activities until the Court had determined whether the operation had a Community dimension. The CFI did not suspend the MTF investigation (as it viewed this to be a substitution of the EC's administrative activities), but supported the MTF decision.[44] In any case, just before the CFI decision was announced, the operation was withdrawn due to a change in the Spanish government in 1996.

The Spanish government then tried to prevent the launch of Canal Satélite Digital with two laws[45] (Llorens-Maluquer 1998: 578–85). The government stated that the laws were enacted to promote pluralism as they required the use of multicrypt (rather than simulcrypt) transmission and mandated the shared use of sports rights. As Canal Satélite Digital was using simulcrypt, this rendered their broadcasts illegal. The Commission opposed both of the laws as anti-competitive and in contrary to the free movement of goods and threatened to challenge them in the ECJ. As Llorens-Maluquer details well, a long battle between the Commission and the Spanish government ensued resulting in a revocation by Spain of both laws (1998).[46] In a parallel development, CDS challenged one of the laws (Real Decreto Ley 1/97) in a Spanish court (Tribunal Supremo), which referred the case in turn to the ECJ. Long after the Real Decreto had been revoked, the ECJ ruled with the Spanish court, and against the Spanish government, in January 2002.[47]

In 1997, two Spanish cases dealt with the cable television company Cable I Televisio de Catalunya (CTC), in the Spanish region of Catalonia. In the first case,[48] joint acquisition of CTC was proposed by the electric company, Endesa, the gas company, Gas Natural (the principle suppliers of electricity and gas in Spain), Stet (the Italian telecommunications operator), and Caixa Catalunya (the leading Catalan bank). In the second case,[49] the American companies General Electric (through Cableuropa) and Bank of America (through SpainCom) proposed partial acquisition of CTC. The European companies were dubbed 'the European partners' and the American companies, 'the American partners'. The MTF authorized the acquisitions in both cases,

---

[44] 1996 Case T-52/96 Sogecable SA v Commission of the European Communities. [12.07.96, ECR 0797].

[45] 1997 Real Decreto Ley 1/97 incorporation of the EC Directive 95/47/CE; and 1997 Ley 17/97 (conversion into law of the decree law) Regulation of the Emission and Retransmission of Competitive Sport (Reguladora de las Emisiones y Retransmisiones de Competiciones Deportivas).

[46] Ley 1/97 amends Leys 1 and 16/97 with the changes mandated by the Commission.

[47] Case C-390/99 Canal Satélite Digital V. Spain 2002 [22.01.02].

[48] Cable I Televisio de Catalunya (CTC). Case No. IV/M.1022 [28.01.98].

[49] Cableeuropa/SpainCom/CTC, Case No. IV/M. 1091 1998 [28.01.98].

establishing joint control between the American and European partners in CTC. The Commission could not justify an intervention under the 1989 EC Merger Regulation and approved the cases. However, the MTF expressed dissatisfaction with the ruling (European Bulletin 1/2 1998: 25, 1999: 14).

With the amendment of the Merger Regulation in April 1997, paragraphs 1 and 3 of Article 85 have been extended to joint ventures to determine whether or not a dominant position is created or maintained. Even though turnover thresholds have been lowered from five to two-and-a-half billion ECU under the new rules, only a small number of cases are expected to utilize the new lowered thresholds due to the organizational requirements involved (Fine 1997).[50] The new rules entered into effect on 1 March 1998. The Telenor case, which related to the provision of Internet and audio–visual interactive services in Sweden, represented the first media case to which the new rules applied in 1998. The number of media cases is on the rise, but since 1999, when Van Miert left office, the EC has made no negative decisions in the media sector. This section has shown that the EC's MTF has had a strong influence on the development of media markets in Europe, particularly in the case of digital television and the prevention of market concentration at the national level.

The Commission and New Modes of Governance

Sections 'Vertical Europeanization via EC Merger Policy' and 'The Commission and New Modes of Governance' looked at vertical mechanisms of Europeanization—how decisions of the ECJ and MTF have influenced national media markets and laws. This section looks at the horizontal mechanism. The Commission is facing a number of problems in producing media directives due to limitations in the EU Treaties, reliance on economic policy instruments, and politicization of policy processes. Depoliticization of the policy process during TWF negotiations was hard won by the Commission. Subsequently, the Commission met with insurmountable political obstacles during policy processes for the EC initiatives on *media ownership* and *convergence* (this is the convergence between telecommunications and media markets). These political obstacles have limited the Commission's capacity to regulate the media sector. However, although media regulation has represented a significant impasse to conventional policy making (in the form of directives), the Commission has since found new ways of governing media markets. These are through the suggestion of best practice solutions to domestic policy problems

---

[50] Even the old rules have proved difficult in this respect. For example, when the MTF decided negatively on the Canal Plus/Metro joint venture, the decision had to ratified by six national authorities.

(in green papers) and the establishment of media forums at the European level which have been used to diffuse suggested policy instruments.

In 1993, the Commission came up with a new idea for regulating media markets: audience share.[51] This policy instrument first appeared in a one-hundred page study commissioned by DG XV and sent out to national authorities in 1993. This, along with other technical studies on regulating media markets, was sent out to interest groups in 1995 during consultation on the EC's media ownership draft directive. The instrument has subsequently been adopted to regulate media markets in three countries: Germany, the United Kingdom, and Ireland. Diffusion of the idea in Germany was aided by the organization of meetings at the national level by an EC head of unit, wherein national media experts discussed solutions to growing media concentration. Audience share was adopted as a key regulatory instrument in the 1996 inter-state treaty. Under the German 1996 Interstate Treaty on Broadcasting, broadcasting companies are limited to a 30 per cent share of national audience.

The United Kingdom and Ireland also adopted audience share as an instrument for regulating domestic media markets. The UK 1996 Broadcasting Act introduces audience share to limit of broadcasters to 15 per cent (for both television and radio stations). In the United Kingdom, the civil servant drafting the 1996 Act adopted the idea of audience share directly from the EC studies. With the new instrument, there is now no limit in the United Kingdom on ITV license ownership, as long as the combination of company ownership and their corresponding license-holding does not exceed 15 per cent. The 15 per cent limit has remained intact under the new 2002 Broadcasting Act. In Ireland, the same instrument was adopted in Ireland's 2001 Broadcasting Act.

The necessity to implement the 1997 *Television Without Frontiers Directive* at national levels resulted in the adoption of new media acts in most member states and prompted many countries to re-examine their regulation of national media markets. At this point in time, a number of countries (specifically Italy, Spain, Switzerland, Slovenia, and the United Kingdom) chose to embrace the EU's convergence initiative. In 1996, the Commission produced its convergence green paper which recommended a new joint authority for both media and telecommunications. The Commission's ISPO group, which includes national experts from all member states, aided in diffusion of the idea.

Italy and Spain were the first to regulate for convergence. Italy's 1997 New Media Act established an Authority for Communications (Autorità per le garanzie nelle comunicazioni), which was set up in 1998. It replaces the *Press and Broadcasting Authority* and is situated within the new Ministry for Communications. It was the first regulatory authority in Europe to regulate

---

[51] The concept of audience share was created by FCC consultant William Shew in the study *Measures of Media Concentration* (American Enterprise Institute), commissioned by News International and sent to the European Commission in 1989 (Harcourt 2003).

both telecommunications and media under one roof. It both issues broadcasting licences and regulates telecommunications companies. The new Authority monitors media mergers and acquisitions taking place across all related media markets, including telecommunications and new services. Spain also passed an Act in 1997 which set up a joint regulatory authority for both telecommunications and media markets. Switzerland (2000), Slovenia (2001), and the United Kingdom (2002) soon followed suit with new media acts setting up new joint authorities.

Conclusion

This chapter has shown that national media market regulation has been effected through the interplay of horizontal and vertical mechanisms of Europeanization. The first mechanism consists of formal decision making by the European institutions in the form of directives, competition decisions, and ECJ decisions. The horizontal mechanism consisted of the transfer of policy instruments through forum politics (high level working groups, committees, platforms of regulators). Taken together, the two mechanisms have led to a Europeanization of media market regulation at national levels in the form of formal changes to media laws, the adoption of suggested policy instruments, and regulatory approaches at the national level.

The first mechanism concerned formal decisions of the ECJ and MTF that have been shown to require changes to national laws in Belgium, Greece, the Netherlands, Spain, and the United Kingdom. The section 'The Impact of ECJ Decisions on National Regulation' showed how the ECJ was an important actor in promoting Europeanization by taking an assertive role in expanding EU legal competence in the media field. Its decisions are effecting national legislation. The ECJ's decision that broadcasting be considered a service places broadcasting in the realm of economic policy to be determined at the European level and removes it from cultural policy which resides with the member state. The Court has been consistent in upholding this decision throughout all of its media cases. From 1994, the ECJ has supported the clause in *TWF* which maintains that broadcasting be governed by the laws stemming from the state of transmission and not the state of reception. The court's position on public service has differed from that of member states in that it found that public service broadcasters should be considered equivalent to commercial broadcasters. Section 'Vertical Europenization via EC Merger Policy' discussed how the MTF has been increasingly interventionist in national media markets by narrowing the definition of media product markets and thereby expanding its own competence. The MTF was shown to have taken an active role in determining the structure of the media industry in Europe. The examples of

Spain and the Netherlands were given to show how the MTF had promoted greater sector liberalization than desired by member states. The second horizontal mechanism showed how the Commission has influenced national policies through the suggestion of policy instruments in EU level forums. The implementation of European Directives (particularly the 1989 and 1997 *Television Without Frontiers* directives) prompted overhauls of national laws. When drawing up new media acts, national civil servants choose to embrace EU policy solutions in domestic laws. This has occurred with the adoption of the Commission idea of audience share in the German 1996 Interstate Agreement, the British 1996 Broadcasting Act, and the 2001 Irish Broadcasting Act; and the embrace of the Commission-inspired 'convergence' initiative in the 1997 Spanish Law on Telecommunications, the 1997 Italian New Media Act, the 2000 Swiss Broadcasting Act, the 2001 Slovene Media Act, and the 2002 UK Broadcasting Act. Apart from the countries under examination in this chapter, recent media acts were introduced in Austria, the Czech Republic, Denmark, Estonia, France, Greece, Holland, Hungary, Luxembourg, Portugal, Poland, and Sweden (on the transfer of media regulation models in the context of EU enlargement see Harcourt 2002). Indeed, all EU member state media laws have shown effects of Europeanization, which has resulted in an overall convergence in national policies at the national level.

REFERENCES

Butterworth's Merger Control Review (1995). 'Article 8 Decisions: Nordic Satellite Distribution—Case No. IV/M490', *Butterworth's Merger Control Review* 5(3): 12–15.
Cini, Michelle and Lee McGowan (1997). *EU Competition Policy* (London: Macmillan).
Communications and Information Technology (CIT) (2001). *The Media Map of Western and Eastern Europe* (London: CIT).
EIM (1994). *La Transparence Dans Le Contrôle Des Médias*.
Fine, Frank L. (1997). 'Recent Developments in EC Merger Control', presented at the *Future of Merger Control in Europe* conference, European University Institute, Florence, 26.09.97.
GAH (1993). *Audience Measurement in the EC*.
GAH (1994) *Feasibility of Using Audience Measures to Assess Pluralism*.
Harcourt, Alison J. (2002). 'Policy Transfer, the Regulation of Media Markets in First Wave Accession States', *European Law Journal* 58(12).
——(2003). *European Institutions and the Regulation of Media Markets: New Modes of Governance* (Manchester: Manchester University Press).
Kon, Stephen (1996). '*Competition Law and the Audio-visual Industry*' (S. J. Beowia & Co.).

Korthals Altes, W. (1993). 'European Law: A Case Study of Changes in National Broadcasting', *Cardozo Arts and Entertainment Law Journal* 11: 313–35.

Lang, John Temple (1997). 'Media, Multimedia and European Community Antitrust Law', typescript, European Commission.

Llorens-Maluquer, Carlos (1998). 'European Responses to Bottlenecks in Digital Pay-TV', *Cardozo Arts and Entertainment Law Journal* 16(2): 425–49.

Snoddy, Raymond (1997). 'UK: EU Raises Doubts on Digital TV Licence Bid', *Financial Times* 04.06.97.

Snyder, Francis (1990). *New Directions in European Community Law* (London: Weidenfeld and Nicolson).

Wilks, S. and McGowan, L. (1995). 'The First Supranational Policy in the European Union: Competition Policy', *European Journal of Political Research* 28: 149–69.

Wolf, Dieter (1997). 'Position on the Subject of "Commission and National Competence – A Debate"', presented at the *Future of Merger Control in Europe* conference, European University Institute, Florence, 26.09.

9

The Impact of the European Union on Environmental Policies

MARKUS HAVERLAND

Introduction

Focusing on environmental policies, this chapter aims to contribute to the debate on the politics of Europeanization by presenting the conceptual and theoretical state of the art of research into this specific sector of potential EU impact on domestic political systems. As environmental policy can be regarded as one of the best-researched fields of the domestic impact of the European Union, this focus on environmental policy will yield some more general lessons for the theory and analysis of Europeanization. This chapter employs a minimalist notion of Europeanization: Europeanization is defined as national responses to European integration, or, more precisely, as national adaptation to European Union policies (see Featherstone, this volume). As this chapter is sector-oriented, national adaptation is confined to sector-specific policies rather than domestic political structures and structures of representation and cleavages more generally (see Börzel and Risse, this volume; Radaelli, Figure 2.1, this volume).

The chapter first provides some background information on the essential properties of environmental policy and on the development of EU environmental policy. This is done to explicate the defining characteristics of this sector vis-à-vis other sectors.

The chapter then reviews three recent theoretically informed comparative case studies on the determinants of national adaptation to EU environmental policy requirements (Knill 1998; Börzel 2000; Haverland 2000). These studies

An earlier version of the paper was presented at the Netherlands School of Government research seminar 'The search for convergence: Assessing the impact of the European Union on the member states', Leiden, 17–18 May, 2000. I would like to thank the participants of the workshop and also Bertjan Verbeek for their helpful comments, and Joy Burrough, who advised on the English.

are informed by either sociological institutionalism or rational choice institutionalism (see Börzel and Risse, this volume; Hall and Taylor 1996). They arrive at different and partially competing explanations for the variation in national adaptation to European environmental policies. Despite disagreement about the relative importance of the factors and mechanisms of Europeanization, the results of the comparative case studies offer elements for a theory about the conditions of policy adaptation and, by implication, about convergence. Building upon these findings the chapter suggests elements for a future research agenda. I advocate a research strategy that is based on theoretically informed comparative case studies that gradually include new policy sectors and countries. In addition, I propose to use counterfactual arguments to isolate the causal impact of the European Union. Such a strategy has the potential to ultimately address not only sector-specific policy change, but also broader issues such as domestic institutional change and the changing structures of representation and cleavages.

European Environmental Policy

What are the defining properties of environmental policy in comparison to other policy sectors? Environmental policies typically aim at regulating the use of energy and natural resources, or the environmentally harmful emissions from consumptive and productive behaviour or both. Environmental policy is regulatory rather than redistributive; it usually employs either substantive or procedural standards for potentially harmful activities and products; and it focuses either on specific environmental media such as water, air, or soil, or it assumes a more integrated form, across media (Turner *et al.* 1994).

   Radaelli (this volume) has advanced three generic policy characteristics that affect the likelihood of Europeanization. Depending on the characteristics in question, environmental policy is a moderately likely case, a most likely case, or a least likely case. Radaelli argues, for instance, that Europeanization is more likely in policy areas where pro-European technocrats can be isolated from pressure groups and public opinion. In this respect environmental policy is a moderately likely case. To some extent, setting environmental standards is a technocratic process, typically involving experts such as scientists, civil engineers, and economists. Yet a large number of actors from different branches and levels of government are typically affected and involved, as are environmental NGOs and a multitude of business interests. The latter include, for instance, polluter interests versus environmental technology interests (Haverland 1999). With regard to the second characteristic advanced by Radaelli, the relative importance of policy formulation versus implementation for success of the policy, environmental policy is clearly a policy sector for which implementation is very important. Policy effectiveness depends largely on the cooperation between the implementation agencies and the target groups (Jordan 1999; Knill and Lenschow 1999). This dependence may make Europeanization comparatively unlikely. In terms of Radaelli's third characteristic, policy discourse, however, Europeanization is quite likely. Economists and other experts have argued convincingly in favour of the centralization of policy making. As environmental policy is aimed at correcting market failure and providing common goods, centralization of decision making at the EU level will help to mitigate external effects and free riding behaviour (see Turner *et al.* 1994). Moreover, it is widely believed that most environmental problems extend across national frontiers and therefore transcend the problem-solving capacity of individual nation states. Accordingly, Eurobarometer surveys consistently document that most citizens in most EU countries believe that environmental issues should be decided at EU level rather than at national level (see, for instance, European Commission 2001).

How has environmental policy evolved? Until three decades ago, environmental policy was primarily adopted at local level and focused on safeguarding public health and personal well-being. National environmental protection policies grew in importance from the late 1960s on, gradually broadening the scope of protection to the environment in a more comprehensive ecological sense. It was not until the Single European Act (1986) that environmental protection was formally recognized as a competence of the then European Community. However, the treaty provisions concerning environmental protection merely formalized legislative activities that had been well under way for some time already. The legislation had been based upon a creative reading of either of both Article 100 and 235 of the Treaty of Rome (McCormick 1999*a*: 195). The Treaties of Maastricht (1992) and Amsterdam (1997) refined the primary legal base for environmental policy. The overall goal was defined as sustainable growth (Maastricht) and, later, as sustainable development (Amsterdam). The principles of precaution and subsidiarity have been increasingly emphasized, and most measures are now subject to the codecision procedure, which provides the European Parliament with a veto in policy making (for overviews on EU environmental policy, see McCormick 1999*b*; Weale *et al.* 2000).

The first European environmental protection policy was adopted as far back as 1967. And from the mid-1970s to the mid-1990s, a continuous stream of legislation was produced at the rate of about eight major legislative items per year on average. Thereafter, legislative activity was mainly concerned with amending existing legislation rather than creating new laws (Jordan *et al.* 1999).[1]

---

[1] It is notoriously difficult to quantify the environmental acquis. Scholars who focus on 'major' environmental legislation arrive at some 300 items, while those who employ a broader concept of what constitutes the acquis arrive at 500 or more (see Jordan *et al.* 1999; McCormick 1999*a*, 1999).

Environmental policy belongs to the group of sectors in which formal competencies are now roughly equally distributed between the European Union and its member states. Other examples of this category of policy sectors include 'competition' and 'health and safety' at work (Schmitter 1996; see Schmidt 1999).[2]

EU regulations and directives stipulate requirements that the member states must implement. EU environmental policies are examples of positive integration rather than negative integration, because the EU describes a model instead of dismantling national barriers to trade or obstacles to competition (see Scharpf 1999: 45).

In the case of positive integration, the degree of adaptation depends on the extent to which European requirements are implemented and enforced; in the case of negative integration the degree of Europeanization depends on the dynamics of regulatory competition. Moreover, Europeanization of national domestic environmental policy, if it happens, follows the vertical mechanism of coercion rather than the horizontal mechanisms of mimetism, framing, or normative pressure (Radaelli 1997; Knill and Lehmkuhl 1999; Radaelli, this volume).

Now that it has become widely accepted that European law is superior to national law, the legitimacy of coercion has increased. The pressure to implement and enforce European legislation has further been strengthened over the years by European Court of Justice case law. For instance, the European Court of Justice has ruled that European directives must come into full effect and that member states are held liable if the desired results are not achieved. Moreover, much EU legislation confers rights on individuals, who can rely on these rights in *national* courts, the so-called Direct Effect. The European Court of Justice has ruled that in such cases member states could be held liable if individuals suffer damage because of inaccurate implementation (see Prechal 1995).

Although the mechanism of coercion is dominant, 'horizontal' Europeanization via policy learning, or, in the words of Radaelli, the diffusion of ideas and discourses about the notion of 'good policy', is also present (Radaelli, this volume). Both the properties of the 'environmental protection' sector and also the characteristics of the European decision-making process are conducive to learning about policies. Environmental policy is still a relatively new policy field with plenty of scope for innovation and experimentation in regard to standards, policy instruments, and regulatory structures. Moreover, as it regulates the allocation of goods and activities rather than their distribution,

---

[2] The free movement of goods, services, capital, and labour, together with external economic relations, agriculture, and, most recently, monetary policy, which were once the domains of the nation-state, nowadays belong almost exclusively to the competencies of the European Union. The classic domains of the state in which the European Union is gradually becoming more important include home affairs, justice, foreign affairs and defence. Areas such as education, social exclusions, and redistributive social policy do still belong almost exclusively to the domestic domain.

public and private actors have an incentive to search for alternatives and modifications that increase the efficiency of allocation, in other words to create win–win situations.

The EU decision-making structure and procedures are also conducive to policy learning. The development of regulation typically takes place in issue-specific subsystems. Expertise plays an important role in these subsystems and issues are frequently depoliticized. Depoliticization and the emphasis on expertise may facilitate the diffusion of ideas and lessons learned from experience elsewhere. Certain features of the EU decision-making procedures facilitate policy learning further. To give just two examples: first, under the conditions of majority voting, member states try to build either passing or blocking coalitions. They generally do so after all kinds of options suggested by member states or the Commission have been exhaustively explored, and careful studies of existing national programmes. Second, member states have to notify any draft law that might actually or potentially restrict intra-EU free trade in goods. There is an EU committee that discusses in depth these hundreds of notifications of national laws, decrees, etc. and comes up with comments or detailed opinions, or both. 'Nowhere in the world is there such an intense, routine-based process of understanding one another's regulations. Learning is likely to be considerable here' (Pelkmans 1997: 4).

The Determinants of National Adaptation to European Environmental Policy: A Review of Recent Studies

If European regulations and directives deviate from national environmental policies these national environmental policies must be adapted. Since the mid-1980s, studies on the implementation of European policies have gradually increased in number and in theoretical and methodological sophistication. Whereas most of the early work comprised descriptive single case studies, some recent examples are theoretically more advanced and are based on cross-national or cross-issue comparisons or actually combine both perspectives.[3] As reviewing such studies offers the prospects of accumulating knowledge and developing theories, I propose to compare three recent studies (Knill 1998; Börzel 2000; Haverland 2000).[4]

The studies under review follow an intensive research design, focusing on a few countries and one or a few directives. Together they cover six environmental directives and one Council regulation: in chronological order of

---

[3] An early example of a systematic and empirically comprehensive comparative study is Siedentopf and Ziller (1988*a,b*).

[4] Note that this chapter focuses on the adaptation of national environmental policies rather than on national environmental administrations (see for the latter Weale *et al.* 1996; Jordan 2001).

adoption these are the Drinking Water Directive (80/788/EEC), the Directive on Air Pollution of Industrial Plants (84/366/EEC), the Environmental Impact Assessment (EIA) Directive (85/337/EEC), the Large Combustion Plant (LCP) Directive (88/609 EEC), the Access to Information (AI) Directive (90/313/EEC), the Environmental Management and Audit System (EMAS) Regulation (Regulation EEC, No. 1836/93), and the Packaging and Packaging Waste Directive (94/62/EC).

Although relatively small in number, these policies are sufficiently diverse to represent an appropriate sample of EU environmental policy over the last three decades. The Drinking Water Directive, the LCP Directive, and the Industrial Plant Directive stipulate substantive standards for specific environmental media, whereas the AI Directive, the EIA Directive, and the EMAS Regulation provide procedural standards and follow an integrative, across media, approach. The Packaging and Packaging Waste Directive entails both procedural and substantive standards. In addition, it is also an example of product regulation.

The countries under investigation include the environmental front runners the Netherlands and Germany, the somewhat more reluctant United Kingdom and France, and the alleged environmental laggard Spain (see Andersen and Liefferink 1997; Börzel 2000).[5] As will be elaborated below, these countries also vary significantly in their policies and regulatory styles, hence for any European policy adopted they display, to a varying degree, pressure to adapt.

The comparative case studies reviewed emphasize different determinants for the adaptation of national policy to European integration. At the same time, each study presents solid empirical evidence for its theoretical claim. This puzzle is attributable to the studies' focus on somewhat dissimilar cases. Having demonstrated their explanatory strength for particular cases, the determinant can serve as building blocks for a general theory on national policy adaptation to the European Union. Future research is needed to show the relative importance of the determinants identified in these studies and the interaction between them (see final section).

The Impact of National Administrations

The first systematic comparative case studies concentrated on national public administrations, the main agents involved in the implementation of European policies. These studies depart implicitly or explicitly from an institutional perspective developed by the sociological branch of neoinstitutionalism. This approach assumes that actor behaviour is guided by standard operating procedures, based upon the logic of appropriateness, rather than that such behaviour is guided strategically—that is, based upon the logic of consequentialism

---

[5] For the sake of brevity, results for France will not be reported.

(March and Olsen 1984; Hall and Taylor 1996; see Börzel and Risse, this volume). Accordingly, the aforementioned authors emphasize the stickiness of national administrative structures and practices in situations of environmental change. The general idea is that implementation and national adaptation are made more difficult, if not impossible, if European policies and their administrative implications differ significantly from national arrangements and standard operating procedures.

Knill (1998) (see Knill and Lenschow 1998) presents a particular systematic, theoretically informed, and empirically rich study in this respect. Essential to his argument is the concept of pressure to adapt, which is defined as the degree of institutional incompatibility between national structures and practices and EU requirements (see Börzel and Risse, this volume; Radaelli, this volume). Institutional compatibility is inferred from the nature of the EU policy requirements, the degree of embeddedness of those features in national administrative styles and structures, and the national capacity to change these administrative features; in other words, the 'embeddedness of embeddedness' (Knill 1998: 24). To give an example: the EIA Directive requires a regulatory style that is based on procedural interventions and great flexibility. This requirement does not fit in the German regulatory style, which is characterized by substantive intervention and legalism. This misfit constitutes the first dimension of incompatibility. Next, the legalistic regulatory style is difficult to change because it is strongly embedded in the German tradition of *Rechtsstaat* that is based on a superior role of the state vis-à-vis society, as well as the binding of the administration to law. The latter limits how much flexibility and discretion implementation that agencies enjoy. This is the second dimension of institutional incompatibility.

In addition, the third dimension of incompatibility is that adaptation is hampered by the low institutional capacity for administrative change. German federalism generates a multitude of institutional veto points, and the likelihood of adaptation is further reduced by legalistic procedures in combination with administrative fragmentation and differentiation.

Knill argues that in cases of *high* adaptation pressure, implementation of European requirements is likely to be ineffective, since European policies require the core structures and practices of national institutions to change fundamentally. In cases of *no* or *low* adaptation pressure, effective implementation is achieved because European requirements are compatible with existing national arrangements. The explanation becomes more complex for cases where EU legislation demands changes within the core of national tradition but does not challenge this core as such. In these instances of *moderate* pressure, the degree of adaptation is shaped by the preferences and resources of domestic coalitions, mediated by institutional structures such as veto points (Knill 1998: 25).

Knill applies the argument to the implementation of the Drinking Water Directive, the AI directive, the EIA directive, and the EMAS regulation in three countries (Germany, France, and United Kingdom). In order to identify the degree of adaptation pressure, he assesses the administrative implications of the directives in terms of the regulatory style (type of intervention and character of interest intermediation) and regulatory structure and confronts them with the prevalent features in the respective member states. The empirical findings are consistent with the theoretical argument.

Germany, for instance, implemented the EMAS Regulation appropriately because it caused only moderate adaptation pressure and was supported by environmental and industrial organizations. The EIA Directive and the AI Directive were implemented ineffectively, however, because there was much pressure to adapt. In these cases the problem was not only the misfit of European requirements with national administrative traditions; in addition, a 'thick institutional core' aggravated the adaptation problem, that is, these national administrative traditions were ideologically rooted in paradigms denoting, among others things, the very concept of the state and were also tightly linked to other sectoral and general institutions.

The explanatory framework also serves well for the British case. The EMAS Regulation generated only low adaptation pressure as its self-regulatory, procedural, and flexible approach fitted the British regulatory style very well. The implementation record for the EIA has been less successful, due to moderate adaptation pressure and a lack of domestic support. The Drinking Water Directive and the AI Directive have been successfully implemented, though they initially generated adaptation pressure. Public sector reforms at the core of public administration that were not wholly related to the European Union, however, reduced adaptation pressure and strengthened domestic actors that supported the directive, such as consumer and environmental groups. These reforms included the privatization of the water industry and administrative changes aiming at increasing public accountability. It was for these reasons that the two directives could be successfully implemented. The occurrence of domestic administrative reforms points to the low degree of embeddedness of British administrative arrangements and the great capacity for institutional change that is the result of the high degree of political centralization in the United Kingdom.

Reluctant Governments Pulled by Domestic Mobilization

The research discussed above concentrated in particular on the impact of national administrations and their traditions on the implementation of European directives. In addition it started out with a neoinstitutionalist theoretical framework. Following the methodological concept of decreasing abstraction, it confined the analysis to institutional factors as long as these factors were capable of explaining the observed patterns (see Lindenberg 1991; Mayntz and Scharpf 1995; Knill 1998: 25). Only in cases where institutional factors did not match the empirical observation was the analysis supplemented by actor-oriented factors such as domestic support.

The paper by Börzel (2000) presents a study that departs from the explicit focus on national administration and the institutional perspective by taking society into account and by employing a more actor-oriented approach, hence concentrating on domestic mobilization (pull) and supranational actors (push). Like Knill, Börzel too focuses on the Drinking Water Directive, the EIA Directive, and the AI Directive. But, unlike Knill, she includes the Industrial Plant Directive and the LCP Directive rather than the EMAS regulation. Moreover, she compares Germany with Spain, rather than with France and the United Kingdom.[6]

As in Knill's study, adaptation pressure—the misfit between EU policies and national administrative structures and traditions—is an important obstacle to national adaptation. Börzel translates this institutional feature into her actor-oriented approach by stating that 'legal and administrative changes involve high costs, both material and political, which public authorities are little inclined to bear' (2000: 148). In other words, she assumes rather straightforwardly that the government's willingness to implement European directives depends on the degree of adaptation pressure.

In her framework, however, adaptation pressure is a necessary but never a sufficient condition for non-compliance.[7] Non-compliance and implementation failure will only occur when there is no domestic mobilization that directly or indirectly, the latter is via the Commission and the Court, succeeds in forcing public authorities to comply despite a policy misfit. Domestic pressure can emanate from political parties, environmental organizations—especially via mass media—and business and industry groups. The domestic 'pull' is especially effective when it is combined with a supranational 'push', that is the EU Commission starting infringement procedures. Börzel hypothesizes that 'the higher the pressure for adaptation and the lower the level of domestic mobilization, the more likely is that non-compliance will occur' (2000: 148–9). As is the case with Knill's study Börzel's theoretical argument is capable of explaining the variations found. Spain's non-compliance with the Drinking Water Directive and the Industrial Plant Directive is associated with policy misfit and lack of domestic mobilization. Policy misfit in combination with domestic mobilization, by environmental groups and in some cases also by local municipalities, political parties, and trade unions, led to Spain being more compliant,

---

[6] Note, however, that a case study by Jordan suggests that Börzel's finding also holds for the United Kingdom. Jordan analysed the implementation of the EU coastal bathing water policy in that country (Jordan 1997).

[7] The terms 'effective implementation' and 'compliance' are used interchangeably.

with regard to the LCP Directive, the AI Directive, and the EIA Directive, and to Germany complying with the AI Directive and the EIA Directive. Due to low adaptation pressure, Germany had no problems in complying with the Industrial Plant and the LCP Directive.[8]

The Importance of Institutional Veto Points

For my own contribution to the debate on national adaptation to European integration, I studied the implementation of the Packaging Waste Directive in Germany, the Netherlands, and the United Kingdom (Haverland 2000). My paper built upon the work of Knill. Like Börzel's study, however, my paper places less emphasis on adaptation pressure and public administrations and considers domestic mobilization more explicitly. In contrast to Börzel, however, I do not assume that central governments are unwilling to implement directives in the case of a policy misfit (adaptation pressure). Related to this, domestic mobilization can work in two ways: unwilling governments can be pushed to comply with European requirements; but governments willing to change their policies in order to comply with European directives can be blocked by domestic opposition that favours the status quo. This blockage is particularly effective in countries that provide institutional veto points, such as a second chamber of legislation, to domestic oppositions.

Briefly, like other studies, I analysed a case where a European directive caused member states to be exposed to adaptation pressure to a varying degree. The Directive on Packaging and Packaging Waste (Packaging Directive) challenged the core of the British waste policy and regulatory style. The government was forced to impose—from a national point of view—demanding packaging waste recycling and recovery standards. It was also forced to depart from its traditional regulatory style—broad objectives to be translated into individual obligations by bilateral government–company negotiations—by imposing a scheme on industry that was based on uniform and quantified targets. The Dutch government, however, was only exposed to moderate adaptation pressure. The Directive demanded modifications to the Dutch pragmatic covenant scheme, but did not fundamentally challenge it. Meanwhile, the German policy and regulatory style were faced with comparatively low adaptation pressure, so the ambitious domestic recycling objectives and the administrative arrangements to achieve them could remain intact. Yet, in contrast to Knill's study, I found that the differences in the degree of adaptation pressure cannot explain the pace and degree of adaptation to European requirements. Britain, the country with the biggest misfit between national practice and European requirements, implemented the Packaging Directive comparatively successfully, while Germany had huge problems in implementing even incremental changes.

[8] The implementation of the Drinking Water Directive in Germany is a special case. There was a 'push' from the European Commission without domestic mobilization (2000: 150–1).

Moreover, unlike in the cases studied by Börzel, I found that the central governments were willing to implement the directive despite policy misfit. Germany had to adapt a provision concerning drink packaging, the so-called refillable quota. There was considerable domestic mobilization by German retailers and parts of the beverage industry in favour of changing this provision and bringing it into line with the European directive. The German central government was in favour of doing so, especially as environmental issues had become less important in the public perception and new environmental research had questioned the environmental effectiveness of the existing provision. The Netherlands had to introduce legally binding individual obligations in addition to its packaging covenant scheme. Though this was at odds with the flexible target group approach of Dutch environmental policy, central government was actually in favour of doing so, as there was a real danger that the existing covenant would not achieve the targets set, particularly due to the problem of freeriding. A legalistic approach would have helped to tackle this problem more effectively. In both countries the preferences of governments had changed and the European directive provided central executives with the opportunity to put new preferenes into practice; circumventing domestic constraints by invoking the European Union as 'vincolo esterno' (Dyson and Featherstone 1996; see Grande 1996). The British willingness to adapt is more surprising. Preferences did not change and no domestic constraints had to be circumvented. What is more, the European directive challenged the core of British waste management policies. The British government accepted substantial changes in the form and substance of its national environmental policies, however, because it assigned overriding importance to the second element of the Packaging Directive: the free movement of goods. The British government had pushed for an EU directive to effectively tackle the trade distortions resulting from the existing German packaging regime. As has been documented elsewhere, in the decision-making process at the European level, member states strive for unanimous solutions (see Hayes-Renshow and Wallace 1995; Kerremans 1996). Since a bad solution was preferable to no solution, the United Kingdom had made concessions and had accepted higher standards and a formalization of its environmental policy.

Given the willingness of central governments to implement the Packaging Directive, the explanation of the variation in degree of adaptation must be sought in the domestic groups *opposing* the implementation of the European directive. In all the aforementioned three countries, there was such opposition. Given the divergent character of the adaptation required, the nature and goals of the opposition varied between the countries. The weakening of the German refillable quota was opposed by environmentalists and by producers of drinks in refillable bottles, who tried to protect their markets against producers who market their drinks in one-way bottles. The legalistic turn of the Dutch packaging waste policy was initially criticized by almost the entire Dutch industry.

As the free-riding problem became more pressing, however, opposition to the mandatory character of the new regulation concentrated on those companies and their associations who did not participate in the covenant scheme. The more ambitious and more legalistic approach needed in the United Kingdom to comply with the Packaging Directive was largely opposed by industry, especially by the more domestically oriented companies that did not suffer from the negative trade effects of the German packaging regulation.

Given that there was domestic opposition by interested groups in all three countries, the variation in implementation record cannot be attributed to opposition alone. This result highlights the importance of the domestic institutional opportunity structure. In Britain, the adaptation generated much political conflict. The important point was, however, that the domestic opposition had no effective veto point at which it could substantially delay the process or modify the outcome of the implementation of the Packaging Directive.[9] The institutional structure of the United Kingdom effectively sheltered central government from societal demands. The British packaging regulation was adopted eight months after the official deadline for doing so, but this was nonetheless earlier than the Dutch or the German regulation was adopted. The same holds also for the Netherlands. As in the United Kingdom, the opposition did not control an institutional veto point. But, in contrast to the United Kingdom, the process of adaptation was less adversarial. The problem-oriented and active approach of Dutch government and industry and the existence of sophisticated machinery of corporatist interest intermediation enabled the central government to reconcile European and domestic demands in a flexible manner and implement the policy properly and not long after the United Kingdom. Germany, however, facing a veto in the *Bundesrat*, implemented rather late and inappropriately.[10] Any attempt of the German government to weaken the refillable quota met with strong resistance by the German *Bundesrat*. The opposition parties in the Federal parliament controlled the *Bundesrat*, representing the German states (*Länder*). These parties, the Social Democrats and the Greens, represented the interests of the groups opposing the adaptation.

Hence, the case study suggests that, institutional veto points tend to shape the timing and quality of implementation regardless of differential gaps in the

[9] Veto points refer to all stages in the decision-making process on which agreement is required for a policy change (Immergut 1992).

[10] This is not to say that European requirements as such can be ultimately rejected at domestic institutional veto points. But in practice, European legislation is mostly 'packed' with additional provisions to ensure effective implementation. These provisions are necessary to make directives fit with the domestic (legal) situations or to create specific legislative conditions for application (Streinz and Pechstein 1995). However, such provisions often depend on the assent of other institutional players; most importantly, second chambers of the legislature. If these chambers represent regional actors, the government has a strong incentive to get assent even when this not formally required, because central governments often rely on these actors for the practical implementation of European legislation, for which the central governments nevertheless remain legally responsible and liable. This was the case in Germany.

goodness of fit between European requirements and national traditions. In other words, institutional veto points matter not only in situations of moderate adaptation pressure but also in instances of low and high adaptation pressure. Granted, adaptation pressure is important because it can activate domestic opposition, but whether the opposition is successful or not depends on the availability of veto points. This finding corroborates the contention of Börzel and Risse that adaptation pressure is a necessary but not a sufficient condition for Europeanization (see Börzel and Risse, this volume).

Towards a New Research Agenda

The comparative case studies discussed were informed by general political science theories, but their findings driven by the characteristics of the cases. Knill could concentrate on public administrations to make sense of the observed variation of the dependent variable. Likewise, Börzel's assumption of unwilling governments pulled by domestic mobilization did a good job in explaining the variance she found. The existence of willing governments and unwilling opposition in my case study sheds light on how variations in institutional veto points explain the pattern of implementation records. Taken together, the case studies identified four conditions shaping the degree of the European Union's impact on domestic policy, as will be elaborated below.

Misfit/adaptation pressure: In all three studies adaptation pressure was identified as a major obstacle to adaptation. Knill provides the most elaborate conceptualization of adaptation pressure, which he has further refined in a study with Lenschow (Knill and Lenschow 1998). Like Börzel and Risse (this volume), Knill and Lenschow make a difference between policy misfit and institutional misfit. The former refers to policy-specific regulatory styles and structures, whereas the latter refers to the institutional embeddedness of the national policy, that is, 'the degree of institutionalization or institutional stability of sectoral administrative arrangements' (Knill 1998: 5). In contrast to Börzel and Risse, however, Knill and Lenschow further refine institutional misfit, as they make use of Krasner's distinction between the depth and the breadth of institutionalization (Krasner 1988: 74–7). The depth of institutional embeddedness is related to the degree to which policy arrangements are ideologically rooted in paradigms, or, one might add, in core beliefs (Sabatier 1998). Examples are beliefs about the role of the state in society or the function of the legal system. The breadth of institutional embeddedness is constituted by the number and tightness of 'inter- and intrainstitutional linkages that need to be broken or rerouted in order to comply with EU legislative requirements' (Knill and Lenschow 1998: 603).

This conceptualization of misfit goes a long way towards providing the degree of precision of the concept of 'goodness of fit' and 'adaptation pressure' envisaged by Radaelli (this volume).

Government willingness to implement: Börzel's study has explicitly considered government preferences, arguing that in cases of policy misfit governments are reluctant to implement. The case of packaging waste shows, however, that under certain circumstances governments are willing to implement despite adaptation pressure. Preferences may change due to changes in domestic or external conditions, but also due to policy learning. As argued earlier, properties of the 'sector' environmental policy, such as its focus on allocation rather than redistribution, as well as characteristics of the European decision-making structure and procedures favour policy learning.

Domestic mobilization in favour of EU requirements: Knill considers the role of domestic mobilization only for cases of moderate adaptation pressure, whereas Börzel assigns general importance to this factor. She is also most elaborate about actors in and processes of domestic mobilization. Among the actors pulling for adaptation are political parties, environmental organizations, and business and industry lobby groups. Though strong domestic mobilization in favour of adaptation is important when governments are reluctant, when governments are willing, weak domestic mobilization against policy adaptation may be an important condition for adaptation.

Veto points controlled by pro-EU groups: The emphasis on the interaction of government and society in processes of adaptation points to the importance of the opportunity structure for domestic groups. Institutional veto points are of particular importance in this respect, as those controlling these points have a legal—sometimes even constitutionally guaranteed—right to veto changes of the status quo. These institutional veto points are most decisive where it is likely that the party or party coalition that controls them differs from the one controlling the central government. This is the case, for instance, for incongruent systems of bicameralism, that is, systems of government in which the second chamber is elected according to a different voting method (see Lijphart 1999).

Note that the role of veto points may be more ambiguous than stated by Börzel and Risse (this volume). Whereas they argue that the existence of veto points empowers actors to resist Europeanization, I argue that under certain circumstances veto points may also facilitate Europeanization. I acknowledge that when opposing groups control these veto points, willing governments might face serious obstacles to adaptation. However, when actors supporting Europeanization control the veto points, reluctant governments might be forced to adapt.

The relative importance of these four conditions identified by the comparative case studies reviewed, and the way they interact merit further investigation. The scope of the analysis should be gradually extended to other environmental policies and other European member states. The next step might be to carry out cross-sectoral comparisons. It is likely that by changing national policies and sectoral regulatory structures the European Union also affects domestic institutional structures and structures of representation and cleavages more generally (see Radaelli, Figure 2.1, this volume). Policy-oriented case studies of the new generation should consider these broader effects.

I advocate continuing with an intensive research design, rather than conducting large '*n*' studies. The latter typically seek to establish causal relationships by correlating policy inputs with policy outcomes without identifying the relevant causal mechanisms. This is not without problems, as it is important to note that policy development and institutional change towards a European model or more similar systems across EU member states may not be causally related to the European integration process. Domestic or global forces can cause political change. In these instances, the causal relation with European factors is spurious. To give an example outside the environmental policy field: the liberalization of telecommunication is a worldwide phenomenon rather than a European one (Eliassen and Sjovaag 1999). Few would argue that in all member states the European Union is the main cause of national telecommunication liberalization. For a number of countries, the timing, process, and specific design of the regulatory framework might be influenced by European policies, but not liberalization as such. Moreover, convergence might not be the outcome, even if the European Union is causally important. If Europeanization is defined as *any* response to European integration, the European Union may even cause divergence, as in the case of the Italian transport policy (Héritier *et al.* 2000). Only a rather intensive study would be able to pinpoint the processes and underlying forces by which policy change came about and to rule out rival explanations (see Radaelli, this volume).

A case study design would also enable governments to be disaggregated in order to arrive at a more differentiated view of the adaptation process (see Featherstone, this volume). Many studies on Europeanization do already differentiate between national and subnational governments. Yet, most studies take central governments as unitary actors. However, research into environmental policy suggests that, by analysing intragovernment conflicts, for instance, between ministries of the environment and those of trade, industry, or transport, a fuller understanding of Europeanization can be achieved.

A supplementary device for this strategy would be to make the counterfactual claim that is implied in Europeanization research explicit and to justify it. Drawing on Fearon, the statement that European integration has resulted in a particular outcome implies that if there had been no European integration, a particular outcome would not have occurred. Making this statement explicit allows researchers to develop the counterfactual scenario in which they can substantiate their view that the European Union has indeed been causally important. One can do so by adding observations and invoking general principles (Fearon 1991: 183; Ned Lebow 2000).[11] In my research, for example, I have sought to demonstrate that without the European Packaging Directive there would not have been a shift from the Packaging Covenant to generally binding regulation in the Netherlands. To support this view I presented the facts that environmental protection has lost in salience, and that much of industry opposed the regulation, and I argued that in principle policy-makers do not engage in reforms against business unless the reforms have public legitimacy (Haverland 1999).

In this context I would like to caution against another research strategy that is sometimes advocated as a panacea for isolating the impact of the European Union: comparing EU member states with non-members. This strategy is based upon two assumptions. The first assumption is that European integration only affects members. Hence, if policies become more similar across members and non-members alike, then the European Union is not causally important. However, it is likely that the European Union affects non-members too, for instance, via policy learning and imitation. In this respect, research on non-member states such as Switzerland and Norway is revealing. Not only do these countries move in similar directions as EU member states, which would intuitively lead to a rejection of the EU-matters thesis, but also the timing and content of the policy changes are so similar to EU requirements that one is inclined to argue that the European Union matters even more in these countries than in EU member states. Norway, for instance, has been portrayed as a very adaptive non-member (Sverdrup 1998; see Kux and Sverdrup 2000). The second assumption of the member-non-member design is that the countries show enough similarities in all other theoretically relevant conditions, so that variation in the outcome can be unambiguously attributed to the presence/absence of the European Union. It is probably easier to meet the needs of such a most similar system to satisfy than the first assumption. Still one should be careful when choosing non-members, in particular if choosing countries outside the—geographical—reach of the European Union, to forgo the problems associated with the first assumptions. There are only a few countries that are sufficiently similar—New Zealand and Australia, for instance. Countries from East Asia or Latin America are probably too different to allow one to control for other potentially influential factors.

In short: a counterfactual research design is more promising than comparing actual cases of members and non-members, as the latter design is based on one implausible assumption and one assumption that restricts the potential candidates to only a few countries. An incremental research strategy based

---

[11] Counterfactual reasoning should not result in unlimited speculation, however. Based upon earlier work by Tetlock and Belkin, Ned Lebow has developed eight criteria for counterfactual reasoning to become meaningful and relevant. These include, for instance, logical, theoretical, and historical consistency (Ned Lebow 2000: 581–5).

on carefully selected intensive comparative case studies, supplemented by counterfactual arguments has the most prospect of ultimately providing theoretically, methodologically, and empirically sophisticated contributions to debate on the Europeanization of the nation state.

REFERENCES

Andersen, M. S. and Liefferink, D. (eds) (1997). *European Environmental Policy: The Pioneers* (Manchester and New York: Manchester University press).

Börzel, T. A. (2000). 'Why There is No "Southern Problem". On Environmental Leaders and Laggards in the European Union', *Journal of European Public Policy* 7(1): 141–62.

Dyson, K. and Featherstone, K. (1996). 'Italy and EMU as a "vincolo esterno": Empowering the Technocrats, Transforming the State', *South European Society and Politics* 1(2): 272–99.

Eliassen, K. A. and Sjovaag, M. (eds) (1999). *European Telecommunications Liberalization* (London: Routledge).

European Commission (2001). *Eurobarometer Report Number 54* (Brussels: Directorate-General Press and Communication).

Fearon, J. D. (1991). 'Counterfactuals and Hypothesis Testing in Political Science', *World Politics* 43: 169–95.

Grande, E. (1996). 'Das Paradox der Schwäche. Forschungspolitik und die Einflusslogik europäischer Politikverflechtung', in M. Jachtenfuchs and B. Kohler-Koch (eds), *Europäische Integration* (Opladen: Leske and Budrich), 373–99.

Hall, P. A. and Taylor, R. (1996). 'Political Science and the Three Institutionalisms', *Political Studies* 44(4): 936–57.

Haverland, M. (1999). *National Autonomy, European Integration and the Politics of Packaging Waste* (Amsterdam: Thela Thesis).

——(2000). 'National Adaptation to the European Union. The Importance of Institutional Veto Points', *Journal of Public Policy* 20(1): 83–103.

Hayes-Renshow, F. and Wallace, H. (1995). 'Executive Power in the European Union, the Functions and Limits of the Council of Ministers', *Journal of European Public Policy* 2(4): 559–82.

Héritier, A., Kerwer, D., Knill, C., Lehmkuhl, D., and Teutsch, M. (2000). *Differential Europe: New Restrictions and Opportunities for Policy Making in the Member States* (Lanham: Rowman and Littlefield).

Immergut, E. (1992). *Health Politics. Interests and Institutions in Western Europe* (Cambridge: Cambridge University Press).

Jordan, A. (1999). 'The Implementation of EU Environmental Policy: A Problem Without a Political Solution', *Environment and Planning C: Government and Policy* 17 (1 February): 69–90.

——(2001). 'National Environmental Ministries: Managers or Ciphers of European Union Environmental Policy', *Public Administration* 79(3): 643–63.

Jordan, A., Brouwer, R., and Noble, E. (1999). 'Innovative and Responsive? A Longitudinal Analysis of the Speed of EU Environmental Policy-making, 1967–97', *Journal of European Public Policy* 6(3): 376–98.

Kerremans, B. (1996). 'Do Institutions Make a Difference? Non-institutionalism, Neo-institutionalism, and the Logic of Common Decision-making in the European Union', *Governance* 9(2): 217–40.

Knill, C. (1998). 'European Policies: The Impact of National Administrative Traditions', *Journal of Public Policy* 18(1): 1–28.

——and Lehmkuhl, D. (1999). 'How Europe Matters. Different Mechanisms of Europeanization', *European Integration Online Papers* 3(7).

——and Lenschow, A. (1998). 'Coping with Europe: The Impact of British and German Administrations on the Implementation of EU Environmental Policy', *Journal of European Public Policy* 5(4): 595–614.

——and——(1999). 'Neue Konzepte—alte Probleme? Die institutionellen Grenzen effektiver Implementation', *Politische Vierteljahresschrift* 40(4): 591–617.

Krasner, S. (1988). 'Sovereignty. An Institutional Perspective', *Comparative Political Studies* 21(1): 66–94.

Kux, S. and Sverdrup, U. (2000). 'Fuzzy Borders and Adaptive Outsiders, Norway, Switzerland and the EU', *Journal of European Integration/Revue d'intégration Européenne.*

Lijphart, A. (1999). *Patterns of Democracy. Government Forms and Performance in Thirty-Six Countries* (New Haven and London: Yale University Press).

Lindenberg, S. (1991). 'Die Methode der abnehmenden Abstraktion: Theoriegesteuerte Analyse und empirischer Gehalt', in H. Esser and K. G. Troitzsch (eds), *Modellierung sozialer Prozesse* (Bonn: Informationszentrum Sozialwissenschaften), 29–78.

March, J. G. and Olsen, J. P. (1984). 'The New Institutionalism: Organizational Factors in Political Life', *American Political Science Review* 78(2): 734–49.

Mayntz, R. and Scharpf, F. W. (1995). 'Der Ansatz des aktuerszentrierten Institutionalismus', in R. Mayntz and F. W. Scharpf (eds), *Gesellschaftliche Selbstregulierung und politische Steuerung* (Frankfurt and New York: Campus).

McCormick, J. (1999a). 'Environmental Policy', in L. Cram, D. Dinan, and N. Nugent (eds), *Developments in the European Union* (Basingstoke: Macmillan), 193–210.

——(1999b). *Environmental Policy in the European Union* (Basingstoke: Macmillan).

Ned Lebow, R. (2000). 'What's So Different About a Counterfactual?', *World Politics* 52: 550–85.

Pelkmans, J. (1997). 'Competition Among Regimes in the EU, between Ideas and Sober Reality' *Paper presented at the Conference Institutions, Market and (Economic) Performance: Deregulation and its Consequences.* Utrecht, December 11–12, 1997.

Prechal, S. (1995). *Directives in Europe and Community Law. A Study of Directives and their Enforcement in National Courts* (Oxford: Clarendon Press).

Radaelli, C. (1997). 'How does Europeanization Produce Policy Change? Corporate Tax Policy in Italy and the UK', *Comparative Political Studies* 30(5): 553–75.

Sabatier, P. (1998). 'The Advocacy Coalition Framework: Revisions and Relevance for Europe', *Journal of European Public Policy* 5(1): 98–130.

Scharpf, F. W. (1999). *Governing in Europe. Effective and Democratic?* (Oxford: Oxford University Press).

Schmidt, M. G. (1999). 'Die Europäisierung der öffentlichen Aufgaben', in T. Ellwein and E. Holtmann (eds), *50 Jahre Bundesrepublik Deutschland. Rahmenbedingungen, Entwicklungen, Perspektiven* (Opladen/Wiesbaden: Westdeutscher Verlag), 385–94.

Schmitter, P. (1996). 'Imagining the Future of the Euro-polity with the Help of New Concepts', in G. Marks, F. W. Scharpf, P. Schmitter, and W. Streeck (eds), *Governance in the European Union* (London, Thousand Oaks, New Delhi: Sage), 121–50.

Siedentopf, H. and Ziller, J. (eds) (1988a). *Making European Policies Work – Volume I, Comparative Syntheses* (Brussels and London: EIPA/Sage).

—— and —— (eds) (1988b). *Making European Policies Work—Volume II, National Reports* (Brussels and London: EIPA/Sage).

Streinz, R. and Pechstein, M. (1995). 'The Case of Germany', in S. A. Pappas (ed.), *National Administrative Procedures for the Preparation and Implementation of Community Decisions* (Maastricht: European Institute of Public Administration), 133–60.

Sverdrup, U. (1998). 'Norway—an Adaptive Non-member', in K. Hanf and B. Soetendorp (eds), *Adapting to European Integration—Small States and the European Union* (London: Longman), 149–66.

Turner, R. K., Pearce, D., and Bateman, I. (1994). *Environmental Economics* (New York, London, Toronto, Sydney, Singapore: Harvester/Wheatsheaf).

Weale, A., Pridham, G., Cini, M., Konstadakopulos, D., Porter, M., and Flynn, B. (2000). *Environmental Governance in Europe. An Ever Closer Ecological Union?* (Oxford: Oxford University Press).

Weale, A., Pridham, G., Williams, A., and Porter, M. (1996). 'Environmental Administration in Six European States. Secular Convergence or National Distinctiveness?', *Public Administration* 74(2): 255–74.

IV

Interest Groups and Europeanization

10

Europeanization and Organizational Change in National Trade Associations: An Organizational Ecology Perspective

JÜRGEN R. GROTE AND ACHIM LANG

The Paradigm of Europeanization and Business Interest Associations

Triggered primarily by the volume published by Green Cowles *et al.* (2001) on Europeanization and national processes of change, some of the political science research on Europe has begun to deal with the question as to what extent one can speak of Europeanization in terms of the relationship between new forms of governance located at the level of the European Union and the more traditional forms of nationally and subnationally anchored statehood. The main focal point centres around scenarios of adaptation of national political patterns to European political patterns in which different mechanisms and modes, varying in terms of orientation, interests, and policy specifics, can serve as stimuli for institutional change. The following *mechanisms* are believed to be possible. Adaptation can take place through:

(1) imposition of unilateral political pressure without remarkable discretionary space for actors concerned (positive integration);
(2) institutional coevolution, a process by which the most heterogeneous institutional structures conform to new environments even independently of authoritative parameters;
(3) organizational learning and socialization processes in a multilevel hierarchy, where the emphasis is primarily placed on changes in cognitive behaviour patterns;

We would like to thank Michael Dobbins (Konstanz) for his linguistic assistance, Volker Schneider, Frank Janning (both Konstanz), and Simone Leiber (MPI-Cologne) for their comments, and the participants of the Florence (European University Institute), Amsterdam (Institute for Advanced Labour Studies), and Mannheim (MZES Mannheim) conferences for further conceptual inputs. Responsibility for the arguments presented here lies, of course, fully with the authors.

(4) the horizontal diffusion of *best practice* through the sharing of mutual experiences (isomorphism and mimicry);

(5) predominantly market-opening measures (negative integration), through which existing opportunity structures and power differentials are eroded at and eventually lead to a new equilibrium.

Regarding the *results* of the process, the main candidates are absorption, accommodation, transformation, retrenchment, and institutional inertia, whereas the two mentioned last are treated as a special case of negative Europeanization (Radaelli this volume). Due to their embeddedness into specific national paths of development, these results can manifest themselves either in form of convergence or divergence of institutional structures, predispositions, world views, logics (*appropriateness* and *consequentialism*), and procedures. The predominant *stimulus* triggering adaptation finally is *goodness of fit* or *misfit* (see Risse and Börzel, this volume).

The menu of possible mechanisms, results, and stimuli at our disposal is therefore, extraordinarily comprehensive. It is no simple task to undertake a systematization or to attempt a classification in terms of underlying theories of political science and organizational sociology. At this point in time it is hardly foreseeable as to whether a general model of institutional or cognitive change can be derived from this amalgam of distinct approaches and points of view. On a purely abstract level, numerous systemizing and definitional attempts do now exist (see e.g. Featherstone, this volume; Radaelli, this volume; Green Cowles *et al.* 2001; Olsen 2002). It is not our intention to add yet another to this.

For the sake of simplicity, if we restrict ourselves to an overview of the primarily descriptive material existing to date, we come to the conclusion that the majority of articles can be assigned to three categories. The first comprises research dealing with the Europeanization of policies and the second includes analyses of the Europeanization of national institutions in a more narrow sense (in particular administration and administrational units). Finally, present contributions to the debate can be distinguished by as to whether they adopt a vertical perspective, according to which Europeanization is a matter of top-down imposition of rules or of learning in hierarchies, or, alternatively, a more horizontal perspective, according to which adaptation comes about by a transnational exchange and sharing of experiences of best practice. The majority of the existing literature can be assigned to the category 'studies of policy change across the hierarchical layers of multi-level governance'. In our view, the policy networks within which this change may take place are more adequate for an examination of Europeanization processes than, for instance, the individual units of these networks, for example, administrations and agencies. With the network–analytic techniques now available, relational change of this sort may also be easier to study. Anyway, while networks are more adept at facing new challenges through a restructuring of their relationships without making larger internal modifications, individual units of these networks tend to depend more strongly on the institutional paths along which they have developed (see below). If at all, organizational change here takes place by means of transnational learning and the mutual exchange of experiences, or by copying the characteristics of especially successful species[1] while changes in political network structures predominantly occur within vertically organized forms of the European multilevel system.

The fact that organizations are more resistant to change than network-like configurations has already been established in earlier analyses of administrative adaptation. Since this tradition is much closer to our own interest and research target than, for example, policy analysis or the study of state–society relations, we will present it more thoroughly. For instance, Page and Wouters (1995: 203) argue that national administrations are becoming Europeanized due to 'the decisions of the European Union (...) increasingly becoming part of national decision-making processes', but they also point to the fact that 'there is no strong reason to believe that this (...) brings with it any substantial change in the national administrative structures (...)'.

Harmsen (1999), above all, must be given credit for making us aware of what we believe to represents one central difference in processes of institutional adaptation. In an analysis of forms of reaction of Dutch and French administrations and administrational units towards the pressure applied by the European Union, he refers on the one hand to the factual 'Europeanization of national administrations, in the sense of a pronounced increase in the range and frequency of contacts between the national and the supranational levels' (ibid: 81), but also finds that, 'despite these increasing contacts, there is little evidence of the Europeanization of national administrations in the sense of a convergence towards a common institutional model (...). The administrations of the member states have, for the most part, retained their distinctive structures and operating procedures' (ibid.: 81–2). Obviously, this applies not only to adaptation within vertically structured multilevel games, but also to transnational, that is, horizontally organized, processes of sharing common experiences.[2] What Harmsen indicates here is the difference between

---

[1] Attempts at copying, as has been demonstrated by the literature on population ecology, extremely rarely lead to perfect replications of the original and thereby increase the pool of variance from which the environment (or particularly ambitious managers of organizations) selects (see McKelvey and Aldrich 1983).

[2] Harmsen elaborates on this by stating that 'even a minimal convergence, produced by a shared search for best practice in the face of common pressures, does not appear to be taking place'. Much more predominant is a 'persistence of distinctive national models of decision-making, which seems relatively impervious to a diagnostically based process of cross-national learning' (Harmsen 1999: 83).

relational and attributive properties of actors. The difference becomes particularly evident when neither policies nor policy networks or other macropolitical phenomena are at the focus of the analysis, rather than the micro- and meso-political units of these networks, such as individual institutions or, in our case, interest associations or entire associational systems. It would be daring to trace Europeanization directly back to the integration of these actors into broader constellations.[3] This, at least, is also suggested by the few existing studies of organized collective action on Europeanization and/or internationalization. Although being macropolitical and mostly influence-biased studies,[4] they do tend to support Harmsen's results.

Coleman (1997), for instance, comes to the conclusion that—despite their increasing internationalization and market liberalization—interest associations can be considered to be very resistant to change, to have expanded their relationships to public institutions, to have kept their individual interest domain, and to have remained the most relevant actors in the development of collective identity (see also Coleman and Perls 1999; or, for the impact of internationalization on private interest governments, Schmitter 1997; for Europeanization, Kriesi 2003; Pestoff 2003).

Finally, regarding the *stimuli* of adaptation predominant in the literature, a limitation of the perspective to different extents of *goodness of fit* also seems to be inadequate for the case of organized business interests. Most of all, this is related to the fact that there are simply no relevant organizational reference points on the European or international level to whose structures collective actors active on the nation state level could be related analytically. Despite conflicting views, the majority of EU interest group populations remain, for the time being, an appendix of national associations and not vice versa. In the majority of cases European interest groups are not equipped with a negotiation mandate and practice thus very frequently 'the politics of an empty chair' (Streeck 1995: 115; see also 1999). At any rate, they are more than likely additional beachheads for the expression of national business interests without a policy monopoly of any sort (see also Bennett 1997; Kohler-Koch and Quittkat 1999; Greenwood and Webster 2000). The '*goodness of fit*' metaphor, therefore, can easily seduce us into rash generalizations.

For example, Green Cowles (2001) analyses the organizational impact of the Transatlantic Business Dialogue, which is based primarily on individual company membership and the relationship between government and business

---

[3] Similarly diverging logics and structures were found in a project carried out at the MZES-Mannheim several years ago on processes of adaptation within and across European regions (see Grote 1998).

[4] We observe that the vast majority of studies on business interest intermediation is bound by an influence bias and tends to disregard membership-related developments. This influence bias corresponds to what could be called the relational bias of Europeanization research.

in the United Kingdom, Germany, and France. She comes to the conclusion that 'there is a misfit between the German and the European business-government relationship, and one can expect there to be some difficulty' (ibid.: 166) in terms of the adaptability of organized interests. The British associations are esteemed to be those with the most superior *goodness of fit*. Vivian Schmidt (2002), focusing on a comparable question at a higher level of abstraction—the repercussion of EU policies and politics on domestic state–society relations—comes to entirely different results. For her, 'Germany is (. . .) the least affected by European integration, mainly because of the better fit of its government practices with Europe (. . .). European governance structures and processes have had much less impact on Germany (. . .) than on either France or Britain' (ibid.: 166). Both authors primarily concentrate on the analysis of relations. If such diverging outcomes already arise in the study of relational structures which, as we have argued, may be easier to observe and to analyse, one can assume that an application of the institutional *goodness of fit* metaphor is inappropriate for the analysis of organizational change. Organizations certainly do adapt to their environment, but in the case of the latter we are dealing with an exceptionally complex phenomenon that cannot be reduced to one single aspect, nor to a single level or dimension. Second, it would be overdrawn to expect environmental adaptation to take place exclusively via the '*goodness of fit*'.

It should not be concealed that we first worked with the metaphor of Europeanization in our project ourselves and operationalized it in form of four possible scenarios.[5] After a first glance at preliminary results, and after intense interviews with leading representatives of business associations both in the United Kingdom and in Germany, it became clear that Europeanization plays at best a subordinate role in the context of organizational change. Neither in terms of possible adaptation mechanisms nor in view of possible results or stimuli did we come across any material that came close to convincing us of anything else. From the perspective of individual institutions and organizations at least, the concept of Europeanization is deeply teleological. In the very last instance, it targets the abandonment and relinquishment of central characteristics and organizational properties and thereby the very *raison d'être* of national interest associations. Despite being a concept oriented towards the study of change, it is not capable of capturing the process of change in a wider sense. The focus on Europe, and preferably on politics and policies, poses an obstacle to the consideration of other relevant environments for change and adaptation. Furthermore, the concept is limited in a contingency theoretical sense for it postulates or at least tends to suggest a *single-best-solution*

---

[5] The original research design distinguishes between transference, retrenchment, mutual reinforcement, and irrelevance (see Schneider *et al.* 2000).

for all kinds of change. However, environmental adaptation in the real world follows rather different paths and ends in diverse configurations, whose relative degree of fitness can only be judged analytically after the demise of less successful variations.

For these reasons above all, we have decided to drop the concept for the time being and search for more adequate candidates to theoretically ground our questions. The approaches of organizational theory are among the main candidates. However, they concentrate primarily on the analysis of micropolitical, that is, internal structural processes of change, and are almost continually marked by the blending out of the category of actors we are most interested in, that is, intermediate organizations and business interest associations.[6] We therefore revert to the fundamental reflections drawn from the only systematic project on organized business interest to date, known to a wider audience under the acronym OBI.[7] In this case as well, however, some of the concepts developed by OBI cannot easily be transmitted into our context without friction. The project design borrows in some essential points from established organization-theoretical approaches, but often does not specify these, which inhibits us from systematically 'hooking up' with these traditions. Along with that, OBI lacks both the dynamic perspective as well as the inclusion of factors responsible for processes of change lying beyond the borders of the nation state. We thus attempt to overcome the shortcomings of the previous literature by establishing an extended approach without blending out the results of micropolitical and 'specifically' interest association-based theoretical approaches relevant for our context. This more comprehensive theoretical construct to which we bestow the attribute 'meso-political' in allusion to Bogumil and Schmid (2001) is the approach of organizational ecology, which has become increasingly relevant within the area of organization studies (see in particular Baum and Clegg 1996; Baum 1999, 2002). This approach will be presented briefly before we move onto the description of both the sectors and the populations within them.

---

[6] The approaches of behavioural-sciences decision theory (in particular March and Simon 1958; March and Olsen 1976; March 1988) quoted and recommended by Bogumil and Schmid (2001), which apply to the analysis of micropolitical processes, strategic organizational analysis (in particular Crozier and Friedberg 1979), and configuration analysis (Mintzberg 1991), are of a certain relevance for our research and in particular for the analysis of change within our focal associations. The exclusive concentration on micropolitical processes of change would, however, be just as reductionistic as lingering on the macropolitical level alone.

[7] Vg.: Schmitter and Streeck 1999. The Organization of Business Interests. Here we refer to the most recent version of the original project design of 1981 published by the Max-Planck-Institut für Gesellschaftsforschung in Cologne.

Change in Sectoral Business Associations: An Ecological Perspective

The Europeanization debate's one-sided focus on the political repercussions of the integration process neglects the contingencies of organizational action through other factors, which along with governance structures and institutions lead to a limitation of the organizational 'room to move'. Here we should mention foremost economic, technological, and societal factors, which can limit and change the repertoire of strategies within the population through exchange relationships with other organizations. The four mentioned factors—and this is what decisively distinguishes our perspective from the EU focused view sketched out at the beginning—can impinge on populations and individual interest groups not only via national and European channels, but also through international channels. To avoid the teleological bias of the debate we will speak in the following neither of Europeanization nor of internationalization or renationalization, but, rather, of the challenges and effects emanating from the processes of change on these levels onto the field of business associations. These latter occupy an intermediate position between two (initially) independent populations with sufficient resources: between enterprise, on the one hand, and the state and its institutions, on the other hand. Since both populations can in principle come into contact without making use of intermediate actors, interest groups must be so structured that they can offer both specific services which the other actor is unable to supply. In other words, business associations must offer (potential and effective) members sufficient incentives in order to obtain the necessary resources for their own organizational reproduction. On the other hand, they must offer the state specific goods in order build up a capacity for exerting political power (Lehmbruch 1994; Traxler and Schmitter 1994; Schmitter and Streeck 1999).

Business associations are, therefore, exposed to influences from their immediate environment which is composed of interactions with a multitude of organizations and populations.[8] Changes in these populations can have direct and indirect effects on the actions of associations and comprise several different factors: technological and ecological developments find their

---

[8] Organizational sociology distinguishes between different concepts of environment. *Organization sets* are determined by the pespective of a focal organization, *organizational population* comprises all organizations of the same type, *interorganizational community* unites the organizations of a geographical region, and organizational spaces aggregate the space of institutional life (a good summary is given by Scott 1998; see also Baum and Clegg 1996). In the following equal organizations will be integrated under the term 'population'. These populations interact with other populations in an organizational space. Community and organizational space are used synonymously. The term 'community' has its origin in population ecology and has nothing in common with the term *interorganizational community*.

entrance into associative action through their members, while political factors have access via the configuration of the sectoral structures of regulation. Of further relevance are socially relevant factors, which impact business associations by being conveyed through media and/or social movements in particular.

One especially adequate approach of illustrating the interactions between organization and environment is the organization ecological approach which postulates an integrated perspective of the factors of influence on organizational action.

'Organizations, populations, and communities of organizations constitute the basic elements of an ecological analysis of organizations. A set of organizations engaged in similar activities and with similar patterns of resource utilization constitutes a population (...). Populations themselves develop relationships with other populations engaged in other activities that bind them into organizational communities. Organizational communities are functionally integrated systems of interacting populations; the outcomes for firms in any one population are fundamentally intertwined with those for firms in other populations in the same community' (Baum and Clegg 1996: 78).

In this approach, organizations are open systems whose ability to survive essentially depends on an exchange of resources with the environment to obtain or increase inner order (Buckley 1967; Bertalanffy 1968; Scott 1998). Thus open systems are basically two types of processes at the stratum: morphostasis and morphogenesis.[9] Morphostatic processes emphasize the maintenance of the momentary structure with the help of feedback loops from the environment with which deviations from the state of being at the beginning (outcome equilibrium) can be recorded and adjusted. In contrast, morphogenetic processes stress the deviations from states of equilibrium and further development through organizational learning. Both processes refer to systemic adaptation to environmental stimuli. 'Complex adaptive systems are indeed nothing more than hierarchically graduated networks of mutual effects between agents, who themselves represent complex adaptive systems in their own right. These agents have access to internal models of the outer world, are able to learn and capable of rule-guided behaviour, that is, to pursue goals in a boundedly rational manner' (Kappelhoff 1999: 350).

The evolution of an adaptive system does not take place as an assimilation to a static environment, but instead occurs as interplay between adaptive systems which are centralized in a network. The actions take place within a realm

---

[9] 'The former refers to those processes in complex system-environment exchanges that tend to preserve or maintain a system's given form, organization, or state. Morphogenesis will refer to those processes which tend to elaborate or change a system's given form, structure, or state' (Buckley 1967: 58).

of possibilities, that is, bounded by environmental limitations (Buckley 1967; Kappelhoff 1999). The coevolution within and between organizations is thus the result of management actions and environmental and institutional effects (Fombrun 1988; Lewin and Volberda 1999).

If we carry this over to the realm of business associations, then we must first determine the elements underlying the coevolution of interest populations and their members. On the basis of Schmitter and Streeck's research design, four types of organizational properties can be distinguished: domains, resources, structures, and outputs. Domains determine the interest and action space of the association. Resources can be financial, personal, or legitimatory. The latter is made available through state institutions, while the first two are generally supplied by the members. The structures of an association comprise the operative core, in which inputs are turned into outputs.[10] Outputs can be divided into two broad categories: supply of services and lobbying activities.

In our more encompassing perspective, how are these properties linked to an association's changing environment? First, on the input side, inflows of resources represent the interface through which organizational reproduction is being sought or guaranteed. The main providers of these resources are public authorities and enterprises. Public authorities supply associations with strategically relevant information or with legitimacy, but they may also grant them a monopoly of representation or the like. Enterprises, of course, also provide information but, first of all, function as main sources of an association's income. In a context where the environment is not restricted to domestic politics and markets, as was the case when OBI took off in the early 1980s, the nature of both public authorities and firms is substantially different. At least since the event of the Internal Market, and since the introduction of a number of international regulatory settings, national trade associations are moving on a wider terrain, while the state has lost its monopoly in the provision of authoritative and information resources. In a number of areas, it shares this activity with European institutions and, in exceptional circumstances, with international players.

While the institutions of the nation state are still likely to remain the most important source of legitimacy, this may be different for the income supplied to associations by member firms. In a number of sectors, associations increasingly depend on the subscription fees of large multinational corporations and

---

[10] Following population ecology approaches, the associational structure can further be subdivided into 'core' and 'periphery'. The 'core' refers to identities, standing operating procedures, and routines in the division of tasks, while the periphery consists of 'organizational maps' and subunits of the organization. A widely shared consensus exists that the 'core' generally tends to institutional inertia, while the periphery is used as a buffer against environmental influences.

this may create dependencies detrimental to the interests of smaller and more traditional firms operating in domestic markets. Even more important are the implications of economic developments resulting in the restructuring of larger companies (mergers, buy-outs, takeovers, etc.). Some associations may lose their prime source of income and will have a hard time collecting what is left of those who now turn to their core business, thus dropping marginal or less profitable product lines. While economic and technological developments can hardly be controlled and most often hit an association in an indirect way, that is, via their membership, this is different for political and/or societal challenges. Changes of this type emerge within the influence dimension of associative action and it is here where an association is more directly affected, but also better equipped to react through the implementation of appropriate strategies.

Among other things, this can be done by applying changes to the organization's output. Again, outputs have two dimensions. Parts of what an association offers to actors within its environment is aimed at the maintenance of influence. Membership compliance or information about the Domestic Encompassing Interest (DEI)[11] may be such goods and they are today supplied to both national and supranational authorities. Associations may increase or decrease their lobbying activities vis-à-vis either of these authorities, but they may also increase or decrease the type and amount of services offered to members or generate completely new organizational tasks. In any case, economic and technological internationalization as well as political and societal challenges may substantially alter the internal structure, as well as the inputs and outputs, of business associations.

Intraorganizational change of the above type apart, they may also alter the domain of an association, that is, the structures of the population and of the wider community. This occurs by way of coevolution of organizational properties and manifests itself at various levels:

On the level of *Organization–Population* the main focus is put on the interactions within the population of business associations and their impact on the organizational properties. Interaction primarily occurs between the poles of competition and cooperation. Decisions by associations at this level (e.g. expansion of the domain, new lobbying strategy, new financial sources, etc.) change the relative fitness of interest groups within the associational landscape and may lead to adaptive reactions on the part of the other interest groups as a consequence.

On the level of *Organization–Community* the opportunity space is concerned with where the activities of interest groups are taking place. On the one

---

[11] 'The DEI concerns the needs and interests of a sector in the domestic market and the domestic political and social arena' (Bouwen 2001: 8).

hand, it contains the pool of resources from which a group (or the entire population) draws, and, on the other, the selection mechanisms for associational activity. Selection mechanisms can be institutionalized expectations of rational group activity (on the part of the members) or the taking into account of the position of interest associations on the part of public authorities.

Changes in the populations of the community lead to pressures to assimilate in the focal population and, therefore, to reactions of the respective individual organization. However, no specific direction towards a desirable structural configuration is made out by this pressure to adapt as postulated, for instance, by contingency models in organizational sociology. Instead, organizations have access to a multitude of alternative actions which may lead to comparable outcomes.

Linking the resource-dependence approach to institutionalist arguments, we are offered a repertoire of strategies which organizations can make use of to confront external challenges (Thompson 1967; Pfeffer and Salancik 1978; Oliver 1991). We can now argue that organizations have a choice of many different strategies of action to overcome the situations of uncertainty caused by resource-dependencies and institutional requirements. These could be subdivided into measures oriented towards the inside (absorption and compensation) and those oriented towards the outside (integration, cooperation, and intervention).

Absorption and Compensation

These internal measures aim for internal assimilation which can be improved by the successful management of insecurity. In the area of absorption, they comprise the flexibilization of the organizational structure, the construction of buffers, as well as the use of reserves. Moreover, there is a possibility of risk compensation through measures that diminish the difficulties arising from resource dependencies and institutional expectations. This is mainly achieved through internal diversification (Thompson 1967; Pfeffer and Salancik 1978; Oliver 1991).

Integration

The second action strategy associations may select consists of the integration of the source of uncertainty by taking over the respective organization, or through the fusion of both systems (Pfeffer and Salancik 1978).

Cooperation

The third strategy to reduce environmental uncertainty is cooperation. In the present context, cooperation may imply a loss of autonomy for the system to be paid as the price for overcoming uncertainty (Thompson 1967; Pfeffer and Salancik 1978; Oliver 1991).

Intervention

The fourth type of measure implies intervention into the system of interdependencies by which organizations are connected. Intervention aims at weakening the power base of the critical organization. This mostly occurs through the involvement of third parties, that is, through political influence strategies such as lobbying or the mobilization of the public (Pfeffer and Salancik 1978: 188).

Corresponding to our project design, we shall now present the most crucial factors which potentially trigger change. We conceive these as an association's environment which can be subdivided into different dimensions and levels. Having described the most important types of environmental influence (input), we then present the historical paths of development of the two sectoral populations as well as the strategy we have chosen for boundary specification, that is, the identification of our samples. Subsequently, network structures of the focal organization sets will be presented and then a few words will be said on mergers and alliances within populations. Finally, we discuss some cognitive aspects, such as the perception of change within the management structures of the associations (throughput), before turning to a brief description of how our analytical targets use their resources and implement their tasks (output).

Change-Inducing Environmental Factors

We distinguish between political, economic, technological, and social environments that influence the individual groups and group populations in different ways according to sectors via national, European, or international channels.

Political Environment

The political framework of the *Information and Communications Sector* has changed in a fundamental way since the 1980s in several areas. The liberalization and harmonization process in the telecommunications sector triggered by the Green Book of the Commission (1987) served as an impulse for further community activities in the entire ICT sector. The further extension of liberalization competencies approved by the European Court of Justice brought about comprehensive EC-parameters and climaxed in the liberalization directive, which set the path for the introduction of unrestricted competition in the telecommunications market and the admission of alternative networks as of

1 January 1998. The directive also included provisions on the creation of national regulation authorities, whose arrangement remained at the discretion of the member states, however.

In the audio-visual sector, the directive 'television without borders' became the central norm for content transmission across borders. It primarily serves to secure the provision of services beyond borders and the maintenance of program standards. In the content area there are no community regulations that go beyond the network infrastructure.[12] These areas are dominated by national provisions. In Germany the legal framework for the entire ICT sector comprises a plethora of laws that correspond to a fragmentation of responsibilities across the federal level and the level of the *Länder*. This division of tasks is regulated by the State Treaty on Media Services ('Mediendienste-Staatsvertrag') of 1992 and the Law on Information and Communication ('Informations- und Kommunikationsdienste') of 1997. In the domain of telephone services and telecommunications the competencies lie in the hands of the national government, while the media services are under the authority of the *Länder*. In practice, however, competencies often overlap because many new media escape attempts at classification.

The EU competencies in the *Chemicals Sector* are even more comprehensive and above all are based on a longer tradition. The most relevant policy domain involved is the Union's environmental policy. For the time span which we have analysed, continual growth of European regulation activities can be demonstrated. Between 1980 and 1996, thirty-one laws were passed (Regulations, Recommendations, Decisions, and Directives) by both the Council and the Commission. In addition, there have been twenty-three changes to Directives which directly affected the Chemicals Sector (Munz 2001: 44–8). Regulatory density, considerably increased in the 1990s, especially after the ratification of the Single European Act. Various decisions of the Commission (twelve in total) fall within the timeframe 1991–6. After the Council of Ministers for Environment (on 25 June 1999) requested the Commission to bring forward proposals for a policy on chemicals, the latter ratified a White Book 'Strategy for a Future Policy on Chemicals' in February 2001.[13] The White Book provides that the 2700 new and about 100,106 old

---

[12] With the exception of the areas of telecommunications and radio mentioned above. In the radio sector, the content regulation is only of a rudimentary character and primarily applies to advertisement times.

[13] See European Commission (2001). The White Paper basically concerns a review of four existing legal instruments governing chemicals in the Community: Council Directive 67/548 (classification, packaging, and labelling of dangerous substances); OJ 196 of 16.8.67:1; Directive 88/379 (classification, packaging, and labelling of dangerous substances), OJ L 187 of 16.7.1988:14; Council Regulation 793/ 93 (evaluation and control of risks of existing substances), OJ L 84 of 5.4.1993:1; and Directive 76/ 769/ EEC (restrictions on the marketing and use of certain dangerous substances and preparations) OJ L 262 of 27.9.1976:201.

substances, which were previously examined according to different standards, be subject to a comparable control procedure within the framework of a unified system by 2012 which comes under the acronym REACH.[14] This is currently the main political challenge for the Chemicals Industry and its associations. The White Book and its soon to be implemented Directives on specific individual aspects absorb and bind a large number of organizational resources of many of the branch associations.

Regulatory activity by European Institutions thus is relatively high in both sectors, but it would be an exaggeration to assume the existence of dramatic changes over the past decade. The political environment remains relatively stable for the timeframe relevant to us, with the exception of the guidelines not to be implemented until the new millenium. This also holds for supply-side measures and support programs of the Commission in the area of biotechnology and ICT. They may indeed be considerable in individual cases and pose an incentive to some branch associations as well, but will have a more indirect impact on these latter to the extent that they are mostly oriented towards individual firms.

Technological Environment

The technological revolution within the *Information and Communications Sector* began at the end of the 1970s with the introduction of integrated circuits. The continual further development of the microelectronic components led to a steady size and cost reduction, with low energy consumption and higher information storage at the same time. Simultaneously, the process of digitalization set in, allowing for the packing and transmission of larger and larger quantities of information in binary codes. This technology permits computers to exchange data directly through the telephone network without having to first convert the information into analogue signals. This 'merger' between telecommunications and computers into a telematic sector paved the way for a multitude of innovations in the services and hardware market. Additionally, the infrastructure for data transmission also improved through the production of newer satellites, the spread of newer materials for cable networks, and the usage of radio frequencies. The radio and printing sectors were not yet affected by this convergence process between telecommunications and computers (Latzer 1997; Sandholz 1998). The technological fusion into a mediamatic sector has been taking place since the end of the 1980s as a consequence of the increased data transmission capacities and the linkage of different networks. Thereby the interactivity of the infrastructure was enhanced and abolished the restriction to terrestrial networks in the transmission of radio

---

[14] REACH, that is, Registration, Evaluation, and Authorization of Chemicals.

programmes. The rise of the Internet finally created a platform on which the diverse, and previously incompatible services could be offered (European Commission 1997; Latzer 1997).

Within the *Chemicals Sector*,[15] which is extremely research-intensive in its own right, it is biotechnology, thus, the activity areas 'health' and 'agriculture' which are commonly described as 'Life-Science-Business', which deserves special attention from the perspective of technological change. The volume of the European market for products of this most research intensive subsector will be multiplied fourfold in the coming ten years (DIB 2000: 4). While Germany initially performed poorly in an international comparison, its biotechnology sector with its 280 young biotech-companies has now become Europe's forerunner, even ahead of the United Kingdom (DIB 2000: 6; VCI 2000: 10). The biotech revolution has thus gained great significance, although, in comparison to ICT, technological innovations in this area do not (yet) comprise and affect the sector in its totality. In this sense technological change in the chemicals sector remains more moderate, while it is of a radical nature in the ICT sector. Furthermore, technological innovations take place internationally and are not restricted to national or European borders.

Economic Environment

Economic developments in the German *ICT sector* throughout the 1990s were characterized by great fluctuations in market growth between the subsectors, so it is difficult to map out a unified sector trend. At the beginning of the decade the entire sector reached rock bottom, and the deepest crisis was experienced in 1993 with losses between 5 and 43 per cent of the market in individual subsectors. The service providers in the areas of radio, television, and telecommunications had to swallow massive decreases in profit. From that point onward, things started to turn around in office configuration, cable, and the electronics industry. Starting in 1996 the other subsectors also followed this positive trend. With the liberalization of the sector in 1998, market growth excelled with average growth rates of over 9 per cent (OECD 2000). The trade balance has been described as being chronically deficitary. It increased from slightly less than eight billion DM in 1990 to over eighteen billion DM in 1998. In particular, the area of IT hardware contributes around 80 per cent to this deficit. At the same time, over 60 per cent of the German hardware production is exported. This area is very internationalized. The import–export ratio in the services area, though, only amounts to around 7 per cent (OECD 2000).

---

[15] With more than 7.5 billion euros in the year 2000 (VCI 2001: 97; Chemiewirtschaft in Zahlen), the German Chemical Industry is rated second behind the automobile industry (*c.* sixteen billion euros) in terms of its expenditures for R&D.

German *Chemicals* is more internationally active than any other economic branch. The export quota averaged 44 per cent in 1980 and reached *c.*76 per cent in the year 2000, while the worldwide direct investments mounted to thirty-five billion euros in total (1999). Particularly impressive are the continually rising profits within the timeframe we are studying (1980–2000). With *c.*107 billion euros, its percentage of the entire profit of the manufacturing industry is over 15 per cent. The export statistics have been more than doubled in the past twenty years and the import statistics have been tripled. The companies in the German chemicals sector reap about half of their profits abroad. Their main customers today are the member states of the European Union (53 per cent), the United States (13 per cent), and Asia (12 per cent). In terms of the number of people employed in the sector and the import–export data, Germany is in second place worldwide behind the United States, but in front of Japan, while holding the first place in Europe ahead of France, the United Kingdom, and Italy. Together these four EU countries produce *c.*65 per cent of chemicals output in Europe. This is significant, especially in light of EU initiatives to unify and streamline regulation in that area (e.g. the White Book on Chemicals) which hold for the entire Union, although only a small number of member states are affected in reality.

More than half of the investments abroad are allocated to the North American Free Trade Area (NAFTA)—in 1991 41.1 per cent alone in the United States. More than a quarter of the investments (29.8 per cent in 1999) go to Western Europe,[16] thus into a region which is now considered to be the home market of many German companies already. The extraordinarily strong orientation to the world market has led to distortions in the firm population within this sector and this in particular has a direct impact on the branch association of the VCI.[17] As a rule we are dealing primarily with two different, but

---

[16] From another angle, investments by foreign companies in the German chemical industry mount to 59.6% from EU countries, 28.6% from the United States, and 40.2% from all non-EU countries in total.

[17] What was described in the middle of the 1990s as 'Baustelle Hoechst' (Construction Site Hoechst) reached a preliminary conclusion with the merger of Hoechst AG and Rhône Poulenc to Aventis in 1999. Meanwhile, relevant restructuring processes have also taken place within BASF, and despite selling Knoll AG—at about seven billion US dollars the largest merger in the Chemicals sector with German participation to date—one can hardly make a prognosis on how the company will present itself in a few years. In contrast to Hoechst, BASF followed the opposite pattern by selling its entire pharmaceutical sector to the American drug company Abbott in 2001, and it presents itself today as a mere chemical company. BASF is now expanding in the area of plant protection and its takeover of the agro-chemistry business from American Home Products (AHP) for four million US dollars two years ago was the largest acquisition in the history of the company. Henkel, the most significant producer of consumption goods, laid off over 3000 (Frankfurter Allgemeine Zeitung, 13 November 2001: 30) employees and thereby entered the list of renowned large companies trying to overcome the weak business cycle in the world economy by means of drastic layoffs and restructuring. The fourth largest German company of

closely related, developments of differentiation and de-differentiation of the peak association's population of enterprises. 'First of all chemical firms are starting to increasingly concentrate on what they consider to be their core business areas (...). Second the internal company growth within the business areas defined this way is often not sufficient to persist in the rapidly growing world markets. The consequence of this is a considerable number of mergers and company takeovers, which bring about lasting changes on the number and types of firms in a given area' (VCI 2001: 12–13; own translation).

Societal Environment

For the *ICT Sector* influences from the part of societal forces are less relevant. There are indeed negative externalities which can be felt within other sectors (vulnerability of cyberspace, e.g. in banking) or within society as a whole (digital divide, privacy protection; see for this Schneider 2002), but the groups affected by this are often not capable of organizing or hardly willing to organize. There is an entirely different scenario in the *Chemicals Sector*. The chemicals industry has the worst possible reputation in terms of environmental protection and has been perceived to be the largest polluter of all since way back in the 1980s (Schneider 1988: 117). Since then, however, a clear differentiation has taken place. If one were to position individual branches of the sector (and the associations representing them) in a cross table with plus and minus along the dimensions dispensability of use and compatibility with the environment, there are today considerably more products than twenty years ago that could be listed in the positively rated list of 'indispensable' and 'environmentally compatible'. Among the more traditional branches, this holds true, for example, for the plastics industry, which likes to present itself as a branch of lifestyle products. Regardless of the present debate on Genetic Engineering, this may at least pertain to the development of vaccinations, medicines, and diagnostics as well. The socially most negatively perceived branch continues to be the one that produces pesticides and fertilizers used in agriculture. However, advances in plant manipulation have also contributed to making this branch more socially acceptable.

the sector, Bayer, does not seem interested in remaining the only department store (Gemischtwarenladen) of the sector. The four segments of Bayer are (percentages of profit for 2001): health (thirty-four), agriculture (thirteen), plastics (thirty-seven), chemicals (sixteen). In December 2000, the main office was turned into a holding, thus, the four segments have ever since obtained much greater autonomy. In particular, after taking over Aventis-Agrochemikalien, the label 'construction site' was also slung onto this company. In the case of the abolishment of the chemicals sector, Degussa would be willing to buy it. Degussa in its present form originated in 2001 as the 'scraps' of the merger of Viag and Veba.

Pressure applied to industries by social and, in particular, environmental movements are endemic, at least for the chemicals sector. Its interest groups have been getting accustomed to this for decades now and consider political marketing in this area to be one of their main tasks. It would be an exaggeration to speak of radical change, however. What has changed are the sources of this pressure, which increasingly are being shifted from the national to the European or international level.

Change in an Intra- and Interorganizational Perspective

In this section, we will describe our interest group population, make a few statements on the identification of our samples and the focal organizational sets dominating both sectors, and will finally turn to some selected results, which shed light on both the ways that leading representatives of trade associations perceive external challenges and the related modifications in the application of resources.

Interest Group Populations and Focal Organizations

There are approximately 1750 chemical companies in Germany. Close to 100 per cent of these are organized by the VCI and its divisional interest associations. An analysis of the interest groups operating in the interest domain of the sector is therefore practically an analysis of the 'VCI world'. The VCI is subdivided into eight territorial or *Länder* associations, twenty branch associations (Fachverbände), and ten divisional incorporations (Fachvereinigungen), thus in total around thirty-eight subunits. The branch associations are relatively autonomous organizations, while the incorporations are directly subordinated to the VCI main executive. Anyone who has joined a branch association or is directly affiliated to the VCI can become a member of a Fachvereinigung. The VCI is internally divided into a total of thirty-nine committees and permanent task forces (Fachausschüsse), which are headed by leading executives of the largest participating member firms.[18]

Our entire population initially comprised well over eighty interest groups.[19] After detailed research, though, it turned out that many of these organizations no longer exist. Through questioning a panel consisting of five experts on

---

[18] Bayer has a total of fifteen committee executives (Fachausschuß-Vorsitzende) and deputies (Stellvertreter), BASF fifteen as well, Degussa 8, Henkel four, and Aventis and Boehringer 2 each.

[19] This number is the result of comprehensive Internet research while adding other available source material. Very important at the beginning was the consultation of the Max-Planck-Institute's (MPI-Cologne) data bank on business interest associations (see Visser *et al.* 1999).

interest associations, we were able to limit the number of associations we are interested in to sixty-three. Those who obtained the highest reputation values were treated separately as a so-called focal organisation-set. The interest groups from whom we have obtained completely filled out questionnaires are our overall sample. It is composed of thirty-five organizations in total. The response rate in the case of the sixteen focal organizations was 100 per cent. We visited these associations and conducted both structured and semi-structured interviews. The corresponding numbers for the information and communications sector are as follows. The population here comprises all national interest groups active in the ICT domain. There are thirty-eight in total, from which the focal associations were traced, as in the case of chemicals, by means of reputational analysis. The response rate for these associations is 89 per cent, in comparison to 61 per cent of the entire population. The material presented in the following is based on the answers of the thirty-five and thirty-eight associations and their executives and, hence, comprises seventy-two groups from both sectors in total.

The VCI is probably the broadest German sectoral association based on voluntary membership and has no equivalent in any other EU member state because of its quasi-representational monopoly. Within our complete sample of thirty-five interest associations, six associations in total have been created since 1980. Except for the case of the biotechnology association DIB and the Association of Research-Intensive Drug Producers (VFA), these are foremost spin-offs of previously existing associations.[20] Thanks to this, the VCI was able to establish itself as the central umbrella organization of the sector. Outside this umbrella organization no other differentiation processes arose within the population. Differentiation in the German chemicals sector exclusively took place in an intra-organizational fashion. There are some recent signs of turbulence within the population—marked, for instance, by the break-off of the VFA from the BPI and by their move to Berlin[21]—but in general this so far exceptional case should not be overstated.

In the network of its population, the VCI towers over the other associations. Its main headquarters are located at the centre of the network and its satellites in Berlin and Brussels are extremely well connected with the different branch associations.[22] Compared to the early results of Wyn Grant (1986), see also

---

[20] Within the focal organization sets this is the IHO (1991) and the VFA (1993), and within the complete sample the IGV (1990), the BfT (1985), and an association of producers of soft foam rubber (1989).

[21] With a few exceptions having to do with the geographical location of the company headquarters of the most important member firms, almost all branch associations of the VCI are located in Frankfurt 'under one roof' in the most literal meaning of the words.

[22] We draw this information from an empirical network analysis of the chemicals' associational population, but we will refrain from a more detailed description of this due to lack of space.

Groser (1983) and Grant *et al.* (1988), we do not detect any real changes: 'There are very pronounced and integrated relationships between the VCI (...) and the specialized subsector associations (...). The heads of the various associations meet once a month, one director comparing the relationship between the VCI and his associations as like that of a father and his grown-up children' (Grant *et al.* 1988: 70). If there really is a business interest association whose properties perfectly correspond to those of the corporatist prototype described by Schmitter and Streeck, then this clearly is the VCI.

The situation in ICT is completely different. The dynamics within the organizational population are unequally higher than in the chemicals sector. For this reason, the number of interest associations rose by 31 per cent between 1985 and 2000 (16 per cent in the chemicals sector). It must be noted that we are not dealing with branch associations like in the case of chemicals but, rather, with independent organizations which are not integrated into a central peak association. Above all, interest groups operating at the interfaces of the subsectors and smaller segments of the industry have established themselves in the associational landscape throughout the 1990s. In 1990 the Association of Private Radio and Telecommunications (*Verband Privater Rundfunk und Telekommunikation* or VPRT) originated through the merger of previously independent associations. In 1995, the German Multimedia Association (Deutscher Multimediaverband) was founded and comprised practically all subsectors of the domain, while in 2000 three independent associations and one divisional association for each subunit of the *Zentralverband Elektrotechnik und Elektroindustrie* (Central Association for Electric Technology and Electric Industries or ZVEI) and the Association of German Mechanical and Plant Engineering (*Verband Deutscher Maschinen- und Anlagenbau* or VDMA) merged to become the largest ICT association known to date: BITKOM (*Bundesverband der Informationswirtschaft, Telekommunikation und Neue Medien*, or the Federal Association of Information Economy, Telecommunications and New Media). It has taken on the task of putting an end to the dissipation of the associational landscape and of representing the entire ICT sector under its umbrella. For this purpose it also has cooperative relationships with other associations which have joined BITKOM as members. As a rule, intergroup cooperation plays a large role in the ICT sector.[23] For example, in 1996 five associations joined forces under the umbrella of the leading association of the German software industry (SVDS) to offer members from the software technology area a common platform. In the 1990s more than half of all associations were involved in mergers and cooperation arrangements.

---

[23] In terms of the forms of population competition presented in the theoretical section, these could be considered to be integration and cooperation in the ICT sector, and in the chemicals sector as absorption.

These population dynamics have also left their mark on the positioning of the associations in the population's contact network. In the 1980s the ICT's interest system was dominated by two associations, the ZVEI and the VDMA. Among the branch associations, they represented the private part of the sector which was not under the supervision of the present-day Telekom (at that time, the Federal Post Office). At the beginning of the 1990s more and more actors joined them (in particular the VPRT), thus breaking up the representational monopoly (Schneider and Werle 1991). This constellation was completely changed in 2000. ZVEI and VDMA were pushed out of the centre of the ICT branch by other associations which had been founded just a couple of years before. The dominating actors since the start of the new millenium are now the DMMV, BITKOM, and the VPRT.

External Challenges

We are interested in whether, and to what extent, members of both sectoral samples and the leadership of their associations are able to discern the thrust induced by internal or external environmental challenges and determine which dimension this pressure reverts back to and from which material level it is exercised.[24] We must set apart here that the questionnaire distinguishes between pressure exercised from within the influence and/or the membership dimensions. With the latter we are primarily referring to changes within one's own association as well as within the population of firms such as company mergers, takeovers, high domestic investments by foreign capital, new associational tasks, etc. In the case of the chemicals' associations there were great variations in the distribution of responses between more influence—and more membership-induced challenges: 51.4 per cent of the respondents believed that the bulk of adaptational pressure is due to factors internal to the populations of firms and associations (25.7 per cent influence-related factors). In the ICT sector there was a more balanced distribution (50 and 50 per cent each). Therefore in the following we will limit ourselves to commenting on those external factors described in terms of the environment that is, economic,[25]

---

[24] We are aware of the fact that changes in perception among interest group leaders only cover parts of the structural segment of organizational properties, that is, of the operational core and periphery. Further analysis of our data will show that these cognitive changes are also reflected in the strategies of the groups being documented in annual reports and similar material.

[25] Note that, in the case of the chemicals' associations, 90% of the respondents considered company restructuring and mergers to be a decisive risk for their association (score: important and very important). Both factors can be directly traced back to economic developments—a fact that increases the weight attributed to economic pressure—although only indirectly.

TABLE 10.1. *Different types of challenges (general and from within different levels)*

Challenges	Associations	General	National	European	Global
Economic	Chemicals	45	31	26	23
	ICT	56	35	26	35
Technological	Chemicals	31	20	14	37
	ICT	65	0	17	74
Political	Chemicals	89	20	51	0
	ICT	73	39	48	4
Societal	Chemicals	55	60	14	3
	ICT	31	61	13	17

technological, political, and societal challenges, and the way they are perceived by the association leadership (see Table 10.1).

Consider, first of all, that the associations' leaders in both sectors feel organizationally challenged by more than just changes in their environment (Column 1: General). Primarily political factors are mentioned here (89 and 72 per cent), but economic, technological, and societal factors also obtain high scores. For representatives of the ICT sector, for instance, technological changes are almost as important as political ones, while representatives of the chemicals' industry attest a great significance to societal and economic challenges. We should therefore underline that the thrust conveyed by the organizations' environment is by no means restricted to the political domain.

More significant are the judgements apropos the territorial levels identified as a source or origin of these challenges. The highest scores here contain the following combinations with a high level of intersectoral agreement: technological and global (37 and 74 per cent); political and European (51 and 48 per cent), as well as societal and domestic (60 and 61 per cent), while the pressure exercised by economic processes of change are predominantly expressed as coinciding with national sources (31 and 35 per cent). The latter score is quite astonishing, but may be due to the fact that the dynamics of international markets do not strike directly, rather indirectly and conveyed by the members of the association. As argued above, the actual effects of many of these changes (mergers, etc.) primarily manifest themselves within the national space. Another phenomenon to which reference was made in many of the interviews carried out in both sectors and both countries, and which also becomes manifest on a primarily national scale although being triggered by economic internationalization, is the growing presence of foreign and mostly American CEOs in German multinationals companies. They are accused of not being able to relate to German associational culture and of being difficult to 'socialize' into the system,[26] due to the short periods of time they spend in their positions (secondment).

The political challenge perceived as being the most significant is EU regulatory activity. This should not astonish us, especially when taking into account that the issueing of the Commission's White Book on Chemicals occurred at the same time as the interviews. However, the branch associations of the VCI are extremely well prepared for this challenge and had already built up intensive contacts with diverse EU actors over the past decades. The network analysis that we carried out reveals almost identical centrality scores for the Environmental Ministry, the DG Environment (DG Umwelt) of the European Commission, and EU branch associations (see below).

Changes in the technological environment or technological challenges receive the highest score of all (74 per cent) in the case of the ICT associations. Their origins clearly lie within the international dimension. The rather remote significance granted to this factor by the chemical associations (37 per cent) should not obscure the fact that technological changes in particular triggered the foundations of the only new associations in the sector (VFA and DIB) at that time.

Societal challenges also received relatively high scores—astonishingly, from representatives of both sectors. Less astonishing is the fact that, above all, the national level plays a significant role. In the section dedicated to the societal environment we pointed to a dispensability and compatibility matrix for typical products in the chemicals sector. Our interviews pertinent to this have demonstrated that the branch associations of this sector apply considerable financial resources to move upwards on the dispensability axis and down on the risk axis. In some individual cases the resources invested for marketing, image building, and press and media presence outweigh those which were traditionally available for lobbying or services to members.

With respect to possible scenarios of Europeanization, we should like to stress that there is hardly a need for a one-sided adaptation of association structures or strategies. Albeit being mentioned as a possible source of structural changes and as representing a political threat, the European Union is consistently ranked in last place among the other levels and dimensions.

Internal Distribution of Resources

Apart from modifying the cognitive maps within an association's structure, the consequences of the environmental changes envisaged above also have

---

[26] 'More and more companies are managed by the "country manager" of a multinational on a three-year stint (. . .) as part of an international career. Indigenous chief executives are increasingly subject to the "Four Years and You're Out" syndrome common in the United States. There is a danger that participation in trade association activity will become a second-order issue to chief executives' (Macdonald 2001: 9).

TABLE 10.2. *Allocation of resources to different organizational tasks*

Type of task	Sectors			
	Chemicals	Rank	ICT	Rank
Lobbying (national)	15	4	24	1
Lobbying (EU)	9	6	12	4
Lobbying (societal)	11	5	9	6
Lobbying (total)	35		45	
Consultation of members	17	3	13	3
Information for members	17	2	12	4
Conferences	22	1	14	2
Side benefits	1	9	6	7
Training	4	7	4	9
Other	4	7	6	7
Membership investments	65		55	

implications for an organization's output. Along with the processing of environmental information, organizations may also apply effective internal measures to improve their fit to surrounding landscapes. Ecological approaches in organizational sociology describe absorbing and compensating measures on the part of the organizations with whose help uncertainties emerging from the environment can be intercepted and buffered. This primarily involves changes in the organizational characteristics in the direction of more flexibility and diversity.

A central indicator for change in organizations is the effective allocation of resources or their changes. In Table 10.2 the activities of the associations are listed according to task areas and scope of functions in terms of percentage of the total output. In both sectors, the expenditure for services mainly made available to members dominates. With 65 and 55 per cent of the activities of the ICT associations, they rank far in front of the resources that are invested in lobbying.

In the area of lobbying, the national contacts and lobbying channels are much more predominant than their European counterparts. In the chemicals sector, even societal lobbying (i.e. resources invested for influencing the public) is more important than European lobbying. Our network analysis of communication contact reveals that, in the ICT sector, the most frequently mentioned reference points for associations are federal ministries, in particular the Federal Ministry for the Economy, followed by the political parties of the *Bundestag*. On the European level, contacts to the EU Commission are the most predominant, followed closely by the European branch associations. The European Parliament plays only a subordinate role. This testifies to the low relevance of the supranational level in several segments of the sector where the Commission hardly possesses the authority to enforce norms and standards or secure the freedom of movement of goods and services. On the other hand, telecommunications and related branches are subject to strong regulation by the EU Commission, which results in the fact that associations from this domain are also active in Brussels.

As already mentioned, the density, frequency, and weight given to the links with European institutions and organizations are particularly high in the chemicals sector. To mention just a few selected statistics, we refer to the leading centrality positions occupied by several actors (for details see Grote and Schneider 2002). For a total of forty-two public and private organizations, we have asked our respondents to report the strength and quality of their ties along five types of relations:

(1) influence reputation;
(2) communication contact;
(3) supply;
(4) receipt of strategically important information;
(5) the building of alliances with a view to influencing public decisons.

If we isolate only the strong and most frequent relations, code the indegrees (choices received) of the respective organizations, and classify the results in terms of ten positions, then the following emerges.

The sector's peak association, the VCI, consistently occupies the leading position across all types of relations; national ministries hold the positions 2, 2, 3, 3, and 8, respectively; and the General Directorates of the Commission the positions 3, 7, 5, 6, and 8. Interestingly, the EU branch associations around CEFIC—the peak association of European chemical producers and the EU's strongest interest association overall (Greenwood 2001)—score higher than all other EU level organizations (8, 4, 2, 2, 2), while CEFIC itself occupies rather marginal positions (10, 9, 8, 8, 5). What is important to note is that the associations divide their contacts and other relations in a relatively balanced way across the most important actors at both the national and the supranational levels—an activity that absorbs an increasing proportion of their resources.

Cross-section analyses can only give clues on the course that organizational change takes. In order to trace these changes, we must investigate the longitudinal section of resource allocation in the economic associations. As an indicator for the change in resource allocation, we use the number of times that significant modifications in partial areas of the activity spectrum are mentioned. In the timeframe since 1995, the individual associational activities have been subject to considerable changes. In particular, lobby activities have witnessed an increase, which is nearly equally distributed between the national and European levels (between 30 and 40 per cent in the case of both sectors). From the perspective of interest groups, European integration can thus not be depicted as a zero-sum game in which shifts of authority to the European level are compensated for by losses at the national level. Instead, the member states still have the possibility of exhausting their discretionary space, especially during the implementation phase of the policy cycle. In addition, the selection mechanisms of lobbying have distinguished themselves in parallel to the shifts of competencies, and therefore pose greater demands on the associations' strategies. Limiting itself to one lobbying channel drastically reduces the chances of an association's position being selected in the political process. As many others have argued, only a combination of national and European strategies can now maximize success.

There is currently no clear picture as to the logic of membership. The proportion of resources allocated to services for members has grown in total, in the various areas to different extents, however. In the chemicals sector it is primarily the expenditures for member information that have increased, while in the ICT sector the services for further education and trade fairs have experienced growth (rubric 'other').

Final Remarks

It is difficult, if not impossible, to draw a unified picture of organizational change in national trade associations. This is especially true if one considers that hardly any comparable material on this topic exists, that organizational sociology almost completely blends out organized business interests from its research agenda, and that in the current debate on Europeanization they are foremost marked by their absence. Accordingly, we have limited ourselves to present a number of aspects which appear to be essential to us. In a comprehensive and international comparative perspective guaranteed within the project by the British and US cases (both chemicals and ICT), the variances will become much more clear and our theoretical arguments will be substantiated in a more convincing manner.

However, it should be evident here that relevant influences on national trade associations conveyed via the European level can indeed be partially verified, but do remain relatively limited in the entire context of organizational change. National interest associations will remain national for the time being. Nevertheless, they will map out parts of their environment in their operational core, continue to further differentiate their organizational periphery, structure their contact portfolio, and learn primarily through sharing experiences and best practice with associations from other national contexts. To describe this as Europeanization is, in our view, exaggerated because associations are doing all of the above with respect to their overall environment. As we have seen, the European level plays only a limited role in this process.

The organizational ecological perspective applied here suggests that we are dealing with processes of coevolution. Organizational phenomena such as the ones described here do not occur in an isolated fashion. The transformation of political space and the repercussions of this process in the minds of associational leaders cover only part of what is going on objectively and what is being perceived subjectively. With the exception of technological developments, in terms of objective changes in the environment we are mostly dealing with modest transformations of the dimensions studied, which are however, met by greatly diverging reactions within the groups of our samples. In the case of the ICT sector, this results in interorganizational shifts which are then intercepted in the form of integrative or cooperative competition, while the associational population in the chemicals sector has been organized under the roof of an encompassing peak association right from the start. As a whole, we observe both processes of differentiation and dedifferentiation, without witnessing a quantum leap towards the type of organizational form that the adoption of a Euro-centred perspective would perhaps have suggested.

REFERENCES

Baum, J. A. C. (1999). 'Organisational Ecology', in S. R. Clegg and C. Hardy (eds), *Studying Organisation. Theory and Method* (London, Thousand Oaks, New Delhi: Sage Publications), 71–108.

—— (ed.), (2002). *The Oxford Companion to Organisations* (Oxford: Blackwell Business).

—— and Clegg, S. R. (eds), (1996). *Handbook of Organisation Studies* (London: Sage), 77–114.

Bennett, R. J. (1997). 'The Impact of European Economic Integration on Business Associations: The UK Case', *West European Politics* 20(3): 61–90.

Bertalanffy, L. V. (1968). *General System Theory* (New York: George Braziller).

Bogumil, J. and Schmid, J. (2001). *Politik in Organisationen. Organisationstheoretische Ansätze und praxisbezogene Anwendungsbeispiele* (Opladen: Leske und Budrich).

Bouwen, P. (2001). *Corporate Lobbying in the European Union: Towards a Theory of Access*, SPS No. 2001/5 (Florence: EUI Working Paper).

Buckley, W. (1967). *Sociology and Modern System Theory* (Englewood Cliffs: Prentice Hall).

Coleman, W. D. (1997). 'Associational Governance in a Globalizing Era: Weathering the Storm', in J. R. Hollingsworth and R. Boyer (eds), *Contemporary Capitalism. The Embeddedness of Institutions* (Cambridge, Massachusetts: Cambridge University Press), 127–53.

—— and Perl, A. (1999). 'Internationalized Policy Environments and Policy Network Analysis', *Political Studies* XLVII: 691–709.

DIB (2000), *BioTech (2000). Die wirtschaftliche Bedeutung von Biotechnologie und Gentechnik in Deutschland* (Frankfurt/Main: Deutsche Industrievereinigung Biotechnologie).

European Commission (2001). *White Paper on the Strategy for a Future Chemicals Policy, COM (2001) 88 final, 27.2.2001* (Brussels: EU Commission).

Fombrun, C. J. (1988). 'Crafting an Institutionally Informed Ecology of Organisations', in G. A. Carroll (ed.), *Ecological Models of Organisations* (Cambridge: Ballinger), 223–39.

Grant, W. (1986). 'Associational Systems in the Chemical Industry', in A. Martinelli (ed.), *International Markets and Global Firms. A Comparative Study of Organized Business in the Chemical Industry* (London, Newbury Park, New Delhi: Sage Publications), 47–60.

——, Paterson, W., and Whitston, C. (1988). *Government and the Chemical Industry. A comparative Study of Britain and West Germany* (Oxford: Oxford University Press).

Green Cowles, M. (2001). 'The Transatlantic Business Dialogue and Domestic Business–Government Relations', in M. Green Cowles, J. Caporaso, and T. Risse (eds), *Transforming Europe* (Ithaca, London: Cornell University Press), 159–79.

——, Caporaso, J., and Risse, T. (eds) (2001). *Transforming Europe* (Ithaca, London: Cornell University Press).

Greenwood, J. (2001). *Inside the EU Business Associations* (Basingstoke, New York: Palgrave).

—— and Webster, R. (2000). 'Are EU Business Associations Governable?', *European Integration Online Papers—EIOP* 4(3) 14 February 2000 (http://eiop.or.at/eiop/texte/2000003a.htm.

——, Grote J. R., and Ronit, K. (eds), (1992). *Organized Interests and the European Community* (London, Newbury Park, New Delhi: Sage Publications).

Groser, M. (1983). *Die Organisation von Wirtschaftsinteressen in der chemischen Industrie der Bundesrepublik Deutschland*, unpublished paper.

Grote, J. R. (1998). 'Regionale Vernetzung: Interorganisatorische Strukturdifferenzen regionaler Politikgestaltung', in B. Kohler-Koch *et al.* (eds), *Interaktive Politik in Europa. Regionen im Netzwerk der Integration* (Opladen: Leske und Budrich), 62–96.

—— and Schmitter, P. C. (1999). 'The Rennaissance of National Corporatism: Unintended Side-effect of European Economic and Monetary Union or a Calculated Response to the Absence of European Social Policy?', *Transfer* 5(1–2): 34–64, http://www.etuc.org/etui/Publications/Transfer/GROTEFO.pdf.

—— and Schneider, V. (2001). *The Europeanization of (Organized) Business Interests. A First Approximation*, paper presented at the IPSA World Congress, August 2000, Montreal, Canada.

——, and —— (2002). *International Challenges and Organisational Change in National Trade Associations. First Insights from a Comparative Research Project*, Paper Presented at the Workshop on 'The Europeanization of Interest Politics', Amsterdam Institute for Advanced Labour Studies (AIAS), University of Amsterdam, 16–17 May 2002.

Harmsen, R. (1999). 'The Europeanization of National Administrations: A Comparative Study of France and the Netherlands', *Governance* 12(1): 81–113.

Kappelhoff, P. (1999). 'Komplexitätstheorie und Steuerung von Netzwerken', in J. Sydow and A. Windeler (eds), *Steuerung von Netzwerken* (Opladen: Leske und Budrich), 347–89.

Kohler-Koch, B. and Quittkat, C. (1999). *Intermediation of interests in the European Union*, Arbeitspapiere 9/1999, Mannheimer Zentrum für Europäische Sozialforschung.

Kriesi, H.-P. (2003). 'Institutional Filters and Path Dependency: The Impact of Europeanization on Swiss Business Associations', in W. Streeck, V. Schneider, J. Visser, and Jürgen R. Grote (eds), *Governing Interests: Business Associations in the National, European and Global Political Economy*.

Latzer, M. (1997). *Mediamatik—Die Konvergenz von Telekommunikation, Computer und Rundfunk* (Opladen: Westdeutscher Verlag).

Lehmbruch, G. (1994). 'Dilemmata verbandlicher Einflußlogik im Prozeß der deutschen Vereinigung', in W. Streeck (ed.), *Staat und Verbände* (Opladen: Westdeutscher Verlag), 370–92.

Lewin, A. Y. and Volberda, H. W. (1999). 'Prolegomena on Coevolution: A Framework for Research on Strategy and New Organisational Forms', *Organisation Science* 10(5): 519–34.

Macdonald Report (2001). *The Business of Representation. The Modern Trade Association. A Report to the Trade Association Forum by Alistair Macdonald* (London: Department of Trade and Industry and Trade Association Forum).

McKelvey, B. and Aldrich, H. E. (1983). 'Populations, Natural Selection, and Applied Organisational Science', *American Sociology Quarterly* 28: 101–28.

March, J. G. (ed.) (1988). *Decisions and Organizations* (New York: Blackwell).

—— and Olsen, J. P. (eds) (1976). Ambiguity and Choice in Organizations (Bergen: Universitetsforlaget).

—— and Simon, H. A. (1958). Organizations (New York: Wiley).

Metcalfe, L. (1994). 'International Policy Co-ordination and Public management Reform', *International Review of Administrative Sciences* 60: 275–90.

Munz, C. M. (2001). *Europäisierung und verbandliche Orientierungen: Eine Inhaltsanalyse der Wahrnehmung von Umweltveränderungen durch den Verband der Chemischen Industrie* (Universität Konstanz: Diplomarbeit).

OECD (2000). *Measuring the ICT sector* (Paris: OECD).

Oliver, C. (1991). 'Strategic Responses to Institutional Processes', *Academy of Management Review* 16: 145–79.

Olsen, J. P. (2002). *The Many Faces of Europeanization*, Arena Working Papers 01/2, Oslo.

Page, E. and Wouters, L. (1995). 'The Europeanization of the National Bureaucracies?', in J. Pierre (ed.), *Bureaucracy in the Modern State: An Introduction to Comparative Public Administration* (Aldershot: Edward Elgar).

Pestoff, V. (2003). 'Globalization, Business Interest Associations and Swedish Exceptionalism in the 21st Century', in W. Streek, V. Schneider, J. Visser, and Jürgen R. Grote (eds), *Governing Interests: Business Associations in the National, European and Global Political Economy*.

Pfeffer, J. and Salancik, G. R. (1978). *The External Control of Organisations* (New York: Harper and Row).

Sandholtz, W. (1998). 'The Emergence of a Supranational Telecommunications Regime', in W. Sandholtz and A. Stone Sweet (eds), *European Integration and Supranational Governance* (Oxford: Oxford University Press), 134–63.

Schmidt, V. A. (2002). 'The Effects of European Integration on National Forms of Governance. Reconstructing Practices and Reconceptualizing Democracy', in

J. R. Grote and B. Gbikpi (eds), *Participatory Governance. Political and Societal Implications* (Opladen: Leske und Budrich), 141–77.

Schmitter, P. C. (1997). 'The Emerging Europolity and its Impact Upon National Systems of Production', in J. R. Hollingsworth and R. Boyer (eds), *Contemporary Capitalism. The Embeddedness of Institutions*, op. cit.: 395–430.

——and Streeck, W. (1999). *The Organisation of Business Interests. Studying the Associative Action of Business in Advanced Industrial Societies*, discussion paper; Max-Planck-Institute for the Study of Societies, Cologne.

Schneider, V. (1988). *Politiknetzwerke in der Chemikalienkontrolle. Eine Analyse einer transnationalen Politikentwicklung* (Berlin, New York: Walter de Gruyter).

——(2002). 'Private Actors in Political Governance: Regulating the Information and Communication Sectors', in J. R. Grote and B. Gbikpi (eds), *Participatory Governance. Political and Societal Implications*, op. cit., 245–64.

——and Werle, R. (1989). 'Die Eroberung eines Politikfeldes. Die Europäische Gemeinschaft in der Telekommunikationspolitik', *Jahrbuch zur Staats- und Verwaltungswissenschaft*, 3: 247–72.

——, Dang-Nguyen, G., and Werle, R. (1994). 'Corporate Actor Networks in European Policy-Making: Harmonizing Telecommunications Policy', *Journal of Common Market Studies* 32: 473–98.

——, Schmitter, P. C., and Grote, J. R. (2000). *Die Veränderung von Einfluß- und Mitgliedschaftslogiken sektoraler Dachverbände im Kontext von Europäisierung und Internationalisierung*. Projektantrag an die Deutsche Forschungsgemeinschaft, März 2000.

Scott, W. R. (1998). *Organisations: rational, natural, and open systems* (Upper Saddle River: Prentice Hall).

Streeck, W. (1987). 'Vielfalt und Interdependenz. Überlegungen zur Rolle von intermediären Organisationen in sich ändernden Umwelten', in *Kölner Zeitschrift für Soziologie und Sozialpsychologie*, 39. Jg., Heft 3, 471–95.

——(1995). 'Politikverflechtung und Entscheidungslücke. Zum Verhältnis von zwischenstaatlichen Beziehungen und sozialen Interessen im europäischen Binnenmarkt', in K. Bentele, B. Reissert, and R. Schettkat (eds), *Die Reformfähigkeit von Industriegesellschaften*. Fritz W. Scharpf, Festschrift zu seinem 60. Geburtstag (Frankfurt/M.: Campus), 101–28.

——(1999). 'Entscheidung durch Nichtentscheidung: Zur Logik transnationaler Interessenpolitik', in W. Streek (ed.), *Korporatismus in Deutschland. Zwischen Nationalstaat und Europäischer Union* (Frankfurt, New York: Campus), 112–23.

Thompson, J. D. (1967). *Organisations in Action* (New York: McGraw-Hill).

Traxler, F. and Schmitter, P. C. (1994). 'Perspektiven europäischer Integration, verbandlicher Interessenvermittlung und Politikformulierung', in V. Eichener and H. Voelzkow (eds), *Europäische Integration und verbandliche Interessenvermittlung* (Marburg: Metropolis), 45–70.

VCI (2000). *Fakten, Analysen, Perspektiven, Chemie 2000, Jahresbericht* (Frankfurt/Main: Verband der Chemischen Industrie).

—— (2001). *Chemiewirtschaft in Zahlen* (Frankfurt/Main: Verband der Chemischen Industrie).

Visser, J., Streeck, W., and Hauser-Ditz, A. (1999). *Some Preliminary Results from the EOI Database Project* (Köln: Max-Planck-Institut für Gesellschaftsforschung), unpublished paper.

11

Differentiated Europeanization: Large and Small Firms in the EU Policy Process

DAVID COEN AND CHARLES DANNREUTHER

Introduction

Europeanization is usually discussed in vertical terms of how top-down pressures for change are received and implemented at the national level (Goetz and Hix 2000; Cowles *et al.* 2001; Schmidt 2001; Radaelli 2002). In this chapter, the issue of Europeanization is explored primarily at the horizontal level of European Union (EU) policy formulation and the adaptation and Europeanization of large and small business interests in the new opportunity structures of Brussels (Grande 1996; Coen 1997, 1998; Mazey and Richardson 2001). That is to say, we are looking less at the Europeanization of policy domains and implementation and more at the differentiated Europeanization of actors and institutions in the policy processes. Recognizing that EU institutions have increased their regulatory competencies and that the process of business representation has taken on a very distinct logic at the European level with the development of forums under an activist Commission (Coen 1997, 1998; Richardson 2000), we explore how SMEs and large firms have reacted to these opportunities in diverse ways. Specifically, we identify how multinational firms have established a strong EU presence and distinct European business–government relationship, and assess the ability of SMEs to coordinate European strategies. In studying the Europeanization of business representation we explore the nature of the evolving EU public policy process, the requirements for EU interest representativeness, and the differential impact that this has on organized vs. disorganized economic interests.

The movement of business and other societal interests towards the European level has long been associated with a neofunctional perspective on European

The authors would like to thank the organizers and participants of the Bradford University Conference on Europeanization, Andreas Broscheid, Mark Duckenfield, Burkard Eberlien, Fabio Franchino, Dieter Kerwer, Sabine Saurugger, and Wyn Grant for comments on various drafts.

integration and societal change. Business interests have always been associated with the changes in policy and polity described by the term Europeanization, begging the question 'how does the study of "Europeanization" add to our understanding of European business lobbying'? To answer this we define in Section 'Europeanization and the Application to EU Public Policy' what we understand Europeanization to be, and set out a number of European policy-making process propositions to be explored empirically in Section 'The Europeanization of Business Interests in a Differentiated Policy Process'. While recognizing that EU business interests have a pedigree in terms of a pluralist/corporatist analysis (Streeck and Schmitter 1991; Mazey and Richardson 1993; Greenwood 1997), we turn our attention to: how institutional and organizational capabilities have affected representative ability over time (Coen 1998, 2002; Young and Wallace 2000); how firms, of all sizes, have developed 'venue shopping' strategies in a multilevel governance structure (Coen 1997; Kohler-Koch 1999; Mazey and Richardson 2001); and, finally, in resource dependency terms, we explore how firm size affects the distinct rules and norms of interest representation with the European Commission

Europeanization and Application to EU Public Policy

The study of Europeanization focuses not on polity building, as European integration studies were concerned with, but on policy making (Jachtenfuchs 2001). This theoretical orientation of the public policy literature towards the Europeanization debate is one emphasized in the theoretical introduction to this volume (Radaelli 2002) and supported for two reasons in this chapter. First, public policy analysis fits the incremental and piecemeal nature of the processes associated with Europeanization (Richardson 1996; Mazey and Richardson 2001). Moreover, the analytical frameworks for public policy analysis were constructed in relation to national level case studies, so once applied to the European level they facilitate both the comparison of European with national levels and then the interaction between them (Borzel and Risse 2001; Heritier *et al.* 2001; Schmidt 2001). In short, public policy analysis works well with Europeanization as it bridges the two political arenas and so helps us to compare like with like.

The second reason relates not so much to the explanatory powers of public policy analysis as to the limits of European integration theory. Theories of European integration owe their intellectual and disciplinary origins to international relations literature. Implicit in this body of literature was the focus on the state and its preservation, through realist approaches, or eradication, through functionalist approaches. More specifically, in the EU context, the intergovernmentalists posited the view that EU institutions were acceptable to nation states only insofar as they strengthened, rather than weakened, their national interests (Hoffman 1966; Moravcsik 1993). However, the Maastricht Treaty and the subsequent increase in EU regulatory competencies demonstrated to actors and academics alike that we had to move beyond 'state centrism' and towards independent interests operating in 'multilevel governance' structures (Marks *et al.* 1996). These studies unpack the idea of the nation state as a unitary actor, often using comparative politics and public policy analysis, to examine the interaction of sets of institutions, norms, and values that react to and influence international relations. The study of Europeanization is part of that move, only this time it is unpacking domestic political institutions to examine how states interact with the European Union. This chapter advances the public policy position further by examining Europeanization not in the institutions of the state, but of society in the form of societal interest groups.

We look at interest group politics because they are such an essential element to politics and to public policy analysis (Richardson 2000). Interest groups can therefore help us to understand the effect of a political system on an external actor—how insiders treat outsiders and how these outsiders have to react. Gaining credibility is a large part of the political process for all political actors and institutions, but especially interest groups that do not necessarily enjoy the weight of administrative support, political authority, and Treaty protected privileges enjoyed by member state actors in the European Union. This chapter therefore examines how business interest groups from member states have Europeanized at the European tier of a multilevel system. We do not seek to explain the 'top-down' Europeanization of national association, since, in line with Grote and Lang in this volume, we observed limited alterations to national business–government traditions and institutions. Rather, we assess the effect of Europeanization on the policy process by analysing how it has provided new venues to agenda-set or veto depending on the nature of the policy domain (distributive or regulatory) and the policy cycle (Schmidt 1997; Coen 1998; Coen *et al.* 2002). Thus, we focus on how the European opportunity structure has affected how societal interests behave and changed over time. This allows us to examine the Europeanization of society which, unlike national bureaucracies and political parties, is operating outside the state and so can adapt its business cultures and institutional arrangements more readily.

But while business interests provide us with a clean slate upon which to examine the processes of Europeanization, they also present us with an analytical problem. Europeanization is most often investigated with the dependent variable as national political systems—that is, in the actors and institutions of nation states. But if we remove the dependent variable, that is, the actors and institutions of the member state, how can we understand Europeanization to have taken place? What should we look at to begin our investigation? To answer this question we need to explore the public policy literature again. In recent years the public policy debate has developed a number of behaviourist assumptions for application to the European Union as a political system (Hix 1999), as a regulatory state (Majone 1997; Thatcher 2000), and as a system of multilevel governance (Marks *et al.* 1996; Streeck *et al.* 1997). Hence, today we have had a number of actor-based studies of agenda-setting and advocacy coalitions within the Brussels black box (Coen 1998; Sabatier 1998; Kohler-Koch 1999; Young and Wallace 2000; Mazey and Richardson 2001). These actor based approaches are complemented by a range of institutionalist approaches that introduce structuring variables by focusing on the changing arenas in which these policy makers make their decisions, and agendas are set (Pierson 1996; Armstrong and Bulmer 1998; Schneider and Aspinwall 2001). More recently a third body of literature has emerged that examines the impact of beliefs and norms on EU policy making (Haas 1992; Radaelli 2002), and draws on the methodological frameworks of constructivism and the sociological institutionalism school (Powell and DiMaggio 1991).

These three methodological orientations provide us with a set of starting propositions in the investigation of the Europeanization phenomenon. These start with the proposition that Europeanization may be the consequence of actors perceiving their interests as being best pursued at the European level. The second proposition would argue that a change in the rules of the game has changed incentive structures to encourage actors to move to the European level. Finally, we are able to move beyond a functional debate to investigate the significance of the discursive constructions of Europeanization, as seen in norms and shared beliefs, and examine how they construct the political realities that affect business–government relations. As pointed out by Featherstone in the introduction to this volume, we can see all these theoretical approaches—agency, structure, and beliefs—as underpinning the Europeanization literature.

Drawing on these methodologically informed approaches to Europeanization, we develop a number of propositions for investigating the Europeanization of business interests. First, we examine how and why large and small businesses participate at the European level and the reasons that refined the logic of action at the European level. In so doing we examine the initial 'bottom up' and 'top down' aspect of the Europeanization of business interests, and examine how different sized firms have different lobbying venues (Mazey and Richardson 2001). The movement of large firms to the European level, as demonstrated by the birth of the European Round Table of industrialists, took place more readily than for small firms, who had to rely on the nationally embedded peak business associations and Economic and Social Committee. We can explain this assertion in resource dependency terms because large firms, with their clear and internally defined interests and well funded Brussels based offices, were able to organize in ways that small businesses representatives, with their conflicting interests and competing national tradition, were unable to.

Second, we can examine the impact of rule changes at the European level and look at the ability of the actors to respond to the new incentives and opportunities structure of the multilevel and institutional environment. Thus we can recognize a two-level game, where the newly Europeanized actors can bring influence to bear on member states and member states' interests can shape European positions. In response to the changed rules, business interests that once fought each other moved towards more conciliatory or even collaborative arrangements at the European level. In some areas, collaborating in Commission-sponsored forums has become a requirement for access, while creating ad hoc '*strategic issue alliances*' is commonplace (Coen 1998, 2002). Moreover, flexible *advocacy coalitions* of wide groupings of societal interests increasingly play states and EU institutions off against each other (Young and Wallace 2000). In this complex advocacy environment we again expected to see stark differences between the way that large and small business react to the attempts of EU institutions to manage the proliferation of interests and opportunities at the European level through the new rules of the lobbying game. So the larger business representatives responded well, adopting *issue identities* and competing for European '*insider*' status at the Commission. SMEs, on the other hand, were disadvantaged, as national representative organizations were unable to present a unified voice for European SMEs to the Commission and other institutional 'allies', such as the European Parliament, presented competing, yet legitimated, representations in the name of the SME business community.

Third, we examine the proposition that Europeanization of business representation has developed unique styles of behaviour and norms for large and SME representatives. This socialization of business interests has been most clearly seen in the increased scrutiny placed on the processes of interest definition and in the obligations placed on actors with the development of forum politics. Since the Social Dialogue was introduced, a number of reports have been published on the *representativeness* of actors, identifying qualitative factors, such as participation in national level social partnerships and participation in ILO conferences, as well as quantitative characteristics of representatives involved in the process. In addition, in some sectors, such as SMEs, where the quality of information has sometimes been criticized, new sources of information have developed objective, scientifically sanitized representations of SME interests in a way that is qualitatively different to the subjective information provided by interested parties. In short, the rules of interest definition have come under European governance, as much as the interaction between those interests, so indicating the need for a certain kind of 'actorness' in the European arena. The advent of *forum politics* at the EU level operationalized many of the representativeness criteria and encouraged a form of institutional isomorphism where the EU institutions demanded a style of behaviour in return for access to the EU policy process (Coen 1997; Broscheid and Coen 2002). In the case of large firms, with the resources to play this new EU game, we observe a mimicking of successful lobbyists and the gradual establishment of norms of behaviour based on sophisticated advocacy alliances. Conversely, while EU institutions have attempted to encourage the access of SMEs to the EU policy debate, we observe a limited Europeanization of SME representative identity in Brussels and even that as a result of harsh costs of European lobbying.

Finally, we make the distinction, like others in this volume, between the European public policy *process*, with its evolving business–government interaction in Brussels and the Europeanization *policies* that result in greater EU competencies in the member states (Kohler-Koch 1996; Radaelli 2002). Seeing Europeanization as a governance process allows us greater flexibility in the analysis of the dynamics of individual policy processes and potentially removes the traditional assumptions of top down and bottom up policy making. We therefore accept the idea of incremental changes occurring in both member states and at the EU level (Bulmer and Burch 2001; Ladrech 1994). However, the degree to which national and European public policy structures converge is more questionable (Radaelli 2002). We argue that, while changes occur at both levels through a gradual process of learning, it is possible to see greater institutional isomorphism at the European public policy level than between the national public policy levels (Coen and Héritier 2000; Coen and Thatcher 2000; Héritier *et al.* 2001). That is to say, while Europeanization is often associated with convergence between national regulatory regimes, the reality is that is it is not a prerequisite.

In line with the above assertion, we observe that limited contagion or Europeanization of large or small business–government traditions has occurred in member states (Schmidt 1998; Grote and Lang 2002). However, significantly, today we are seeing the Commission attempting to take an increasingly coordinating lead via the advent of EU regulatory agencies and network committees of national regulatory bodies (Majone 1997; Radaelli this volume, Chapter 2; Eberlien and Grande 2000; Coen and Doyle 2001). Thus, for the purposes of this chapter, we do not see Europeanization as the harmonization of national policymaking or regulatory governance, but rather as a guiding principle that allows for interpretation and incorporation by both national and supranational actors.

The Europeanization of Business Interests in a Differentiated Policy Process

In recent years, large multinational firms have established a strong EU presence and distinct business–government relationship in Brussels, yet question marks continue to exist over the ability of SMEs to coordinate European strategies. Recognizing that business interests are an important mechanism through which citizens make their ideas, needs, and views know to policy-makers, it is important that we understand how they enter the policy process via formal consultation or ad hoc lobbying arrangements and how the recourses they bring to the debate vary with the aims and openness of the policy-makers. In theory EU institutions have always provided a number of opportunity structures that have been favourable to interest groups, but, as the following sections demonstrate, access and influence to the European debate has varied over time for economic interests (Richardson 2000). In the 1990s, the creeping competencies of the European institutions resulted in a large shift of political resources, by economic interests of all sizes, from the national to the European level (Coen 1997; Pollack 1998; Falkner 2000). Accepting that the European Union has limited impact in the areas of health care, education, and crime, it is fair to say that much EU lobbying activity has been dominated by business interests (Coen 1998; Grant 2000; Richardson 2000).[1] Accepting that the EU Institutions have become significant policy actors, we must note that the degree of activity in Brussels is a function of the policy cycle, with economic interests focusing on the formation of EU directives and regulations, the implementation of directives and 'day-to-day' regulatory monitoring in the domestic markets (Coen and Héritier 2000), and the resources that the actors can mobilize. As a result we can no longer see Europeanization of business lobbying in terms of 'bottom up' management or 'top down' coordination, but as a managed multilevel process with numerous feedback loops and entry points constrained by budgets and political experience. In light of the stated aim of the European Governance White Paper to improve interest representativeness in the 1400 EU forums (European Commission 2001), we assess below how business interests have Europeanized, adapted to the new opportunity structures, and aligned with other societal interests to create new identities.

Redefining the Preference Level for Business Interest Representation

Business interests have played an important role in the European project since the early days of economic integration in iron, steel, and agriculture. Not surprisingly, for a European Economic Community based on Christian Democratic traditions, the early business–government relations attempted to foster a continental style corporatist arrangement, based on national sector

---

[1] The DTI has estimated that some 70% of legislation affecting British business now emanates from Brussels (Grant 2000).

associations and European peak organizations. This structured and hierarchical business relationship was driven by the desire to foster a one-stop shop for information and a European business elite that could act as a constituency vis-à-vis member states. Yet for all desire to create a structured and hierarchical arrangement the reality was a more fragmented 'bottom-up' arrangement where business interests would lobby via national governments and/or established national associations feeding into the European associations (Streek and Schmitter 1991; Aspinwall and Greenwood 1998).[2] The national focus was thus reinforced by the recognition that national lobbying strategies avoided European compromises and lowest common denominator policy. Consequently, both large business and SME representation contributed little to the European policy debate and was perceived by Brussels policy-makers as reactive and destructive to the European initiative.

Gradually, after years of European stagnation, big business recognized the potential economic significance of the single market, both in terms of economies of scale and as a potential barrier to entry, and instigated a positive European lobbying campaign (Sandholtz and Zysman 1989). The most visible expression of this change of emphasis was the creation of the European Round Table of Industrialists (ERT) in 1984, which initially brought together seventeen of Europe's largest industrialists with the prime objective of lobbying for the creation of a single market (Cowles 1995).[3] Working closely with the established American Chamber of Commerce (Amcham) and the Union of Industrial and Employers' Conference of Europe (UNICE), it was able to agenda-set on 'big ideas', such as the Single European market (van Apeldoorn 2000), without getting into the nuts and bolts of policy making (Cowles 1996).

The success of ERT could be attributed in part to the desire of the Commission to have fast and effective information, but much of its 'insider' status can be explained in terms of the Commission's desire to have high profile and important industrialists involved in the European programme. Hence, access for those firms involved in the ERT was very open and considered legitimate. Finally, being a company/actor driven organization it quickly introduced large firms to the benefits of direct proactive lobbying of the EU institutions and the importance of a permanent EU presence. Hence, by the early 1990s, some 200 large firms had located political representation in Brussels to complement the functional roles of the associations and UNICE.

The SME lobby did not instinctively move to the European level as big businesses did. Rather, the presence of SMEs on the EU agenda needed a significant

[2] Aspinwall and Greenwood (1998) estimated that 66% of the 265 EU business federations they surveyed were associations of associations.
[3] Today the ERT has some forty-five CEO members and is still active in raising the business agenda.

injection of political effort from the EU institutions. This took the form of designating 1981 as the European Year of SMEs by the European Parliament and organizing many large-scale consultations, conferences, and discussions on SMEs. In order to achieve as wide a consensus as possible, these discussions were coordinated across many levels of governance and sectors by a Commission chaired committee. At the supranational level there was a formal attempt to coordinate SME representation via two Commission sponsored 'contact groups'. These two contact groups, called 'EUROGROUP' (Contact Group 1) and 'ESME' (Contact Group 2), allowed national SME representatives to work at the European level without being seen to collaborate with their opposite numbers at the national level. After two years ESME disappeared as its member organizations stepped out on their own, while EUROGROUP continued to receive support until 1994.[4] The representational politics of small firms therefore offers some similarities to the description of the competitive environment of the large firms. There was some consolidation in the strategies that corresponded with large business, in that there was an attempt to centralize interest representation and that the Commission led this initiative.

But without the resources to mobilize directly they had to continue to rely on the 'bottom up' presence of national associations and the creation of the directorate for small enterprises (DG XXIII) to monitor their interests. Recognizing that their voice was marginal in many of the larger EU trade federations and that demand for their input within most directorates was limited, SMEs sought to exert influence and voice via the social partners of the Economic and Social Committee (Grote 1995). However, the ESC was itself a marginal institutional player, especially in comparison to the European Commission and the ERT alliance, and much of the political agenda for SMEs was set by the European Parliament's Industrial Policy and Monetary Committee. As a peak organization, UNICE also attempted to represent the SME positives via the small firm working parties, but in reality the larger sector federations and big companies dominated its agenda (Cowles 1998; Grant 2000). Finally, and to complicate the SME representation process further, a conference held in Avignon in 1990 resulted in a split between small businesses and the accepted 'generic' description of 'enterprise'. Now, rather than there being one small firm constituency, that had enjoyed the politically fashionable identification with the term of enterprise, there were two—SMEs and craft businesses—which would become formalized in both policy debate and outcomes. This further complicated the coherence of the SME lobby and its ability to provide a unified voice to the Commission.

---

[4] This funding was released to help support information dispersal and conferences under a budgetary procedure known as 'B5-234'. Even as late as 1994, this source of funding was the only formalized mechanism for recognizing SME representation in the European Union.

In comparison to the access of larger business representative organizations, such as UNICE, and direct big business lobbying of the EU institutions, the quality of access for SMEs was poor. Yet, it should be noted that the access problems of small business in the European Union were not merely due to lack of political will to consult with them; SMEs have been more actively supported in accessing the European Union than almost any other group. Rather, it has been a failure of the small business sector to organize in a way that has been seen as legitimate by the Commission and the policy-making community in the European Union. This failing has essentially been in the lack of organizational resources available to small firm representatives to establish a European-level presence. Consequently, at this important and early stage of the evolution of interest group politics in the European Union, SME representation remained compromised by the political values of the national representative organizations, which limited the collaboration that the Commission sought and compromised the objectivity of their representations at the European level.

New Rules of Interest Intermediation in Brussels

In the late 1980s the European Union institutions were faced with an unprecedented boom in economic and social interests. This increase in European-level interest associations, national interest associations with Brussels offices, and direct representation by large firms can be explained in terms of the creation of the single market, the loss of the national veto at the Council of Ministers, and the concomitant transfer of regulatory competencies to the EU institutions (Mazey and Richardson 1993; Coen 1997). However, while this explosion of European level representation provided greater legitimacy for the European integration programme, it put a great strain on the existing open EU business–government relationship (Richardson 2000). These changes led to a significant change not only in the opportunities for influence open to businesses but also in the management by the Commission of the increased number of interests that arose at the European level.

The rapid expansion of direct European lobbying capabilities introduced a proliferation of lobbying practices into Brussels. Lobbying in the European Union was therefore experienced according to the type of actors, policy areas, and issue under consideration. Of the business nationalities to have established EU representation, US firms had the largest and most visible presence, followed by the British and German multinationals. However, not surprisingly, with the increasing regulatory and redistributive competencies of the EU institutions, it was not only big business that was attracted to Brussels. Significantly, the Commission estimated that more than 3000 public interests were active in the EU public policy process and that 1674 of these new pressure groups represented business interests in some capacity (Greenwood 1997). Faced with these new European 'countervailing pressure groups', business recognized that it needed to reorganize its collective voice as well as its ad hoc and individual direct lobbying strategies at the European level. Had there been fewer actors or fewer styles, it may have been possible for one method of representation to prevail naturally. But given the diversity of lobbying styles and number of actors it was the Commission that would now take the lead in the organization of lobbying, via the creation of policy forums.

In this competitive environment, the Commission established a wide variety of committees, working groups, conferences, and other forums. These policy committees and forums ranged from the formal committology committees, which serve as oversight bodies of the Commission, to the informal commission committees that seek to benchmark and coordinate national markets.[5] Recognizing the importance of these policy forums, firms sought to gain access via active participation in EU policy networks like the ERT[6] and the EU Committee of Amcham.[7] Thus gradually '*insider*' firms evolved and were invited to participate in EU agenda setting fora such as the Competitiveness Advisory Group and the Bangerman forums on "Trans-European networks", "Information Society", and "competition and competitiveness"'. On more narrow industrial questions in the Enterprise DG, the formation of the G-10 group illustrates how a topical policy debate on intellectual property rights and patient times can be coordinated around a steering group made up of ten insider players, three of which are large multinational pharmaceutical firms and two are sector federations.

In recognizing a need for some form of regulated interest representation, the European Commission was faced with the problem of how to balance its informational needs and representative requirements against a manageable number of interests. Despite the fact that large firms favoured direct lobbying of EU officials, it soon became apparent that the Commission had to limit the number of participants in EC Committees if decision making was to function effectively.[8] Hence access to the Commission policy committees was limited

---

[5] The Commission has launched eleven initial '*best procedure projects*'. The idea being to analyse and identify best practice in member states to improve industrial performance. http://www.europa.eu.int/comm/enterprise/enterprise_policy/best/best_report.htm

[6] Significantly, it has also built alliances with Amcham and in 1997 formalized its relationship with UNICE, which has always had a favoured position in the EU public policy debate. Moreover, the ERT being the sum of large industrialists (CEOs), as opposed to firms, has political weight with states.

[7] The EU Committee represents the views of 135 American businesses operating in Europe.

[8] That is to say, the legitimacy of the group increases with numbers of actors and interests, but the speed and effectiveness of policy making is reduced, and lowest common denominator policies made. This problem is magnified in the European Union with national markets in different stages of liberalization, variance in implementation, and different business cultures.

to those firms that had established some form of *issue identity* or *European profile* (Coen 1998). However, as the recent European Governance White Paper notes, there is increasing concern at the explosion of unaccountable sector forums and dominance of business interests. Thus, with an estimated 1400 forums in Brussels today, there are now calls for the rationalization of numbers and reorganization of membership to be more representative of societal interests (European Commission 2001).

For large firms, the Commission's closer management of interest interaction through the creation of a European-level institutional apparatus provided opportunities for business to gain wider social credibility and so access to the Commission. Moreover, as the direct voices of large businesses, their position as representatives were rarely challenged. But because of the diversity and volume of small businesses in European Union, other institutional channels were able to exercise influence in the SME policy process (Dannreuther 1999). From the early 1980s, national SME representatives were organized through European level groups (EUROGROUP, EUROPMI, UEAPME) or worked through sectoral lobbies that related specifically to SMEs (such as EUROCOOP or EUROCOMMERCE). But in addition to these more conventional lobbying routes, SME interests were also disproportionately influenced, even *defined*, by the policy-making institutions, such as the EP and the Council of Ministers, that were involved in the political process. MEPs, keen to represent small businesses in their constituencies, formed an SME Intergroup, while the Industry Council of Ministers held SME Councils with ministers from the various ministerial positions that held responsibility for SMEs in the member states. Unsurprisingly, each presented the interests of SMEs in very different ways. For example, one of the EP's earliest Resolutions on SME policy was extremely radical.[9] The EP argued that '...the largest single impediment to the creation and growth of new firms lies in low returns on capital invested in productive enterprise rather than any shortage of capital...', advocating tax cuts, reductions of public expenditure, and the controlling of deficits, supplemented by reforms of the financial services sector.[10] The member states response was less enthusiastic keeping a tight grip over SME policy's development at the EU level and limiting the ability of the Commission or EP to exercise significant policy leadership. Other than in the SME multi-annual programmes, the Council kept SME policy in the form of soft law, and focused on suggesting measures designed to augment national, rather than develop European, initiatives (Dannreuther 1999). We might suggest that in addition to the countervailing interests of big business and other actors, small business representatives also had to deal with the problem of 'countervailing access points' for small businesses through the EU's institutional architecture.

[9] 24 May 1984, OJ No C172, 2.7.1984, page 190.   [10] Ibid. page 191.

We therefore see that institutional change in the lobbying environment had an important impact on the representation of business interests, both large and small. Big business was forced to get its house in order if it was to respond effectively to the increased variety of countervailing interests lobbying against it. The evolution of coordinated mechanisms of representation for big business was very much a response to the lobbying environment. But for small business the institutional arena had already been determined by the events of the early 1980s. The number of institutionalized interests, in the form of the EP, Council, and ESC, that argued for small businesses compromised the influence and credibility of the small business interest groups. The divergence of interests in small business expressed by the institutions of the European Union made it hard for small business to set agendas, provide a coherent voice, and, more importantly, challenge the other formal channels of interest through which other, especially national, small business constituencies were making themselves heard.

Identity Politics, Isomorphism, and the Convergence of EU Lobbying Styles

The creation of new forums, which included many of the ERT committee members, suggested the development of an inner core of policy makers and the institutionalization of big business in the EU policy process. The European Industrial forums listed above were reinforced and guided by the success of groups like the Amcham. Firms and the Commission recognized early that firm-based groups like Amcham, which drew on its US lobbying experience, could provide early and detailed information. Hence, the traditional European federations began to restructure their membership and decision-making processes to allow for the direct participation of large firms (Coen 1997; Greenwood 1997). Rather than aggregating the interests of their members, these federations became gatekeepers to privileged access and influence. The outcome of this restructuring was an increase in direct representation by multinationals of federation positions at the Commission. Thus, while new industry forums continued to pursue collective EU agendas, they benefited from a smaller membership of like-minded firms, with the significant payoffs outlined below. Issues that could no longer be resolved at a collective level were effectively tendered out into new ad hoc political alliances that grew around and dissolved on single issues. In light of these developments, the SME voice and those channelled through the traditional sector federations were increasingly marginalized. In addition, the degree of autonomy that small business groups were able to exert on the way organized and presented information to enjoy political access was also contained.

But the benefits for big business of forum politics were more than simple access. It also raised their influence in the power politics of inter-DG rivalry, has given them quasi and policy-making and agenda-setting status in certain strategic areas. While pressure for new alliances and political groupings came from the increasingly disaggreggated political goals of large firms, it was also significant that competition between Director Generals encouraged the creation of forums and networks. The advantage of specialist forums, in addition to the focused policy making and ability of the Commission to demand specific access criteria, was that it provided the individual Commissioners with their own political/economic constituencies within Brussels and vis-à-vis member states (Broscheid and Coen 2002). The most visible recent forums have been Liikanen's Enterprise and Innovation group on how EU enterprise policies contribute to competitiveness, growth, and employment, and Prodi's eEurope initiative.

While the greatest lobbying benefits to business come via the formal Commission lead forums, it is possible to observe a secondary trend towards formalized business groups taking the policy lead in a form of public–private policy making. A visible example of such a grouping is the Trans-Atlantic Business Dialogue (TABD), set up in 1995 as a joint initiative of the Commission and US State Department to circumvent trade issue problems at the WTO. Gradually it has evolved into a quasi-policy-making organization which fast tracks business-led trade and product standards to the EU and US regulatory bodies (Coen and Grant 2001; Cowles 2001). The ERT has also reasserted itself in the integration process, in light of the Lisbon 2000 summit Declaration. Here the European Council leaders committed themselves to the ambitious goal of making the European Union the most competitive and dynamic knowledge-based economy in the world by 2010. This business friendly agenda explicitly recognized the importance of entrepreneurs as a means to growth and job creation and attempted to create an innovative environment through the reduction in compliance costs and coordinated and benchmarked regulation within the internal market. Significantly, in line with the above, the ERT and UNICE agreed to work with the Commission to develop relevant benchmarks applicable across the European Union to give a comparative picture of how business rates perform.

Such institutionalized big business representation has advantages in terms of the delivery of policy and the credibility of the actors involved in the policy process. Notably the Commission enjoys credibility while the large firms gain access—both sides of the arrangement gain in a relatively equal partnership. Central to this arrangement has been not only the Commission's ability to dictate terms for access but the ability of big business and their representatives to make the required changes in their behaviour to win the prize of privilege in access, influence, and agenda setting powers. Clearly business had to change its behaviour in response to the rules of game described in the previous section. But to enjoy benefits of insider status, big business had to win the trust of the Commission by becoming European in its identity too.

The Commission also launched forums to help SME representation. In a follow-up to the 1990 Avignon conference for crafts and small businesses, Heinrich von Moltke, the former Director General of DG XXIII, called for the consolidation of small business representation so that they could participate in the standards setting.[11] On a Commission request, NORMAPME was established by UEAPME in March 1996, incorporating UEAPME, EUROPMI, JEUNE, EMU, EEC, IFD, GCI, EFTC, and FEPD.[12] NORMAPME both consults with membership organizations and, through a technical committee, selects standards on which to campaign. Since the Portuguese Presidency in 2000, there have been a number of other initiatives to promote small business policy generally (notably the European Charter for Small Enterprises[13] adopted by the European Council at Santa Maria de Feira in June 2000). Commissioner Erkki Liikanen has established an Enterprise Policy Group (EPG).[14] This was divided into two advisory committees to advise on the development of Enterprise policy: the Directorate General policy group, which is composed of high level member state policy officials in charge of SME policy, and the Professional Chamber of individuals appointed for their experience and ability to provide advice. The formal policy-making status of both is of less importance than the ability of the Commission to access rapid advice and promote the coordination of policies amongst member state stakeholders (Dannreuther 2000). This was partly on account of Commission initiatives, such as the Social Dialogue,[15] and partly because of the demand for technical as opposed to solely political information from small businesses. The process of political identity formation has been particularly onerous for the small business sector because the divergence of national traditions in small business sectors persists. Thus, while the Commission has provided definitions for SMEs, these are made to ensure that competition policy on state aid is not abused. Competing notions of what small business interests are therefore remain, guaranteeing that competing notions of small business interests will too.

---

[11] NORMAPME's webpage is at http://www.ueapme.com/normapme/english/info_e.htm
[12] These acronyms stand for UEAPME/EUROPMI (European Association of Craft and SMEs), JEUNE (Young Entrepreneurs in the European Union), EMU (European Metal Union), EBC (European Builders Confederation), IFD (International Federation of Roofing Contractors), GCI (Génie Climatique International), EFTC (European Federation of Timber Construction), and FEPD (Federation of European Dental Laboratory Owners).
[13] The charter is available at http://europa.eu.int/comm/enterprise/enterprise_policy/charter/index.htm
[14] The EPG website is at http://www.europa.eu.int/comm/enterprise/enterprise_policy/epg/index.htm
[15] Small firms are also able to influence through a direct consultation mechanism called Interactive Policy Making which encourages direct consultation between SMEs and policy makers on selected issues. The website is at http://europa.eu.int/comm/enterprise/consultations/index.htm

While large businesses enjoy access to the Commission far beyond that of information provision, the Commission found that basic data on the SME sector from the representatives was inadequate. An SME Observatory was established to coordinate reports from national research institutes and compile an annual report on the fortunes of the SME sector. While SMEs are given places on the new EPG, they are not granted these positions on the basis of their association with the interest groups, in the way that large businesses gain privileged access through the federations as outlined above. Indeed, and as if to further distance the Commission from the SME representatives, the incoming Commissioner appointed an SME Envoy in December 2001 to supplement and facilitate dialogue with small business and the various representative organizations.

The pressures on small business representatives to merge have been irresistible for some time from both the Commission and the increasing costs of the Brussels lobby. There has been further rationalization of small business representation, with the two main organizations UEAPME and EUROPMI merging after protracted negotiations in 1998. At last small businesses spoke with almost one voice and were able to exercise more proactive influence in the Framework 6 research programme, but at the price of their autonomy (Schranz 2001). But still not all national groups have joined UEAPME as opposition to merger came from some members of the old EUROPMI, who established a rival organization called ESBA. Financial concerns apart, it was the heavy influence of the Statutory Chambers in UEAPME that was at the core of the disagreement, revealing once again the tension in the politics of small business representation.

While large businesses continue to gain access by growing the credibility of their identities as European actors, small business lobbyists are compromised by the dominance of national level identities in the representative process. While larger firms enjoy ever-increasing access and influence, smaller businesses, despite their centrality to the EU's future economic well-being, find themselves sidelined by uncooperative representatives at the EU level. While SMEs have made strides in unifying themselves into a main single group, they have some way to go before they present themselves as the coherent and thoroughly European constituency of their larger cousins. Only then will they enjoy the bounty of privilege that comes from insider status.

Conclusion

Accepting that there is more to Europeanization than our case study of business–government relations can capture, we assessed how firms play the political options in the multilevel regime and the potential advocacy coalitions of state actors and societal interests. We assert that the very nature of *'forum politics'* in Brussels encourages firms to create sophisticated multilevel webs that utilize national channels and that this process is reinforced when the national regulatory bodies are the focus of political activity—such as in periods of implementation or setting of state aid. However, accepting the continued existence of national business government traditions, a strong argument for a distinct EU lobbying style can be made.

The study demonstrates those societal actors experience different dynamics of Europeanization to state actors. First, we note that not all societal actors instinctively see their interests as best pursued at European level, as all member states do. Second, not all societal actors enjoy the financial resources to act nor the organizational capacity to express the clearly defined interests that are required to cut through the noise of opinions at the European level, as nation states do. Finally, not all societal actors are able to play by the rules of the game to enjoy insider status as some interests can—a status that all the member states are guaranteed in the Council of Ministers. So we might expect the process of Europeanization to be experienced in a very different way for societal actors in comparison to state officials.

More specifically, this chapter illustrates empirically that, in the crowded European political market, greatest influence and access are given to those firms that are prepared to establish positive European identity and policy credibility over time. From the firm's perspective, the most effective means of establishing reputation was to develop a broad political profile across a number of issues and to enter into complex political alliances with a vast array of interest groups. While improving the decision-making and informational flow at the institutional level, forum politics has created a European-level political market where large 'outsider' firms can no longer allow rivals to establish themselves. Accordingly, firms that had previously chosen to 'free ride' on others' contributions have been forced to reassess their political strategies and step up their European presence.

Small businesses have, in comparison, struggled at the European level. Despite their early presence in the ESC, the agendas for SMEs have been controlled by the institutions of the European Union since the early 1980s. SME, or enterprise, interest forums have been overshadowed by EU's policy-making institutions, each with its understanding of SMEs and their interests. For the small business representative organizations, achieving 'European credibility' has been costly. They have had to merge with competing small business organizations and collude with arch rivals, while their credibility has been compromised by the development of alternative sources of information on SMEs. While the status of small business representation at the European level has therefore been greatly improved, it has not been able to wrest itself from the national level, where traditional national styles of small business representation have been entrenched.

Finally this chapter has implications for the analytical distinction between Europeanization, as the study of policy making, and European integration, as the study of polity building. Drawing from the public policy literature we can understand the process of Europeanization through a number of methodologically derived propositions. While these may stall the pursuit of a singular definition of Europeanization, we would assert that this is a strength to the approach. Clearly Europeanization is not experienced in a similar way by state and society, nor even by the relatively homogenous set of interests of the business community. Furthermore, the divergent experience of the Europeanization of big and small business interests indicates that the Europeanization of political functions, such as representation, have implications for the sort of polity that the European Union will become. While it may be that the European Union is uniquely open and accessible for those with clearly defined interests, those parts of European society that lack these organizational resources, or remain too embedded in national tradition, to match the stringent requirements for interest articulation, may find themselves excluded from the emerging European polity.

REFERENCES

Armstrong, K. and Bulmer, S. (1998). *The Governance of the Single European Market* (Manchester: Manchester University Press).

Aspinwall, M. and Greenwood, J. (1998). 'Conceptualising Collective Action in the European Union. An Introduction', in J. Greenwood and M. Aspinwall (eds), *Collective Action in the European Union* (London: Routledge).

Borzel, T. and Risse, T. (2000). 'When Europe Hits Home. Europeanisation and Domestic Change', APSA. Washington DC 2000.

Broscheid. A and Coen, D. (2002). 'Business Interest Representation and European Commission Fora: A Game Theoretic Investigation', *Max Plank Institute for Study of Society, Discussion Series*, Cologne.

Bulmer, S. and Burch, M. (2001). 'The "Europeanisation" of central government: the UK and Germany in Historical Institutionalist Perspective', in G. Schneider and M. Aspinwall (eds), *The Rules of Integration: Institutional Approaches to the Study of Europe* (Manchester: Manchester University Press).

Coen, D. (1997). 'The Evolution of The Large Firm as a Political Actor in the European Union', *Journal of European Public Policy* 4(1): 91–108.

——(1998). 'The European Business Interest and the Nation State: Large-firm Lobbying in the European Union and Member State', *Journal of Public Policy* 18(1): 75–100.

——(2002). 'Business Interests and European Integration', in R. Blume, D. Chabanet, and V. Wright (eds), *L'action Collective en Europe* (Paris: Presses de Sciences Po).

—— and Doyle, C. (2001). 'Designing Economic Regulatory Institutions for European Network Industries', *Current Politics and Economics of Europe* 9(4): 83–106.

—— and Grant, W. (2001). 'Corporate Political Strategy and Global Public Policy: A Case Study of the Transatlantic Business Dialogue', in *European Business Journal* 13(1): 37–44.

—— and Héritier, A. (2000). 'Business Perspectives on German and British Regulation: Telecommunications, Energy and Rail', in *Business Strategy Review* 11(4):29–37.

——, ——, and Böllhoff, D. (2002). *Business Perspectives to Utility Regulation: An Anglo-German Comparison.* Anglo-German Foundation Report July 2002.

—— and Thatcher, M. (2000). 'Introduction: Reform of Utility Regulation in the EU', in D. Coen and M. Thatcher (eds), *Utilities Reform in Europe* (New York: Nova Press).

Cowles, G. M. (1995). 'Setting the Agenda for a New Europe: The ERT and EC 1992', *Journal of Common Market Studies* 13: 501–26.

—— (1996). 'The EU Committee of AMCHAM: The Powerful Voice of American Firms in Brussels', *Journal of European Public Policy* 3(1): 501–26.

—— (2001). 'The TADB and Domestic Business-government Relations', in Cowles *et al.* (eds), *Transforming Europe: Europeanisation and Domestic Change* (London: Cornell University Press).

——, Caporaso, J. and Risse, T. (2001). *Transforming Europe: Europeanisation and Domestic Change* (London: Cornell University Press).

Dannreuther, C. (1999). 'Discrete Dialogues and the Legitimation of SME Policy in the EU', *Journal of European Public Policy* 6(4): 102–20.

—— (2000). 'The Political Limits to Economic Governance—a Study of Hierarchy', *Current Politics and Economics of Europe* 10(2): 167–87.

Eberlein, B. and Grande, E. (2000). 'Regulatory and Infrastructure Management: German Regulatory Regimes and the EU Framework German Policy Studies', http://www.spaef.com/GPS-PUB/index.html

European Commission (2001). *European Governance A White Paper* COM (2001) 428 Final.

Falkner, G. (2000). 'Policy Networks in a Multi-Level System: Convergence Towards Moderate Diversity?' in S. Hix and K. Goetz (eds), *Europeanised Politics? European Integration and National Political Systems* (London: Frank Cass).

Grande, E. (1996). 'The State and Interest Groups in a Framework of Multilevel Decision-making: The Case of the European Union', *Journal of European Public Policy* 3(3): 318–38.

Grant, W. (2000). 'Pressure Groups and British Politics', *Contemporary Political Studies* (London: Macmillan).

Greenwood, J. (1997). *Representing Interests in the European Union* (London: Macmillan).

Grote, J. (1995). 'Relevance of Size and Territory for the Organisation of Business Interests in Europe', in J. Greenwood (ed.), *European Casebook on Business Alliances* (London: Prentice Hall).

Haas, P. (1992). 'Introduction: Epistemic Communities and International Policy Co-ordination', *International Organization* 46(1): 367–90.

Héritier, A. (2001). *Policy-making and Diversity in Europe* (Cambridge: Cambridge University Press).

——, Kerwer, D., Knill, C., Lehmkuhl, D., Teutsch, M., and Douillet, A. (2001). *Differential Europe—EU Impact on National Policy Making* (Boulder: Rowman and Littlefield Publishers).

Hix, S. (1999). *The Political System of the European Union* (London: Macmillan).

—— and Goetz, K. (2000). 'Introduction: European Integration and National Political Systems', in S. Hix and K. Goetz (eds), *Europeanised Politics? European Integration and National Political Systems* (London: Frank Cass).

Hoffman, S. (1966). 'Obstinate or Obsolete? The Fate of the Nation State and the Case of Western Europe', *Daedalus* 95: 862–915.

Jachtenfuchs, M. (2001). 'The Governance Approach to European Integration', *Journal Of Common Market Studies* 39(2): 245–64.

Kohler-Koch, B. (1996). 'Catching up with Change. The Transformation of Governance in the European Union', *Journal of European Public Policy* 3(3): 359–80.

—— (1999). 'The Evolution and Transformation of European Governance', in B. Kohler-Koch and R Eising (eds), *The Transformation of Governance in the European Union* (London: Routlege).

Ladrech, R. (1994). 'Europeanisation of Domestic Politics and Institutions: The Case of France', *Journal of Common Market Studies* 32:69–88.

Majone, G. (1997). *Regulating Europe* (London: Routledge).

Marks, G., Hooghe, L., and Blank, K. (1996). 'European Integration from the 1980s: State Centric Versus Multi-level Governance', *Journal of Common Market Studies* 34:341–78.

Mazey, S. and Richardson, J. (1993). *Lobbying in the European Community* (Oxford: Oxford University Press).

—— and —— (1996). 'The Logic of Organisation: Interest Groups in Richardson', in J. Richardson (ed.), *European Union Power and Policy-Making* (London: Routledge).

—— —— (2001). 'Interest Groups and EU Policy Making: Organizational Logic and Venue Shopping', in J. Richardson (ed.), *European Union: Power and Policy Making* (London: Routledge).

Moravsik, A. (1993). 'Preferences and Power in the European Community: A Liberal Intergovernmentalist Approach', *Journal of Common Market Studies* 31(4):473–524.

Ohmae, K. (1995). *The End of the Nation State: The Rise of Regional Economies* (New York: Free Press).

Pierson, P. (1996). 'The Path to European Integration: A Historical Institutionalist Analysis', *Comparative Political Studies* 29: 123–63.

Pijenburg, R. (1998). 'EU-lobbying by Ad-hoc Coalitions: An Exploratory Case Study', *Journal of European Public Policy* 5(2).

Pollack, M. (1998). 'Defused Interests in Europe', *Journal of European Public Policy* 4(4):572–90.

—— and Shaffer, G. (2001). *Transatlantic Governance in the Global Economy* (Maryland: Rowman and Shaffer Publishers).

Powell, W. and DiMaggio, P. (1991). *The New Institutionalism in Organisational Analysis* (Chicago: University of Chicago Press).

Radaelli, C. (2002). 'The Europeanisation of Public Policy', in C. Radaelli and K. Featherstone (eds), *The Politics of Europeanisation* (Oxford: Oxford University Press).

Richardson, J. (1996). 'Policy-Making in the EU: Interests, Ideas and Garbage Cans of Primeval Soup', in *European Union Power and Policy-Making* (London: Routledge).

——(2000). 'Government, Interest Groups and Policy Change', *Political Studies* 48(5):106–25.

Sabatier, P. (1998). 'The Advocacy Coalition Framework: Revisions and Relevance for Europe', *Journal of European Public Policy* 5(1): 98–130

Sandholtz, W. and Zysman, J. (1989). 'Recasting the European Bargain', *World Politics* 42: 1–30.

Schmidt, V. (1997). 'European Integration and Democracy: The Differences Among Member States'. *Journal of European Public Policy* 4(1): 128–45.

——(2001). 'Europeanization and the Mechanics of Economic Policy Adjustment', *American Political Science Association* National Meetings (San Francisco, 30 August–2 September 2001).

Schneider, G. and Aspinwall, M. (2001). *The Rules of Integration: Institutional Approaches to the Study of Europe* (Manchester: Manchester University Press).

Schranz, J. (2001). 'Small and Medium Sized Enterprise Representation in Brussels: UEAPME's Influence in the Formulation of the EU's Research and Technology policy: Scratching the Surface of a Deeper Lobbying Agenda', College of Europe, Bruges (2001)—supervisor: Rudolf Hrbek.

Streeck, W., Sharpf, F., and Marks, G. (1997). *Governance in the European Union* (London: Sage Press).

—— and Schmitter, P. (1991). 'From National to Transnational Pluralism', *Politics and Society* 19(2): 133–64.

Thatcher, M. (2000). *The Politics of Telecommunications: National Institutions, Convergence, and Change* (Oxford: Oxford University Press).

Young, A. and Wallace, H. (2000). *Regulatory Politics in the Enlarging European Union: Weighing Civic and Producer Interests* (Manchester: Manchester University Press).

Van Apeldoorn, B. (2000). 'Transnational Class Agency and European Governance: The Case of the European Round Table of Industrialists', *New Political Economy* 5(2): 157–81.

V

Understanding 'Europe' as a Policy Model

12

The Idea of the European Social Model: Limits and Paradoxes of Europeanization

DANIEL WINCOTT

Introduction

While both 'positive' and 'negative' integration can produce 'Europeanization', the former, which generally implies the specification of a 'European model', is more likely to be politically loaded with explicit normative content (of a 'European' sort). The latter relies upon social and economic agents taking advantage of the opportunities provided by the removal of barriers to generate 'Europeanization' from below. The 'European Social Model' (ESM) is arguably the clearest example of a normatively loaded (putative) 'European model'. Partly as a result, the lessons that the history of the ESM can teach us are not those of Europeanization producing a gradual and steady convergence (whether normative, cognitive, or policy) of national practices and policies based on a positive model. Instead, it suggests that the processes of European integration and of Europeanization are not wholly distinct and neatly separated stages or phases, nor is Europeanization itself necessarily clear and coherent.

The history of the ESM is one of fragmentation and competition in the European Union, both between national visions of a legitimate Europe and within and among EU level institutions, often forcefully articulated and saturated with normative meaning. It emphasizes the contested politics of competing 'European' projects, not a rational and technocratic policy-making process. This approach contrasts with most existing theoretical accounts, which tend to assume, usually implicitly, that the European Union is—or EU policies are—internally coherent and consistent. For example, influential applications of historical institutionalism to the European Union emphasize the tendency of social and political complexity to 'lock-in' whatever pattern is initially developed

This chapter forms part of the research for an ESRC funded project 'Globalisation and the European Social Model' (Grant: 213252043) which forms part of the 'One Europe or Several?' Programme. I would like to thank the editors Kevin Featherstone and Claudio Radaelli for their helpful comments on an earlier version of my argument.

(see Pierson 1998). While this position need not assume that the patterns are wholly coherent, it certainly suggests that they do not display strong internal tensions, never mind contradictions. An alternative vision of complexity would envision it as encompassing internal tensions and/or contradictions, for example, viewing them as the precipitates or residues of completing political projects, none of which is ever wholly realized (see, e.g. Wincott 1996). Skilled political actors, policy entrepreneurs, and political movements may be able to recombine elements from this complex history into a novel discourse or project and hence alter the dominant characteristics of the governing ethos or regime.

If the meaning of the ESM is unclear, so too is the level at which it is alleged to operate or 'exist' (European Union and/or national). Taken at face value as an empirical model, the ESM's most robust empirical reference was/is arguably to national, not European Union, social policies, practices, or values. To qualify as a 'European model' these policies, practices or values would have to be common, originating in and/or perhaps exclusive to European states. Placed within the context of the political maelstrom of Europe in the 1980s, however, the ESM is better seen as an elite attempt to articulate a normative vision for Europe for purposes of political mobilization and the construction and coordination (see Schmidt 1999) of a political project. Viewed in this perspective the 'outcomes' of this projected 'model' for Europe are paradoxical. It is always difficult and potentially dangerous to try to sum up the political resonance of an idea that is the subject a large and complex discussion. Nevertheless, taken at face value, the ESM generally seems to have suggested a policy regime, or broad configuration that exists (or existed) and was shared by the member states, the European Union level at least aspired to bolster this model. Yet, as we shall see, the initial period during which the idea of the ESM had some currency was when EU social policy took a 'regulatory form' that some have described as 'American' in style. The implications of the more recent discussion of the ESM (the 'modernization' which is now the focus of attention) are as yet much more difficult to discern. *One possibility* is that it will serve to reinforce the influence of US style approaches (by way of the British government) to social and employment policy (workfare and labour market flexibility).

Taken as a whole, the implication of my argument here is that there is considerable analytical value in distinguishing between European integration and 'Europeanization'. The latter notion, however, needs to be subjected to rigorous conceptual analysis if it is to be useful to scholars. In the complex and contested politics of the European Union, it is all to easy to elide analytical concepts and ideas deployed in political projects. It is only if we can distinguish these elements *for analytical purposes* that we can make sense of apparent paradoxes of Europeanization, for example, that Europeanization (in the analytical sense) has resulted in the growth of (what some scholars identify as) 'American style' regulation in the social field.

This chapter is developed in a further five sections. After this introduction, the next section considers the concept of Europeanization, emphasizing *both* its analytical value *and* the difficulty of applying it to the European Union, given the difficulty of identifying the character of the Union clearly. If this point is worth making in relation to the European Union in general, it is even more valuable when the idea of the ESM is considered. Before we can consider its relationship to the European Union and Europeanization, the character of the ESM must be identified. The Section 'Is There a Common Social Model in Europe' analyses whether a common ESM can be identified across the states of the European Union. Of course, if the ESM is predominantly a common national model, then it would hardly be a product of Europeanization. I find that while there are some shared values, these states certainly do not share a common model of policy. Even at the level of values, it is hard to discern a model that is restricted to European states. Instead, the ESM discourse emerged primarily from the French political context. It embodied French cognitive and normative frames (being constructed in opposition to Anglo-Saxon 'hyper' liberalism—a construction that gained in plausibility through being reflected back in the similar structure Thatcherite world view). It was also a good deal more complex and nuanced that is usually recognized. In section 'Is the European Social Model a Product of Europeanization?', I turn to the question of whether the ESM was a product of Europeanization. Ironically, however, when we turn to the European level, we find that the consequence of European social politics in the 1980s was the emergence of a regulatory state—a pattern of economic and social regulation—fairly aptly characterized as being 'American' in style. While rich and persuasive analysis exists of the dominant empirical tendencies of the European Union 'Regulatory State' (*inter alia* Majone 1996), its significance remains widely misunderstood. In a final twist, the section 'The European Social Model II' analyses the reappearance of the ESM on the European Union policy agenda as a part of the legitimizing discourse surrounding the 'Open Method of Co-ordination' (OMC), introduced at the Lisbon meeting of the European Council in 2000. The significance of the OMC has yet to be settled—it could produce a further 'Americanization' in Europe (albeit in a fundamentally different *form*), but might equally provide part of the basis for a new European welfare settlement (Wincott 2001*a,b,d*). A brief conclusion returns to issues of and debates about Europeanization.

'Europeanization': Conceptual Issues

That the analysis of the ESM requires us to consider aspects of European integration alongside 'Europeanization' does not imply that the two are identical. The debate about 'Europeanization' requires greater discipline. As Claudio

Radaelli has argued, unless there is greater clarity about the concept, the plethora of studies of Europeanization will create a mountain of confusion (Radaelli this volume). Specifying the scope and limits of the concept, distinguishing it from other, perhaps related, notions and the identification of different forms or domains of Europeanization are all indispensable elements of the conceptual analysis and necessary prerequisites to useful empirical work. In all this, Radaelli's recommendations are powerful and persuasive. It is appropriate to limit the concept of Europeanization to the impact of the European Union within states, particularly the member states (with prospective members and near neighbours also likely candidates for analysis). The question of the direction and degree of impact should be left to empirical research (rather than assuming convergence as its consequence). The impact of Europeanization on domestic political structures must be distinguished from its cognitive and normative consequences and influence on national policies.

Nonetheless, the most potentially significant contribution of a clearly specified concept of Europeanization (and especially any empirical work generated within the resulting analytical framework) might initially appear odd. It is the opportunity to nest Europeanization within, and use it to challenge widely held assumptions of, broader debates and discussions on such topics as globalization, European integration and convergence, and divergence in contemporary capitalism. Thus, it is helpful to distinguish between ontological (European integration) and postontological (Europeanization) aspects of European Union related research (Radaelli this volume), even although ultimately many analysts, political leaders, and citizens will wish to cash out claims about what the European Union is in terms of its impact. So long as the distinction is recognized as part of an analytical strategy, distinguishing these two aspects and the development of careful and conceptually clear empirical research in each area may help our understanding of the interaction between them. In the final analysis research on Europeanization should filter back into our understanding of what the European Union is (on an abstract level) and might even influence the process of European integration itself. For example, an understanding of the European Union as a robust supranational order based on the rule of law is difficult to sustain if Europeanization were found to have had little or no impact in core European policy domains. Indeed, the nature and origins of the conceptual confusion that currently reigns in Europeanization research may be instructive. Rather than being a simple consequence of sloppy academic analysis, it may have roots in the phenomenon under investigation—in the character of the Union itself.

The EU policies and models often draw, sometimes heavily, on the practices of certain member states. More generally, as Majone recognizes, evidence of the turn towards regulation in western Europe during the 1980s can be found at the national as well as the supranational level. Even so, he argues that the supranational level rapidly became the source of creativity and dynamism in the development of regulation (Majone 1996). Some regulatory policies may result in the replacement of (whatever) national regulatory structures (existed) by European regulation. In the social sphere, however, regulatory policies typically involve a fusion of European and national elements, particularly through the courts and through the administrative enforcement mechanisms. As with other aspects of 'Europeanization', the accent in social regulation may still be on diversity alongside elements of and pressures for convergence.[1] In other words, while it is analytically crucial to make a conceptual distinction between European integration and Europeanization, the substantive focus of analysis is unlikely to be so clear. Turning to the more recent emergence of 'European' 'policy' developed through the OMC, the distinction between the creation of the policy and its impact becomes even more difficult to establish. If the OMC can produce Europeanization effects, then it would do so through cognitive and normative mechanisms, as it does not give policymakers access to the binding (quasi-)coercive mechanisms of the law.

Is There a Common Social Model in Europe?

Even within Europe, the burden of comparative analysis of welfare over the past twenty years emphasizes the diversity of capitalist democracies. Famously, Esping-Andersen has suggested that there are three ideal types of (capitalist) 'welfare state regime' (1990). The states that approximate most closely to two of these types ('socialist' Sweden and 'conservative' Germany) are members of the European Union. Moreover, since Esping-Andersen, a number of different analysts have suggested that there are four distinct welfare state regimes, rather than three, and each one nominates a different state, or group of states as regime number four. While the best known candidate for the fourth regime—the 'radical' regime proposed by Castles and Mitchell (1993)—seems to be modelled on Australian experience, some European states—the United Kingdom and perhaps Ireland—are included within it. The other two candidates for 'regime number four' are both European—in turn the Dutch and Southern European models (Kloosterman 1994; Ferrera 1996). The case that European states show diversity rather than similarity does not end here. Even within 'socialist' Scandinavia, scholars have come to emphasize differences among these states. For example, analysts of gendered aspects of these regimes often emphasize difference.[2]

---

[1] See Kilpatrick (1998) for a discussion which touches on the pattern of diversity created by the dialogues between national courts on the ECJ in the area of sex equality.

[2] With Norway differentiated from more progressive Sweden and Denmark, see, for example, Leira (1992).

Jacques Delors, President of the European Commission 1985–95, himself makes a sharp distinction between France and what he calls 'the social democracies', while identifying both Scandinavia and 'the German countries' as social democratie. (Of course, the implications of much other research is that the social policy differences between the Scandinavian and Germanic countries are more significant than their similarities—indeed that the Germanic countries may share more with France than they do with Scandinavia.) He argues that 'the historical characteristics which have marked the social democracies count for a great deal. The Scandinavian countries did not experience to the same extent the destabilization of the social authorities that was caused elsewhere by the conditions in which democracy was established. The German countries have repressed like a nightmare the memory of that destabilization (the Weimar Republic, Austria between the world wars, Nazism), and it is the legitimacy that has been maintained or recovered by major social forces (trade unions, vast and non-specialized associations, churches) that are independent of the states, but share the public arena with it, which has made possible in German-speaking Europe a certain form of social dialogue'. He suggests that the 'gap is so wide between French realities and...the historical facts which underlie the social democracies, that invoking *that* model amounts to little more than gloomy rhetoric...' (Delors 1992: 53).

In debates on the welfare state, the features of models or ideal types and those of national policy configurations are often confounded (for a related discussion see Wincott 2001c). In other words, many describe Germany as *being* a Conservative Welfare State, rather than as the example of a real world regime that is closest to the ideal type of the Conservative Welfare State Regime. 'Actually existing' state welfare (policy) configurations combine elements of more than one conceptual 'type'. The diversity of real world welfare configurations dilutes empirical relevance of the sharp conceptual distinctions between welfare regime types. At first glance this dilution might make it appear easier to place the accent on shared features of European states. Closer investigation reveals that the range of concrete experience becomes greater when the variety of combinations of features usually conceptualized within particular regime families is taken into account. On the other hand, when considered *more* abstractly there is a sense in which the general notion of the welfare state has analytical relevance for all European countries. Unfortunately, this does little to rescue the notion of a distinctly *European* model, as its features would have to be defined so broadly or loosely as to *extend* the concept such that it would also include many non-European states. It is hard to find a level of abstraction at which a conception of 'the social' (understood as a policy regime or configuration) can be developed that includes the relevant states of 'Europe', while excluding the Antipodes and North America.

Conceptual work needs to be done at the level of the general and abstract notion of the welfare state. In particular, discussion of citizenship being partly composed of social rights often involves the mixing of empirical and normative elements in an unhelpful combination. Retaining a unified conception of citizenship, the idea of social rights can be used in empirical comparisons of the social aspect of state–citizen relations. Equally, social rights of citizenship— and particularly the notion of 'social citizenship'—can be used as a normative ideal against which the features of national regimes might be compared. Still more work is required at the more concrete level. Here the common language of analysis can obscure the diversity of historical experience. It is dangerous to assume, as many appear to, that the generic and analytical language of the 'welfare state' reproduces the language of 'welfare' policy and 'welfarist' struggles across Europe. Thus, for example, while Sweden is widely regarded as an apotheosis of the social citizenship welfare state, there is no Swedish word for 'citizen'. Equally, the perfectly acceptable translation of the French phrase 'l'etat providence' as the welfare state may distract attention from the resonance of the French phrase in the particular history of French social policy development. Similar arguments can be made in other cases; for illustrative purposes I will discuss one case in greater detail.

The assumption that the notion of the social state in Germany corresponds to the idea of the 'welfare state' either as deployed in other countries or as an analytical construct requires much more careful consideration than it is given typically. So too does the idea that the 'social state' signifies the same thing throughout the post-war period. It is worth raising the question of whether the Federal Republic of Germany should be considered to *be* a welfare state at all. Germany does not meet the tough criteria that the most influential analysts offer as definitions of welfare state status—neither the primary purpose nor main activity of the state is welfare (Esping-Andersen 1990: 18–23; cf. Therborn 1989). The preference of some analysts for the expressions *Sozialpolitik* and *Sozialstaat* over *Wohlfahrtsstaat* may be an indication of this difference. The *Sozialstaat* concept is entrenched in the Basic Law (Articles 20 paragraph 1 and 28 paragraph 1) and, for some, should be distinguished from the latter which, they argue, has a generally negative ring and patronizing implications in German (Zapf 1986: 132).[3] Esping-Andersen's caution (in one incarnation—compare 1990: 20 with 1994: 716) about the self-made claims of states to be welfare states seems to me to be appropriate in the German case, and many others. Social policy is not an egalitarian incubus or portent within German capitalism. The ideology and practices of equality and vertical redistribution are weakly articulated within it. Instead, it reflects and

[3] Ginsburg (1992: 68) makes a similar point more equivocally; but compare with Schmidt (1989: 66–69).

may (re)produce status divisions associated with employment (blue collar, white collar, and higher Civil Service—see Esping-Andersen and Korpi 1984; Schmidt 1989: 66–7; Esping-Andersen 1990). To the extent that social policy, and by extension the welfare state, is associated with the ideal of equality, or of a common 'social citizenship', it may not be appropriate in the German case.[4]

In addition, there are good reasons for believing that meaning or significance of the *Sozialstaat* has both shifted in the course of the post-war period and has been politically contested throughout the period. In the early history of the BRD, for example, tensions within Christian Democracy might be traced in significantly different understandings of the significance of the 'social' aspect of the social state and social market. These tensions were to some extent embodied in the figures of Adenauer and Erhard, reflecting the Chancellor's paternalism and the Finance Minister's interest in ordo-liberalism. According to the latter, the emphasis on the 'social' was, to an important extent, an assertion that a properly ordered market, within which competitive pressures were nurtured, would produce socially acceptable—perhaps even optimal—outcomes. 'Monopoly control is the main "social" component of this economic order' (Leaman 1988: 52). Even those keen to emphasize the distance of Erhard from ordo-liberalism ('he was not a dogmatic economics professor nor a purist neoliberal'—Berghahn 1986: 158) agree with the following key point. He was convinced that 'the best social policy was one which relied on the dynamism of a production- and consumption-oriented capitalism which would provide a decent living standard "for all" and, through further growth, even increase it' (Berghahn 1986: 159). Adenauer's vision of social insurance as a largely untainted, authentically German tradition valued social policy more highly as a balancing element in both the Constitution and day to day politics. Subsequently, and particularly after *Bad Godesberg* and the 'Grand Coalition' of the 1960s, the latter interpretation became more influential. Some analysts interpret Erhard's own position as moving in this sort of direction by the mid-1960s, especially after his formulation of the *'Formierte Gesellschaft'* notion (although the emphasis here was on *Gesellschaftspolitik* rather than *Sozialpolitik*). By the end of the 1960s, however, it might not be inaccurate to regard the SPD as following a strategy of 'social democratizing' the *Sozialstaat*, in both policy and discursive terms. This strategy was altered significantly as the Social-Liberal governments of the 1970s came to concentrate on matters of individual liberty particularly in matters of family policy, on which they could make common (un- or even anti-clerical) cause. Ultimately, the space for 'social democratization' of *Sozialpolitik* (and *Arbeitsmarktpolitik*)

---

[4] None of which is to argue that the social state notion is either devoid of normative content or insignificant for the character of the German state.

in the 1970s was tightly circumscribed by the *Bundesbank's* confrontation with the SPD in government.

If comparative analysis of European policy regimes or configurations show relatively little evidence of a clear common structure, then how do these regimes appear when viewed as a group in comparison with states elsewhere? Are there 'European' features that stand out by contrast with United States (regulatory) capitalism and/or Asian Identity/Culture/models? Moving to the higher level of abstraction required for a sweeping comparative regionalism of this sort restricts the scope for detailed investigation of the particular features of individual, social, and public policy configurations. Moreover, we have already seen enough to recognize that patterns of commonality and difference cut across regional boundaries, at least to some extent. However, the more sweeping comparisons implied by contrasting global regions with one another generally tend to move the focus of comparison from the more concrete policy domain, to the normative and/or abstract field of 'values'. Closer inspection of the statements of key political actors in the debates about Europe's social dimension since 1980 reveal that the dimension of values is accented. Indeed, Delors himself rarely if ever spoke of the 'European Social Model', instead deploying the notion of the 'European Model of Society', which is at once much more broad *and* makes less specific claims about the detailed organization of social policy. Notwithstanding his equally strong dismissal of a detailed policy commonality between France and 'the Social Democracies', Delors does argue that French values are not distant from the values underpinning social democracy (1992: 53). Furthermore, he claims that

'there is a European model of society to which the great majority of Europeans are committed. Everyone agrees that we must adapt it, in order to respond better to the dual challenge of economic competition and solidarity. Nevertheless, most people want to retain its spirit and its political foundations'. (Delors 1992: 157–8)

Closer examination does not provide a direct and clear specification of the nature of the European model of society, but it does provide some revealing indirect hints about its character. While emphasizing the consensual nature of the discussion of the European model, Delors also hints at the limits to that consensus. 'Many French people would be amazed if they knew that in the European councils which bring together the heads of state and government of our twelve nations,[5] a broad consensus emerges, on the problems of society or on the social dimension of Europe's construction, between two of the major political currents in our Europe: the Socialists and the Christian Democrats' (1992: 157). This statement (first published in French in 1988) should be seen (at least in part) as a specific political intervention in a particular conjuncture.

[5] There were twelve members at the time Delors wrote.

Published after the period when the main outline of the internal market was already complete, the text should be seen as an attempt to think through the political possibilities of the period after that episode of market making. It was also probably intended to recruit members of the French—and perhaps also wider European political elite—for a 'post market' project of some sort. Equally, however, it was published as the quality of the relationship between the British government and both Delors and the governments of many other member states declined rapidly. The broad consensus to which Delors referred excluded the government of the United Kingdom at that time, which was neither socialist nor Christian democratic. The idea of a European model of society, then, may be sustainable at the level of values, if it excludes Thatcher's Britain. Picking up on long-standing themes in French political discourse, then, the European model of society seems to be set up in opposition to Anglo-Saxon liberalism. Thus the United States, and its 'European' representatives in the United Kingdom, appear to be the defining 'other' for the European model of society. The plausibility of this argument was powerfully enhanced by the readiness of the Thatcherites themselves to embrace it.[6] At more or less the same time as Delors and his colleagues were publishing their book in France, Mrs Thatcher was repudiating European integration as an attempt to roll forward the 'frontiers of the state' from Brussels in her famous speech at The College of Europe in Bruges.

While the opposition between the European model of society and Anglo-Saxon liberalism might seem most stark during Mrs Thatcher's period of office, it is not merely a feature of a particular(ly right wing) British administration, at least according to some commentators. From such a perspective, evidence that Britain is deeply marked by Anglo-Saxon liberalism can be found in the putative persistence of neoliberalism under a 'Labour' administration. Thus Eric Hobsbawm has argued that the 'Blair idea ... is of a centre-left which is between the Democratic Party in the United States and New Labour. He believes that is the model for the centre-left. But the alternative is New Labour or the traditional European centre-left, marxist, social democratic, and social christian. And there is a great difference between the two. The American tradition is fundamentally not that of the European social state. It may be that as between Republicans and Democrats, the Democrats are, in terms of class composition and topographical position, the Left. But they are not the same as the European tradition. If you look at the reaction, for instance, from Blair and others to the election of the Left in France, and Clinton in the United States, it is very different. Whatever it is, New Labour is not a centre-left government in any traditional sense in which we in Europe

---

[6] For a critical discussion of the effects of the polarizing dichotomy between neoliberalism and regulated capitalism, see Wincott (2000).

perceive it and that includes not only socialist but demo christians, the whole of the social state which is the central tradition of the nineteenth and twentieth centuries on the continent' (Hobsbawn 1998: 11). ✓✗

The ESM (as used by representatives of the European Commission) and the European model of society (espoused by Delors) were based on an idealization of some characteristics of certain national policy regimes—or perhaps even of broader forms of 'civilization'. It was used to motivate a political project at the EU level and to recruit supporters from among Europe's political, policy, and intellectual elites for the purpose of coordinating and communicating this project.

Is the European Social Model a Product of 'Europeanization'?

If Jacques Delors celebrated a broad consensus in support of a European model of society and Mrs Thatcher perceived a 'socialistic threat' from the European Union, we might expect to see evidence of a major attempt to impose a distinctively European (and perhaps socialist) 'model' during the 1980s and early 1990s. There is precious little such evidence. Indeed, it is well known that the record of EU economic policies in the 1980s and early 1990s was of a massive and continuing liberalization. Moreover, an influential strand of analysis suggest that European integration represents a form of 'subversive liberalism', in which transnational liberalization undercuts national social models (Rhodes 1996). There has been considerable debate about the impact of the relationship between the states and the European Union on the policy options available at both levels. I do not wish to be drawn into a discussion of these issues here. Instead, my attention is more narrowly focused on the EU's social policy itself.

What may be less widely recognized, however, is that the development of the EU's social 'dimension' itself may be at odds with the objective of constructing a social model with a distinctively 'European' quality (at least with the resonance usually attributed to the ESM notion). The characterization of the Union as a Regulatory Order, or even a Regulatory State, which is particularly associated with the work of Giandomenico Majone (see, *inter alia*, Majone 1996, 1998, 2000) is undoubtedly influential. Majone has explicitly applied the regulatory perspective to the making of EU social policies. Majone and others (notably Laura Cram 1993) have analysed the ability of the European Union—and specifically the European Commission—to carve out a substantial set of competences in the 'social' domain (and, or including, gender, environment, and consumer areas) by concentrating on regulatory rather than redistributive—tax and spend—policies. Cram and Majone are influential scholars, but the implications of the regulatory analysis for the idea of the 'European Social Model' seem not to be drawn fully drawn out by some policy-makers and analysts. The lack of a vigorous debate between Majone's perspective and advocates of the ESM is striking, especially in the period since Majone has explicitly developed the normative aspect of his work (see e.g. 1998). Indeed, for those wedded to the ESM, Majone's early characterization of the emergence of the European regulatory order as introducing 'American-style' regulation might appear a provocation. So, far from seeing European integration as producing or supporting an 'ESM', Majone discerns the rise of an American style 'Regulatory State' at the EC level, one which is distinguished from what he sees as the traditional European model of the 'Keynesian Welfare State' (Majone 1996: 54–5).

If we are to take seriously the idea that the EU's 'social dimension' is better characterized as social regulation than social policy, this position has major implications for how we understand its nature and potential. Majone is hardly alone in asserting that the prospects for the development of a European level welfare state are poor (1998). Yet, his formulation provides deeper reasons for its failure than do many others. Majone clearly values the market highly—or at least argues that European societies have come to place increasing value on it. He is equally clear, however, that this valuing of the market amounts to a good deal more than laissez-faire (Majone 1996: 54–6). In other words, Majone takes seriously the idea that the market is not self-organizing. For markets to operate effectively, they need a legal and regulatory (and, I would add, 'policy') framework (similar—but not identical—sentiments can be found in the work of one of Mrs Thatcher's advisors who argued that 'The task of proclaiming the virtues of free markets and the vices of government ownership and control is altogether more exhilarating than that of setting out the legal framework—the weights and measures stuff—which is a precondition if the free market is to enjoy the political and moral acceptance which will enable it to survive' (Mount 1992: 240)). One way of signalling this distinction is to label Majone's regulatory perspective as a form of *market* liberalism, in order to distinguish it from *neo*liberalism. The latter is attached to the idea that the market is self-organizing and can provide (more or less) an entire social ethic, while the former draws attention to the administrative and perhaps even 'political' prerequisites of market operation. Although I am not wedded to these *labels* (pragmatic and purist neoliberalism might work equally well), the *distinction* is important.

Once the administrative and/or political dimension of market liberalism is accepted, a difficult question is raised about where the boundary between acceptable and unacceptable regulation should be drawn. Majone stresses that regulation is not necessarily limited to market making narrowly defined. 'Progressive' social, environmental, and consumer regulation has expanded rapidly in Europe, often without a strong legal basis in the Treaties. For

Majone, regulation in these areas tends to protect diffuse interests, while imposing costs in a concentrated manner. He points to an 'apparent paradox: the same supranational institutions so often criticized for their "democratic deficit" or for their distance from domestic political concerns, may in fact be the best advocates of diffuse interests which do not find adequate expression in national political systems' (Majone 1996: 78). These are powerful arguments. Others have made related points. Carol Harlow, for example, has suggested that progressive political and legal activists would do better to 'make the most' of EC law, rather than bemoan the democratic deficiencies of the European Polity (1992). In other words, notwithstanding the absence of an opportunity to develop a European Welfare State, there is considerable scope for the pursuit of a progressive social agenda in the European Union. Indeed, issues and groups that have traditionally received short shrift in the existing 'social models' of Europe's nation-states might expect to be much better represented at the EU level.

Equally, however, the fact that a new (vibrant?) social 'policy' dynamic operating according to a distinct logic has emerged at the European level, requires greater attention. Although social policy and social regulation are not necessarily in tension with one another, neither need they be wholly compatible. *If* and *to the extent* that they are incompatible, we might even arrive at the conclusion that, in addition to the pressures that some see as emerging from supranationally driven economic liberalization, supranational social regulation—the EC's social dimension—may further increase the strain on national social policy. This point requires further development. It might be a simple matter of emphasis. National authorities may be required to divert attention from the always on-going routine maintenance and redevelopment of their social policy regimes in order to ensure that they are compatible with developing supranational requirements. On the other hand, it is also perfectly possible for new social 'rights' developed at the European level to have a corrosive influence on the existing social policy practices of (some) member states. For those inclined to defend traditional social policy regimes in the member states, the 'nightmare' scenario could involve the development of US-style 'social victimization'. According to Rosanvallon, where social policy has atrophied, some social demands may become inappropriately reexpressed in 'civil' terms through rights and regulation, a condition he identifies in the United States (2000). Rather than regarding some 'unfortunate' outcomes as a matter for collective social responsibility, particular agents must be found to be 'to blame' for them, (re)casting the others as their victims. The unleashing of a logic of social victimization, with the result of ratcheting up the level of litigation across Europe, could have a devastating impact on national social policy systems. Of course, even if the increased importance of social regulation does exacerbate such pressures, there will nonetheless be normative reasons to support it (equal pay may put pressure on a National Health Service, but that is not a reason to oppose it). Moreover, the contrast between supranational social regulation and national social policy is undoubtedly too stark. National regimes have long contained regulatory elements, and tendencies towards social regulation are themselves rooted in deep processes of individualization in western societies. Nonetheless, although Majone, for one, does note the turn to the market and regulation in the nations of western Europe, he places considerable emphasis on the EC as the creative centre of the rise of the regulatory state in Europe. The key point to make is that there is more than one way of developing a 'social dimension'.

Paradoxically, then, the promulgation of the ESM discourse coincided with and may have had the effect of partially disguising the rise of a 'regulatory order' appears to 'Americanize' European (Union) public policy, in both the economic and social domains. Although Majone defends regulatory policies as being basically oriented to 'efficiency' (see e.g. 1998), nonetheless in Europe as in the United States there is considerable scope for (political) debate and disagreement about the scope of regulation. It is hardly unknown for business organizations to argue that they labour under an unfair burden of regulation, perhaps especially when regulation serves social or environmental purposes. However, these observations should not be allowed to distract our attention from the significance of the distinction between regulatory and other forms of policy, perhaps especially in the social domain. While there is plenty of evidence of EU social regulation having an impact on national regimes and policies, as with Europeanization more generally, it is less clear that this impact has produced unequivocal converge of some sort.

Although Majone's analyses of European regulation are well known, the full implication of these approaches is not always recognized. Thus, for example, an influential perspective on the political economy of European integration during the 1980s characterizes the period as one of a clash between neoliberalism and regulated capitalism, and generally comes to the conclusion that neoliberalism was victorious (see e.g. Marks and Hooghe 1999). We have already seen that the upshot of the processes of integration and Europeanization in the 1980s is more accurately characterized as a form of regulated market capitalism, than of full blown neoliberalism (at least if neoliberalism is understood as a ideology of the 'unfettered' market). This point would be a matter of mere scholasticism, except that it helps to cast light on an odd paradox of the 1980s. When the history of the European Union in the 1980s is analysed as a competition between regulated capitalism and neoliberalism, the two are generally conceived as 'projects'. A political 'project' suggests that some strategic agent or agents deliberately attempt to make an intervention to change or defend some regime or configuration. In other words, we should be able to identify the agents of neoliberalism and regulated capitalism as European projects. Moreover, if the neoliberal 'European' project 'won', then we might expect to identify the victorious neoliberal 'agents'. While it is easy enough to stack up 'regulated capitalism' agents with a clear and articulated strategy—from Delors to Gonzalez and Mitterrand and even, arguably, to Kohl—it is much more difficult to identify neoliberal agents from the age of the Single European Act. Most of the candidates are British—and those with a clearly articulated strategy for a European 'neoliberalism' are mostly Commissioners—particularly Cockfield and then Brittan. We will return to the question of the position of Mrs Thatcher in a moment.

Even if we agree that British Conservatives were unambiguous European neoliberals, it nonetheless remains odd that a neoliberal project could 'win' in the face of substantial opposition from all the other member states (if we accept Hobsbawm's formulation for a moment) and from most of the Commission. If such a victory did indeed occur, it was partly due to the relative (but only relative) ease of achieving deregulation and negative integration by comparison with positive integration and reregulation. Yet as we have seen, the European project did indeed involve a considerable regulatory effort. Moreover, by the end of the 1980s Britain was largely standing outside of the process of monetary union, a powerful process of 'neoliberalization' through positive integration.

But it is hard to agree that most British Conservatives were *unambiguous* European neoliberals. Mrs Thatcher did have a vision of a neoliberal Europe, to be sure. But this vision of a Europe of free trade (narrowly defined as deregulation) was arguably more informed by the necessity of finding a form of economic liberalism that could be made consistent with her visceral and atavistic nationalism. Free trade neoliberalism would leave the formal features of national sovereignty relatively unchallenged. It suited Mrs Thatcher's ideological position to depict what has lately come to be seen as a period of profound liberalization as one in which a socialist inspired statism was being reimposed on Britain by the European Community. A good deal of the confusion about the character of European regulation is due to market-making and shaping regulations being misconstrued as fundamentally anti-market. Of course, not all of the explanation of the turn to the market and economic liberalization in Europe can be explained as a result of misconceptions (although they do go a long way towards explaining the confusion of the European debate in the United Kingdom). Equally, the increased acceptance of the market by agents usually associated with the 'regulated capitalism' project needs to be recognized. Delors and others recognized that major changes—a 'modernization'—of Europe was required and that the market would play a much larger role in that 'modernized' Europe than it had done previously (and particularly than it had in earlier Left strategy). The Delors strategy was one of

'Russian dolls', according to which market integration was to be followed by social reregulation and perhaps even the (re)construction of some form of 'organized capitalism' in Europe. In this sense, there is a little more to Mrs Thatcher's position than I have acknowledged so far. She may have been reacting against the future 'projected' by Delors. Indeed, this opens the ironic possibility that notwithstanding her repudiation of the European Union (in the form that eventually emerged), which became ever more wholehearted by the end of her period in office (and vitriolic after she left office), Mrs Thatcher's oppositional stance may have been instrumental in blocking the more ambitious later stages of the construction of a 'Social Europe'. Despite bemoaning her European failure, thinking herself 'tricked' into a socialist inspired integration project, Mrs Thatcher may have helped to cause the liberalization of Europe.

In the end, while Mrs Thatcher's opposition surely had some influence, it was largely in blocking or limiting some forms of consultation and involvement of 'social partners' in European policy making and in restricting the development of certain kinds of socially oriented regulation. As Majone's regulatory analysis suggests, there were other, much more powerful forces, which were also dispersed much more widely across the territory of the Union, at work. They made the emergence of a social model at the European level that engaged in large-scale activities of a redistributive nature highly unlikely. Indeed, we need only examine the politics of monetary union, from which British Conservatives largely excluded themselves, to learn that other actors were deeply sceptical about supranational level redistribution (Dyson and Featherstone 1999). Such an analysis shows that developments at the European level need to be nested within wider international or global tendencies as well as related to national trends. Thus, we have already noted that the turn to market liberalization at the EU level was rooted in some tendencies of the same sort in most national settings. Moreover, while patterns of national economic liberalization have indeed been strongly influenced from the EU level (representing a form of 'Europeanization'), this influence is necessarily refracted through the national politics of policy making. While such liberalization has typically met with some (and on occasion considerable) national resistance and opposition, it generally requires that some domestic actors are committed to carrying the process forward, while empowering those actors. Equally, external changes, not least in the normative/cognitive sphere, cast an influence within Europe (at both supranational and national levels). So, for example, a certain version of the 'sound money' paradigm among professional and academic economists, including central bankers and officials of international organizations, was increasingly dominant. This approach strongly influenced Europe's central bankers as they constructed European monetary union, to the point that an 'epistemic community' developed (Dyson and

Featherstone 1999). As a consequence, of course, developments in Europe may have further entrenched the dominant view.

Rather than seeing the outcome of European integration in the 1980s as a victory for neoliberalism, it may be better understood as a (partial) failure of the Delors strategy. In turn, this may have been rooted in a variety of factors or conditions. For example, first, the detailed character of the 'Social Europe' that Delors was committed to protecting, constructing, or modernizing/reconstructing may not have been clear. Second, those developing this strategy may have miscalculated the balance of forces. Third, the strategy may have been an inherently 'risky' one, which unfolded in a manner that left Delors on the losing side when the dice were thrown. For whatever reason, by the end of his period as President of the Commission, Delors' strategy seemed to change somewhat. In his search for a unifying symbol or objective that would motivate a more substantial project of reregulation (and possibly also of redistribution), Delors seemed to downplay 'Social Europe', instead replacing it with the idea of a sustainable development model for Europe. The project for organising capitalism in Europe suggested towards the end of his term in the White Paper on Competitiveness, Growth and Employment was of a sustainable 'development model' rather than a European model of society. Indeed, some commentators interpret this White Paper more as the institutionalization of liberal economics than as seeking a basis for an alternative reregulatory, reorganizing project. To the extent that the White Paper looked towards a project of the latter sort, the 'sustainable model', while certainly including social elements, owed more in its underlying ethos to environmentalism than social activism.

The European Social Model II: A 'Triumphant Return' or 'Second Time as Farce'?

Although Delors himself may have changed the emphasis of his project for 'reregulation', the ESM did not vanish from official discourse. The Commission's Social Policy Directorate-General continued to use the idea of an ESM as a central organizing concept for its work into the mid-1990s, without ever generating a distinctively 'European' approach. However, in the complex and contradictory world of the European Union, the White Paper on Competitiveness, Growth and Employment provided resources that new actors later took up and deployed in a politics that eventually involved an attempt to rearticulate a positive normative discourse of the ESM. Delors' last throw of the dice, which seemed to move away from 'Social Europe' as an organizing concept, ironically may have led later to a redeployment of the idea of the ESM, albeit in a modified form, through the OMC named at the

Lisbon European Council meeting 2000. The question how far Delors himself endorses the new politics of the ESM remains open, as indeed does the issue of whether the changes now introduced in the name of the ESM represent policies that could be endorsed as distinctively 'European' and 'Social'. It is certainly possible that they might do so. The OMC encompasses policies that move decisively beyond classic regulatory policies, covering such areas as education and social protection that are right at the heart of the welfare state. However, the *form* of the OMC reinforces some aspects of the regulatory analysis. Specifically, the 'cost' of the OMC moving beyond the domain of regulatory policies is that it does not deploy the (quasi-)coercive mechanisms available under the Community Method.

Instead, the OMC is based on cooperation between the member states, based on benchmarks, guidelines, and targets, but lacking formal/legal sanctions should a state fail to achieve set objectives. In this sense, while the OMC might produce strong moral or political pressure on a state to conform, it in principle it does not encroach on its independence of action. At best, the OMC might provide a forum for policy learning, based on cognitive and normative processes. Importantly, while the OMC has been extended to a wide variety of policy areas, its core domain is arguably in precisely those areas of employment and social policy in which the European Union has not traditionally proven able to legislate under the Community method. In institutional terms the OMC is, effectively, led by European Council. Characteristically states sign up to a set of benchmarks, targets, and so on at European Council meetings. They then must produce national reports on the degree to which the objectives set have been achieved. The Commission plays a key coordinating and monitoring role. In particular, it typically synthesizes national positions into a joint European document, highlights both successes and failures, and points towards possible future policy paths (for more on the OMC, see Wincott 2001a and forthcoming; Trubek and Mosher 2001).

Finally, we turn to the issue of the place of the OMC in the political architecture of the European Union. The fact that the OMC does not amount to an autonomous and authoritative European dynamic, is of course, part of its attraction. We have already seen that there are good reasons why the Community Method tends to produce 'social regulation' rather than 'social policy'. To the extent that the process of integration throws up demands for policy development that are ultimately difficult to resist in areas that are not amenable to social regulation, an alternative method is required. Such a 'method' should not impose binding rules at the national level, while creating a 'European' profile in and dimension to social policy. At best, the OMC might be able to serve this function. At worst, it will encroach upon, and perhaps undercut, the distinctive features and politics of the Community Method.

Under the OMC 'Europeanization' takes an even more voluntary form, based largely on cognitive and normative mechanisms, and especially those associated with policy learning. In the employment and welfare fields, the OMC seems to build upon elements drawn from countries as diverse as the United Kingdom and Denmark, France and the Netherlands. In other words, to the extent that a (pan) 'European' model is developed, it is clearly built from national elements. As a result, the OMC might make very little difference to national trajectories (states already embarked on reform will continue, those that have not need not change). Given that the OMC does not impose substantial sanctions on states that fail to achieve the targets set by the common policy, this might mean that the OMC amounts to little more than a 'merely' symbolic policy or sloganeering. It could be used to give the impression that 'something' is being done about problems that are either intractable, or which national leaders wish to duck. If the OMC does produce change, it might move in one of at least two possible directions—the substantive impact (if any) of OMC-style policy in the employment and welfare fields, then, remains an open question.

If the OMC is effective only when it builds upon existing tendencies in (a significant number of) member states, it may still serve a useful purpose. Nevertheless, it could provide a forum and set of mechanisms that do indeed facilitate cognitive and/or normative convergence which selects from and builds on some national tendencies, while also perhaps introducing new policy ideas to certain states. In this case the convergence is on the activation of welfare policies and the integration of economic and social policies. Alternatively, the OMC could once again move 'Europe' in the direction of an 'Anglo-Saxon' policy regime in the name of modernizing the European Social Model (albeit using a quite different set of policy instruments to those deployed in the social regulation). The OMC is at the heart of Blair's European strategy to place Britain at the leading edge of EU development, shaping its form, not 'taking' policies shaped elsewhere. If New Labour is as close to the 'US model' as such commentators as Hobsbawm suggest, this scenario of Anglo-Saxonization appears plausible. On the other hand, after twenty years of competitive austerity, social policy may be entering a period marked as much by reform as by retrenchment (I discuss the new dynamics of welfare reform in Wincott 2001*d*). The OMC may provide a framework within which new patterns of convergence and divergence in European social policy can be worked through. And of course, such novel patterns need not follow the welfare regime 'clusters' that are the staple of comparative analysis (on which see Wincott 2001*c*).

What does the evidence of OMC style policy in the welfare and employment areas tell us? The European Employment Initiative—one of the most active working groups in the history of the Party of European Socialists—was launched in September 1993. It took up and attempted to rework some of the themes of the White Paper of the same year. Strongly influenced by its Nordic members organized in SAMAK, the EEI may have reflected distinctive Nordic traditions of social democracy and policies that connect issues of welfare and employment. It developed into the European Employment Strategy through the Essen European Council Meeting of 1994 and eventually provided the foundation for the Employment Title of the Amsterdam Treaty (Johansson 1999). While the EES had certainly developed significantly before Amsterdam, it was not yet a fully formed approach to European policy making. After Amsterdam, the initiative was taken forward decisively, first at the Special 'Jobs' Summit in Luxembourg and then in the Lisbon European Council meeting, when the Employment Policy became the model and leading example of the 'new' OMC (Goetschy 2000). At Lisbon a strategy of 'modernizing' the European Social Model, through the 'activation' of the Welfare State, was set out (Wincott 2001*a*,*b*).

The political significance of the slogan of 'modernizing the European Social Model' remains contested. It might amount to the introduction of another US policy style into Europe—that of US 'workfare' policy. This, of course, is policy of a very different form from 'regulation'. In this context, the strong leadership role taken by the United Kingdom in the development of the Lisbon strategy may be important. Here, the position of the United Kingdom becomes important. Do UK policy developments point in a US direction, with 'workfare' amounting to a punitive alternative to expensive training aimed at delivering high level skills, or is it consistent with the trajectory of 'welfare-to-work' policy in such countries as the Netherlands and Denmark?

European commentary at the time of the Lisbon summit tended to treat Blair's Britain and Jospin's France as the opposite extremes of 'new' social democratic politics. Indeed, for many, Blair was hardly a social democrat at all and seemed to derive more of his inspiration from the United States than from Europe. He was, however, profoundly enthusiastic about 'modernization'. Jospin, on the other hand, led a government that seemed much more deeply wedded to 'European' social traditions. Yet both felt able to sign up to a set of proposals for the modernization of the ESM. The 'activation' or welfare policies could build on deep traditions in some parts of Europe (e.g. the Nordic states) and strongly emergent tendencies in others (France—see Coron and Palier 2002—the Netherlands, the United Kingdom), including states with notably 'passive' welfarist *traditions*.

Judging from the OMC as it has developed so far, both of these alternatives remain possible. But in order to adjudicate between them, the character of active welfare, particularly in relation to work–welfare connections, must be clearly conceptualized. As with the widespread misunderstanding of the regulatory nature of EU social policy developed under the traditional Community Method, the character of active welfare is often poorly understood. If 'workfare' type policies can lead to modifications of social policy so as to minimize its impact on the adjustment of the labour market, then they might be regarded as consistent with a market-oriented perspective. However, in general 'active' welfare policies are likely to be predicated on the view that market adjustment is *inefficient* and require political supplementation. Moreover, active welfare policies are *either* voluntary, in which case they are likely to be expensive in order to make them sufficiently attractive to induce people to take them up, *or* they contain coercive elements that have the effect of forcing people to take them up. In the former case, the presumption that policy is more effective or desirable than market outcomes must be strong; in the latter the state typically assumes that it is better placed to judge what is in individuals' best interests better than those individuals themselves.[7] The former argument is likely to be characteristically social democratic; conservatives have deployed arguments of the latter sort, as have some social democrats. Neither argument sits particularly easily with liberal ideology, particularly in its economic or 'neo-' liberal forms.

Viewed in this light, the dramatic changes to US welfare policy over the past decade represent a mixture of a directive, autocratic conservatism with a brutal form of market liberalism. Directive elements emerge in the workfare aspects of the policy, while the strictly limited amount of 'welfare' an individual can claim within a lifetime shows the punitive side of liberalism. While national experiments in 'workfare' policy have been pursued in several (particularly northern) European states, they have been neither as brutally conservative, nor as brutally liberal. Indeed, in some parts of Europe the introduction of 'workfare' has been construed by some analysts as amounting to a form of social democratization (see Torfing 1999).

The paradox of 'Europeanization' in the social domain is that the impact of European policy on national regimes has been to introduce and/or reinforce a 'new' policy style—of social regulation—that has been influentially identified as 'American'. In the name of the ESM, it seems, the European Union has moved Europe in an 'American' direction. More recently, the ESM has become associated with the OMC, as part of the normative rationale for an activation of welfare provision. What impact, if any, the OMC will have on welfare provision in Europe remains an open question; but again, one possibility is that it will be part of a process of Americanization, facilitating the introduction of US style workfare. Another is that it could become one element supporting (a) renovated welfare model(s) in European states.

---

[7] Strictly, it is only necessary that the state is making an assumption about the general interests of society.

Conclusion

What does this discussion of the ESM tell us about Europeanization? First, it suggests that considerable care should be taken in the identification of 'models' at the European level. There is no easy translation between the putative 'models' invoked by political actors in their pursuit of particular projects and the conceptual 'models' required for analytical purposes. The ESM does not amount to a conceptual model of the latter sort. Second, there is a risk that some research is too ready to identify the EU—ontological—level as ordered, coherent, and consistent, providing a clear basis from which to develop claims about 'Europeanization'. Even those theoretical perspectives that emphasize the complexity of the European Union, such as historical institutionalism, deploy complexity as a force 'locking' integration in to a particular form (Pierson 1996). A contrasting vision of complexity views the European Union as always still in formation, built through political contests and struggles, in which every protagonist is likely to have some successes, each of which will leave a trace of some sort. The structures thus created will characteristically leave a mixture of resources. Each successive generation of political leaders can make use of these resources and (re)deploy them within political projects. In turn, these projects on occasion have the capacity to alter the structure of the Union significantly. A further aspect of this complexity is that it makes the strict distinction of European integration as the ontological aspect and Europeanization as the post-ontological aspect both more difficult to draw and analytically indispensable.

REFERENCES

Berghahn, V. (1986). *The Americanization of West German Industry* (Leamington Spa: Berg).

Coron, G. and Palier, B. (2002). 'Changes in the Means of Financing Social Expenditure in France Since 1945', in C. de la Porte and P. Pochet (eds), *Building Social Europe through the Open Method of Co-ordination* (Bruxelles: P.I.E.- Peter Lang).

Castles, F. and Mitchell, D. (1993). 'Worlds of Welfare and Families of Nations', in F. Castles (ed.), *Families of Nations: Patterns of Public Policy in Western Democracies* (Aldershot: Dartmouth).

Cram, L. (1993). 'Calling the Tune Without Paying the Piper? Social Policy Regulation: The Role of the Commission in European Union Social Policy', *Policy and Politics* 21: 135–46.

Delors, J. (1992). *Our Europe* (London: Verso).

Dyson, K. and Featherstone, K. (1999). *The Road to Maastricht* (Oxford: Oxford University Press).

Esping-Andersen, G. (1990). *The Three Worlds of Welfare Capitalism* (Cambridge: Polity Press).

——and Korpi, W. (1984). 'Social Policy as Class Politics in Postwar Capitalism', in J. Goldthorpe (ed.), *Order and Conflict in Contemporary Capitalism* (Oxford: Oxford University Press).

Ferrera, M. (1996). 'The Southern Model of Welfare in Social Europe', *Journal of European Social Policy* 6 (1): 17–37.

Ginsburg, N. (1992). *Divisions of Welfare: A Critical Introduction to Comparative Social Policy* (London: Sage).

Goetschy, J. (2000). 'The European Employment Strategy', *ECSA Review* 13 (3).

Harlow, C. (1992). 'A Community of Interests? Making the Most of European Law', *Modern Law Review* 55: 331–50.

Hobsbawm, E. (1998). Contribution to Marxism Today Seminar, 4–6 September, printed in *Marxism Today* Special Issue Nov/Dec 1998.

Johansson, K. M. (1999). 'Tracing the Employment Title in the Amsterdam Treaty: Uncovering Transnational Coalitions', *Journal of European Public Policy* 6 (1): 85–101.

Kilpatrick, C. (1998). 'Community or Communities of Courts in European Integration? Sex Equality Dialogues between UK Courts and the ECJ', *European Law Journal* 4 (2).

Kloosterman, R. (1994). 'Three Worlds of Welfare Capitalism? The Welfare State and the Post-Industrial Trajectory in the Netherlands after 1980', *West European Politics* 17: 166–89.

Leaman, J. (1988). *The Political Economy of West Germany, 1945–1985: An Introduction* (London: Macmillan).

Leira, A. (1992). *Welfare States and Working Mothers: The Scandinavian Experience* (Cambridge: Cambridge University Press).

Majone, G. (1996). *Regulating Europe* (London: Routledge).

——(1998). 'Europe's "Democratic Deficit": The Question of Standards', *European Law Review* 4(1): 5–28.

——(2000). 'The Credibility Crisis of Community Regulation', *Journal of Common Market Studies* 38(2): 273–302.

Marks, G. and Hooghe, L. (1999). 'The Making of a Polity: The Struggle Over European Integration', in H. Kitschelt *et al.* (eds), *Continuity and Change in Contemporary Capitalism* (Cambridge: Cambridge University Press).

Mount, F. (1992). *The British Constitution Now* (London: Heinneman).

Pierson, P. (1996). 'The Path to European Integration: A Historical Institutionalist Analysis', *Comparative Political Studies* 29: 123–63.

—— (1998). 'Irresistible Forces, Immovable Objects: Post-Industrial Welfare States Confront Permanent Austerity', *Journal of European Public Policy* 5(4): 539–60.

Rhodes, M. (1996). 'Subversive Liberalism', *Journal of European Public Policy* 2(3): 384–406.

Rosanvallon, P. (2000). *The New Social Question: Rethinking the Welfare State* (Princeton: Princeton University Press).

Schmidt, M. (1989). 'Learning From Catastrophes: West Germany's Public Policy', in F. Castles (ed.), *The Comparative History of Public Policy* (Cambridge: Polity).

Schmidt, V. (1999). Discourse and the legitimation of economic and social policy change in Europe, *Paper prepared for delivery for Roundtable 4, "Les effets d'information. Mobilisations, préférences, agendas." Association Française de Science Politique, 6è Congrès*, Rennes, France 28–31 Sept. 1999.

Therborn. G. (1989). ' "Pillarization" and "Popular Movements": Two Variants of Welfare State Capitalism: The Netherlands and Sweden', in F. Castles (ed.), *The Comparative History of Public Policy* (Cambridge: Polity).

Torfing, J. (1999). 'Workfare with Welfare: Recent Reforms of the Danish Welfare State', *Journal of European Social Policy* 9(1): 5–28.

Trubek, D. and Mosher, J. (2001). 'New Governance, EU Employment Policy, and the European Social Model' Contribution to the Symposium: Mountain or Molehill? A Critical Appraisal of the Commission White Paper on Governance *Jean Monnet Working Paper* No. 6/01 http://www.jeanmonnetprogram.org/papers/01/011501.html.

Wincott, D. (1996). 'Federalism and European Union: The Scope and Limits of the Treaty of Maastricht', *International Political Science Review* 17(4): 403–17.

——(2000). 'New Social Democracy, the Third Way and European (Union) Welfare Reform', in L. Funk (ed.), *Contemporary Aspects of the Third Way in the New Economy* (Berlin: Verlag für Wissenschaft und Forschung), 98–112.

——(2001a). 'Beyond EC Social Regulation? Luxembourg, Lisbon and New Social Policy Instruments' Paper presented to the European Community Studies Biannual Conference, Madison Wisconsin, May.

——(2001b). 'Looking Forward or Harking Back? The Commission and the Reform of EU Governance', *Journal of Common Market Studies* 39(5): 897–911.

——(2001c). 'Reassessing the Social Foundations of Welfare (State) Regimes', *New Political Economy* 6(3): 409–25.

——(2001d). 'La nouvelle social-démocratie, l'État-providence et l'avenir de la gauche en Europe', *Le Banquet: Revue Politique* Décembre 2001 No. 16.

——forthcoming (2003). 'Beyond Social Regulation? New Instruments and/or a New Agenda for Social Policy at Lisbon'? *Public Administration*.

Zapf, W. (1986). 'Development, Structure and Prospects of the German Social State', in R. Rose and R. Shiratori (eds), *The Welfare State East and West* (Oxford: Oxford University Press).

13

Europeanization Goes East: Power and Uncertainty in the EU Accession Process

HEATHER GRABBE

Introduction

The European Union (EU) matters in eastern Europe, but how? The candidate countries of central and eastern Europe (CEE) have been taking on all the obligations of EU membership for some ten years now, so the domestic effects of transferring policies and institutions to them are likely to be comparable to the effects of the European Union on its current member states. However, the political relationship between the applicants and the European Union is very different, which affects how Europeanization occurs.

The first section sets out a prima facie case for extending the study of Europeanization to include the EU effects in CEE, arguing that the effects are likely to be similar in nature, but broader and deeper in scope. The second section discusses how theoretical and empirical work on Europeanization in the EU-15 can usefully be applied to the applicants for membership, particularly the CEE countries that have sought to join since 1989. It sets out a typology of routes of influence through which the European Union can affect domestic changes in CEE.

The third section presents an analysis of two major reasons why Europeanization is different in the case of central and eastern European countries. The first reason is that they are candidates rather than members of the Union, in an asymmetrical relationship which gives the European Union more coercive routes of influence in domestic policy making processes. The applicants cannot influence EU policy making from the inside, and they have a stronger incentive than existing member states to implement EU policies because they are trying to gain admission. The second reason is the uncertainty built into the accession processes. This uncertainty has at least five dimensions, and each can help explain the differential impact of the European Union across domains of public policy in CEE. The constraints on EU influence point towards analytical problems in assessing to what extent different policy domains are Europeanized in CEE.

This chapter restricts itself to just one domain of Europeanization—public policy. Unquestionably the European Union also affects cognitive–normative structures in CEE as well, but there is still very little convincing empirical work on which to draw in the case of the candidate countries. This is a promising area for future research, however.

The Case for Comparability with the Existing European Union: Nature and Scope

The Europeanization literature is relevant to the CEE applicants[1] because these countries are already subjected to substantially the same pressures of adaptation to EU policies as current member states. Europeanization mechanisms identified in the literature on the European Union are likely to operate for the applicants too, given that the same policy structures and implementation procedures are used.

Previous studies of Europeanization have dealt almost exclusively with countries that have already joined the European Union (Goetz 2000 is a welcome exception), yet the European Union exerts similar pressures on the applicant countries. Many of the phenomena identified in the Europeanization literature can also be seen emerging in CEE, but the EU's influence on the applicants has the added dimensions of conditionality and accession negotiations. The *acquis communautaire*[2] has to be adopted by the candidates in its entirety, and the negotiations are primarily concerned with determining how much of it should be implemented prior to accession and which parts of the *acquis* will be the subject to a transitional period after joining.

The CEE candidates approached EU accession with different starting conditions from previous applicants, following over four decades of central planning and state socialism. The fact that they are such different candidates offers the researcher an opportunity to test hypotheses about Europeanization outside the cultural, political, and economic particularity of advanced West

---

[1] There are ten CEE applicants for membership, and three Mediterranean ones. Six of the applicants (the Czech Republic, Estonia, Hungary, Poland, and Slovenia, plus Cyprus) began accession negotiations with the EU in March 1998, and three of them (the Czech Republic, Hungary, and Poland) joined NATO in 1999. Bulgaria, Latvia, Lithuania, Romania and Slovakia (plus Malta) opened EU accession negotiations in February 2000. This chapter is concerned with the post-communist CEE applicants and does not discuss the Mediterranean ones in detail, but the same accessions conditions apply to Cyprus, Malta, Turkey, and any country that seeks to join the EU in future.

[2] *'Acquis communautaire'* is the term used to refer to all the real and potential rights and obligations of the EU system and its institutional framework; the accession *acquis* is the whole body of EU law and practice (see Grabbe 1999).

European democracies with developed economies. The CEE candidates thus provide valuable new cases to compare with studies of the existing European Union. At the same time, empirical work on how post-communist political economies react to an external influence such as the EU offers insights into the transformation of public policy processes after 1989, thus adding value to the study of post-communist transition and democratization.

However, this chapter does not advocate using Europeanization indiscriminately as a theoretical framework. In using the concept, with reference to the CEE region, it is particularly important not to overestimate the EU influence. It is easy to do so when a study is looking for evidence of EU effects. Moreover, there is already a tendency in parts of the literature on transition to exaggerate the EU impact. For example, scholars working on democratization have tended to assume that the European Union has vigorously encouraged democratization by pressing the CEE countries into implementing democratic human rights regimes and open political systems (e.g. Linz and Stepan 1996; Kopecký and Mudde 2000). Although the European Union has enormous potential influence, scholars should not prejudge the extent to which the European Union has shaped governance overall. A systematic examination of the limitations on EU influence is an essential part of assessing the degree to which the European Union is responsible for the changes that have taken place.

The pressures on CEE for adaptation and policy convergence are considerably greater than those on previous applicants, owing to the Union's much more advanced state of policy development—because of the completion of the single market in 1992, the integration of the Schengen area of passport-free movement into the EU treaty framework in 1997, and the launch of the single currency in 1999. These pressures are more comparable with those on member states in the 1990s than on Mediterranean applicants in the 1970s and 1980s because of the development of eastern accession conditionality. The creation of formal accession conditions has given the European Union much wider leverage to get these applicants to comply with its demands than previous ones. It has also reduced the ability of applicants to negotiate concessions such as transitional periods and derogations in comparison with previous enlargements. The European Union is applying the accession conditions for CEE in a way more similar to the Maastricht convergence criteria for monetary union than to its approach in previous enlargements. The conditions are set in advance and national governments have to meet them before they can join—as with the convergence criteria.

The prima facie Case for EU Influence

What kind of convergence between EU and CEE policies should we expect? The experience of the EU's current member states would suggest the scope is not wide, but I argue it will be considerably greater for CEE. Within the existing

Union, there has been only limited convergence of policies and institutions, and the continuing diversity of member states has been well documented (Kohler-Koch and Eising 1999; Cowles *et al.* 2001; Héritier *et al.* 2001). For example, there has been little convergence towards a European 'model of capitalism' (Crouch and Streeck 1997; Rhodes and Apeldoorn 1998, among others). National economic systems have remained diverse partly because of the characteristics of EU policy making. In particular, the EU's key governance function is regulating social and political risk rather than resource redistribution (Majone 1996; Hix 1998). Moreover, the EU's policy framework for regulating the single market—which is one of its most extensively developed policy areas—remains a patchwork (Héritier 1996). In addition, member states can mitigate the impact of regulatory alignment on their domestic political economies, leading to uneven implementation and hence differentiated effects on national regimes (McGowan and Wallace 1996).

However, three factors point towards a hypothesis that the European Union accession process is pushing the applicant countries towards greater convergence with particular policy models than has occurred within the existing European Union. The first factor is the speed of adjustment. The formal accession process sets out to adapt CEE institutions and policies to the European Union much faster and more thoroughly than the adaptation of current EU-15 members. It took Greece well over a decade to adapt to the EU single market norms (Featherstone 1998). By contrast, prospective CEE members are expected to have oriented their institutions and policies to the European Union prior to membership, which means less than a decade in practice. Moreover, they have done so from a much lower starting-point and with very limited scope for negotiating transitional periods. The European Union has been able to push CEE policy reforms faster than they would otherwise have gone because of the priority accorded to accession by their governments and because of the institutional lacunae resulting from communist era. Since 1989, most of the candidates have been building market regulation from only the most basic of foundations, and introducing policies where previously they had none, for example, in competition policy, migration, asylum, and protection of minorities.

The second factor is the openness of CEE to EU influence owing to the process of post-communist transformation. The CEE applicants are working from different starting points in terms of institutional development, with gaps left by communist systems (Batt and Wolczuk 1999). They did not start with an institutional *tabula rasa*—far from it (see Lijphart and Crawford 1995)—but the communist legacy means that some EU policies meet with less institutional resistance than in the current member states. What was called 'deregulation' under the single market programme means radical reregulation in the CEE case, and sometimes imposing regulation where there was none—for most financial services, for example. The candidates are in the process of throwing off communist-era legislative frameworks and creating new ones for a capitalist market economy. This process has made them more receptive to regulatory paradigms than the EU's member states were, because EU models were being presented at the same time as CEE policy-makers were seeking a model to implement.

The third factor is the breadth of the EU agenda in CEE. The CEE applicants have no possibility of opt-outs from parts of the agenda, such as those obtained by the United Kingdom on the Social Chapter, Schengen, or monetary union. Hence the applicants are committed to converging with a maximalist version of the EU policies. In areas like social policy, where there is resistance to greater integration from some member states, the Commission has tended to define a 'maximalist' version of the *acquis communautaire* for CEE (Brusis 1998).

The EU's agenda in CEE has also become wider than that for current member-states through the membership conditions established for the eastern applicants. The conditions set at Copenhagen in 1993 go beyond those for any previous applicant, stating that not only do prospective members have to take on the 'obligations of membership'—i.e. the *acquis communautaire*—but they also have to have a 'functioning market economy' and 'the capacity to cope with competitive pressure and market forces within the Union', as well as 'stability of institutions guaranteeing democracy, the rule of law, human rights, and respect for and protection of minorities'. The European Union has no specific test to determine whether or to what extent these conditions have been met. That gives the European Union a licence to involve itself in domestic policy making to an degree unprecedented in the current member states. Moreover, mitigating the impact of EU policies is more difficult for applicant countries than it was for states that had already gained membership, owing to the continuous monitoring of implementation of every part of the *acquis*, including annual reports from the Commission.

Because of the political and economic Copenhagen conditions set for this enlargement, the European Union is having a twofold impact on CEE public policy making. First, it is influencing areas like market regulation and sectoral policies by presenting rules and norms that have to be adopted inflexibly, with very limited transitional periods. Second, the European Union can present other demands for changes in regulations and policies to CEE ad hoc. The very general nature of the conditions thus allows the European Union (particularly the Commission, which formulates and manages accession policy) a wide margin for policy entrepreneurship in setting demands that change the policy and institutional frameworks of these countries. Since 1993, the EU's demands on the applicants have become progressively more specific as it has defined more clearly what would constitute meeting the Copenhagen conditions. The Commission's 1995 Single Market White Paper set out the market regulation part of the *acquis* for adoption, building on the Europe Agreements (which cover trade liberalization and competition policy, among other areas) signed from 1993 onwards. The Accession Partnerships issued from 1998 onwards present a huge range of demands. The candidates have to implement the Accession Partnerships to move forward towards accession, and also to qualify for EU aid and other benefits.

Conditionality for accession now extends the reach of EU influence considerably more deeply into domestic policy making in CEE than it has done in the member states, which have only had to implement policies resulting from 'the obligations of membership' (the third condition) and have never been judged on the other two conditions. The democracy and market economy conditions have led the European Union (in the form of the Commission and Council) to influence many policy areas beyond the reach of Community competence in the member states. Although only some policy domains have moved to supranational level in the European Union (Stone Sweet and Sandholtz 1997), the distinctions between Community and national competences that are so extensively debated within the European Union are not acknowledged in the agenda presented to CEE. Indeed, the conditions cover several areas where member states have long been very resistant to extending Community competence for themselves. The political criteria take the European Union into areas such as judicial reform and prison conditions; the economic criteria are interpreted to include areas such as reform of pension, taxation, and social security systems; and the measures for 'administrative capacity to apply the *acquis*' brings EU conditions to civil service reform in CEE, for example.

Hence we may expect a large number of parallels with the impact that Europeanization has had on less-developed member states, but also some contrasts. Particularly important are the potential parallels with the southern EU member states in the impact of importing political philosophies; of advantaging small circles of actors (and reinforcing a democratic deficit) and privileging technocrats; of penetrating state administration practices; and of aid-dependence. Europeanization has had the effect of empowering modernizers to change specific policies (particularly macroeconomic policies) and also to reform political institutions. This effect has been observed not only in the case of later joiners like Greece (Featherstone 1998), but also in founder-members like France (Ladrech 1994) and Italy (Francioni 1992; Amato 1996). However, contrasts immediately arise too. The CEE countries have undergone deep reforms in a much more globalized economy and an era of much greater liberalization of trade and capital flows. Finally, flows of aid to CEE have been much less than those to the main recipient member states as a proportion of GDP. But as the CEE applicants move closer to membership, all these contrasts will start to diminish, and they could become more directly comparable with the existing member states' experiences of Europeanization.

How to Study Europeanization in the Candidate Countries

The previous section has argued that we may expect the EU influence in CEE to be similar in nature to that in the EU-15, but wider and deeper in scope. This section explains how the concept of 'Europeanization' can be used to investigate the effects that the European Union is having on public policy in the candidate countries. It categorizes the different mechanisms of Europeanization at work in CEE public policy, distinguishing between those that are similar to the mechanisms in the EU-15 and those that are particular to the accession process.

What Europeanization is—and is not—in the Case of Enlargement

The definition of Europeanization presented by Radaelli in this volume is highly relevant to CEE:

Europeanization consists of processes of (a) construction, (b) diffusion, and (c) institutionalization of formal and informal rules, procedures, policy paradigms, styles, 'ways of doing things', and shared beliefs and norms which are first defined and consolidated in the EU policy process and then incorporated in the logic of domestic (national and subnational) discourse, identities, political structures, and public policies.

This definition stresses the importance of change in the logic of political behaviour, which is a useful way of distinguishing Europeanization effects from the many other processes of change at work in the post-communist political context. In applying this heuristic concept to CEE, I am primarily investigating (b) and (c), looking at how the outcomes of EU policy processes have been diffused and institutionalized in CEE. The typology of Europeanization mechanisms presented below is primarily concerned with 'hard transfer', how the European Union has transferred rules, procedures, and policy paradigms to CEE. However, the importance of soft transfer—of styles, 'ways of doing things', and shared beliefs and norms—is also increasingly evident (as pointed out by Schimmelfennig 2001; Sedelmeier 2001).

This chapter is also confined only to certain dimensions of Europeanization in CEE: its main subject is public policy, not political structures, structures of representation, or cognitive and normative structures (to use Radaelli's typology of potential subjects of Europeanization). However, the European Union is undoubtedly having an effect on political structures in CEE, as early work on the Europeanization of interest groups (Fink-Hafner 1998) and political parties (Pridham *et al.* 1997; Szczerbiak 2001; Taggart and Szczerbiak 2001) shows, and these effects will increase after the CEE candidates join the Union. Moreover, there is an interaction between policy dynamics and political structures in the European Union (Héritier and Knill 2000; Coen in this volume) to be investigated in CEE.

Before proceeding, we must define what Europeanization is not, lest it become a catch-all for any process of domestic change. In studying the European Union, Radaelli (this volume) makes a series of analytical distinctions between Europeanization and convergence, harmonization, and political integration, while recognizing that in the real world Europeanization and EU policy formation are interconnected. Three further distinctions are necessary when applying the concept to the CEE applicants:

1. Europeanization is not a theory of EU Enlargement

Theories of enlargement address the question 'Why does the European Union decide to enlarge and why do applicants want to join?' (e.g. Schimmelfennig 1998; Fierke and Wiener 1999). They seek to explain why the enlargement process is happening, that is, the ontological stage of research, whereas Europeanization is post-ontological in being concerned with the effects of the enlargement process. This distinction parallels that made by Caporaso (1996) between EU ontology and post-ontological perspectives in Europeanization and political integration in the European Union. Clearly Europeanization is linked to the politics of enlargement in practice, through a two-way process that causes feedback effects from Europeanization in CEE on to reformulation of accession policy. However, formation of enlargement policy and Europeanization should be kept separate at a conceptual level.

2. Discrimination between differences of kinds as well as differences of degrees

Radaelli draws on Sartori (1991) to remind us of the danger of 'degreeism', where if we are unable to tell the difference between a cat and a dog, we talk of degrees of cat–dog. If we are always looking at the extent of Europeanization, we may fail to notice that other processes are producing the effects. It is easy to overstress the role of the European Union when we are looking for it as a specific variable. This is a particular danger in studying the accession process, because both EU and CEE policy-makers tend to exaggerate the extent of EU influence for political purposes. Both the main sources for evidence of Europeanization (i.e. EU institutions and candidate country governments) have a vested interest in claiming that the European Union is the principal driver of most reforms. The CEE officials tend to talk up the EU role to emphasize the scale of preparations and how ready they are, and to blame the European Union for unpopular reforms. On the EU side, both officials and politicians like to promote enlargement as a commitment device in post-communist transition, claiming that the Union has been the principal driver of beneficial political and economic reforms in CEE. As is the case in the European Union, institutional isomorphism is used as a source of legitimacy (Radaelli 2000).

Both sets of claims are justified to a large extent, but they often exaggerate the EU's specific influences in any given policy area. There are many other exogenous forces and endogenous processes of change at work in post-communist contexts. It is particularly important to distinguish Europeanization from globalization (a powerful exogenous process) and from post-communist transition (endogenous factors). The CEE domestic structures and public policies were very different from EU norms at the start of the accession process, and the simultaneous processes of political and economic transition interact with the accession process as well as with each other (see Offe 1991 on the 'triple transition'). At the same time, it is important to resist assuming that changes in political behaviour will be the same as those identified in the member states, given the candidates' very different starting circumstances and the fundamental nature of post-communist reforms.

We need to discern where the nature of outcomes is clearly the result of EU-driven change and where other, non-EU processes are at work. This is necessary to control for rival alternative hypotheses, something that is rarely done systematically in Europeanization research (as observed by Goetz 2000). This distinction is difficult to maintain in practice because of the interaction between domestic, international, and European variables. Europeanization happens at the same time as the CEE polities are undergoing modernization and post-communist reform, and the interaction between Europeanization dynamics and transition processes is an increasingly important research area. Moreover, Europeanization effects are a continuum, and work on the European Union has shown the importance of parallel processes of national and EU-level reforms (e.g. Héritier and Knill 2000 on transport; Radaelli 1997 on taxation). However, research design needs to start a consideration of how to distinguish between Europeanization and endogenous processes, as well as with other exogenous pressures.

3. Distinguishing between Intentional and Unintentional Effects of the European Union

We cannot assume that the European Union will achieve the effects it explicitly aims for just because of its power relationship through conditionality and the breadth of its agenda. 'EU influence' operates through many different actor constellations and its goals are often unclear, so the overall impact can be very diffuse (as discussed by Harcourt, this volume). One must therefore look carefully at whether EU pressure actually had its intended effects. It is equally important to be sensitive to unintended consequences, because the European Union can effect change by example-setting and unintended policy transfer. The European Union has been a significant source of models for political actors seeking outside guidance on policy and institutional change.

'European' norms and models are frequently cited in CEE political debates to legitimate political choices of various kinds (see e.g. Fowler 2001 on regional reforms). However, 'EU norms' can also be invoked in contexts where the European Union has not asked for compliance, such as constitutional models.

Mechanisms of Europeanization

The EU accession involves different processes that effect some degree of institutional and policy transformation in CEE. I call these processes 'mechanisms', because they are largely used instrumentally by the European Union. This section tackles the question 'what is Europeanized?', by dividing the mechanisms into five categories:

- *Models*: provision of legislative and institutional templates
- *Money*: aid and technical assistance
- *Benchmarking and monitoring*
- *Advice and twinning*
- *Gate-keeping*: access to negotiations and further stages in the accession process

Two of these processes have long caused Europeanization effects in the EU-15 countries: the European Union has provided models for implementation in the existing European Union, along with regional aid funds and other fiscal transfers from the Community budget. The third mechanism has also begun to be used in the EU-15 in the past few years, with benchmarking becoming an increasingly important method of European integration within the existing European Union. Indeed, some of the benchmarking and monitoring methods developed for accession may have feedback effects, as the Commission uses its experience in CEE to apply the same methods to existing member states. The last two mechanisms are primarily reserved for applicant countries, and have particularly strong Europeanization effects in CEE.

1. Models: Provision of Legislative and Institutional Templates
The candidate countries have to take on all the EU's existing laws and norms, so they are subject to the same Europeanization pressures as member states in the policies and institutional templates that they 'download' from EU level. Legal transposition of the *acquis* and harmonization with EU laws are essential to becoming a member state, and they have so far been the central focus of the accession process and preparations by the candidates. Legislative gaps and institutional weaknesses are also identified by the screening process that takes place with each applicant prior to negotiations on the thirty-one negotiating 'chapters'.

As with the current member states, this transfer of models involves both 'vertical harmonization' and 'horizontal harmonization' (Radaelli, this volume), depending on whether the policy area in question involves positive or negative integration (Knill and Lehmkuhl 1999). However, a critical difference is that the candidates cannot 'upload' their own preferences into those European-level policies. They are only consumers, not producers, of the outcomes of the EU's policy-making processes. That means that they cannot object if an EU policy fits very badly with their domestic structures or policies. Moreover, the candidates have less room for manoeuvre in implementing EU models because they are under stronger pressure to attempt close mimetism, as they have to prove themselves to be worthy potential member states.

The candidates are also increasingly subject to the EU's 'framing' mechanisms of Europeanization as well. This occurs through all three 'soft' Europeanization mechanisms identified by Radaelli. The candidates are encouraged to comply closely with minimalist directives and non-compulsory directives, in order to convince reluctant member states that they will be good partners in sensitive policy areas. For example, they were invited to shadow the 'Lisbon process' of economic reform, even though it is not officially part of the accession *acquis*, and the candidates have voluntarily signed 'Joint Assessment Papers' with the Commission that will guide their labour market policies. Another example of where the candidates have been encouraged to do more than is strictly required by the *acquis* is social policy, where the Commission has presented a maximalist version of a largely non-binding *acquis* to the applicants (Brusis 1998). CEE activity in both of these policy areas also involves cognitive convergence, where the European Union does not have a coherent corpus of directives, but the CEE countries nevertheless look to the European Union for guidance on what is a good policy. The CEE governments have a double incentive to respond to framing integration: one is to show the European Union that they are willing and able to play a full part as member states and take on the future *acquis* as it develops; the other is to show their domestic electorate that they are taken seriously by the European Union as a full partner, and to legitimate their policy programme by reference to EU policies.

However, the extent to which references to EU norms actually result in changes in policy depends on the domestic political context and on the policy area in question. One of the problems in analysing the EU's impact in CEE lies is distinguishing how far an actual EU model has been used, and how much the EU's own diversity has provided multiple points of reference in the CEE debates. The European Union often lacks a single model to export (as discussed by Mörth, this volume), and its own diversity can undermine its effort to export a single model of governance. For example, an appeal to 'Europe' is a constant feature of the Hungarian domestic debate about sub-state reform (see Fowler 2001). All sides and all political parties make this appeal, yet the European Union is a confusing model, as CEE actors can point to the very different examples of substate governance in EU member states to support their positions. This provides ammunition for different sides in domestic political battles.

Candidate countries tend to engage in anticipatory adjustment to EU policies as well, adopting EU norms or practices before the European Union tells them they must do so. In the first years of post-communist economic transition, policy-makers in central Europe frequently made reference to EU economic models and EU regulatory and competition policies to justify their policy choices, even before the European Union required conformity. More recently, candidates have adjusted their domestic policies and institutions in advance of specific EU requirements to do so in the area of justice and home affairs. All of the candidates have rapidly adopted the EU's still sketchy *acquis* for border control, police cooperation, asylum, migration, and crime prevention. After the terrorist attacks in New York and Washington on 11 September 2001, several leading candidates (e.g. Hungary and the Czech Republic) quickly put forward plans for tighter border controls and cooperation with United States and EU intelligence and police forces that go beyond official requirements for accession. They have done so because current member states could veto their membership if their capacity to control cross-border crime and other threats is judged to be inadequate (see Grabbe 2002). Candidates also have to show willing and prove that they take these issues seriously, because member states' acceptance of the candidates' readiness to join will be largely based on confidence in their border controls and legal systems, rather than on technical standards.

2. Money: Aid and Technical Assistance

The European Union is the largest external source of aid for CEE, providing funds administered by the European Commission and also bilateral programmes from individual member states. The amounts transferred to CEE are relatively small in comparison with the fiscal transfers to current member states under the structural and cohesion funds. However, they have an important role in reinforcing the transfer of EU models, because the aid helps to pay for implementation and the technical assistance builds institutional capacity to use EU practices. The co-financing requirements force applicant countries to allocate public resources to particular policy areas too, so EU aid can change the order of priorities on a government's agenda.

3. Benchmarking and Monitoring

Progress towards EU accession is a central issue in CEE political debates, so the European Union can influence policy and institutional development through ranking the applicants, benchmarking in particular policy areas, and providing examples of best practice that the applicants seek to emulate. Monitoring is a key mechanism in the conditionality for membership, through the cycle of 'Accession Partnerships' and 'Regular Reports' published by the European Commission on how prepared each CEE applicant is in different fields. Conditionality for aid and other benefits is based on implementing the Accession Partnerships issued to each applicant since 1998. These documents provide a direct route into domestic policy making in CEE, because the European Union sets out a list of policy 'priorities' that have to be implemented within the year or in the medium term (defined as five years). The European Commission then reports on each applicant's progress in meeting each priority in the autumn of the year, and may publish a revised Accession Partnership for a particular candidate for the following year.

The experience of setting standards and creating monitoring mechanisms for the applicants has been an important learning process for the European Commission. Several key officials have used this experience in planning monitoring processes for the existing member states. The Commission discovered benchmarking almost by accident (Begg and Peterson 1999), and it is increasingly used as a powerful vector of Europeanization for both candidates and member states.

4. Advice and Twinning

The European Union has a direct line into policy-making structures in CEE through its 'twinning' programme. Twinning pays for the secondment of civil servants from EU member states to work in CEE ministries and other parts of public administration. That provides a direct route for cognitive convergence, as EU civil servants work alongside CEE counterparts. However, because twinning projects use civil servants and focus on implementation, most twinning agents are concerned with standards and technical issues rather than overall institutional models or policy direction. Moreover, the advice and expertise offered by the twinning agents are not controlled centrally by the European Union, so the impact on CEE public administrations is likely to be diffuse rather than reflecting any consistent European model. Indeed, one of the main principles of the twinning programme is the recognition that the present member states implement the EU legislation by different means. The advice offered on how to transform institutions is somewhat random in that it depends on the experience and assumptions of the individual preaccession advisor, which are in turn influenced by his or her nationality and background. Whether an advisor is German, Greek, British, or Swedish could make a big difference to the advice offered on how to meet EU standards in a given policy area, given the divergence in 'policy styles' between the member states.

5. Gate-keeping: Access to Negotiations and Further Stages in the Accession Process

The EU's most powerful conditionality tool is access to different stages in the accession process, particularly achieving candidate status and starting negotiations. Aid, trade, and other benefits can also be used to promote domestic policy changes, but they have not had such direct and evident consequences as progress towards membership. It has taken a decade for the European Union to evolve an explicit use of conditionality in a gate-keeping role, where hurdles in the accession process are related to meeting specific conditions. For several years after the conditions were first set in 1993, it was not clear exactly which elements of the political and economic conditions had to be fulfilled for an applicant to be admitted to which benefits. However, by the time of the Luxembourg 1997 and Helsinki 1999 European Councils, a rough progression had emerged of stages in the accession process.

This sequence of moving into an ever closer relationship with the European Union provides a coercive tool to reinforce other mechanisms of Europeanization, such as transfer of models and benchmarking. But it also works as a Europeanization mechanism in its own right, because the European Union can attach specific conditions to particular stages in the accession process. At the Helsinki European Council in 1999, the European Union explicitly made fulfilment of the democracy and human rights conditions for accession a prerequisite for starting negotiations—and excluded Turkey from negotiations on these grounds. The Commission also imposed specific tasks for Bulgaria (on nuclear power) and Romania (on economic reform and state orphanages) before they could join negotiations in 2000. This was an innovative move for the European Union, in making an explicit linkage between benefit and specific tasks for applicants, and it may herald the start of more targeted use of conditionality.

Although access to negotiations and other stages in the accession process is the EU's most powerful political tool for enforcing compliance, it is not a precise instrument that can cause complex changes. Rather, it is a blunt weapon that has to be used judiciously for priority areas only. Its main value is as a shock tactic, to embarrass applicant governments into making dramatic changes owing to the domestic repercussions of failing to meet a major foreign policy goal. This results in 'shaming', whereby governments are forced into complying with EU requirements by the international and domestic press coverage and political pressure.

Criticisms made in EU reports can have a powerful impact on domestic debates about public policy and a CEE government's political fortunes. Conversely, gaining international approval is an important way of legitimizing political choices in the post-communist context. The European Union has also made exceptional criticisms of undemocratic practices in particular countries in '*démarches*',[3] that is, public criticisms that are intended to embarrass CEE governments into making particular institutional or policy changes. As Schimmelfennig (2001) points out, this process of 'socializing' CEE countries into international norms happens through 'reactive reinforcement' rather than active conditionality: 'internalization is rewarded but a failure to internalize the community rules is not punished beyond withholding the reward'. (p. 2). It only works if governments and political elites as a whole are committed to EU accession. In other words, the conditionality only works as a carrot, not as a stick.

Intervening Variables: Power and Uncertainty

The previous section has demonstrated that the European Union has powerful mechanisms to shape institutional development and policy making in CEE. But how (and how far) have the routes of influence analysed above actually driven change? It is difficult to say at this point in time, given the dynamic nature of the process, the wide range of potential effects, and the fact that accession has not yet happened. The European Union has no specific test of institutional change or compliance with its requirements, and it is difficult to see how an identifiably 'European' influence on institutional and policy change could be detected in all but a few cases.

However, it is clear that there remain persistent differences between the CEE candidates; for example, there is little evidence of convergence towards a standard model of governance (Goetz and Wollmann 2001). Empirical research on CEE also demonstrates the wide differences that have persisted in policy making between the candidates, despite a similar pressure on all the countries studied, namely the impact of EU accession conditions. For example, in regional policy, the candidates have reacted differently to the EU requirement that they establish subnational administrative structures (Hughes *et al.* 2001; Fowler 2001). Likewise, they have created widely varying structures of microeconomic governance (Hare *et al.* 1999). This outcome parallels the limited convergence that has happened in EU member states (see Risse and Börzel, this volume); indeed, it is the continuing diversity of member states' institutions and policy preferences which inhibits the emergence of a fully fledged blueprint for CEE policy-makers.

Adaptational pressure is not the best predictor of how a country responds to Europeanization (Radaelli, this volume). There can be a number of intervening variables that determine the EU's impact in a given policy area and country, and other chapters in this volume explore how they work, both empirically

---

[3] *Démarches* are issued as part of EU foreign policy by unanimous intergovernmental agreement between the member states.

and conceptually. Several of the variables at work in CEE are familiar from the study of the European Union: one is the interaction between Europeanization and other processes of change, driven externally and internally. Another is the complexity of actor constellations involved in EU policy making. In the case of the candidate countries, there are additional constraints owing to the diffuse nature of EU influence (see Grabbe 2001*a*). This section highlights two major intervening variables that are specific to the context of candidacy as opposed to membership of the Union. One is the asymmetry of the relationship with the European Union; the other is the uncertainty built into the accession process.

The relationship is one of obvious asymmetry of interdependence, and hence power—after all, 'power arises from an asymmetrical interdependence'.[4] The EU has all the benefits to offer (principally accession, trade, and aid), and far from all of its component member states are sure they want all the CEE applicants to join. The CEE countries, by contrast, have little to offer the European Union, given their tiny economic size, and little to bargain with, because the desire of their political elites to join is generally much greater than that of the member states to let them in. This asymmetry of interdependence allows the European Union to set the rules of the game in the accession conditionality. However, the candidates have an opportunity to mitigate to some extent the impact of EU influence in the way that they implement the *acquis*. The implementation stage is critical to understanding how the European Union has affected policy and policy making in CEE: it is the interface between domestic and foreign policy, and it determines the impact of conditionality. The EU influence on detailed policy formation and implementation is mediated by domestic actors, and determining the manner and extent of this mediation requires empirical enquiry. The EU member states have frequently used implementation to mitigate the impact of EU-level policies on their domestic political economies. The tight conditions for accession and continuous monitoring by the Commission mean there are fewer opportunities to do so in CEE than there were for the current EU-15 (McGowan and Wallace 1996), but opportunities nevertheless exist.

There are thus a number of intervening variables which remain to be explored. This chapter considers in more detail one variable which has rarely been conceptualized in the study of Europeanization: uncertainty.

Five Dimensions of Uncertainty

There are at least five dimensions of uncertainty built into the accession conditions, each of which acts as an intervening variable in the implementation of policies to meet the conditions.

---

[4] See, for example, Knorr (1977: 102).

1. There is uncertainty about the *policy agenda* that should be undertaken by the applicants. In mature policy areas like the Single Market—where the European Union has developed a large *acquis* over many years that has been implemented by member states—the agenda is fairly certain because the requirements have been tried and tested already by the existing member-states. Uncertainty can remain about the timing and standards to be achieved, and how important the area is politically, but the tasks are relatively clear because of the solid legal basis and established case law. But there are also nascent policy areas that have started being developed recently, where the future shape of the policies is still unclear, and the extent of Europeanization in the member states still unknown—for example, justice and home affairs (Grabbe 2002), social policy (Falkner 1998), and direct taxation (Radaelli 2001). The agenda is uncertain because the tasks have not yet been fully determined for the member states either. In the cases of social policy and direct tax policy coordination, the uncertainty is heightened by the fact that the most common method of integration used is framing integration rather than positive integration. The *acquis* in these areas contains a much less specific agenda because the initiatives involve soft law rather than Community legal instruments. However, the European Union has often had to harden such soft parts of the *acquis* because it had to define them more clearly for the candidates.

The level of uncertainty is even higher in policy areas where the European Union has set conditions for the candidates, but there is no Community competence in the European Union. This is the case for the political conditions for membership, where the European Union requires candidates to achieve the rule of law, human rights, and respect for and protection of minorities. The European Union itself has no institutional template for any of these conditions, because they remain outside EU-level responsibilities. The Charter of Fundamental Rights endorsed at Nice in 2000 makes reference to them, but is not legally binding, and member states exhibit a wide variety of democratic systems and policies in areas like protection of minorities. The European Union has been very slow to develop a definition of its political values, and has no single, harmonized model to export to CEE in such policy areas.

2. Uncertainty about the *hierarchy of tasks* was a major characteristic of accession policy (and much criticized in CEE) between 1993 and 1998. The CEE policy-makers complained that they did not have sufficient information about the relative importance of the different conditions to sequence their preparations for accession. The EU official position was that all 80,000-plus pages of the *acquis* had to be implemented; yet it was obvious that some pages of the *acquis* were more important than others. Moreover, it was unclear what the European Union would judge as an adequate pace of preparations to clear hurdles in the accession process, such as joining negotiations.

Partly in response to such criticism, this uncertainty about sequencing and prioritization was reduced owing to the introduction of the Accession Partnerships. However, this dimension of uncertainty has not entirely disappeared as a result. There can be discrepancies between the formal priorities set out in the published Accession Partnerships and the signals (e.g. advice and informal communication) that the applicants are given by different EU actors over the relative importance of the various priorities. These discrepancies can arise from changes in the political agenda in the European Union over the year between publication of the Accession Partnerships; for example, an issue that looked very important one year may be considered less important by the following year owing to changes in government in large member states. Likewise, issues can rise up the agenda quite rapidly over the course of the intervening year; for example, treatment of the Roma and border controls rose up the agenda prior to Autumn 1999 owing to flows of asylum-seekers to the United Kingdom and Finland over the year between the Accession Partnerships, and the change of government in Austria. Essentially, the uncertainty arises because of incomplete information. The information may be lacking on the CEE side, when it is about the politics of different policy issues in the European Union. However, it may also be unknowable information that all actors lack because of uncertainty about issues that may come up unexpectedly on the political agenda after annual priorities have been set.

Uncertainty can also emerge because the European Union does not rank clearly the different items on its political agenda; after all, the Union can make multiple demands, and is not forced to make trade-offs between the different tasks it sets for the applicants. There can be uncertainty about which will be veto issues for membership and which negotiable. Uncertainty about prioritization also remains where an applicant lacks the administrative capacity to fulfil all the demands made in its Accession Partnership, and so is forced to choose between them. For the countries furthest from membership (Bulgaria and Romania), this is a particular problem because of the severe limitations on their financial and human resources.

3. *Timing* has been identified as a dynamic factor in Europeanization by Goetz (2000), who borrows the categories of time, timing, and tempo from Schmitter and Santiso (1998). However, the applicants face several problems of uncertainty concerned with timing. First, there is the timing of costs and benefits. The ultimate reward of accession is far removed from the moment at which adaptation costs are incurred, so conditionality is a blunt instrument when it comes to persuading countries to change particular practices. There are, of course, intermediate rewards, such as aid and trade liberalization. But in the end, accession is tied to overall readiness, and membership benefits are not disaggregated to reward partial readiness. Since the accession reward comes in one big step—and at the end of a very long and highly politicized

process—CEE policy-makers may believe there is time to make up deficiencies closer to the accession date. It is thus difficult to use EU membership conditionality as a precision tool to sculpt institutions and policies during the accession process; rather, it is a mallet that can be used only at certain points in the process to enforce a few conditions at a time.

There are also timing issues involved in negotiations. All of the *acquis* has to be implemented eventually. But which areas absolutely have to be fully in place prior to accession and which can be left until afterwards? The CEE countries still have to calculate where concessions on transitional periods are likely to be made, in order to decide where to invest in full compliance and where to try for a transitional period and invest only in partial implementation. Incomplete information causes uncertainty about the allocation of resources across time. The EU's position on timing will change according to the politics of enlargement in the European Union. For example, the debate about social and environmental 'dumping' was very lively in the mid-1990s and caused the European Union to emphasize implementation of process standards in the Europe Agreements and Single Market White Paper (Sedelmeier 1994). But later this pressure eased as the cost implications became clearer, and the candidates faced little opposition to their requests for transitional periods in environmental policy once they had attached financing plans to them in July 2001 (see Grabbe 2001*b*).

How does timing affect implementation and the impact of Europeanization? Do CEE policy-makers have more or less scope for using time, timing, and tempo than member states? They use sequencing and stalling, both in the domestic context and with the European Union. But the timetable for negotiations and the cycle of priority-setting and annual monitoring reports reduce the scope for stalling, because the timing is defined to within a year or even a few months. Moreover, there is much greater pressure on CEE to adapt more quickly than member-states because of the incentive to gain rapid accession. Indeed, the European Union has more scope to use tempo as a trade-off to gain concessions in negotiations than CEE, because the candidates are much more keen to get into the European Union quickly than the member states are to accept them.

4. The applicants face uncertainty about *whom to satisfy*. Who is the veto-player for a given policy area? In the case of Single Market regulation, it is likely to be the Commission, which is most zealous in demanding full compliance because of its role as guardian of the treaties and regulator of the internal market. However, in justice and home affairs, the Council has tended to predominate both in establishing the *acquis* and in judging compliance with it. Different policy areas attract differing levels of concern from the member states, so only some of them may be potential veto-players on JHA compliance; for example, Germany and Austria might veto an applicant for

accession because its borders were not seen as sufficiently secure, whereas Ireland or Portugal is unlikely to do so. For the candidate countries, there is an immediate calculation to make about whom to satisfy in a given policy area in a given year, and there is also longer-term uncertainty about who might emerge as a veto-player over another, possibly unexpected issue, later in the accession process. For example, in 1997 it would have been hard to predict that the United Kingdom would become so adamant about treatment of the Roma minority following an influx of asylum-seekers in 1998. Likewise, most Czech policy-makers did not expect Austria to threaten to block their country's accession owing to the opening of the Temelin nuclear power station in Autumn 2001.

In addition to the issue of veto-points in negotiations, the actor constellations involved in the accession preparations are very complex. Different parts of the European Union—both its institutions and member states—give different advice and signals, and different actors even in the same institution do as well (e.g. individual Directorate-Generals within the European Commission stress different tasks). Twinning has added to the complexity of actor constellations: at any one time, CEE policy-makers may be dealing with pre-accession advisors from national administrations, Commission officials, national experts from the Council, and civil servants and politicians from individual member states, plus a range of joint parliamentary committees and representatives from the European Parliament and ECOSOC. It is hardly surprising that they are often unsure exactly what the EU requirements are.

5. The final dimension is uncertainty about *standards and thresholds*. What will count as meeting the conditions and complying with the various EU demands? EU conditionality is not based on quantitative targets like those established by the international financial institutions such as the International Monetary Fund and World Bank. The conditions are much less transparent because the judgment about whether they have been met is made by the same actor who set them—the European Union—but there are no published measurement techniques or indicators. The requirements are complex, and they are often not amenable to quantitative targets that show explicitly the extent to which they have been fulfilled. The European Union does not have clear benchmarks to show progress, although it is now working towards producing them in some areas. The Commission's 1997 Opinions and annual Regular Reports use a variety of sources for their analyses, but these are not published, and the precise criteria used are never specified. Moreover, member states and previous applicants have been allowed a wide margin of tolerance in how fast and how thoroughly they have implemented the *acquis*—witness their differing performances in complying with single market regulation in the annual 'Single Market Scorecard' produced by the Commission. How much margin will be allowed to each applicant in assessing compliance?

The answer depends on which candidate, which policy area, and by whom the decision is made.

Overall, Europeanization effects will depend not only on the individual uncertainties in a given policy area, but also on the interaction between these different dimensions of uncertainty. Where uncertainty about the agenda, timing, and standards are high but the political salience is also high (as in the case of justice and home affairs), the European Union may have a large impact despite its uncertain agenda because CEE policy-makers endeavour to meet whatever criteria are hinted at. Where uncertainty about the agenda, timing, and standards are high but political salience is relatively low (as in the case of social policy), the European Union is likely to have a small impact because the incentives to second-guess EU requirements are low and CEE policy-makers can use the uncertainty to implement the *acquis* less strictly.

The explanatory value of uncertainty thus depends on the priority that the European Union attaches to the policy in question, and the degree of domestic resistance to it in CEE. Its explanatory value also depends on the type of policy under consideration. In framing integration, uncertainty about standards and thresholds is much higher because so many of the concrete measures are a matter of national discretion. Moreover, degrees of uncertainty also change across time; for example, the European Union did not establish a clear *acquis* in the area of justice and home affairs until the very end of the 1990s, so uncertainty diminished suddenly between 1997 and 2000.

Conclusions

This chapter has set out a research agenda for studying the Europeanization of central and eastern Europe. The scope of potential Europeanization in CEE is very wide, owing to the breadth of the accession conditions. Europeanization can penetrate deeply into policy making in the region, given the fundamental transformations taking place in post-communist polities and the importance of EU models in CEE political discourse. However, the European Union does not use its rule-setting powers to their full potential. It is often sporadic in its attention to particular policy areas, and inconsistent in its communications with the candidate countries. In several major policy areas—minority protection, social policy, macroeconomic policies—the Union has not used its routes of influence consistently to enforce a particular policy agenda.

How does such a failure of influence occur? It happens largely through the uncertainty built into the accession conditions, which reduces their potential use as a structure of incentives to encourage institutional and policy change in the applicant states. However, the degree and kind of uncertainty depends on the policy area. The various dimensions of uncertainty outlined in this chapter can thus help to explain the variance of EU influence across different parts of public policy making in CEE.

Europeanization is an area of enquiry as much as a concept. It is a tool to make sense of phenomena in CEE which involve domestic policy processes in a context of international relations. The complexity of the EU's demands for the eastern applicants, and the multifaceted role that the European Union plays in CEE, necessitate deep investigation both of the EU's agenda and of domestic policy processes. Study of Europeanization thus requires greater attention to the details of EU policies than has been paid by comparativist scholars primarily looking at the international relations aspects of EU–CEE relations, such as classifying transition paths. It is also requires more than a simple 'balance of power' research design. Using Europeanization as an analytical framework enables us to investigate processes at both international and domestic levels, and without a simplification of these levels into bargaining games.

Although it is appropriate to use the concept of Europeanization to study the effects of the European Union on the applicant countries, future research needs to go further than just looking for the same effects in CEE as have been observed in the European Union. The key question that remains open is the extent of change. How far has the European Union changed domestic political structures and public policy in CEE? What conditions determine its success in effecting changes in institutions and public policies in CEE? Empirical and theoretical work on the European Union provides a starting point, but the approach now needs greater refinement to capture the particularities of the Europeanization process in a context as different as post-communism. In particular, the case of the applicant countries shows the need for bottom-up research design because both European Union and CEE policy-makers have an incentive to exaggerate the extent of EU influence. Individual policy choices are affected by multiple variables, as this chapter has tried to show, including conflicting demands from different parts of the European Union. The often enthusiastic rhetoric from both candidates and the European Union about the influence of the accession process obscures a complex interaction between the processes of Europeanization, accession, and post-communist transformation.

REFERENCES

Amato, Giuliano (1996). 'The Impact of Europe on National Policies: Italian Anti-Trust Policy', in Yves Mény, Pierre Muller, and Jean-Louis Quermonne (eds), *Adjusting to Europe: The Impact of the European Union on National Institutions and Policies* (London: Routledge), 157–74.

Batt, Judy and Wolczuk, Kataryna (1999). 'The Political Context: Building New States', in Paul Hare, Judy Batt, and Saul Estrin (eds), *Reconstituting the Market: The Political Economy of Microeconomic Transformation* (Amsterdam: Harwood), 33–48.

Begg, Iain and Peterson, John (1999). 'Editorial Statement', *Journal of Common Market Studies* 37: 1–12.

Brusis, Martin, ed. (1998). *Central and Eastern Europe on the Way into the European Union: Welfare State Reforms in the Czech Republic, Hungary, Poland and Slovakia* (München: Centrum für Angewandte Politikforschung).

Caporaso, James (1996). 'The European Union and forms of State: Westphalian, Regulatory or Post-modern?', *Journal of Common Market Studies* 34: 29–52.

Cowles, Maria Green, Caporaso, James A., and Risse, Thomas (eds) (2001). *Transforming Europe: Europeanization and Domestic Change* (Ithaca, NY: Cornell University Press).

Crouch, Colin and Streeck, Wolfgang (eds) (1997). *Political Economy of Modern Capitalism: Mapping Convergence and Diversity* (London: Sage).

Falkner, Gerda (1998). *EU Social Policy in the 1990s: Towards a Corporatist Policy Community* (London: Routledge).

Featherstone, Kevin (1998). ' "Europeanization" and the Centre Periphery: The Case of Greece in the 1990s', *South European Society & Politics* 3: 23–39.

Fierke, Karin and Wiener, Antje (1999). 'Constructing Institutional Interests: EU and NATO Enlargement', *Journal of European Public Policy* 6(5): 721–42.

Fink-Hafner, Danica (1998). 'Organized Interests in the Policy-making Process in Slovenia', *Journal of European Public Policy* 5(2): 285–302.

Fowler, Brigid (2001). 'Debating Sub-State Reform on Hungary's "Road to Europe" ', ESRC 'One Europe or Several'? Programme Working Paper 21/01 (Sussex: Sussex European Institute).

Francioni, Francesco (ed.) (1992). *Italy and EC Membership Evaluated* (London: Pinter).

Goetz, Klaus (2000). 'Europeanising the National Executive? Western and Eastern Style', Paper prepared for the UACES 30th annual conference, Budapest, 6–8 April.

——and Wollmann, Hellmut (2001). 'Governmentalising Central Executives in Post-communist Europe: A Four-country Comparison', *Journal of European Public Policy* 8(4): 864–87.

Grabbe, Heather (1999). *A Partnership for Accession? The Implications of EU Conditionality for the Central and East European Applicants*, EUI Working Paper RSC No. 99/12, San Domenico di Fiesole (FI): European University Institute.

——(2001a) 'How Does Europeanisation Affect CEE Governance? Conditionality, Diffusion and Diversity', *Journal of European Public Policy* 8(4): 1013–31.

——(2001b). *Profiting from EU Enlargement* (London: Centre for European Reform).

——(2002). 'Stabilizing the East While Keeping Out the Easterners: Internal and External Security Logics in Conflict' in Sandra Lavenex and Emek Uçarer (eds), *Externalities of Integration: The Wider Impact of Europe's Immigration and Asylum Policies* (Lanham, MD: Lexington Books), 91–104.

Hare, Paul, Batt, Judy, and Estrin, Saul (eds) (1999). *Reconstituting the Market: The Political Economy of Microeconomic Transformation* (Amsterdam: Harwood).

Héritier, Adrienne (1996). 'The Accommodation of Diversity in European Policy-making and its Outcomes: Regulatory Policy as a Patchwork', *Journal of European Public Policy* 3(2): 149–67.

——and Knill, Christoph (2000). 'Differential Responses to European Policies: A Comparison', Max Planck Projektgruppe Recht der Gemeinschaftsgüter, preprint, Bonn.

——Kerwer, Dieter, Lehmkuhl, Dirk, and Teutsch, Michael (2001). *Differential Europe—New Opportunities and Restrictions for Policy-making in Member States* (Lanham, MD: Rowman and Littlefield).

Hix, Simon (1998). 'The Study of the European Union II: The "new governance" Agenda and its Rival', *Journal of European Public Policy* 5(1): 38–65.

Hughes, James, Sasse, Gwendolyn, and Gordon, Claire (2001). 'Enlargement and Regionalization: The Europeanization of local and Regional Governance in CEE States', in Helen Wallace (eds), *Interlocking Dimensions of European Integration* (Basingstoke: Palgrave).

Knill, Christoph and Lehmkuhl, Dirk (1999). 'How Europe Matters: Different Mechanisms of Europeanisation', *European Integration Online Papers* 3, http://eiop.or.at/eiop/texte/1999-07a.htm.

Knorr, Klaus (1977). 'International Economic Leverage and its Uses', in Klaus Knorr and Frank Trager (eds), *Economic Issues and National Security* (Lawrence: University Press of Kansas), 102.

Kohler-Koch, Beate and Eising, Rainer (eds) (1999). *The Transformation of Governance in the European Union* (London: Routledge).

Kopecký, Petr and Mudde, Cas (2000). 'What has Eastern Europe Taught Us about the Democratisation Literature (and vice versa)?', *European Journal of Political Research* 37: 517–39.

Ladrech, Robert (1994). 'Europeanization of Domestic Politics and Institutions: The Case of France', *Journal of Common Market Studies* 32: 69–88.

Lijphart, Arend and Crawford, Beverly (1995). 'Explaining Political and Economic Change in Post-Communist Eastern Europe: Old Legacies, New Institutions, Hegemonic Norms and International Pressure', *Comparative Political Studies* 28: 171–99.

Linz, Juan J. and Stepan, Alfred (1996). *Problems of Democratic Transition and Consolidation: Southern Europe, South America and Post-Communist Europe* (Baltimore and London: The Johns Hopkins University Press).

McGowan, Francis and Wallace, Helen (1996). 'Towards a European Regulatory State', *Journal of European Public Policy* 3(4): 560–76.

Manjone, Giandomenico (1996). *Regulating Europe* (London: Routledge).

Offe, Claus (1991). 'Capitalism by Democratic Design? Democratic Theory Facing the Triple Transition in East Central Europe', *Social Research* 58: 865–92.

Pridham, Geoffrey, Herring, Eric, and Sanford, George, eds. (1997). *Building Democracy? The International Dimension of Democratisation in Eastern Europe* (London: Cassell).

Radaelli, Claudio (1997). 'How does Europeanization Produce Policy Change? Corporate Tax Policy in Italy and the UK', *Comparative Political Studies* 30: 553–75.

——(2000). 'Policy Transfer in the European Union: Institutional Isomorphism as a Source of Legitimacy', *Governance* 13: 25–43.

——(2001). 'Do the Pieces fall into place? Europeanisation, Enlargement, Transatlantic Relations and the Puzzles of Direct Tax Policy Coordination', Paper delivered to the Robert Schuman Centre Forum, European University Institute, 25 October.

Rhodes, Martin and van Apeldoorn, Bastiaan (1998). 'Capitalism Unbound? The Transformation of European Corporate Governance', *Journal of European Public Policy* 5(3): 406–27.

Sartori, Giovanni (1991). 'Comparing and miscomparing', *Journal of Theoretical Politics* 3: 243–57.

Schimmelfennig, Frank (1998). 'NATO, the EU, and Central and Eastern Europe: Theoretical Perspectives and Empirical Findings on Eastern Enlargement', Paper presented at the 3rd Pan-European International Relations/ISA Conference, Vienna.

——(2001). 'The Community Trap: Liberal Norms, Rhetorical Action, and the Eastern Enlargement of the European Union', *International Organisation* 55(1).

Schmitter, P. and Santiso, J. (1998). 'Three Temporal Dimensions to the Consolidation of Democracy', *International Political Science Review* 19: 69–92.

Sedelmeier, Ulrich (1994). *The European Union's Association Policy towards Central and Eastern Europe: Political and Economic Rationales in Conflict*, SEI Working Paper No. 7, Brighton: Sussex European Institute.

——(2001). 'Sectoral Dynamics of the EU's Accession Requirements: the Role of Policy Paradigms', Paper for the ECSA 7th Biennial International Conference; Madison, Wisconsin; 31 May–2 June 2001.

Stone Sweet, Alec and Sandholtz, Wayne (1997). 'European Integration and Supranational Governance', *Journal of European Public Policy* 4(3): 297–317.

Szczerbiak, Aleks (2001). 'Europe as a Re-aligning Issue in Polish Politics? Evidence from the October 2000 Presidential Election', Paper prepared for the PSA Annual Conference, University of Manchester, 10–12 April.

Taggart, Paul and Szczerbiak, Aleks (2001). *Parties, Positions and Europe: Euroscepticism in the EU Candidate States of Central and Eastern Europe*, SEI Working Paper No 46, Brighton: University of Sussex.

VI

Conclusions

14

A Conversant Research Agenda

KEVIN FEATHERSTONE AND CLAUDIO M. RADAELLI

Europeanization: Fad, Political Concern, or New Research Agenda?

Many readers will have started this book with a basic question: is 'Europeanization' a passing fad, a political concern, or a new research agenda? As shown by Kevin Featherstone in Chapter 1, Europeanization as an explicit focus of study has a history stretching over two decades. What is striking, however, is the acceleration of research in this area and the increasing concern to define Europeanization. Although academics may well have a propensity to herd and follow each other, Europeanization is unlikely to be a passing fad as it relates to major developments affecting states, societies, and the European Union institutions. It connects different levels of analysis and types of actors, thereby posing complex ontological issues, and it displays asymmetries across institutional settings and policy processes. The relevance of Europeanization is significant in each of these respects.

Europeanization is also important, of course, in contemporary political debates: much attention is focused on how far the European Union has gone in constraining domestic political and policy choices and how far it should be allowed to go. The Convention on the future constitution of the European Union is a forum for such discussion. The implications of major projects like the 'euro' and enlargement loom large over public debate, as do fears over the future of the so-called European social model and the prospects for migration policy. Concerns are also evident in some quarters over the supposed liberal zeal of the European Court of Justice and the competition directorate of the Commission. In short, European issues are penetrating domestic political debates across the continent like never before. In this respect, academic interest in Europeanization reflects contemporary political concerns. But the breadth of the existing literature clearly indicates that 'Europeanization' is more than the political preoccupations arising out of the progressive penetration of member states by EU policy (see also Olsen 2002; Bulmer and Radaelli 2003).

We are grateful to Beate Kohler-Koch for having stimulated our interest in this 'big question' during Claudio Radaelli's short visit to the Mannheimer Zentrum für Europäische Sozialforschung in June 2002.

Academically, there are also important differences between the 'old' approach to Europeanization (essentially focused on how member states organize themselves to play European politics and how they implement European Union policies) and the 'new', more theory-oriented approach. In this volume, we have dedicated no less than three chapters to the topic of 'theorizing Europeanization'. This reflects a vibrant process of theory-building and the variety of theoretical suggestions on which researchers draw. In the 'old' studies on Europeanization, it was extremely difficult to find models, mechanisms, and explicit explanations of when and how the European Union 'makes a difference' in domestic polities, politics, and public policies.

The contributions of this volume attest to Europeanization as a possible new research agenda. Markus Haverland, at the end of his chapter on environmental policy, goes so far as to suggest some intellectual trajectories 'towards a new research agenda' (see section 'Towards a New Research Agenda' of Chapter 9). Overall, the contributions presented in this volume show that there is an explicit theoretical orientation, a discussion of concepts and their measurement, a set of scientific questions, and models to control the main hypotheses. They also show that this possible new research agenda is not confined to conventional positivism. Quite the opposite, various contributions to this volume incorporated an interest in discourse, the cognitive dimension of politics, the social construction of reality, and the mutual constitution of structure and agency. As such, Europeanization is open to different epistemologies: yet another indicator of the vitality of this area of research.

However, one should not underestimate the risks that this emerging research agenda may encounter. The main risk is academic isolation. One of the main problems encountered by European integration theory has been the evolution of concepts and frameworks cut off from mainstream international relations, international political economy, and comparative politics. With notable exceptions, the proliferation of ad hoc theorizing has precluded more intense and fruitful collaboration between European integration theorists and other political scientists. The last thing we want to do is to recreate the preconditions for intellectual isolation by segregating Europeanization into an ad hoc vocabulary and models that do not travel outside the territory of a small community. Europeanization would then become a community of discourse, but with minimal cross-fertilization with the rest of political science. One indicator of isolation being overcome in the future will be the number of articles on Europeanization appearing in journals that do not specialize on the European Union.

To avoid intellectual segregation, Europeanization—we would submit—is best seen as representing a pluralist research agenda, dependent on the theoretical approaches developed across different disciplines: comparative politics, political economy, policy analysis, and international relations. To complete the loop, Europeanization research should not only be able to draw on these disciplines, but also to provide theoretical feedback. This can be done, at a minimum, by refining models, by showing how conventional political science explanations do not work well (and therefore need adaptation in the light of findings produced by research on Europeanization), and by integrating theoretical frameworks. Europeanization will then become a conversant research agenda when it accomplishes the double task of drawing creatively on existing disciplines and of providing theoretical knowledge to the disciplines themselves.

Europeanization is not so much a theory as a distinct set of processes in need of explanation. These processes establish foci for research. The latter require theoretical approaches developed elsewhere to be adapted in order to offer suitable explanatory frames. As Claudio Radaelli has argued earlier in this volume, Europeanization involves processes of construction, diffusion, and institutionalization of formal and informal rules, procedures, policy paradigms, styles, and shared beliefs, and norms which are incorporated in the logic of domestic discourse, identities, structures, and policies. We agree these processes may originate directly at the EU level or may be an indirect, cross-national consequence of EU membership or the search for membership. Couched in these terms, the dependence of Europeanization research on theoretical approaches developed elsewhere is already apparent.

The foci of Europeanization research refer to major issues in the social sciences. In political science, they beg a range of questions concerned with the autonomy and adaptation of institutional settings; the convergence and fragmentation of policies, processes, and discourse; the restructuring of power and the strength of actors as veto-points; and the emergence of cross-national networks and new forms of governance. These questions relate to fundamental themes of independence, authority, stability, participation, legitimacy, and identity: themes that have underpinned the study of politics since Aristotle.

Europeanization can suffer from both unwarranted expectations—it is *not* a new grand theory to replace those that have been discarded—and from overly narrow definitions. Its advocates are left to argue that it covers *more than* convergence, penetration, loss of sovereignty, or a new form of governance. It is not captured by, nor does it fully constitute, any single explanatory term. Its eclecticism stems from it not being a single theory, but rather a distinct set of research foci. This is not to lessen its significance, only to emphasize its breadth and complexity.

The contributors to this volume have provided fulsome examples of these features, whilst indicating the relevance of concepts and approaches developed in other areas of political science. Many have highlighted the fact that concepts originally designed for domestic comparative politics, policy analysis, and organization theory travel well when applied to the study of Europeanization. An example is provided by Heather Grabbe working on power and uncertainty by drawing *inter alia* on the literature on policy transfer. Her interest in both traditional 'hard' transfer and the more subtle 'soft' transfer of policy paradigms, 'frames of reference', and 'ways of doing things'—not to mention the whole 'big' topic of uncertainty itself—reverberates the major themes of sociological institutionalism and social constructivism. The latter is also found in the chapter by Ulrika Mörth, who additionally blends the 'received view' of social constructivism in political science with the insights of innovative organizational scholars like Barbara Czarniawska. Marco Giuliani pursues the useful task of drawing upon comparative politics to tackle the daunting question of measuring (in an explicitly comparative framework) the pressure of the European Union on member states. Jurgen Grote and Achim Lang 'import' from new organizational sociology concepts and methodologies; these two authors make their 'imports' travel quite comfortably in the 'Europeanization research mode', and conclude with some propositions that cast doubts on bold claims about the effects of positive integration, the power of the consultation practice of the European Commission, and the EU-level system of organized collective action. In so doing, they indicate that by looking outside the conventional perimeter of EU integration literature, one can gain deeper insights on the limits of Europeanization.

On balance, a recurrent proposition in the chapters of this volume is that particular Europeanization foci require tools developed elsewhere: whether this is the dynamics of administrative and political change (Hussein Kassim and Mike Goldsmith), the contradiction and paradoxes of EU networking on domestic elites (Daniel Wincott), the surprising effects generated by institutional veto points (Markus Haverland), the differential effects of the EU policy process on the business community (David Coen and Charlie Dannreuther), or the interplay between courts, competition policy, and Council decisions in 'engineered Europeanization' (Alison Harcourt). Thomas Risse and Tanja Börzel, and also Markus Haverland, try to complete the intellectual circle from mainstream disciplines to Europeanization and then back to the disciplines. They draw on comparative politics and institutional theory in their models of Europeanization. But they also provide thought-provoking questions for those who are working on institutions and political change, thus producing a feedback effect from Europeanization to other areas of scientific inquiry.

The Contours of Europeanization

What are the substantive results of the earlier chapters in terms of mapping out the processes of Europeanization? There are six questions to be asked of Europeanization studies in this context:

- *Who* promotes Europeanization? Which actor(s) are the carriers of Europeanization?

- *Why*? How are interests, identities, and/or beliefs defined in a manner that leads to action?
- *How*? Which processes or venues, strategies or tactics are effective in promoting Europeanization?
- *When*? Which conditions favour Europeanization and which hinder it?
- *What* is the effect(s) of Europeanization? and
- *Where* are the effects evident?

The studies presented in this volume offer evidence relevant to each of these basic questions. The *types of actor* involved in the process of Europeanization can be many and varied:

- the institutions as collective actors, or individual actors within them (see e.g. Harcourt's and Mörth's chapters)
- national government administrations as collective actors, or individual actors within them (see Kassim, Mörth)
- subnational, regional, and local authorities (see Goldsmith)
- interest associations (see Grote and Lang) or individual firms (see Coen and Dannreuther).

How the *interests, identities, and beliefs* of actors are defined in a manner consistent with action to promote Europeanization requires a conceptual framework along the lines suggested by Börzel and Risse or, for policy-relevant questions, by Radaelli. Such a framework provides a basic ontology, whilst suggesting that synthesis is necessary for completeness: that is, the selected empirical focus determines the conceptual lens, but the focus should be seen as part of a larger whole. The chapters in this volume choose different foci:

- the power and structure of veto-players (see Börzel and Risse, Giuliani, Haverland)
- the shift in identities and/or beliefs (see Coen and Dannreuther, Grote and Lang)
- processes of learning and isomorphism (Radaelli, Mörth, Grabbe).

How actors activate and interpret processes and venues, strategies and tactics, must also be seen in relation to a particular ontology. The chapters by Featherstone, Börzel and Risse, and Mörth argue for structures and agency to be seen as being mutually constitutive. Other chapters give less explicit attention to this dimension. The case study chapters reveal, however, a rich tapestry of actor responses to settings and processes in different locations: national (Kassim, Haverland, and Mörth); subnational (Goldsmith); and EU level (Coen and Danreuther; Harcourt; Mörth). By contrast, more research that is empirical is needed on the choices made by actors with respect to strategies and tactics (see Dyson and Featherstone 1999: 33–47). The rational choice variant of new institutionalism gives a sharp focus to actor interests (exogenously defined) and the resultant strategies. Yet, few studies give much empirical attention to *how* strategies became effective, in the sense of examining the roles played by actors and the tactics they deployed. A leap in analysis is made: strategies are linked to outcomes, without the means receiving much close attention.

By contrast, the conditions *when* Europeanization occurs are being amply explored. Börzel and Risse stress the mediating factors that affect the outcomes of Europeanization pressure, and these vary according to whether the focus is on actor interests (multiple veto-points; formal institutions) or ideas and beliefs (norm entrepreneurs, political culture). Several case studies follow their lead. Haverland makes the point that governments may be willing to implement adaptational shifts, but be held back by domestic veto-points. Grote and Lang delineate a complex transformation process in which the European Union is only one of the factors at work. Coen and Dannreuther stress the importance of actor reputation and credibility in seeking policy influence. Grabbe, in her study of the applicant states of central Europe, gives prime emphasis to the effects of uncertainty—about timing, agency, and standards—on the extent and significance of Europeanization at the domestic level.

Radaelli focuses on the level of the policy process and—drawing on the insights of recent research projects such as Héritier *et al.* (2001)—seeks to qualify the reliance on 'goodness of fit' assumptions drawn from new institutionalism. His purpose is to take account of situations where no EU model exists, but that pressure emanates from softer mechanisms or other types such as regulatory competition. Mörth goes further and highlights the role of individual actors in interpreting, translating, and editing pressures that construct new rules of the game. Each of these studies provide sophisticated refinements of the conditions under which Europeanization shifts occur.

Finally, the *what* and *where* of the effects of Europeanization are also being extensively explored. Several themes emerge from the studies in this volume. Above all, Europeanization is about diversity and asymmetry: one consistent result throughout the chapters is that Europeanization is refracted, translated, and edited in various guises by domestic political systems. There may be instances of clustered convergence, and possibly one case of convergence documented in this volume (Harcourt's chapter), but diversity is the dominant theme. Domestic institutions and discourses are extremely important. Europeanization is not producing a coherent, homogeneous, and harmonized Europe—a result that stands at odds with some political preoccupations about the 'exaggerated power' of European institutions. Diversity is inbuilt in Europeanization, in part because there are still very diverse ideas about models of capitalism in Europe (Hall and Soskice 2001). The role of the state in the economy, the scope of the welfare state, and the functions of social policy and education diverge across the member states for historical reasons. Europeanization has not produced convergence on these fundamental issues.

As explained by Wincott, political leaders are experimenting with fuzzy discourses on the European social model, a key component of any possible European model of capitalism. They are also experimenting with new political technologies, such as the open method of coordination (OMC). The OMC acknowledges the presence of different national preferences and political values. Diversity is built into the OMC, but the result should be a spread of innovation and best practice. One problem with the OMC is that the EU level of discussion and benchmarking is not as ordered, coherent, and consistent as some Europeanization claims assume or assert (see Wincott's chapter). This is yet another nail in the coffin of the top-down approach to Europeanization (as described in Radaelli's chapter): an approach that assumes clear choices made in 'Brussels' and transferred to the national level in a vertical chain of command fashion.

Viewed through the horizontal lenses of the OMC, Europeanization provides insights on the 'nature of Europe' based on the challenging task of producing policy innovation without having clarified some fundamental divergence on what the European model of capitalism should be. It is a task in which competitive pressure (which originates diversity and original solutions) and spread of best practice (which produces homogenization and repetitive solutions) paradoxically live together. Uncertainty and fuzzy discourses make this aspect of Europeanization even more elusive. Under these conditions, collective learning can become a political exercise and conflict can resurface easily. This suggests that more research should be done on the political aspects of learning. The slogan is therefore 'politicizing learning and learning politically'.

Uncertainty is also crucial for the analysis of Europeanization beyond the European Union. In her chapter on enlargement, Grabbe develops refreshing ideas on the modalities of Europeanization. Contrary to prima facie evidence for a 'story' of enlargement based exclusively on the asymmetry of power, conditionality, and strong agendas coming from EU institutions, Grabbe uncovers a 'different story' of uncertainty. Agendas are not clearly set by EU institutions. The ambition of the European Union to act as a standard setter in terms of broad 'models of capitalism' is frustrated by the fact that, as mentioned above, there is fundamental conflict over the coordinates of European capitalism. Additionally, Central European elites can import selectively. Uncertainty about the key actors that must be satisfied and lack of clarity on what counts as 'meeting the EU standards' make Europeanization very different from a linear process of policy transfer.

The road to transfer is even more uncertain and bumpy when one considers that Central European elites have to struggle with the immense task of adopting the *acquis communautaire* with limited time resources in the shadow of domestic instability (electoral and, in some cases, even institutional instability). Consequently, the argument that elites can import strategically from the European Union (in terms of what is more politically convenient at home) should be counterbalanced by the argument that radical uncertainty prioritizes political contingency over strategy.

As mentioned above, a major theme of this volume is that Europeanization has a differential or asymmetrical impact. This can be seen not only at the level of the domestic political system, but also at the level of the impact on society and subnational actors. The contributors looking at business organizations and corporate behaviour have shown how important this point is: Europeanization is neither experienced in the same way by states or societies, nor even by a given set of interests. Goldsmith has considered how the effects of the single European market, globalization, and other processes of deregulation have posed a major set of challenges, opportunities, and constraints for subnational authorities, and how the responses of the latter have differed. Similarly, Kassim highlights the limited scope for generalizations about the convergence of national government administrative systems in the context of EU membership: domestic institutional conditions determine responses. Future research might well follow his lead and open up the issue of the impact of Europeanization on the hard (e.g. procedures) and soft (e.g. administrative culture and values) machinery of government (see Jordan 2002 forthcoming for an attempt in this direction).

As Featherstone discussed, the effects of Europeanization on domestic societies can be further distinguished between constructivist perspectives on identity formation (ranging from a shift in social habits to new perspectives on governance) and debates over reform linked to 'modernization'. The latter is particularly salient in the societies of southern and central Europe where largely liberal elites have historically sought to emulate the 'progress' of western Europe. Domestic cleavages have been defined and intensified on this basis. Thus, domestic social perspectives on Europeanization may well differ between 'centre' and 'peripheral' EU states (see Featherstone and Kazamias 2001). Concluding on this point, the 'what' and 'where' of Europeanization overwhelmingly displays the attributes of diversity and asymmetry. Indeed, 'Europeanization' would have little distinct meaning without both attributes being at the core of any conceptual definition.

Developing a Conversant Research Agenda

Looking beyond this volume, how can Europeanization develop as a pluralist and conversant research agenda? We outline four areas where this seems feasible and fruitful, these cover: *comparative politics, international political economy, theoretical policy analysis*, and *systemic change*. The classic problem of comparative politics is the explanation of stable democratic political equilibrium in terms of the relations between elites, political parties, and public opinion. From this perspective, Europeanization raises the important question of how political equilibrium is altered by the mechanisms triggered by EU integration. In a sense, this is a bottom-up view of Europeanization. One interesting result of this approach is that an increasing number of specialists in (previously domestic) comparative politics are becoming interested in the European Union. This is evidence that a conversant research agenda increases the vitality of this area of studies and attracts scholars.

A second perspective is that of change in interdependent political systems. As such, Europeanization can usefully join forces with international political economy and produce a better understanding of the political consequences of economic interdependence. These consequences, in turn, can be examined with the tools of comparative politics, institutional analysis, and discourse theory (see e.g. Hay and Rosamond 2002; Schmidt 2002). By contributing to the wider debate on globalization, Europeanization can provide useful tests about the strength and autonomy of the state. Whereas the large majority of international political economy research looks at the autonomy of governments under conditions of economic interdependence (Garrett 1998; Swank 2002), Europeanization—by focusing on interdependence in the European Union—enters the additional variable of legal constraints.

A third perspective originates in theoretical policy analysis. Some of the most refreshing work on EU public policy has indeed been produced by authors who, instead of reinventing the wheel, have drawn heavily on concepts and models developed for the analysis of agenda setting, policy change, and implementation. As Coen and Dannreuther remind us at the beginning of their chapter, frameworks originally developed for the analysis of domestic public policy have performed quite well in the EU context. Richardson's successful textbook on the European Union (2001) is the manifesto of those who believe in this programme. The next step for policy analysts working on Europeanization is to feed back into the theoretical debate on policy analysis—an important issue for scholars based in Europe, considering that the European Consortium for Political Research has established a standing group on theoretical perspectives in policy analysis.[1] We have not seen much in terms of Europeanists producing theoretical knowledge for policy analysis. Yet we believe that the amount of work done in several EU policy areas should encourage more adventurous steps in this direction.

Finally, we see the scope for a perspective less interested in 'domestic effects' and more interested in the European Union as a system processing change. In this last perspective, Europeanization is all about understanding how national systems pool sovereignty and adapt to each other. This is perhaps

---

[1] In June 2002 information on this standing group could be found at http://www.essex.ac.uk/ecpr/standinggroups/perspectives/index.htm.

the view which is closest to the classic questions posed by integration theory, with the qualification that the 'adaptation' part of the research agenda is where Europeanization has more potential. As one of the classic questions of European integration was 'what is the nature of Europe once states have decided to pool sovereignty?', one may well pose the question 'what are we learning about the changing nature of Europe as a result of Europeanization studies'? This is focus with the widest canvas: asking questions about the basic political characteristics of our age.

The search for a single grand theory of the European integration process was already futile well before the major changes of the late 1980s and 1990s: the single market, the collapse of communism, the onset of the single European currency, amongst others. It is these objective changes in the political landscape of Europe—indeed, even the definition of 'Europe'—that creates the demand for new analytical frames. Europeanization sharpens the focus on a set of complex and varied changes, the intensity and breadth of which had not been as evident in earlier decades. The sceptical reader looking for a new grand theory must be disappointed. Not only is it not a new theory, it depends upon the application (and often the adaptation) of existing theories. Europeanization points the way to a new set of processes and a pluralist research agenda. As such, it represents an important set of signals: the research task is to pursue these in order that we learn more about the complex reality of a Europe that is both converging and fragmenting. Our understanding of 'Europe' requires that we are sensitive to these fundamental traits.

REFERENCES

Bulmer, S. and Radaelli, C. M. (2003). 'The Europeanization of National Policy?', in S. Bulmer and C. Lequesne (eds), *Member States and the European Union* (Oxford: Oxford University Press).

Dyson, K. and Featherstone, K. (1999). *The Road to Maastricht. Negotiating Economic and Monetary Union* (Oxford: Oxford University Press).

Featherstone, K. and Kazamias, G. (eds) (2001). *Europeanization and the Southern Periphery* (London: Frank Cass Publishers).

Garrett, G. (1998). *Partisan Politics in the Global Economy* (Cambridge: Cambridge University Press).

Hall, P. A. and Soskice, D. (2001) (eds). *Varieties of Capitalism. The Institutional Foundations of Comparative Advantage* (Oxford: Oxford University Press).

Hay, C. and Rosamond, B. (2002). 'Globalisation, European Integration and the Discursive Construction of Economic Imperatives', *Journal of European Public Policy* 9(2): 147–67.

Héritier, A., Kerwer, D., Knill, C., Lehmkuhl, D., Teutsch, M., and Douillet, A. C. (2001). *Differential Europe: The European Union Impact on National Policymaking* (Lanham, Boulder, New York, and Oxford: Rowman and Littlefield).

Jordan, A. (2002). *The Europeanization of British Environmental Policy: A Departmental Perspective* (Basingstoke: Palgrave).

Olsen, J. P. (2002). 'The Many Faces of Europeanization', *Arena Working Papers*, 1/2 Oslo.

Richardson, J. (2001). *European Union. Power and Policy-Making* (London: Routledge) 2nd.

Schmidt, V. (2002). *The Futures of European Capitalism* (Oxford: Oxford University Press).

Swank, D. (2002). *Global Capital, Political Institutions, and Policy Change in Developed Welfare States* (Cambridge: Cambridge University Press).

INDEX

ABC/Generale des Eaux/Canal+/WHSmith
191–2
absorption 37, 38, 226, 235
Access to Information (AI) Directive 208,
210, 211
accession:
gatekeeping 312, 316–17
process 303–24
stages 316–17
veto-points 321–2
Accession Partnerships 308, 315, 320
accommodation 226
acquis communautaire 147, 304, 307–8, 313,
314, 319, 321, 323, 337
adaptation 7–9
and country size 146
empirical test 139–46
new institutionalism view 14
adaptation index 137–9, 153
and consensual democracy 145
and institutional variables 148–9
and VPS 143–5
adaptation pressure 58, 61, 212, 215
analysis 44–6
on CEE 304–9
level of 70, 209–11
adaptive systems, evolution of 232–3
Adenauer 286
adjustment, economic, institutional and
ideational 15
advocacy:
coalitions 49–50, 52, 259, 260
network 67–8
AERM 125
agenda-setting control, government 147–8, 149
Agh 11
agriculture 84, 116
Ahmed Saeed Flugreisen 196
aid 308, 312, 314
Allen 10
Altes, K. 184
Americanization 281, 292, 299
Andersen, S. S. 10–11
Article 296 166
Article 85 (3) 186

Association of European Municipalities and
Regions 124
Australia 218
Austria 64, 124, 146, 201, 322
coordination schemes 95–101
infringement 143
regions 118
automotive industry 113

BAE Systems 172
Balme, R. 128
Bangemann, M. 166, 265
bargaining games, multilevel 14
bargaining relations, restructuring of 9
Belgium 45, 113
coordination schemes 95–101
infringement 140
media 182, 185
regions 117, 123, 125
belief systems 49
Benz, A. 118
Blair, T. 118, 288, 297–8
Bogumil, J. 230
Börzel, T. A. 15–19, 29, 33–4, 37, 40, 44–5,
159, 211–13, 215–16, 334–6
Brittan, S. 293
Bulgaria 316
Bulmer, S. 34
Burch, M. 34
business interests:
ecological perspective 230–6
lobbying 261
preference level for 261–4
see also trade associations

CAP 125
capitalism:
democracy 293–4
regulated 292–3
Caporaso, J. 4, 13–15, 29, 59, 310
Castles, F. 283
central and eastern Europe (CEE) 303–24,
337–8
adaptive pressure on 304–9
aid 308, 312, 314

anticipatory adjustment 314
asymmetrical relationship with EU 318
differences amongst 317
membership conditions 307–8
new regulatory paradigms 306–7
open to EU influence 306
speed of adjustment 306
change 30
measuring 37
paradigmatic 38
resistance to 227–8
see also domestic change
change agents (norm entrepreneurs) 59, 67,
68, 73
Checkel, J. T. 67
Chemicals sector 237, 239, 240–1, 240, 242–4,
248–9, 251
Cini, M. 190
Clinton, B. 288
coal and steel 113
Cockfield 293
codecision 87
Coditel case 182
Coen, D. 19–20, 336, 339
coercion 41, 89
cognitive development 38–9
Coleman, W. D. 228
Commission v. Kingdom of the Netherlands
183–4
*Commission v. United Kingdom of Great
Britain and Northern Ireland* 185–6
Committee of the Regions 123, 124, 126
Common Foreign and Security Policy (CFSP)
10, 166
*Communication on the application of
State aid rules to public service
broadcasting* 188
compensation 235
competition, regulatory 41, 42
competition law 190
Competitiveness Advisory Group 265
concepts:
background 31
extension 31–2
intension 31–2
stretching 31–2
systematized 31
convergence 33, 226, 282
cognitive 16
differing outcomes 64
domestic policy 11–12
economic 73
EU and CEE 305

expectations of 88–9
limited 306
measurement of 71–3
OMC to encourage 43–4
partial 74
policy 72
substantive and clustered 51
cooperation 235–6
cooperative federalism 118
coordination:
importance of 84–5
open method (OMC) 43, 179, 281,
295–9, 337
coordination ambitions 92–7, 102, 105
coordination institutions 102–3
coordination systems
explaining 102–4
national 89–101
similarities 90–1
Council of Ministers 114
Council of Ministers for the Environment
237
country size, and adaptation 146
Cowles, M. G. 29, 37, 40, 44–5, 52, 59
craft business 263
Cram, L. 117, 289
Cyprus 18
Czarniawska, B. 334
Czech Republic 201

Dannreuther, C. 19–20, 336, 339
de Gaulle, C. 114
Debauve case 182
defence equipment 161, 164–72
defensive strategy 9
degreeism 32, 310–11
Delors, J. 115–16, 121, 124–5, 284, 287–9,
293, 295
democracy 316
capital 293–4
consensual 136–7, 140, 145, 153
majoritarian 136–7, 140, 148
democratic deficit 291
democratization 305
Denmark 297
adaptation 144
coordination schemes 92–101, 94–101
infringement 143
deparliamentarization 91
deregulation 112
Direct Effect 206
Directive on Air Pollution 208
divergence 88–9, 226, 282

domestic change:
  absorption 69–70
  accommodation 70
  degrees of 69–73
  logics of 68–9, 73–4
  and misfit 60–3, 69
  transformation 70
  see also logic of appropriateness; logic of
    consequentialism
domestic editing 163, 169–72
Domestic Encompassing Interest (DEI) 234
domestic mobilization 116, 210–12,
  213–14, 216
domestic policy convergence 11–12
domestic reform legitimacy 43
Döring, H. 147
Drinking Water Directive 208, 210, 211
Dyson, K. 9

EADS Aerospatiale/DASA/CASA 172
ecological development 231
economic development 122
economic environment 239–41, 245
Economic and Monetary Union 71
Economic and Social Committee 258, 263
economic systems, diverse 306
Eising, R. 8
Eliassen, K. A. 11
Elliniki Radiophonia Tilorassi-Anonimi Etairia
  v. *Dimotiki Etairia Pliroforissis and*
  Sotirios Kouvelas 185
employment 297
empowerment:
  differential 64
  regional 65
emulation 68
  see also mimicry
enlargement theories 310
Enterprise and Innovation 268
Environmental Impact Assessment (EIA)
  Directive 208, 210, 211
Environmental Management and Audit System
  (EMAS) Regulation 208, 210
environmental policy 203–19
  European 204–7
  historical development 205–6
  national adaptation to 207–15
  properties of 204
EPG 270
epistemic communities 66
Erhard 286
ESBA 270
ESME 263

Esping-Andersen, G. 283
Estonia 201
EU-ization 27, 159
EUROCITIES 124, 125
EUROGROUP 263
Europe Agreements 321
Europe of the Regions 115, 116, 124
Europe with the Regions 116
European Commission 115
  1997 Opinions 322
  and defence equipment 165–9
  DG III (Enterprise) 166
  DG 16 126
  DG IA (Foreign and security policy) 166
  directives 119
  and the first pillar 164–5
  implementation burden 127
  mass resignation 126
  and OMC 296
  policy implementation 121
  regulation of lobbying 265–6
  and SMEs 269–70
  structure 87
  and subnational government 121
  'The European Aerospace Industry' 165
European Communities v. *Kingdom of*
  Belgium 185
European Council of Ministers 85, 127
  and the second pillar 164–5
  structure 87
European Court of Justice 114, 180, 200–1
  impact on national media regulation 180–9
  and national courts 119
European Employment Initiative 297–8
European Employment Strategy 298
European Monetary Union 48, 50–1
European Parliament 126
  budgetary role 114
  environmental policy veto 205
  and SMEs 263, 266
  structure 87
European Political Cooperation (EPC) 10
European Regional Development Fund 122
European Round Table of Industrialists (ERT)
  258, 262
European Social Fund 121
European Social Model (ESM) 279–300
  character of 281, 283–9
  II 281, 295–9
  product of Europeanization 289–95
European Union:
  complex 86–7
  deepening 119

enlargement 337; *see also* accession
exaggerated influence 310–11
failure of influence 323–4
fluid and ambiguous 85–6
fragmentation 87
funds 84–5
intentional and unintentional effects
    311–12
lacks single model 313–14
length of membership 146–7, 149
membership demands 83–8
and national law 204
open 86
patchwork of rules 62
sectorialization 87
supranational state 115
widening 117, 125, 127
European Year of SMEs 263
Europeanization:
of business representation 255–72
causal mechanisms 60
in CEE 303
cognitive and normative dimensions 36
concept 27–34, 281–3, 324; inadequate
    229–30
conceptual framework 12–17
conceptualized 116–17, 134
conditions for 336
contextualization 50–1
definitions 3, 12, 17, 29, 59, 63, 134–5,
    203, 309
effects of 336, 338
as a historical phenomenon 6–7
institutional adaptation 7–9
and integration 280, 281–3
key changes in 19–20
mechanisms 40–4, 312–17; horizontal 41,
    160, 179, 198–200, 200, vertical 41–2,
    45, 179, 200
models of 312–14
paradoxes of 280, 299
of policy-making 256
as political institutionalization 13–14
processes of 161
public policy impacts 9–12
as research agenda 17–19, 332–4
research organization 34–40
of society 257
taxonomy 34–6
as transnationalism 7
typology 5–12
utility of the term 5–6, 19–20
Europeification 27

EUROPMI 270
Eurovision case 186

Farmborough agreement 168,
    169, 173
Fearon, J. D. 217–19
Featherstone, K. 9, 11, 18–19, 25,
    258, 331, 335, 338
Finland 125, 143, 144, 146
Finmeccanica Alenia 172
firms:
    multinational 260, 264, 267
    size 255–72
    see also SMEs
foreign affairs ministries 90
foreign policy coordination 10, 12–13
forum politics 259
frame competition 162
frame reflection 14
France 64, 167, 201, 297, 298, 308
    adaptational pressure 62
    agriculture 84
    business 229
    coordination schemes 91–101
    environment 208, 210
    identity 72
    media 186, 187–8, 188
    misfit 66
    regions 113, 117–19
    SGCI 91, 92–3
    Socialists 75
    values 287–8
fuzzy discourse 337

Germany 42, 45, 64, 136, 167, 212
    adaptational pressure 62
    advocacy network 67–8
    American CEOs 246–7
    BITKOM 244–5
    business 229, 264
    coordination schemes 90–101
    environment 208, 210, 211
    ICT 237
    media 192, 193–5, 195–6, 199, 201
    misfit 66–7
    Rechtsstaat 209
    regions 118, 123, 124, 125
    social citizenship 286
    VCI 240–1, 242–4, 249
Giuliani, M. 9, 52, 334
globalization 9, 112, 282, 339
    effects of 118–19
Goetz, K. H. 13, 34, 48, 50, 52, 320

Goldsmith, M. 18, 20, 129, 338
Gonzalez 293
goodness of fit 15, 16–17, 40, 44–5, 61, 215,
    226, 228–9, 336
government:
    agenda-setting control 147–8, 149
    and domestic mobilization 210–12
    heads 90
    by regulation 114–15
    see also subnational government
Grabbe, H. 18, 20, 27, 333, 337
Grant, W. 242–3
Greece 201, 306
    adaptation 144
    coordination schemes 91–101
    infringement 140
    media 185
    misfit 67
    regions 124
Green Cowles, M. 225, 228
Groser, M. 244
Grote, J. 19–20, 257, 334, 336
Groux 10
Gurbey 10

Hall, P. 37
Hanf, K. 11
Harcourt, A. J. 19
Harlow, C. 291
harmonization 33
Harmsen, R. 89, 227–9
Hassenteufel, P. 28
Haverland, M. 16, 19, 332, 334, 336
Hayes-Renshaw, F. 97
Heinmann 10
Héritier, A. 37, 46–7, 160, 336
Hesse, J. 118
historical institutionalist perspective 17
Hobsbawn, E. 288, 297
Holland Media Group (HMG) 194
Hooghe, L. 114–16, 119
human rights 316
Hungary 201, 313

inconvenience, *see* misfit
Industrial Plant Directive 211
inertia 37, 226
Information and Communications Technology
    (ICT) 117, 236–7, 238–9, 240, 244–5,
    248, 251
infringement proceedings 140, 142
insider status 259

institutionalism:
    new 58
    rational choice 9
    sociological 14, 17, 58–9, 65–6, 89,
        159–60, 160
institutionalization process 13–14, 161–4, 173–4
institutions:
    capacity for change 209
    coevolution 225
    competitive culture 68
    computability 209
    data 137–9
    formal 58, 65, 73
    importance of 149–52
    inertia 70, 226
    informal 68
    isomorphism 72, 136, 174, 260
    misfit 62–3
    variables 136, 148–9
integration 10, 33, 235
    and Europeanization 280, 281–3
    framing 14, 313
    informal 128
    negative 14, 16, 41, 73, 206, 226
    positive 14, 41, 73, 206, 225
    theory 256–7, 332, 340
interdepartmental coordination 90–1
INTEREG 113, 120, 123, 129
interest groups:
    intermediation rules 264–7
    politics 257
    resistant to change 228
Intergovernmental Conferences 85
international relations 159–60
intervention 236
Ireland 322
    coordination schemes 95–101
    media 182–3, 199, 201
    regions 124
isomorphism 41, 226, 335
    institutional 66, 72, 136, 174, 260
issue identities 259
Italy 44, 64
    adaptation 144, 145
    coordination schemes 90–101, 95–101
    and EMU 50–1
    infringement 140
    media 188, 199–200, 200
    misfit 67

Jenkins-Smith 49
John, P. 129

Joint Armaments Cooperation Organization 167
Joint Assessment Papers 313
Jospin, L. 298
judicial review 61

Kassim, H. 18, 20, 338
Katzenstein, P. J. 136
Kazamias, G. 19
Kazan 11
Keating, M. 117, 129
Keatinge 10
Kerr, H. 8
Kerwer, D. 38
Knill, C. 14–16, 37, 40, 42, 46–7, 209, 212, 215–16
Kohl, H. 195, 293
Kohler-Koch, B. 8, 41, 44, 160

Ladrech, R. 12, 28
Laird, F. R. 36–7
Lang, A. 334, 336
Langewiesche 10
Large Combustion Plant (LCP) Directive 208, 212
Lawton, T. 10, 29
learning 65–9, 74, 335
  cognitive development 38–9
  cross-national 128
  double-loop 67
  organizational 225
  policy 206–7, 297
LeGales, P. 128
legitimacy 43, 49
Lehmkuhl, D. 14–16, 40, 42
Lenschow, A. 215
Letter of Intent (LoI) 167–9, 173
liberal intergovernmentalism 62, 63
liberalism:
  market 290
  subversive 289
liberalization 293–4
Liikanen, E. 268–9
Lijphart, A. 136–7, 140, 145, 147, 149, 153
Llorens-Maluquer, C. 197
lobbying:
  business interests 248–50, 261, 262–4
  cost of 260
  national 262
  for single market 262
local government, *see* subnational government
logic of appropriateness 15, 17, 58, 65, 74, 89, 162, 226

logic of consequentialism 15–16, 17, 58–9, 63, 74–5, 162, 226
logic of divergence 89
logic of membership 250
logics of action and interaction 74
logics of domestic change 68–9, 73–4
Loughlin, J. 117
Luxembourg 97, 182, 188–9, 201

McGowan, L. 190
Magill cases 182–3
Majone, G. 117, 282, 289–92, 294
Manners, I. 11
March, J. 15–16, 74, 89, 102
Marks, G. 115, 119
Martin 9
media:
  audience share 199
  convergence 181, 198
  free and pay-access 193
  funding 188
  markets 179–201
  national regulation 181–9
  ownership 43, 180, 198
  television 237
Mény, Y. 11
Merger Regulation (1989) 190, 198
Merger Task Force (MTF) 180, 189–98
Metcalfe, L. 105
methodology:
  bottom-up perspective 51
  impact studies 44, 160
  intervening variables 46–50
  measuring problems 38–40
  research design 50
MFT 200–1
MILAN 124
mimetism 41
mimicry 68, 89, 102, 226
misfit 58, 215, 226
  and domestic change 60–3, 69
  institutional 62–3
  national practice 212
  policy 61, 62, 63, 211
  and socialization 66–7
Mitchell, D. 283
Mitterand, F. 75, 118, 293
modernization 338
monitoring 312, 314–15
Montpetit, E. 33
morphogenetic processes 232
morphostatic processes 232

Mörth, U. 18, 334–5
Müller, W. 95–6, 98
multilevel governance 112, 115–16, 130, 257
mutual interdependence 169

NATO 164
neofunctionalists 63–4
neoliberalism 290, 292–3
Netherlands 113, 201, 212, 297
  coordination schemes 95–101
  environment 208
  media 183–4, 194–5
  regions 123
networks:
  formal 129
  functional and territorial 115
  governance mode of 44
  informal 130
  policy 29
New Zealand 218
NORMAPME 269
North American Free Trade Area
    (NAFTA) 240
Norway 218
NUTS scheme 122

Objective 1 regions 122, 123, 126
Objective 2 regions 122, 123
Objective 5 regions 122
Olsen, J. P. 13, 15–16, 52, 74, 89, 102, 139
Open Method of Co-ordination (OMC) 43,
    179, 281, 283, 295–9, 337
optimization 89
Organization of Business Interests
    (OBI) 230
Organizational Theory 230
organizations:
  coevolution 234–5, 251
  domains 233
  learning 225
  logic 30
  outputs 233, 234
  resistance to change 227–8
  resources 233–4
  structures 233

Packaging and Packaging Waste Directive 208,
    212, 218
Page, E. 227
participation:
  dispersal 8
  public 128
partnership 120, 122

permanent representation 91, 97–101, 124
Poland 201
policies 60
policy:
  convergence 11–12
  discourse and narratives 49
  entrepreneurship 307
  formation 33, 34
  formulation versus implementation 204–5
  learning 206–7, 297
  making 30
  misfit 61–2, 63
  networks 29
  public 9–12, 27–52, 36, 309, 356
  regulatory 16
  uncertainty 319
  variables 48–9
  see also regional policy
policy analysis theory 339
political alliances 267
political culture 59, 68
political environment 232, 236–8, 246
political opportunity structure 103
political parties 147, 149
political structure 309
political systems 105, 339
politics 60, 339
  forum 259
  key changes 19–20
  subnational 112–13
polity 60
Portugal 95–101, 124, 146, 201, 322
Poverty 1–3, 113
power:
  dispersal 8
  index 148–9, 153
precaution 205
Presidency 85
principled issue networks 67
public policy 27–52, 36, 309
  analysis 256
  impacts 9–12

Radaelli, C. M. 16–20, 41, 112, 116, 159,
    173–4, 179, 204, 206, 215, 281–2,
    309–10, 313, 333, 336
regional development 84
regional funding 120
regional government 18
regional offices, in Brussels 124
regional policy 113, 317
  downgrade 126
  formal and informal 121

increasing importance 115
operation of 121–7
partnership 120, 122
and subnational government 120–1
regulation:
acceptable and unacceptable 290–1
increasing 282–3, 289–92
process 117
social 296
regulatory competition 41, 42
regulatory policy 16
Rein, M. 14
research strategy 17–19, 217–18, 332–4
counterfactual scenario 217–18
future 338–40
intensive 217
member/non-member comparison 218
resource redistribution 58, 63–5, 74
RETI 124
retrenchment 38, 226
Richard, A. 172
Richardson, J. 339
Risse, T. 15–19, 29, 59, 159, 215–16, 334–6
Romania 316
Rosanvallon, P. 291
Ross 9
Ruggie, J. G. 174
rules:
constitutive 161–2, 162, 163–5, 169, 173
of interest definition 259
regulative 161, 165

Sabatier, P. A. 49
Sacchi case 181–2
Saeter 10
Salih 10
Santiso, J. 48, 320
Sartori, G. 28, 32, 310
Schimmelfennig, F. 317
Schmid, J. 230
Schmidt, V. A. 15, 40, 229
Schmitter, P. C. 48, 233, 320
Schneider, V. 19–20, 257
Schoen, D. 14
Scotland 117, 123, 125
Screensport/EBU decision 191
second-image reversed perspective 52
Shapley's index of power 148–9, 153
similarity and difference, legal criterion 163
Single European Market 112, 119, 125, 190,
205, 237, 262
Single Market Scorecard 322
SME Observatory 270

SMEs 266
and Commission 269–70
definitions of 269
lobby 262–4
Smith, M. E. 13
Snyder, F. 181
social citizenship 286
Social Dialogue 259
social factors 232
social policy 116, 289–95, 313
socialization 65–9, 74, 225
societal environment 241, 246, 247
sociological institutionalism 14, 17, 58–9,
65–6, 89, 159–60, 161
Soetendorp 11
sovereignty, pooled 339
Spain 45, 64, 146
coordination schemes 95–101
environment 208
media 188, 196–7, 199–200, 200
regions 117, 124, 125
state centred model 114–15, 130, 257
state-society relations 229
states:
porous 160
preaccession 18
strategic issue alliances 259
Streeck, W. 233
structural funds 120, 121–2
subnational government 8, 18, 97, 117–19
and regional policy 120–1
weakness of 126, 127
subnational mobilisation 116
subnational politics 112–13
subsidiarity 123, 125, 205
Surel, Y. 28
sutainable development 205
Sutcliffe, J. 126
Sweden 125, 146, 173, 200
coordination schemes 92–101
infringement 143
media 198
neutrality 170–1, 172
Switzerland 218

Tarrow, S. 14
tax policy 49
technocrats 204
technological development 231
technological environment 238–9, 245
telecommunications 46, 71
Television Without Frontiers (TWF) 180,
182–3, 185–7, 190–1, 199–201

Thatcher, M. 46, 288–90, 293–4
Tierce Ladbroke SA v. *Commission* 187
time 47–8
    temporal sequences 51
    uncertainty 320–1
Tonra 12
Torreblanca, J. I. 11
trade associations 225–51
    and EU regulations 247
    lobbying 248–50
    output 248
    resources 247–50
    see also business interests
Trans-Atlantic Business Dialogue (TABD)
    228–9, 268
transformation 37, 226
    discourse 40
    equilibration 39–40
    interaction 39
    robustness 39
    of the state 51–2
Transnational Defence Companies (TDC) 167,
    169
transparency 322
transport 48, 128
Treaty of Amsterdam 125, 165, 188, 205, 298
Treaty of Maastricht 119, 123, 205, 257
Treaty of Nice 114
Treaty of Rome 205
    Article 85 190, 191
    Article 234 (ex. 77) 119
Tsebelis, G. 136–7, 145
Turkey 18
twinning 312, 315
two level game 259

UEAPME 269, 270
uncertainty 303, 337
    for accession countries 318–23
    policy agenda 319
    standards and thresholds 322–3
    task hierarchy 319–20
    timing 320–1
    whom to satisfy 321–2
Union of Industrial and Employers' Conference
    of Europe (UNICE) 262, 263, 268
United Kingdom 43, 46, 48, 64, 167, 212,
    297, 322
    adaptation 145
    adaptational pressure 62
    business 229, 264

coordination schemes 91–101
defence equipment 171–2
environment 208, 210
Equal Opportunities Commission 65
fisheries 84
infringement 143
liberalism 288, 293–4
media 182–3, 185–6, 187, 191,
    199, 201
National Farmers Union 116
opt-outs 307
regions 113, 117–18, 123, 124
UKREP 99–101
United States 167, 169, 171, 240
    American Chamber of Commerce (Amcham)
        262, 265, 267
    firms 264
    model 297
    political tradition 288
    social policy 291
    State Department 268
    workfare 298–9
URBAN 113

values 287–8
van den Broek, H. 166
Van Miert 195
variable geometry 112
Venturelli 10
veto players 140, 335
veto-points:
    for accession 321–2
    informal 46–7
    institutional 46, 212–15, 216
    multiple points 58, 64–5, 73
von Moltke, H. 269
voting, qualified majority 114, 125
VPS 136–7, 140, 143–4, 148–9, 152
VT4 Ltd v. *Vlaamse Geenschap* 186–7

Waever 11
Wales 117, 123, 125
Wallace, H. 97, 174
Wallace, W. 174
welfare 297
welfare states:
    diversity of 284–5
    European level 290–1
WEU 164
White Book, 'Strategy for a Future Policy on
    Chemicals' 237–8, 247

White Papers
  Competitiveness, Growth and Employment
    295
  European Governance 261, 266
  Single Market 307, 321
Whitman, R. G. 11

Wincott, D. 19, 30, 337
Wolf, D. 196
Wouters, L. 227
WTO 268

Yost 11